To Know Where He Lies

D1561520

# To Know Where He Lies

*DNA Technology and
the Search for Srebrenica's Missing*

Sarah E. Wagner

UNIVERSITY OF CALIFORNIA PRESS
*Berkeley · Los Angeles · London*

University of California Press, one of the most
distinguished university presses in the United States,
enriches lives around the world by advancing scholar-
ship in the humanities, social sciences, and natural
sciences. Its activities are supported by the UC Press
Foundation and by philanthropic contributions from
individuals and institutions. For more information,
visit www.ucpress.edu.

University of California Press
Berkeley and Los Angeles, California

University of California Press, Ltd.
London, England

Library of Congress Cataloging-in-Publication Data

Wagner, Sarah E., 1972–
    To know where he lies : DNA technology and the
search for Srebrenica's missing / Sarah E. Wagner.
        p.    cm.
    Includes bibliographical references and index.
    ISBN 978-0-520-25574-6 (cloth : alk. paper)
    ISBN 978-0-520-25575-3 (pbk. : alk. paper)
    1. Yugoslav War, 1991–1995—Atrocities—
Bosnia and Hercegovina—Srebrenica.   2. Missing
persons—Bosnia and Hercegovina—Srebrenica.
3. DNA fingerprinting—Bosnia and Hercegovina—Srebrenica.    I. Title.
    DR1313.7.A85W34   2008
    949.703—dc22                         2008003976

Manufactured in the United States of America
17   16   15   14   13   12   11   10   09   08
10   9   8   7   6   5   4   3   2   1

This book is printed on Natures Book, which contains
30% post-consumer waste and meets the minimum
requirements of ANSI/NISO Z39.48–1992 (R 1997)
(*Permanence of Paper*).

*za nestale Srebrenice*

To Srebrenica's missing

# Contents

# Illustrations

# Acknowledgments

At its core, this book is a study of absence, yet it would never have been possible but for the presence and contributions of many people. First among them are the members of the Women of Srebrenica, my window into the lives and experiences of families of the Srebrenica missing, without whose support I could not have completed this project. I am profoundly grateful to Hajra Ćatić and Nura Begović for their patience, humor, and, above all, earnest desire to help me understand the identification process from the perspective of those most intimately tied to its results. Among the organization's members, I also wish to acknowledge particularly Rufejda, Hajrija, Naza, Ešefa, Rejha, and Ramiza. Their words and insights, though at times searing the heart, demonstrate a resilience of spirit impossible to forget.

The support of the International Commission on Missing Persons, especially the staff in its Tuzla and Sarajevo offices, was instrumental throughout this work. From the onset, Adnan Rizvić provided important instruction on the evolution of the identification technology as well as feedback on my findings. Moreover, he opened the first door, allowing me to work among his staff and urging me to learn firsthand the DNA-based identification procedures. Beyond his intellectual contributions to this study, Dr. Rifat Kešetović at the Podrinje Identification Project (PIP) extended to me one of the most precious privileges of my fieldwork by allowing me to accompany his staff as they visited family members. I am deeply indebted to those very people, the case managers—Enver,

Senad, Jasmina, and my dear friend Emina. Through their grace in the most sensitive and emotionally taxing work, they showed me how one tells a family member that her relative has been found. Their insights have enriched this work in countless ways; their support was essential. Also at PIP, Laura Yazedjian, Amir Hasandžiković, and Nedim Duraković explained the intricacies of the forensic procedures involved in the Srebrenica cases and caught me up on the history of the Srebrenica identification efforts. At ICMP's other Tuzla facility, the Identification Coordination Division, where I worked as an intern for several months, I benefited from the breadth and depth of its staff's knowledge, as well as the encouragement of many friends, including especially Edin Jašaragić, Amela Sejranić, Sanela Fazlić, Sejdefa Salkić, Jasminka Korlatović, Pakiza Čolo, Abduselam Hukić, Zlatan Bajunović, Djordje Badža, and Asmir Gotovušić. In ICMP's Sarajevo office, Asta Zinbo and Kathryne Bomberger responded to my questions with patience and thoughtful reflection; the Tuzla transplants Irfan Berbić and Elvira Hadžinurbegović always welcomed me into the office; and Amir Sutrović helped me understand just how important identifying the missing can be for ICMP staff members. Finally, former ICMP employee Ed Huffine took the time to clarify aspects of the DNA-based technology that I had not learned while in the field.

In conducting research in Bosnia, I depended on many people whose experiences of the war and its aftermath have left an indelible imprint on this book. Friends in Srebrenica—in particular, Sabra and Minka Mustafić, Šefija and Sadik Salimović, Dragana Jovanović, Behkta "Beba" Softić, and the Strbac family—helped me look beyond the scars of the city and explore both its past and present. Over countless meals and cups of coffee, they inspired my research and, through their generosity, hospitality, and unflagging good humor, offered a welcome respite from the challenges of studying the identification process. In Tuzla, Zlatko and Lela Perić, Emira Pašić, Jelen, Mira, and Jelena Jugović, and the Kurtalić and Altumbabić families opened their homes to me. Staff members at the Forum of Tuzla Citizens, especially Mira Mišić Jugović, Emina Babović, and Jadranka Gajić, have provided constant encouragement from the start of this project. I am especially grateful to Mira, my patient sounding board in the field, for her indefatigable capacity to engage my ideas and challenge my assumptions. Also in Tuzla, Mirsad Sabic instructed me in Bosnian Islamic practice and served as an excellent research assistant at different points throughout the project. I am indebted to Mufti Husejn ef. Kavazović for sharing his perspective on the Islamic Community's involvement in the identification process and the commemoration ceremonies at Potočari. Also in Srebrenica, Abel Herzberger and the volunteers of the Werkgroep Nederland-Srebrenica, especially Jannie Wolfert, helped me find my footing in the early months; enthusiastic fellow traveler Thomas Heyne explored eastern Bosnia with me, and Haris Mešinović was my consummate host in Sarajevo.

From start to finish, Engseng Ho has urged this work on, pushing when necessary, inspiring throughout. His *Graves* shed light on Srebrenica's; his advice made the rest possible. Michael Herzfeld, whose generosity of time and spirit first welcomed me to this discipline, was a pillar of support throughout this project and my graduate studies. Steve Caton introduced key texts about memory and narrative; Gary Urton taught an appreciation for material culture; late in this project, Sheila Jasanoff injected new life through STS insight. My special thanks go to Ellen Elias-Bursac, who initially taught me Bosnian (and Croatian and Serbian) and who provided invaluable assistance with translations; any mistakes with language are mine alone. This project also benefited from the sharp but generous eyes, and in some cases ears, of many colleagues and friends, among them particularly Katrina Moore, Sabrina Peric, Priscilla Song, Darryl Li, Maple Razsa, and Manduhai Buyandelgerin. A collaborative project on "technologies of repair" with Lindsay Smith and Jason Cross, along with the Science and Technology Studies circle at Harvard, helped develop my understanding of Bosnia's postmortem technology. Alex Hinton and Rosalind Shaw invited me to present my findings at pivotal moments during writing. Conversations with Dino Abazović, Kimberley Coles, Elissa Helms, Tarik Samarah, and Peter Lippman, feedback on dissertation chapters from Drew Gilbert, Stef Jansen, and Mark Skinner, and help from Sabina Altumbabić and Andras Riedlmayer shored up form and content along the way. My colleagues at the University of North Carolina Greensboro, Art Murphy, Joan Paluzzi, and Steve Kroll-Smith, spurred new reflections in the final stretch. Last but not least, James Tatum's library on memory rounded out chapters 5 and 6.

Research for this project was supported by the Fulbright-Hays Doctoral Dissertation Research Abroad program, Harvard University Department of Anthropology summer research grants, and the Mellon-MIT Inter-University Program on Non-Governmental Organizations and Forced Migration. A dissertation writing fellowship from the Weatherhead Center for International Affairs at Harvard University allowed me to carry momentum from the field into the writing process. I wish to thank Stan Holwitz, Jacqueline Volin, and Sue Carter at the University of California Press and readers Pamela Ballinger and Harvey Weinstein. This book is much stronger because of their efforts.

I am deeply indebted to my family and friends for all their hard work, patience, and care. Wallace Watson has read and commented on more drafts than should ever be asked of anyone; from conversations to editing, Shannon Wagner and Johanna Wagner devoted hours to this text and Jonathan Wagner offered sage advice throughout. Nathaniel Wagner and Christy Ruff helped get me through graduate school; Dave Camillo made sure I was free from worries whenever I traveled to Bosnia. Beyond their intellectual engagement with this work, Lara Nettelfield and Eric Davis were tireless supporters in the field and back home. I am especially grateful to my mother, Shannon Wagner, whose strength and courage inspire me every day.

Finally, I wish to acknowledge a presence that has been my constant compass during the fieldwork and subsequent writing: the missing men and boys of Srebrenica. To them I dedicate this work.

# Abbreviations

| | |
|---|---|
| AFDIL | Armed Forces DNA Identification Laboratory |
| BCS | Bosnian/Croatian/Serbian |
| DNA | Deoxyribonucleic acid |
| ICD | Identification Coordination Division (formerly the Identification Coordination Center of ICMP) |
| ICMP | International Commission on Missing Persons |
| ICRC | International Committee of the Red Cross |
| ICTY | International Criminal Tribunal for the former Yugoslavia |
| IKV | Interkerkelijk Vredesberaad (Interchurch Peace Council) |
| JNA | Jugoslovenska narodna armija (Yugoslav People's Army) |
| KPJ | Komunistička partija Jugoslavije (Communist Party of Yugoslavia) |
| MPI | Missing Persons Institute |
| NATO | North Atlantic Treaty Organization |

| NIOD | Nederlands Instituut voor Oorlogsdocumentatie (Netherlands Institute for War Documentation) |
| OCME | Office of the Chief Medical Examiner |
| OHR | Office of the High Representative |
| PHR | Physicians for Human Rights |
| PIP | Podrinje Identification Project |
| RS | Republika Srpska |
| SDA | Stranka demokratske akcije (Party of Democratic Action) |
| SDS | Srpska demokratska stranka (Serbian Democratic Party) |
| UN | United Nations |
| UNDP | United Nations Development Programme |
| UNHCR | United Nations High Commissioner for Refugees |
| UNPROFOR | United Nations Protection Force |

# Note on Pronunciation

Attentiveness to language is paramount in Bosnia and Herzegovina for practical and political reasons alike. The three official languages of Bosnia and Herzegovina—Bosnian, Croatian, and Serbian—all derive from what was formerly known as Serbo-Croatian. They may be written in either the Latin or Cyrillic alphabet, though the latter is used primarily in the Republika Srpska. Spelling is phonetic in both scripts.

c          as in ca*ts*

č          as in *church*

ć          as in minia*tu*re

dž        as in *George*

dj         as in a*dj*ourn

j           as in *y*ellow

lj          as in mi*lli*on

nj         as in ca*ny*on .

š           as in *sh*oe

ž           as in trea*su*re

In the original Bosnian pronunciation, the name *Srebrenica* has a gently rolled *r*, the first syllable is stressed, and the final *c* is pronounced *ts* (as in *cats*). Thus: Sre'brenitsa.

Bosnia and Herzegovina. Inset shows the Srebrenica enclave in July 1995.

# Introduction

On July 11, 2003, the cemetery of the Srebrenica-Potočari Memorial Center filled with people in anticipation of the burial of 282 recently identified victims of the Srebrenica massacre. Most attendees had traveled a long and circuitous journey to arrive there that day. Crossing borders and, in some cases, time zones, they had come together to commemorate an act of physical and social devastation, the worst massacre to occur in Europe since World War II. But their presence also reflected another and altogether different achievement: the results of an innovative DNA-based identification technology that had reassembled bodies and for the first time in eight years reattached names—individual identities—to those 282 sets of mortal remains.

Among those gathered in the cemetery on that hot summer day were two boys, not more than six and eight years old, who were kneeling beside a grave. It was not one of the empty plots, the dark pits of earth that pocked the northern end of the cemetery awaiting the coffins, but one that had been filled a few months earlier at the memorial center's first commemoration and mass burial ceremony. Side by side, both boys stared intently at the green wooden marker at the head of the mound. Having just finished reciting prayers for the deceased, the older of the two, who sat closer to the marker, reached out his hand and wiped away the clay-colored dust that had covered the name printed on the small black placard. It was a tender, earnest gesture. Brushing away the stray dirt, he paid homage to a relative whom he probably had never known or, at best, knew only through stories told to him by his family.

That moment encapsulated the experience of identification at the heart of this study—a study of a genetic technology developed to reassociate and recognize thousands of nameless mortal remains resulting from a massacre that occurred in July 1995 in eastern Bosnia and Herzegovina.[1] The boy's gesture of maintenance—not simply of the grave's physical space, but of the dignity of an individual's name, his personhood, and his memory—captured the emotional force at work behind the process of identifying the missing. At the same time, it spoke to an intended legacy of identification, of commemorating collective suffering and completing the personal histories of individuals who disappeared during the war. As I would later come to appreciate, the boy's gesture also represented a personal, spontaneous act that stood apart from much of the scripted and politically infused activities taking place at the ceremony that day and during subsequent commemorations at the memorial center. It gave me my first sense of the cemetery and the rest of the complex as a place of meaning making whose audience is vast and varied.

The scene marks the end point of an identification process that has spanned years, cost millions of dollars, and involved a complex network of people with divergent expectations pinned to the act of reattaching names to unrecognizable mortal remains. This book traces that process, illustrating how the DNA-based technology came into being and what the identification process has meant to those involved in it. By examining the stages of identification and the layers of meaning attached to their results, we see the dynamic, multivalent aspects of the forensic effort alongside the intimate, powerful instances of recognition experienced by families of the missing, such as the two boys at their relative's graveside. We see how memory and imagination intersect with biotechnology, exposing the subjective experiences that permeate the identification process. We also learn the extent of its import—for families, Bosnian national politics, and international interventionism. The postmortem identification system developed in Bosnia not only transformed forensic practice but also changed how surviving families and experts working to identify the missing conceived of absence and presence. The system returned remains to relatives, providing them at long last with a grave to visit and knowledge of their loved ones' fate. It profoundly altered the discourse of victimhood and criminality in postwar Bosnia, raising the stakes of facticity through the scientifically backed identification and reburial of Srebrenica's missing. In so doing, the process has often confounded the aims of its international sponsors. Rather than fostering national cohesion, identifying the missing has at times deepened divisions even as it has accomplished the invaluable act of reconstituting physical and social beings.

## A TECHNOLOGICAL INNOVATION

The DNA-based technology was developed in response to mass atrocity. On July 11, 1995, in a brazen and well-orchestrated military action, the Bosnian Serb Army overtook the United Nations "safe area" of Srebrenica, the enclave of Bosnian Muslim–controlled (Bosniak)[2] territory in the eastern part of the country, otherwise dominated by Bosnian Serbs. The Dutch contingent of UN peacekeeping soldiers stood by as the Bosnian Serb forces, augmented by a handful of Serbian units, began to purge the enclave of its Bosniak inhabitants, an estimated 40,000 people who had fled there in the early months of the war that broke out in the spring of 1992.[3] With the attack under way, an estimated 25,000 people sought shelter at the UN peacekeepers' compound in the nearby village of Potočari. A column of 15,000 men and boys tried to escape through the forest. Once they secured the city of Srebrenica, the Bosnian Serb Army proceeded to the UN compound, where they began to expel from the Srebrenica enclave the 25,000 women, children, elderly, and sick or wounded, busing them to the front line between Bosnian Serb and Bosniak–held territory. Not everyone was allowed to board the buses. "Military-age" men—boys in their early teens to men in their late eighties—were forcibly separated from their families and sent to nearby detention sites as UN peacekeepers looked on. Those detainees were soon joined by thousands of men who had been captured while trying to flee through the forest. Over the next six days, the Bosnian Serb and Serb forces systematically executed an estimated 8,000 men and boys.

Srebrenica has since come to mean many things to many people. Within the context of wartime events, the fall of the enclave marked a turning point in the violence that would displace 2 million people and leave almost 100,000 dead at its conclusion in December 1995.[4] It signaled the intensification of a program of systematic violent persecution conducted by Bosnian Serb and Serbian forces against the Bosniak population in the Podrinje region, the land west of the Drina River that forms the natural border between Bosnia and Herzegovina and Serbia (Tokača

2005). Srebrenica was the culmination of this campaign. According to the legal definition and findings of the International Criminal Tribunal for the former Yugoslavia, the execution and mass burial of the 8,000 Bosniak men and boys constituted genocide.[5] At the conclusion of the war, the country faced an immense challenge: to locate and identify the remains of its missing persons, including victims of this genocide.

Srebrenica's graves were a forensic nightmare. The massacre was remarkable not just because of how the Bosnian Serbs killed their Bosniak captives but also because of how they eventually disposed of the bodies in secondary mass graves. In the months following the executions and before the war ended, Bosnian Serb forces returned to the primary (initial) mass graves, dug up the contents, and scattered the bodies in secondary mass gravesites, creating trenches full of commingled and partial remains (Komar 2008:126). Thus, forensic experts faced the nearly impossible task of piecing together the remains and details of the missing persons' final moments of life and death.

The violence that disrupted the individual identity of the enclave's victims and the physical integrity of their decomposing bodies would spark a remarkable technological response. Because of the appalling conditions of the recovered mortal remains, DNA analysis, usually the last step in identification, became the first. The identification process required collecting blood samples from surviving family members and matching them against bone samples exhumed from mass and surface graves on a scale never before attempted.[6] Compounded by the overall number of missing persons in former Yugoslavia, the particular challenge of Srebrenica would change the way forensic experts approach the identification of victims of mass fatalities whose remains defy traditional methodologies.

## RETURN AND EMPTY SPACES

Identification of the missing was not my research focus when I first arrived in Srebrenica in July 2003. I intended to study the process of return: how Bosniaks, both genocide survivors and those who fled the region when the war started, returned to their prewar residences in Srebrenica and surrounding villages. Since the war's end, the policy of physical return (specifically, the return of internally displaced persons) in Bosnia has been a key strategy within the internationally sponsored project of postwar reconstruction (Toal and Dahlman 2004; Steffanson 2004; Black 2001; Bringa 2001). In the Srebrenica municipality, as in other regions throughout the country, however, return was slow, and it was not until 1999 that Bosniaks began to take up permanent residence on their prewar property. Reconstructed houses, it seemed, addressed the displaced persons' needs only partially; reconstruction facilitated return but by no means guaranteed it.[7] Indeed, by the end of 2005 in the Srebrenica municipality, titles for 97.52 percent of property, including residences, had officially been returned to their prewar owners. But the actual return rate—the permanent return of prewar Bosniak residents—remained conspicuously low, at only 12.18 percent (3,364 returnees) (Ministarstvo za ljudska prava i izbjeglice 2005).

As Bosniaks trickled back to their property in the former enclave, an altogether different story of "homecoming" was galvanizing families of the Srebrenica missing: the recovery, recognition, and return of mortal remains through exhumation and identification procedures carried out by local and international institutions in Bosnia. For these families, the absence of the missing could not be ignored; it pervaded their homes. "Sometimes," writes Gaston Bachelard, "in the presence of a perfectly familiar object, we experience an extension of our intimate space" (1994:199). In the case of the returnees inhabiting their newly rebuilt houses, the opposite was true—the glaring absence of both familiar objects (personal possessions carted off or destroyed after their flight) and family members constricted their intimate space and reminded them of what was now missing. More disturbingly, these absences recalled the violence of July 1995.

Occasions such as holidays and birthdays heightened family members' awareness of the painful and permanent interruption of their domestic lives. I visited a good friend, a returnee, on the first day of *bajram*, the celebration ending the Bosnian Muslim holiday of *ramazan*. She had prepared an entire tray of baklava for the occasion. A labor-intensive dessert with its layers of paper-thin pastry, baklava is a traditional sweet offered to family members and guests visiting homes in the days following *ramazan*. Hajra, my friend, prepared the tray partly out of habit. It would have seemed odd to make only a small dish. Yet on that first day of *bajram*, in her quiet house, as she received the occasional telephone call from relatives now living abroad or in other parts of the country, she was left to contemplate the significance of that tray and its untouched layers of sweet pastry. She had lost both her younger son and her husband in the genocide. At that time, neither had been found, and on days such as *bajram*, in the airy halls of her house, Hajra could not escape the emptiness of its space or her life.[8]

Such experiences illustrate the hold that the missing have over the returnees' lives in Srebrenica. Their absence has seeped into the vernacular of the city. Repeatedly I heard the phrase *"nije došao"* (He didn't come) as an explanation of where sons, husbands, friends, and former neighbors were. Didn't come home? Didn't come back? Didn't survive? I could not quite grasp the oblique reference of place implicit in this simple phrase. Much later, when I began to work more closely with members of the Association of Citizens "Women of Srebrenica" (Udruženje građana "Žene Srebrenice"), one of the survivors' advocacy organizations located in Tuzla, I asked them what these words meant.[9] They could offer no direct and definitive answer, perhaps because the reference was so obvious to them: the men and boys who did not survive the genocide did not "come." They did not make it to "free" territory—that is, the territory controlled by Bosniak and Croat forces in July 1995, and specifically, to Tuzla, a predominantly Bosniak city in the northeastern part of the country. Whether captured and killed during their flight through the forest in the days, even weeks, after the enclave fell, or executed soon after their separation from the women and children at Potočari, they fell into the category of the missing, *nestali*.

## THE MISSING

An estimated 40,000 people were missing as a consequence of the violence that tore apart the territories of former Yugoslavia in the 1990s. Some 13,000 people are still presumed missing in Bosnia and Herzegovina.[10] The International Commission on Missing Persons (ICMP), one of the organizations leading the recovery and identification efforts in former Yugoslavia, defines the concept of missing persons specifically in relation to these conflicts, as "victims of enforced disappearances . . . missing as a consequence of deliberate and systematic actions of the regional governments in power during the various conflicts, or agents acting on their behalf" (ICMP 2003b). The 8,000 men and boys missing from Srebrenica are the most politically significant group of the *nestali*. Their scattered, disassociated, and partial remains pose difficult questions. What exactly does the term *missing* mean in this situation? Does it intimate death? Does it erase hope for the surviving families? Does it affect—somehow alter—the identity of the person now considered to be missing? Rifat Kešetović, chief pathologist and director of the ICMP's Podrinje Identification Project, pointed out to me how insufficient the descriptive term *missing person (nestala osoba)* is for surviving families:

> We all know that it is a very difficult expression, a "missing person." Not just the expression, the feeling that someone is missing. It is clear to all of us that a person cannot go missing, simply that a person has his own fate. It is clear to us that after so many years that person is probably dead. But for me it is also an understandable feeling of the family that it is not satisfactory—for them it is not a satisfactory knowledge that their missing relative is probably dead somewhere.[11]

Dr. Kešetović, who has worked on the Srebrenica cases since the first mass graves were discovered, was speaking to the incomplete, hollow knowledge underpinning the phrase *nije došao* and the term *nestali*. People do not simply disappear.[12] The term *missing* signals the absence of a story, a personal history yet untold, for each victim. For the families of the missing, the label reflects the state of emotional limbo in which they must live until they receive the news that the mortal remains of their missing relative have been identified. Until that point, the missing person for them remains "undead," what Robert Pogue Harrison describes as the "open-ended, unreconciled psychic state of the grievers" (2003:144). Furthermore, the certain knowledge that a loved one lies dead "somewhere" opens the possibility of knowing so many details surrounding his death.[13] The horrific circumstances of the Srebrenica genocide—the torturous detention of the men and boys, the mass executions, and the violent disarticulation of their bodies caused by removal to the secondary mass graves—intensify the anguish associated with the term *missing* for their families. The word encompasses more than just death; for many Srebrenica families, it intimates a heinous violation of their relatives' remains.[14] Those who have traveled back to the area are pained by the thought that they might unwittingly drive past the yet undiscovered mass grave that holds a relative's remains, or the woods where his bones lie scattered, not recognizing that "somewhere."

In the chapters that follow, this study of Srebrenica's missing explores the meaning of the term *nestali*—the meaning of absence. I begin with the basic idea that to be missing is to be absent both in time and in space. For surviving family members, conceptualizing the missing person's absence involves mediating memories, imagination, hope, and resignation. In this heightened state of ambiguity, the missing relative's existence is caught in a web of memory and suggestion. As long as he is missing, family members cannot know definitively whether he has died. And even if they accept the notion of his death without evidence of remains, they still do not know where his bones lie.

Beyond this most intimate state of absence, the missing of Srebrenica have other, more prosaic, meanings. For the forensic specialists seeking to identify nameless sets of mortal remains, the missing exist as objects of scientific scrutiny, a problem to be solved by matching genetic profiles and reconciling postmortem data with families' recollections. For the Bosniak nationalist political and religious leadership, the missing are emblematic of collective suffering and victimhood. Resolving their absence through DNA testing and eventual burial in the Srebrenica-Potočari Memorial Center Cemetery offers visible—indeed, scientifically unassailable—support in countering Bosnian Serb dismissals of genocide. The commemorative space and activities of the memorial center have also helped forge a new sense of nationalism among Bosniaks in the region and beyond, as members of the diaspora return to Srebrenica each year to participate in the July 11 memorial ceremonies.

Finally, the missing of Srebrenica present the international community, specifically certain Western governments, with an opportunity to attempt "social reconstruction"—that is, to repair a postconflict society through a "broad range of programmatic interventions," from security to justice, economic development, education, and rule of law (Stover and Weinstein 2004:5; see also Fletcher and Weinstein 2002; Duffield 2002). In Bosnia and Herzegovina, these interventions were designed to counter wartime damage as well as to remove certain vestiges of the previous socialist system, thereby advancing the democratization process (Coles 2004:556; Bose 2002). Joining other projects of international intervention already in place—from rebuilding houses, schools, and hospitals to restoring power lines and water supplies and reinstituting elections—the humanitarian project of exhuming mass graves and returning remains to families was also intended by its international sponsors to facilitate sociopolitical repair. Thus, across these different registers of meaning and experience, the missing persons' absence creates new spaces that are filled with different, and at times competing, expectations of what their recovery will accomplish.

In exploring the divergent readings of the Srebrenica victims' absence, this analysis draws from several perspectives on the identification process. It follows the course of my fieldwork as it shifted away from return to Srebrenica and toward the biotechnological response to the enclave's missing. I began researching the missing person issue while living among the returnee population in Srebrenica, where news of mass graves and recovered bodies rippled through the Bosniak community, serving as a regular topic of conversation. Spending time in the city itself, among both Bosniaks and Bosnian Serbs, I immediately became aware of the divisive nature of the annual commemorative ceremonies that took place at the nearby village of Potočari. I also became familiar with the wartime enclave as a social and historical place, both through returnees' stories and through my own reading of the signs of damage and loss. These experiences in Srebrenica were critical to understanding the sociopolitical import of the identification process.

By late 2003, though, I realized that I would need to relocate to Tuzla, the city in the Bosniak and Croat–controlled entity of the Federation[15] where local staff members of the International Commission on Missing Persons (ICMP) carried out the day-to-day work of trying to identify mortal remains exhumed from graves throughout former Yugoslavia. The organization's Podrinje Identification Project (PIP), specifically dedicated to the Srebrenica cases, was also located in Tuzla. I became an intern with the ICMP's blood collection and DNA matching center (called the Identification Coordination Division) and eventually began working with staff from PIP. With the exception of a few forensic anthropologists employed at PIP's mortuary facilities, all of ICMP's staff members in Tuzla were local—that is, Bosnian. As a group, they reflected the relative ethnic diversity of the city, known for its wartime resistance to ethno-national intolerance. Though the majority of the staff was Bosniak, there were also Bosnian Serbs, Bosnian Croats, and several people who came from mixed marriages. Many had been working on the Srebrenica cases since the end of the war, first hired by Physicians for Human Rights and later joining ICMP's staff.[16] My decision to conduct research on the identification procedures in Tuzla, rather than those carried out in the capital, Sarajevo, meant that my analysis would emphasize the DNA-based technology and the final stages of the process more than exhumations, and I would have more contact with ICMP's local staff than with its international personnel or with staff from the locally based Federation Commission for Missing Persons. Working in Tuzla nevertheless granted me a privileged view into the daily work of the Srebrenica cases, especially my time spent with the case managers at the Podrinje Identification Project. They were the final link in the entire process—the people who presented families with the news of identification.

Tuzla was also an important place for gaining insight into families' experiences of the identification process. After the war, the majority of Srebrenica's evacuees took up residence there in temporary shelters and later in collective centers for displaced persons or private housing around the city. Many of those same people, particularly women, became politically mobilized in the search for their missing male relatives. I sought the perspectives of surviving family members among this population and found a rich source in the diverse voices of the members of the Tuzla-based Women of Srebrenica. Spending time each day in their office, participating in their regular activities, and traveling back and forth to Srebrenica with the organization's two leaders most weekends, I could evaluate the identification procedures from the vantage points of those most directly connected to the results. My research thus moved between the cities of Srebrenica and Tuzla and among the families and technologists bound together by the identification process.

## ON RECOGNITION

For the Srebrenica missing, being absent often means going unrecognized individually while simultaneously being recognized according to collective categories. The act of *recognition* thus serves as a key concept throughout this study, and the interplay between the term's literal and figurative definitions sheds light on the various levels of meaning that run throughout the identification process. By following these shifts in labels, categories, and outward markers applied to the genocide victims and their mortal remains, I explore three different, though mutually informing, ways in which Srebrenica's missing are recognized. These acts of recognition radiate out from the epicenter of the individual missing person—to his family; to his friends, neighbors, colleagues, and schoolmates; to the extended Srebrenica community; to the Bosniak political and religious leaders; and, finally, to the international community deeply invested in the project of identification.

Given this outwardly expanding flow, the first and most obvious instance of recognition occurs when the identification technology reads human genetic material and reattaches individual identity to mortal remains—the technoscientific production of knowledge. The second is the families' subjective experiences of recognizing their missing when presented with the DNA evidence and other material traces of identity—the reckoning of memories, imaginings, hopes, and fears. The third is the collective recognition of Srebrenica's missing at the annual commemorative ceremonies held in Potočari, an act dominated by Bosniak political and religious leaders as well as representatives of the international community present in postwar Bosnia. My aim is to analyze these processes on their own terms, yet illustrate their points of intersection throughout the various stages of the identification-commemoration process.

## Identity and Identification

By considering how Srebrenica's missing are "recognized," we discern movements in meaning from the intimate encounters of families with the news of identification to the socially constituted acts of collective remembering at the Srebrenica-Potočari Memorial Center. The path leading from the unrecognized to the recognized also forces open the term *identity*. Identity not only signifies the relationship between a name and a set of physical remains but also encompasses the social ties that bind a person to a place, a time, and, most importantly, to other human beings. "The relationships and tensions between identity and identification are closely interdependent, of course, like those between systems of collective and individual registration. The question 'who is this person?' leaches constantly into the question 'what kind of person is this?' Identification as an individual is scarcely thinkable without categories of collective identity" (Caplan and Torpey 2001:3). For example, the majority of the Srebrenica missing still lie physically unrecognized—in mass graves, on the forest's surface, or stored in body bags on a mortuary shelf. Stripped of personal identity, these remains exist wholly unconnected to the individual, social beings whose bodies they once constituted. As victims of mass executions, most of the Srebrenica missing died anonymously, and, in that posthumous state of prolonged anonymity, representations of their identity shift—often strategically—between the individual and the collective. In absentia, individual sets of remains decimated by collective violence become emblems for collective categories: victims, enemies, Bosniaks, Muslims, refugees, martyrs. Even the name of their physical remnants depends on the context of who refers to them: the families of the missing and local media representatives covering the exhumation and identification procedures speak generally of "bodies" *(tijela)*; the more nondescript label of *mortal remains (posmrtni ostaci)* allows for a certain vagueness about what exactly those remains entail—decomposed flesh, hair, or bones.[17] Occasionally they are referred to as merely bones *(kosti)*, and at other times in more clinical terms as skeletal remains *(skeletni ostaci).* In the most sensitive moments, when speaking with families of the missing, the forensic experts know to refer to mortal remains as people, not bodies, framing their absence in human, not forensic, terms. Finally, once identified as belonging to individual persons, remains of the Srebrenica missing are still subject to collective categorizing. As we will see, communal remembering involves the collectivity of hundreds of coffins being interred by families with the extended community of the Srebrenica enclave gathered in the cemetery for the occasion.

*A Technological Resolution of Absence:*
*Recognizing Genetic Profiles*

The first segment of this study examines the process of identification as the initial act of recognition, illustrating the technoscientific production of knowledge. How is individual identity, stripped away through genocide and unmarked graves, recovered from anonymity, and how does such identity eventually reassume its social meaning, connected to an individual human being, a member of a family, and a member of a larger community?

Understanding this transformation begins not with the technology itself, but rather the events and people leading to its creation. Chapter 1 chronicles the fall of the enclave, briefly sketching wartime life in Srebrenica before turning to the events of July 11, 1995. The genocide at Srebrenica stands out not only because of the brutality with which Bosnian Serb forces disposed—literally—of their victims, but also because of the international community's role in the events. UN inaction—indeed the UN's failure to protect the enclave and its Bosniak inhabitants—directly correlates to Western governments' postwar interventions in the Srebrenica municipality and, specifically, the identification efforts developed in response to the Srebrenica graves. Chapter 2 focuses on postwar Srebrenica and the complex layers of its Bosniak and Bosnian Serb populations. Here we glimpse the undercurrents of tension not only between the two ethno-national communities but also among the returnees themselves, as "hierarchies of suffering" (Petryna 2002) shape social relations within and beyond the former enclave. Given that Srebrenica's wartime population remains dispersed, Tuzla exists as a center of political mobilization around the missing persons issue, where the Women of Srebrenica conducts its monthly protests in search of "truth and justice," namely the return of missing relatives' remains.

Chapter 3 turns to the DNA-based identification technology. In and of itself, the innovation in forensic science developed in response to the phenomenon of secondary mass graves and their contents of commingled bones presents provocative subject matter for anthropological study. The scope of the identification effort—not to mention its costs—for the Srebrenica victims alone is enormous: collecting tens of thousands of blood samples from surviving family members, locating and exhuming hundreds of mass and unmarked surface graves, reassociating partial skeletal remains, extracting and analyzing DNA from at least 8,000 bone and tooth samples, and producing DNA matches for each set of recovered mortal remains.[18] Why such effort and expense? In part, this project seeks to affirm the facticity of the July 11 genocide. Srebrenica's missing signifies one of postwar Bosnia's most contentious debates because knowledge of its events, chronology, and participants has not yet passed into the realm of the "matter-of-fact." Around their bones a public (Latour 2005) has formed that increasingly relies on genetics to establish evidence of individual identity and, thereby, the concrete facts of numbers and names of victims. This effort requires collecting, cataloguing, and storing massive amounts of data—that is, the re-presentation of bits and pieces of individuals' lives into Excel spreadsheets and computer database windows. Gradually, this public has generated a bureaucracy of postmortem individual identity, not only through genetic profiles but also through compact portraits of the missing and their relatives as donors of blood samples.

The production of scientific knowledge through the instruments of DNA extraction and analysis has become the primary means of establishing individual identity for the Srebrenica missing. Its language of genetic analysis and statistical certainty has, in turn, inserted a new level of facticity into postwar nationalist discourses that tabulate loss and assign blame. But placing the statistically sound DNA evidence above other forms of human knowledge, including more traditional forensic techniques, draws too strict a line between the realms of science and humanism at work within the identification process. For just as genetic profiles provide signposts for individual identity, so the recollections of family members help to recognize the missing person's remains. Indeed, the technology's success depends simultaneously on the innovations of DNA analysis and the human subjective experiences of remembering and reckoning. Science and memory combine forces, connecting the narratives of the missing with the stories unfolded by sets of genetic codes.

*Families' Recognition: Experiences of Memory and Imagination*

Chapters 4 and 5 explore how memory and imagination intersect with evidence of DNA analysis and other postmortem data during the final stages of identifying a missing person. In these instances, we see the melding and interconnectivity of two worlds—experts and families; science and humanism. These chapters raise several questions about experiences and definitions of identification. For example, how does a mother accept the "facts" of the identification of her missing son's body through DNA analysis when she cannot recognize a stitch of the clothing recovered with those same remains? Does the identification of a partial body signal the end of absence, or an incomplete presence? What happens when a family—once defined along its patrilineal social structure—is missing most if not all of its male members? The transformation of the Srebrenica victims' surviving family structure frustrates the very process of recovering mortal remains. The absence of fathers, brothers, husbands, sons, and uncles—and thus their genetic material as readily available references—has forced the experts to create new methods and seek new avenues to bring about identification. Likewise, those very families must invent new ways of living without their male relatives.

Thus, it is through the surviving families' empty rooms and the barely touched trays of *bajramska baklava* that another side of the missing persons' absence comes to light—that is, the ways in which those most intimately connected with the missing person respond to the fact that *on nije došao* (he did not make it) and, much later, to the news of his identification. While many family members rely on memories to maintain their missing relatives' presence in their lives, significant gaps exist between those memories, recollections that leave off abruptly and painfully with their separation in the enclave or at Potočari, and their present, though incomplete, understanding of the genocide. During this period of absent knowledge, imagination fills in where memory cannot, providing images to complete the stories of missing relatives.

These voids often distress family members because they cannot shut out the brutality that they know occurred, information they gleaned from those who survived the flight through the forest and the executions begun at Potočari. They know firsthand of the violence that took place in the spring of 1992 when Bosnian Serb and Serbian forces carried out campaigns of ethnic cleansing in the Podrinje region; they heard the stories of the Omarska and Trnopolje concentration camps in the western part of the country, where Bosniaks were detained, tortured, and killed. This knowledge adds to their fears of what they imagine happened to their missing relatives. The news of identification often includes information about the missing person's capture, detention, and execution, as well as the whereabouts of his mortal remains over the past several years—information that may dislodge or confirm the imagined circumstances of their relatives' final hours and days.

Although the news of identification shuts out any last hope of the relative's survival, it also grants families knowledge that works to counter the violent rupture of July 1995. Perhaps the most helpful frame of reference for understanding the state of disorder in which the surviving family members of the Srebrenica genocide lived in the days, months, and years after the fall of the enclave is the secondary mass grave. The chaotic physical scene of commingled and partial human skeletons represents a rupture not only of the materiality of the human body, but also of any prevailing sense of social, religious, or political order. The procedures of identification created to disentangle the jumbled bones of Srebrenica's victims start from the premise that order can be fashioned from chaos. The technology of violence implemented by the Bosnian Serb forces required a counterpoint system of technology, one that could take the random and minute pieces of human genetic material and render order to the commingled bones of the mass graves. Once achieved, that order falls first to the individual: the missing person's physical remains and his metaphysical being. Identity is reattached to a body, and those remains are then returned to the families. That restoration of personhood offers the surviving family members a release from the state of ambivalence in which they maintained memories of their missing relatives. It provides them with a burial site and a gravestone—at long last the known whereabouts of their loved ones.

## Commemoration as Collective Recognition

The identification technology is a mechanism for distilling individual identity from the genocide's collective categories, and, thus, resolving the crisis of absence caused by unmarked mass graves. But a resolution for whom? Who desired these narratives, graves, and commemorative placards? The families are not alone in seeking the return of their relatives' mortal remains. Chapters 6 and 7 turn to forms of collective recognition, examining how the various actors involved in the controversy over Srebrenica's missing have participated in the identification process and, subsequently, interpreted the results: remains recognized and reburied.

The Srebrenica-Potočari Memorial Center serves as the final destination and culmination of the identification process and, thus, the primary locus of collective remembering. It is there that the overwhelming majority of Srebrenica families have decided to bury their identified relatives and there that the Bosniak religious and political leadership attempts to forge a new sense of nationalism based on wartime narratives of suffering and loss. The annual commemorative ceremony and mass burial held at the complex each July 11 reveal the interconnected layers of sociopolitical and religious meaning tied to the identification process. Prefaced by political speeches, religious services commemorate individual life, collective violence, and nationhood. Near a side entrance to the cemetery, where families and friends gather to inter the coffins that day, a stone has been erected bearing the following prayer:

| | |
|---|---|
| U ime Boga Milostivog, Samilosnog | In the Name of God, The Most Merciful, the Most |
| Molimo Te Bože Svemogući, | Compassionate |
| Neka tuga postane nada! | We Pray to Almighty God, |
| Neka osveta bude pravda! | May grievance become hope![19] |
| Neka majčina suza Bude molitva: | May revenge become justice! |
| Da se nikome nikad Ne ponovi Srebrenica! | And mothers' tears may become prayers That Srebrenica |
| Reisu-l-ulema Srebrenička molitva Potočari 11.juli, 2001 | Never happen again To no one anywhere! |
| | Raisu-l-ulama Srebrenica Prayer Potočari July 11, 2001 |

Appropriating Holocaust survivors' demand that genocide "never again" be allowed to happen, the prayer (also written in Arabic) articulates the Srebrenica community's insistence on building an enduring and collective memory of the genocide in Bosnia. Intended for a universal audience, its message is invoked at each annual commemorative ceremony when the head of the Bosnian Islamic Community (Islamska zajednica), Reis ul-ulema Mustafa Cerić, addresses the gathering, repeating its phrases.

Given the scope and audience of the commemorative activities that take place there, the memorial center has become a site of sociopolitical division as much as it provides surviving families with a shared space to remember their lost relatives and the events of July 1995. The growing number of mounds capped by slender white tombstones feeds into competing ethno-national discourses concerning wartime losses and responsibility among both Bosniak and Bosnian Serb populations within the region. In response to the complex in Potočari, Bosnian Serbs have built memorials to their own wartime victims. As we will see in later chapters, the "political lives of dead bodies" (Verdery 1999) cultivated and commemorated at these respective sites fit within the broader Yugoslav historical context of World War II unmarked mass graves and unnamed victims; they also recall the subsequent public reburials and debates over numbers of World War II victims that took place during the late 1980s and early 1990s (Denich 1994; Hayden 1994, 1992a; Boban 1990; Duijzings 2007; Ballinger 2003; Verdery 1999). The biotechnological evidence of bodies recovered, identified, and reburied adds a new technoscientific twist to the language of political morality (Herzfeld 1997) embedded within these competing ethnonationalist discourses.

The international community also has a deeply rooted interest in naming and reburying Srebrenica's missing. Given the United Nations' negligent role in the fall of the enclave and the ensuing violence, the recovery of the Srebrenica victims remains a top priority for Western governments and their representatives in the Office of the High Representative, the international protectorate in postwar Bosnia established through the Dayton Peace Agreement. The concrete numbers yielded by the identification process—bodies exhumed, blood samples collected, successful DNA matches—offer these international actors a means by which to measure their investment—if not on a social level, at least on a concrete, material one. As it becomes less and less palatable to support reconstruction efforts in the region because of other, more urgent, humanitarian missions, the international community still recognizes and presses ahead with the overt goal of filling Potočari's cemetery. The memorial center and its burial grounds are seen as yet another means of encouraging return and reconciliation and of advancing the project of nation-building deemed so vital by the Western governments actively involved in shaping the country's future.

### Bosnia's Postmortem Technology: Implications beyond the Balkans

The innovative model of postmortem identification developed to counter the annihilating effects of Srebrenica's mass graves has profoundly changed how forensic science approaches the identification of mass "missing person" populations. Chapter 8 explores the political implications of this cutting-edge biotechnology as it circulates beyond the borders of former Yugoslavia. First tracing precedents in forensic practice, particularly in Latin American states, we see how forensic science has supported human rights investigations by documenting crimes and identifying missing persons. In a similar vein, the Bosnian technology has become an important mechanism of intervention in postconflict-postdisaster societies. ICMP's staff and technology have informed, if not been directly engaged in, identification efforts for victims of the September 11, 2001, World Trade Center attacks; the 2004 tsunami; and, most recently, Hurricane Katrina. Examined together, these examples reveal how states and their proxies employ this costly biotechnology as a critical means of caring for and controlling their citizens—both living and dead—in moments of crisis and disorder.

#### WRITING ABOUT IDENTIFICATION

Studying the identification process entailed working closely with those whose lives were deeply implicated in its development, results, and legacy. It meant eating a slice of Hajra's baklava on *bajram*. It meant sitting in the living room with a family member when she first received the news of her missing relative's identification. It meant poring over case files in the Podrinje Identification Project (PIP) office, incessantly asking questions of staff members, particularly the case managers, and becoming gradually inured to the sight of skeletal remains laid out on the steel examination table at the PIP mortuary. While I explore these concepts of identification, recognition, technology, memory, and commemoration at times in very abstract terms, the insight that I have gained through my interactions with both the "experts" and the family members of the missing is anything but indifferent or impersonal. I use the term *experts* to describe the local and international staff involved in the various stages of the grave-to-grave process.[20] In referencing their training and knowledge, inevitably the word also imparts a sense of distance between these people and the object of their work. While it is true that in their hands, the skeletons and blood samples do not encompass individual identity as defined through social relations—that is, a person whose name conjures up a series of recollections or shared experiences—nevertheless, my friends and colleagues at the International Commission on Missing Persons, and in particular at the Podrinje Identification Project office, demonstrated their emotional connections to the work and the people for whom they labored in myriad and heartfelt ways. One of the forensic anthropologists expressed it most clearly when describing her frustration with journalists who visited her workplace in the days leading up to the tenth anniversary of the Srebrenica genocide. They pressed her repeatedly about how she felt working with these remains day in and day out, and some were put off by her seemingly detached responses. They had failed to appreciate something important. Laura's conscientious approach to her job and to the skeletal remains she so carefully examined each day required that she cultivate an emotional distance. In her mind, shedding tears over each of the hundreds of body bags that passed through her hands meant a disservice to her work and, in turn, to the families who depended on that very same calm, dispassionate manner for the critical results of her examination.

In a sense, I have tried to emulate the careful restraint of people such as Laura and the case managers of the Podrinje Identification Project when writing about some of the most emotionally raw experiences of identification that I witnessed during my fieldwork. I have also tried to respect people's sense of privacy. Though each of my informants whose words I quote refused the option of anonymity when offered, in most cases I have chosen to use only first names. I depart from this practice when the people quoted are already public figures whose opinions and actions are well recognized by their fellow Bosnians and whose words I believe should be directly attributed to them.

I became acquainted with only a fraction of the families of Srebrenica's missing, but their open doors and shared stories enabled

my understanding of the process of identification, and more importantly, of the experience of the missing. It is my hope that these same
stories—the rich words and experiences of the people with whom I
worked in Bosnia—will emerge from this text as vivid testimony of
their dedication to restoring individual identity and human dignity to
each of Srebrenica's missing.

# CHAPTER I

# The Fall of Srebrenica

*A ja sam tada imala samo jedanaest godina. Stajala sam na istom ovome mjestu i za razliku od danas, bilo me je užasno strah. Pored mene je stajalo bezbroj uplašene djece, tužnih žena i skrhanih staraca i svi skupa gledali smo kako mržnja ubija čovjeka. I danas pamtim kako odvedoše oca i njegov posljednji pogled upućen mom prekinutom djetinjstvu.*

And I was only eleven at the time. I stood at this very place and, unlike today, I was scared to death. Numerous frightened children, sad women and broken old men stood next to me and all of us watched the hatred killing human beings. I still remember the moment when they took my father away and his last glance cast at my interrupted childhood.

> Advija Ibrahimović *(Excerpt from remarks at the opening ceremony of the Srebrenica-Potočari Memorial Center, September 20, 2003)*

If inaction characterized the international community's response to the events of July 1995, then documenting the story of the enclave and its fall, its mass graves, and its missing has become a principal means of redressing the failure to act. There are the official governmental reckonings: the United Nations Report of the Secretary General pursuant to General Assembly resolution 53/35 (1999), the report commissioned by the French National Assembly (Assemblée nationale 2001), and the Dutch Parliament–commissioned report of the Netherlands Institute for War Documentation (Nederlands Instituut voor Oorlogsdocumentatie [NIOD] 2002). In addition to detailing the Bosnian Serb forces' crimes, all of these documents address the issue of the international community's complicity in the fall of the safe area and the deaths of more than

8,000 Bosniak men and boys. The International Criminal Tribunal for the former Yugoslavia (ICTY) has also created an extensive body of evidence documenting the event through the trials of indicted war criminals. Official testimony, such as that of Dražen Erdemović, one of the Bosnian Serb Army soldiers who participated in the executions of the Bosniak men, as well as the evidence in the trial of General Radislav Krstić, who was convicted of genocide in 2002, provides a comprehensive chronicle of the circumstances, decisions, and actions that resulted in the deportation and execution of the enclave's residents.[1]

Perhaps the most powerful and shocking evidence of the Srebrenica genocide to reach the public appeared during the trial of former Serbian president Slobodan Milošević. On June 1, 2005, the prosecution showed a video of a Serbian special police unit called the Scorpions (Škorpioni) as its members transported, abused, and finally executed six young civilian prisoners from Srebrenica. Local and international television stations broadcast approximately five minutes of this chilling footage, released to the public by ICTY from the two-hour tape, over the following week and during the days leading up to the ten-year anniversary of the genocide. The horrifying seconds of cold-blooded execution captured by the often ill-trained camera lens thrust the human faces of victims and perpetrators into living rooms throughout the region and the world.[2]

Arguably the most politically significant Bosnian report documenting the fall of the enclave came from the RS Commission for Investigation of the Events in and around Srebrenica between July 10 and July 19, 1995. Compelled by the Human Rights Chamber for Bosnia and Herzegovina in a decision resulting from claims filed by families of the Srebrenica missing, the Bosnian Serb government established the commission in 2003.[3] After stalled efforts and much political arm-twisting, including the decision by the Office of the High Representative (OHR) to remove commission members deemed biased and to reject early drafts of its findings, the commission issued its preliminary report in June 2004. Its contents prompted the first official recognition by the Bosnian Serb government of the war crimes committed at Srebrenica. In a televised appearance, the RS president at the time, Dragan Čavić, stated, "The Report . . . is the beginning of difficult, and probably, for all of us, sometimes the empty road of disclosing of the truth. It is on relevant state bodies and institutions to process these and such results of the Commission's work, and it is on us to continue walking towards the truth. Only this is the way to avoid the situation of having our children hate each other in the future, only because they are Croats, Bosniaks, or Serbs."[4] The RS government accepted the commission's report in its entirety through the adoption of its conclusions in a special session on October 28, 2004.

In addition to the tribunal's growing pool of evidence and the various governmental fact-seeking accounts, several foreign journalists and scholars have written books analyzing the fall of Srebrenica (Honig and Both 1996; Neuffer 2002; Power 2002), the most in-depth and compelling of which include the Pulitzer Prize–winning reporter David Rohde's *Endgame* (1997) and Chuck Sudetic's *Blood and Vengeance* (1998).[5] Both Rohde and Sudetic incorporate testimonial accounts of life during and after the fall of the safe area and thus contain especially character-driven narratives of the event and its aftermath.

Since the end of the war, local nongovernmental organizations have sponsored several factual and analytical accounts of the fall of the Srebrenica safe area. In 1998, the Women of Srebrenica published a collection of testimonies, *Samrtno Srebreničko ljeto '95* (Srebrenica's Deadly Summer 1995; Žene Srebrenice 1998b), which was later translated into Dutch. In 2003, the Women of Srebrenica and former UN translator Hasan Nuhanović produced two texts based on collaborative research conducted among Srebrenica survivors: *Uloga međunarodih elemenata u Srebrenici "zaštićenoj zoni"—hronologija, analiza i komentari* (The Role of International Elements in the Srebrenica "Safe Area"—Chronology, Analysis, and Commentary; Nuhanović 2003) and *Kolekcija 107 izjava o ulozi međunarodne zajednice u Srebrenici "zaštićenoj zoni" UN-a* (A Collection of 107 Statements about the Role of the International Community in the Srebrenica "Safe Area"; Žene Srebrenice 2003).[6] Other works include *Genocid u Srebrenici "sigurnoj zoni" Ujedinjenih nacija, jula 1995* (Genocide in Srebrenica, the United Nations "Safe Area," in July 1995; Čekić, Kreso, and Macić 2001), *Sjećanje na Srebrenicu* (Memories of Srebrenica; Mustafić 2003), and *Knjiga o Srebrenici* (A Book about Srebrenica; Sadik Salimović 2002). Timed for optimal public exposure, a spate of books, scholarly and journalistic, came out during the summer of 2005 to coincide with the commemorative activities (Biserko 2005; Matton 2005; Suljagić 2005).

Finally, there are several films about the genocide, the most notable being the BBC documentary *Cry from the Grave*, Maria Warsinski's *Crimes and Punishment*, and the Federation Commission for Missing Persons' *Marš smrti* (March of Death), all of which include footage of the Bosnian Serb forces entering the enclave, assembled at the compound at Potočari, and later with Bosniak captives. Like the Scorpion tape, these films succeed in placing the more abstract facts of the genocide (the estimated 8,000 missing) within a more visceral context of human suffering because they contain the faces and words of both the victims and the perpetrators. One such moment from the film *Cry from the Grave* has made its indelible mark on my own experience of researching the identification of Srebrenica's missing. In the glare of the midday sun, a father is forced by his Bosnian Serb captors to stand up and call out to his son, who is hiding in the hills above, urging the young man to surrender himself. He cups his hands around his mouth and makes the harrowing appeal, repeating his son's name in the vocative case, "Nermine, Nermine." The scene has remained with me, and whenever I pass along that road, by the spot where this man once begged for his son to join him, I recall his voice and that unsettling plea.

THE START OF THE WAR

The events of July 1995 are often dissected within the narrow confines of the Bosnian war. It is important to recognize, however, that the turmoil punctuating the final decade of the twentieth century in Bosnia echoed earlier periods of unrest in the land of the South Slavs—unrest inextricably bound to shifting political forces internal and external to former Yugoslavia. In the nineteenth century amid the rise of nationalism throughout Europe, changing borders between the Ottoman and Austro-Hungarian empires led to heightened militarization in the region. Stirred by the Balkan Wars of 1912–1913, competing European interests in the South Slav lands, namely those of Russia and the Dual Monarch, culminated in 1914 in the assassination of the Austrian archduke Franz Ferdinand by Gavrilo Princip, a member of the Serbian nationalist movement, Mlada Bosna.

Four years later, the end of World War I ushered in a new era of the nation-state, underwritten by the victors' expansionist principle of self-determination, out of which emerged the Kingdom of Yugoslavia, built around the core land of Serbia. Despite the so-called unification of the South Slavic peoples, tension arising from national claims to territory and resources nevertheless persisted throughout the interwar period. Indeed, once World War II broke out, Bosnia and Herzegovina became an easy target for annexation by the Independent State of Croatia, a puppet regime of Nazi Germany and Fascist Italy.[7] As we will see in chapter 6, the occupation of the region by the Axis powers split allegiances along national and ideological lines—from the Croatian fascists and Serb royalists to the communist Partisans. While Communist Party leader Josip Broz Tito succeeded in tamping down nationalist movements in the post–World War II years, the collapse of socialist Yugoslavia in the 1980s prompted disputes among the autonomous republics over power, territory, and the control of economic resources. Often the political discourse framing these claims recalled the century's two previous wars, recasting the past violence and human loss in predominantly ethno-national terms.

War broke out in Bosnia and Herzegovina in the spring of 1992, following political upheaval and armed conflict already gripping other parts of former Yugoslavia.[8] With Slovenia's declaration of independence from the Federal Republic of Yugoslavia on June 25, 1991, and the ten-day armed conflict with the Serb-controlled Jugoslovenska narodna armija (JNA [Yugoslav People's Army]) opposed to its withdrawal, the state of Yugoslavia unraveled swiftly. Croatia declared its independence on that same day in June and entered into armed conflict with Serbia (that is, the Federal Republic of Yugoslavia, which also included Montenegro) and the JNA shortly thereafter. Five months later, the JNA and local Serbian forces occupied over one-third of Croatia, with 15,000 people killed and 250,000 displaced by the conflict. The UN Security Council imposed an arms embargo on Yugoslavia in September 1991, thus tipping the military balance in favor of Serbia and the JNA.

Embroiled in a war whose front lines were pushing into the multiethnic territory of Bosnia and Herzegovina, Croatia and Serbia began to seek the partition of the land and people that lay between their two states. The most ethnically mixed of the Yugoslav territories, Bosnia's population was made up of three ethno-national groups (narodi):[9] Bosnian Muslims, or Bosniaks (44 percent); Bosnian Serbs (31 percent); and Bosnian Croats (17 percent).[10] With conflict breaking out among their neighbors, Bosnians from all three groups were forced to contemplate their future status within an independent Bosnia and Herzegovina, a Croat-controlled territory, or a territory that remained part of the rump state of Yugoslavia. Many Bosnian Serbs resisted the idea of a Sarajevo-based government, which, they worried, would create a Bosnian Muslim–oriented state (Ramet 2002:118–119; Gagnon 2004:76–77). Bosnian Croats looked to Zagreb for support and direction.[11] The Bosniaks feared the consequences of a war of aggression waged by their Croatian and Serbian neighbors. "The Bosnian

Muslims as a people *(narod)* were blocking a simple two-way partition of Bosnia and Herzegovina, both politically and by their numerically strong presence in all parts of Bosnia and Herzegovina, both rural and urban, where they lived among Serbs and Croats" (Bringa 2002:214). For Bosniaks, the division of Bosnia between those two states posed the threat of their forced displacement or outright annihilation. The brutal targeting of civilian populations by Serbian forces in places like Vukovar only heightened such fears.

In November 1991, Bosnian Serbs, led by Radovan Karadžić, head of the Serbian Democratic Party (Srpska demokratska stranka, or SDS), voted in a referendum held throughout predominantly Serb areas of the territory on whether they wished to remain in Yugoslavia. The overwhelming majority who participated voted "yes" (Bringa 2002:198). Although the Bosnian government declared the referendum invalid, by January 9, 1992, the SDS had already established the Serbian Republic of Bosnia and Herzegovina, later renamed the Republika Srpska (RS). Bosnian voters took up the issue of the territory's political course in a referendum held on February 29 and March 1, 1992. Following the examples of Slovenia, Croatia, and Macedonia, Bosniaks and Bosnian Croats voted for independence. The result, however, was undermined by the Bosnian Serb political leadership, the majority of whose constituency refused to participate in the referendum. Determined to thwart the effort to break away from Yugoslavia, SDS leaders had called on the territory's Serbs to boycott the vote.

On April 6, 1992, the European Community recognized the Republic of Bosnia and Herzegovina, and the United States followed suit the next day. Serb forces laid siege to Sarajevo, and shortly thereafter, violence erupted in the northern and eastern parts of Bosnia, including the Podrinje region, which lay to the west of the Drina River, immediately opposite Serbia. Serbian leaders regarded the central Podrinje region, which included Srebrenica, as strategically significant for establishing a Serbian political entity that would stretch beyond the border of the Drina River. During the Krstić trial at the ICTY, defense witness General Radovan Radinović outlined this objective:

> [Serbs] wanted to live in the same state with other Serbs, and the only
> state that could guarantee that was the former Yugoslavia. . . . the
> Serbs realised that the area of the Central Podrinje had a huge strategic
> importance for them. Without the area of Central Podrinje, there would
> be no Republika Srpska, there would be no territorial integrity of Serb
> ethnic territories; instead the Serb population would be forced to accept

> the so-called enclave status in their ethnic territories. The territory would
> be split into two, the whole area would be disintegrated, and it would be
> separated from Serbia proper and from areas which are inhabited almost
> 100 percent by Serb populations. (ICTY Prosecutor v. Radislav Krstić
> 2001, par. 12)

To seize control of this territory, Serbian paramilitary forces such as
Arkan's Tigers, whose ranks included convicted criminals recruited
from Serbian prisons, swept through the Podrinje region. Working
together with Bosnian Serb forces, they carried out the violent campaign to rid villages and cities of their non-Serb populations. The program of ethnic cleansing involved mass killings, forced displacement,
torture and rape, and the destruction of private and public property,
including religious objects.[12]

The notion of "cleaning up" territory in order to render it ethnically
homogenous for some Serb leaders entailed the complete disappearance of the opposing ethnic group. In the case of the Podrinje region
this meant the disappearance of the Bosniak population. Several
months earlier, when arguing against independence before the Bosnian
Parliament (even though he was not actually an elected official at that
point), Radovan Karadžić spoke about the possible disappearance of
the Muslim people in a thinly veiled threat: "Don't you think that you
are going to lead Bosnia into hell, and probably the Muslim people
into disappearance *(nestanak)* because the Muslim people cannot
defend itself[?]—[It] is going to war" (quoted in Bringa 2002:221).
It is difficult to know precisely what Karadžić intended by the word
"disappearance"—that is, whether he meant the forced displacement
of Muslim populations or their complete annihilation. In any case,
within months, both displacement and mass killings were taking place
throughout Bosnia, and the term *missing persons (nestale osobe,* or
*nestali)* evolved from a mere threat to an actual category of persons in
wartime Bosnia. In its postwar application, *nestali* would become the
primary epithet for the victims of the Srebrenica genocide.

With the bloody attack on Zvornik, the major city on the Drina
River to the north of Višegrad, in early April 1992, Bosniaks in the city
of Srebrenica became nervous. Journalist and teacher Mirsad Mustafić,
who fled Srebrenica in the spring of 1992 and covered the enclave
throughout the war, writes, "In the center of the city people began to
gather in groups and seek more information. After Arkan's men's attack
on Zvornik, a powerful wave of flight had begun. Some headed toward
Montenegro and Macedonia, others toward Tuzla and then on to the

West [Europe]" (2003:36). With a prewar population of about 5,800, Srebrenica was a predominantly Bosniak city. In the larger municipality of Srebrenica, which stretched over 527 square kilometers and had a population of just over 37,000, Bosniaks were the ethnic majority, with 73 percent (27,118) of the total population; Bosnian Serbs made up 25 percent (9,380) (Salimović 2002:205).[13] Like the other majority Bosniak cities and villages in the Podrinje region, Srebrenica lay closer to Serbia than it did to the protection of the Army of the Republic of Bosnia and Herzegovina (Bosnian Army). Local Bosnian Serb leaders considered that part of the country to be Serbian, not Bosnian, "a centuries-old Serbian hearth/home" (Mustafić 2003:37), and as political tensions heightened with the encroaching violence, the Serb representatives seized control of the municipality. On April 13, 1992, Srebrenica's municipal parliament met for the last time. Although SDS representatives declared that there would be no war, they moved that all future meetings be held in Bratunac, the Bosnian Serb–controlled city to the north of Srebrenica, and in Ljubovija, the Serbian city across the Drina River from Bratunac.

On April 18, 1992, paramilitary units from Serbia, supported by local Bosnian Serbs, attacked Srebrenica, setting houses on fire, looting shops, and killing twenty-seven people. The overwhelming majority of residents had already fled in anticipation of the violence. The 365 who remained hid in the outlying hills, watching their city burn from afar. The occupation lasted until May 9, when the Bosnian Army recaptured the city. Srebrenica quickly became a pocket of "free" (i.e., Bosniak-controlled) territory, an enclave into which refugees streamed from throughout the Podrinje region—from Bratunac, Vlasenica, Zvornik, Bijelina, Rogatica, Višegrad, and Han Pijesak. By the end of 1992, with medical and food supplies cut off and Srebrenica's population rising to 30,000, famine, disease, and attacks from Bosnian Serb forces had ravaged the enclave.[14] "The first thing you notice about Srebrenica and its victims is the hunger and sickness. The population is growing sick mostly from basic illnesses such as the consequences of malnutrition. Women are dying in great numbers from childbirth because they cannot bear the exhaustion and then the babies [die] because the mothers cannot feed them. The wounded are a story for remembering. The devastated hospital without basic medicines and instruments received around thirty wounded people a day" (Mustafić 2003:88). Without one trained surgeon among them, the doctors performed operations only during the day because there was no electricity; when alcohol ran

out, they used battery acid to disinfect wounds and performed amputa-
tions using saws without the aid of anesthesia. The Bosnian Serbs cut
off the city's water supply, forcing people to use private wells and wash
their clothes in the local streams, whose water had high concentrations
of minerals that stained the clothing a permanent rust color.

During the first year in the enclave, people were literally starving to
death. The local Bosnian defense, led by Naser Orić, conducted raids
on outlying Serb villages ostensibly to seize food, but, as the ICTY
indictment against him later charged, also to exact punishment on the
local Serb population for the Bosnian Serb Army's harassment of the
enclave.[15] Through these attacks, Orić's troops succeeded in extending
the borders of the enclave to its peak size of 900 square kilometers by
January 1993. On several of the raids, Orić's men killed Serb villagers,
including women and children. The most infamous attack was against
the village of Kravica on the Orthodox celebration of Christmas,
January 7, 1993, when Orić's men killed forty-three Serbs, thirteen
of whom were civilians (ICTY 2005).[16] Following the troops on these
raids, *torbari* (literally, bag people) from the enclave swept through the
targeted villages, cleaning out the food supplies and anything else they
wanted and could carry away.

The looting of nearby Serb villages could not stem the widespread
hunger among the enclave's population and only further angered the
Bosnian Serb forces that surrounded the area. It was difficult to deliver
supplies to the isolated city. The first UNHCR convoy carrying humanitarian aid arrived in November 1992, but the Bosnian Serbs turned back
or looted subsequent shipments. With the Bosnian Serbs' violent recap-
ture of the villages of Cerska and Konjević Polje in February 1993, the
enclave's population ballooned to upward of 50,000.[17] "They take up
residence wherever they arrive. On the Tokoljački hill, a village formed
in a dilapidated house, where entire families live. In the city there's no
longer any room. And the small number of stock that had existed, the
war has eaten up. Epidemics rage through the city. Thousands of people
throughout the day tend fires with a couple of blankets and sleep on the
sidewalks. Filth, despair, and incurable grief" (Mustafić 2003:89).

The United Nations finally responded to the humanitarian crisis in
Srebrenica in March 1993, and its subsequent decisions profoundly
affected the fate of the enclave and its inhabitants. US Air Force planes
began to parachute in pallets of food and supplies, but again, given the
swelling numbers of people and the desperate conditions, the support
did little to allay the suffering. Dismayed by reports she had received

about massacres within the northern section of the Srebrenica enclave, UNHCR director Sadako Ogata sent a letter to UN secretary general Boutros Boutros-Ghali in which she recommended that the UN evacuate the refugees living in Srebrenica to Tuzla. Her letter prompted General Philippe Morillon, commander of the UN forces in Bosnia, to visit the enclave to assess the situation. On March 5 he traveled with an assembly of relief workers and a British military unit to Konjević Polje, the cluster of hamlets in the northern part of the enclave where the Bosnian Serb Army had attacked days before. Unalarmed by what he saw there, Morillon returned to Tuzla later that day and explained to reporters, "'As a soldier, I, unfortunately, have the knack for smelling death. I didn't smell it. . . . The most important thing at the present time is to break this vicious circle. . . . Srebrenica is in no danger'" (Sudetic 1998:176). One of the relief workers, a doctor from the World Health Organization, apparently had a better sense of smell. Having broken off from Morillon's entourage, Simon Mardel walked on from Konjević Polje to Srebrenica, where he saw firsthand the daily death toll, and sent back reports about the enclave's dire humanitarian conditions. On March 10 Morillon was forced to set out for Srebrenica with a convoy that included food trucks. After Serb commanders tried to turn back the column and detain the food convoy, Morillon and a small segment of the initial group of vehicles were allowed to proceed into Srebrenica. The Bosniak leadership in Sarajevo took advantage of the situation, sending word to Naser Orić to detain Morillon. "'Do it in a civilized way. . . . Use women and children'" (Sudetic 1998:179). Surrounded by women of all ages—including mothers who placed their small children under the wheels of his car—Morillon was trapped. They begged for, indeed demanded, help. Late that night, the French general attempted to sneak out of the enclave, hiking to Potočari, where his car was ready to meet him. But his ruse was foiled, and Morillon returned to Srebrenica, to an even more embittered and demanding crowd.

On March 13 General Morillon found the words to win over the refugees and secure his own release. From the rooftop of the post office he shouted through a bullhorn to the people assembled below, "You are now under the protection of the United Nations. . . . I will never abandon you" (Rohde 1997:xv). In his hand he held the UN flag, to be raised over the city of Srebrenica. During my fieldwork both in Srebrenica and Tuzla, I would hear that proclamation repeated, even acted out, by numerous survivors when they described their experiences in the enclave and specifically when they spoke about the United

Nations' role in its tragic end. It was difficult for them to reconcile the promise made by the French general—the commander of UN forces in Bosnia no less—with the events of July 1995. In a message to the UN military headquarters in Sarajevo later that day, which he directed for release to the media, Morillon wrote, "'Fully conscious that a major tragedy was about to take place in Srebrenica I deliberately came here. And I have now decided to stay here in Srebrenica in order to calm the population's anguish, in order to try to save them'" (Sudetic 1998:182). He left shortly thereafter.

With Morillon's departure and his promises of the imminent delivery of more humanitarian aid, many people in the enclave believed their protection was ensured. Others were more skeptical, viewing Morillon within the context of the French government's engagement in the war.[18] Mirsad Mustafić wrote in a newspaper column on April 1, 1993, "Altruism as a strong suit of character is not one the French have ever possessed. Morillon cannot be the exception" (2003:92). Regardless of the context from which it sprung, Morillon's declaration of UN protection changed the enclave's conditions and its status in the eyes of the international community. The humanitarian convoys that subsequently delivered food and supplies to the city also evacuated around 5,000 women, children, and elderly people. Helicopters evacuated another 500 severely wounded.[19]

Just one month later, however, the Serbs, who had slackened their grip on the enclave, once again pounded its defenses, and Srebrenica's leaders sought negotiations for the surrender of the enclave. With Morillon's bold and well-publicized proclamation about Srebrenica being under UN protection, the United Nations Security Council was forced to respond to the renewed Serb aggression. It passed Resolution 819, demanding "that all parties and others concerned treat Srebrenica and its surroundings as a safe area which should be free from any armed attack or any other hostile act" (UN Security Council 1993a). Through the resolution, the Security Council recognized the vulnerable state of the enclave and the danger faced by its civilian residents as long as the Bosnian Serb forces continued to attack it, citing among other points that it was

- concerned by the pattern of hostilities by Bosnian Serb paramilitary units against towns and villages in eastern Bosnia and in this regard reaffirming that any taking or acquisition of territory by the threat or use of force, including through the practice of "ethnic cleansing", is unlawful and unacceptable,

- deeply alarmed at the information provided by the Secretary-General to
the Security Council on 16 April 1993 on the rapid deterioration of the
situation in Srebrenica and its surrounding areas, as a result of the continued deliberate armed attacks and shelling of the innocent civilian
population by Bosnian Serb paramilitary units, . . .

- aware that a tragic humanitarian emergency has already developed in
Srebrenica and its surrounding areas as a direct consequence of the brutal actions of Bosnian Serb paramilitary units, forcing the large-scale
displacement of civilians, in particular women, children and the elderly.
(UN Security Council 1993a)

To protect Srebrenica and the five other Muslim-held enclaves, each
given the status of safe areas (Sarajevo, Tuzla, Bihać, Žepa, and
Goraždje), the UN needed to send troops.[20] Boutros-Ghali told the
Security Council that the mission would require 30,000 soldiers.
"Thanks largely to the American refusal to contribute soldiers and
fatigue among European states with troops already in Bosnia, only a
tiny fraction of the forces needed to man, monitor, and defend these
pockets arrived. President Clinton himself called the safe areas 'shooting galleries'" (Power 2002:303). Conferred with the status of a United
Nations "safe area," Srebrenica received the meager protection of a
contingency of UNPROFOR (United Nations Protection Force) troops
from Canada, a total of 750 lightly armed soldiers. They set up a small
command center in Srebrenica proper (Bravo Company Compound)
and a main compound in the town of Potočari, located five kilometers
north, on the road to Bratunac.

The Bosniak population in the enclave maintained its own defenses,
even though the establishment of the "safe area" had also entailed
a demilitarization agreement, dated May 8, 1993, between Bosnian
Army general Halilović and Bosnian Serb general Ratko Mladić. The
agreement stipulated that "any military operation [was] strictly forbid-
den" (Honig and Both 1996:131).[21] Within the enclave, under the command of Naser Orić, there were three or four brigades of the Bosnian
Army's 28th Division, with an estimated 1,500 active soldiers.[22] Their
munitions included light weapons, machine guns, anti-tank weapons,
and light mortars, and it was rumored that the enclave received arms
shipments periodically from clandestine helicopter runs.

With security increased for the humanitarian convoys, conditions
improved inside the enclave, despite its relative isolation from the rest
of the country's Bosniak-controlled territory.[23] Over the next fourteen
months, life for the estimated 40,000 people residing in the enclave

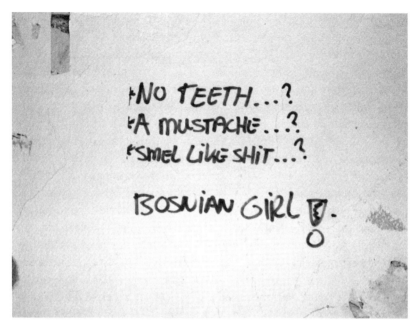

FIGURE I. Graffiti on the wall of the Dutchbat soldiers' compound in Potočari. Photo by the author.

remained relatively stable as the threat of NATO air strikes and the presence of the UNPROFOR troops kept the surrounding Bosnian Serb forces in check. On March 3, 1994, a Dutch battalion of 570 soldiers relieved the Canadian UNPROFOR unit. Frustrated by Orić's troops' disregard for the demilitarization agreement and by the dismal conditions within the enclave, many of the Dutch viewed the refugee population with skepticism or even outright contempt.[24] Some of the soldiers' graffiti in the UN barracks at the Potočari compound still remain on the walls. Written in green marker, the following words reveal at least one soldier's caustic, derogatory depiction of the female Bosnian population: "No teeth . . . ?/A mustache . . . ?/Smel [sic] like shit . . . ?/Bosnian girl!"[25]

In their account of the genocide, Jan Willem Honig and Norbert Both write, "To many of the Dutch soldiers' eyes the refugees did not offer an edifying spectacle. The enclave was overpopulated. People were underfed and badly clothed. Hygiene was a problem. . . . Some Dutch were shocked by the eagerness with which Muslims would await the dumping of rubbish on the tip outside the compound in order to scan it for useable items or food. . . . Many soldiers spoke in disparaging terms of the Muslims" (1996:131). Honig and Both leave off without interrogating these impressions, for example, the lack of basic food supplies for the Bosniak population.[26] Their characterization of the Western European soldiers' relations with the refuges hints at some of the frustrations and biases at play well before the enclave came under attack in the summer of 1995.[27] Reminiscent of the fear, suspicion, and even disgust that displaced persons encountered after their liberation from Nazi concentration camps, the atmosphere in the enclave between the refugees and the UN soldiers was tense, often marked by mutual distrust.[28] For some Dutch soldiers, conditions of squalor and acts of desperation rendered the refugee population less, rather than more, pitiable. The graffiti on the walls of the army barracks and reports of Dutchbat soldiers' disgust with the Bosniak population reveal a level of indifference present not only among some of the very soldiers charged with protecting the civilians within the safe area, but also among the UN bureaucrats in the Zagreb and New York offices. As Michael Barnett argues in his analysis of the failed UN peacekeeping effort in Rwanda, the production of such indifference is closely tied to the bureaucratiza-tion of peacekeeping, a tragically unsuccessful UN endeavor during the early to mid-1990s. Just as members of the secretariat reportedly dismissed concern over UNAMIR troops as "not our boys" in the Rwandan case (Barnett 1997:559), so some among the Dutch troops had drawn subtle, culturally based lines between themselves and the Bosniaks of the enclave. "The identity of the bureaucracy . . . represents the emotional and cognitive mechanisms for producing exclusion and apathy" (Barnett 1997:563).[29] Although in constant contact with the refugees, even the strong arm of the bureaucracy was not immune to the numbing effects of indifference.

## THE FALL OF SREBRENICA

In April 1995, for reasons unclear at the time and that many would later find dubious, Naser Orić was recalled to Tuzla, leaving a power vacuum in the Bosniak military leadership. By June 1995, the situation in the enclave had changed significantly. The effects of a command issued by Karadžić in March, entitled "Directive 7," began to appear: it called for the creation of "an unbearable situation of total insecurity with no hope of further survival or life for the inhabitants of Srebrenica" (ICTY Prosecutor v. Radislav Krstić 2001, par. 28). Following several days of skirmishes between Bosnian Serb and Bosniak forces, the Bosnian Serbs defied UN Security Council Resolution 819 in early June by capturing two Dutchbat observation posts along the southeastern perimeter of the enclave. The action triggered an exodus of 3,000 to 4,000 refugees from that area toward the city of Srebrenica.

In a newspaper column, Mirsad Mustafić condemned the Dutch soldiers' ineffectual defense: "The Dutch 'warriors' did not resist them at all and in a gentlemanly fashion gave up this industrial zone and the communication route of Banja Bašta-Skelani-Milići-Vlasenica to Karadžić's chetniks. The Dutch weren't bound by handcuffs like their colleagues in Pale because the Serbs were more than sure that the American 'phantoms' wouldn't be bombing" (2003:110).[30] By now the Dutchbat troops numbered only 429, half infantry and half medical and support troops.[31] On July 6, the Dutchbat observation posts in the southeastern part of the enclave received direct fire from a range of Bosnian Serb weaponry, including mortars, artillery, and tanks. Rather than returning fire, Dutchbat commander Tom Karremans decided to surrender the posts. One after another, over the course of the next several days, the UN positions fell to the advancing Serbs. Unclear as to the local Bosnian Serb commanders' intentions, the Dutch commanders requested air surveillance to assess the position and movement of Serb troops. A debate arose over what Bosnian Serb general Ratko Mladić was planning—either to seize the southern portion of the enclave or to attack and take control of the entire safe area.

By July 9, Bosnian Serb forces began to attack the city itself from the southern entrance of Zeleni Jadar. The Bosnian Army's defenses succeeded in repelling the thrust of the advance, but the Dutch were indecisive and ill prepared to take on the new threat posed by the Bosnian Serb Army. "The problem was the UN Security Council Resolution 836, which defined the UN's mandate in the safe areas. France demanded that air strikes be used to defend the safe area. Heeding the advice of Chairman of the Joint Chiefs of Staff Colin Powell, the Clinton administration insisted that NATO airpower should be used only to defend UN peacekeepers" (Rohde 1997:78). Out of this distinction emerged two options: air strikes, which entailed NATO's large-scale bombing of a wide area around Srebrenica in response to Serb attacks, or Close Air Support, which would allow NATO planes to target only specific, individual pieces of artillery or tanks. Weighing these options, General Cees Nicolai, the UN chief of staff, decided against air strikes and in favor of Close Air Support. He then devised a plan that would force the Serbs to show their hand. They would be given an ultimatum: if they attacked a specific position—a blocking position that the Dutchbat would assume within the city of Srebrenica—the UN would order the NATO Close Air Support. Nicolai outlined the plan to Colonel Karremans, who later claimed to have understood the warning given by Nicolai to mean that if the Serbs did not withdraw, they would face massive air strikes.

Almir Bašović's play *Priviđenja iz srebrenog vijeka* (Ghosts from the Silver Age) became one of Bosnia's most poignant artistic critiques of the Dutchbat's—and by extension the international community's—failure to protect Srebrenica. In one of the final scenes of the play, a family discusses the growing threat of the Serbs' full-scale attack on the enclave. The father has faith that as a UN "safe area," the enclave will be protected:

> *Father:* How did it go on the guard?
>
> *Son:* This morning some chetnik raids were observed around the UNPROFOR observation points.
>
> *Father:* That's nothing. If it were something serious, they would warn us from Sarajevo.
>
> *Son:* God, old man, how will they warn you from Sarajevo about what's happening right in front of your own nose?
>
> *Fatima [mother]:* My fear is that they'll betray us.
>
> *Father:* Who?
>
> *(Pause)*
>
> *Fatima:* These foreigners. The blue helmets. They're hungry. I heard that people don't go digging through their garbage anymore because it's not worth it. How are they going to defend us when they're hungry? Besides, what does Srebrenica mean to them? They don't even know how to pronounce it.
>
> *Father:* What is it, what is it? A safe area, that's what it is. They have to defend us. They signed on it.
>
> *Son:* Yeah, they did. And they even sealed it. If we hadn't returned Morillon to them when he set out to flee on foot, they would have signed with the devil.
>
> *Father:* It's just the way things have to be. We are now property of the United Nations. That means property of the entire world.
>
> *Son:* Hungry, lice-infested. . . . It'll come out whom we belong to. Better yet, recommend to your guys in the City Hall that they ban even riding a bicycle around

the square with the name General Morillon on it. He
liked to go on foot.

*Father:* Leave off about the general. He was as good as
could be expected. Now they have to defend
us. If it's necessary, even with airplanes.

*(Pause)*

*Father:* They have satellites. They can read a newspaper on
the ground with those things.

*Son:* Where around here can you find a newspaper?

*Father:* Come on, stop kidding around. I'm just saying that
they have all kinds of scientific wonders.

*Son:* Stop. My god, the wonder is this bread of Fatima's.
Mom, where on earth did you get this flour?
(Bašović 2003 "Posljednja večera")

Through this dialogue, Bašović underscores the division of opinion
among the residents of the enclave. The mother, Fatima, speaks of an
ominous sign—the Dutchbat soldiers' hunger—and questions whether
they will defend the refugees if they themselves are suffering. Moreover,
she points out their abiding indifference: "they don't even know how to
pronounce it." The young university-schooled son is deeply skeptical of
the UN's promises, and he mocks his father and the enclave's civilian
leadership for their blind faith. Morillon's promises, he reminds his
father, were made under duress: the man tried to escape the enclave in
the dead of night "on foot" rather than face the nearly hysterical crowd.
The father, on the other hand, believes in that promise, in the international community's responsibility for Srebrenica's security. Furthermore, he believes in the power of their sophisticated technology, their
"scientific wonders." Science, more precisely awe-inspiring scientific
invention, is a synonym throughout the play for the paradoxical cou-
pling of the so-called advancement of civilization with the development
of new technologies of violence. The Western governments' satellite
images and high-precision bombs could have stopped the advancing Serbs. Like the father in the play, many of the enclave's residents
thought the UN would act in their defense. Others were convinced that
the enclave was being sacrificed by the UN, by the Bosnian Army, or by
President Alija Izetbegović in a land swap with the Bosnian Serbs.

For its own part, the Bosnian Army command within the enclave
had relied upon the UN's informal and formal promises of protection—from Morillon's pledge to the language of UN Security Council

Resolution 836. Honig and Both state cynically, "The Bosnians had also concentrated on a risky strategy. Rather than fight themselves, they believed their best chance of defending the enclave [was] with forcing the UN to intervene on their behalf" (1996:180). Yet by not responding to the Serb attacks, the Bosniaks were following instructions from both Sarajevo and the UN troops not to engage. With one piece of weaponry, a Yugoslav Army M-48 field artillery gun that had a range of three miles, the Bosniaks could have disabled infantry and, with a direct hit, even taken out Serb tanks. On July 9, a Dutch soldier spotted the gun and warned the Bosniaks guarding the weaponry not to fire it. If they fired, NATO would not strike, he explained to them. A Bosniak soldier replied that NATO would not strike, but for a very different reason: the Serbs held thirty Dutch troops prisoner and the lives of those Dutch soldiers were more important than the lives of the 30,000 Bosniaks in the enclave (Rohde 1997:67–69).

By 8:55 A.M. the next morning, July 10, Colonel Karremans had filed his third—and still unheeded—request for Close Air Support. The UN headquarters in Sarajevo had balked because the Dutch could not say with 100 percent certainty that the Serbs had fired on their blocking position. By 10:30 A.M., there were forty planes circling above the Adriatic Sea (only six of which could execute strikes), waiting for the command to head toward Srebrenica. At the meeting in UN headquarters at Zagreb later that morning, General Bernard Janvier, force commander, expressed his suspicion that the Bosnian Army (the Bosnian Muslim defense in Srebrenica) was trying to draw the UN into a conflict. Yasushi Akashi, civilian head of the UN mission, agreed: "'The BH [Army] initiates actions,' he said, 'and then calls on the UN and international community to respond and take care of their faulty judgment'" (Rohde 1997:102). Akashi's distrust of the Bosniak forces in the enclave supports what Barnett sees as a shift in the UN's approach to its peacekeeping missions during that period. Whereas previously "the Security Council and the Secretariat routinely noted that they had a responsibility to help those who could not help themselves, they were now suggesting that they could only help those who were willing to help themselves. . . . By and large, 'the people' no longer meant the victims of violence but those who controlled the means of violence" (1997:569).

With clear evidence that Serbs, not the Muslims, had fired on the Dutch blocking position, Karremans sent his fourth request for Close Air Support at 7:15 P.M. By 7:50 P.M., back in Zagreb, the UN officials were debating the logistics of a nighttime strike. Notoriously indecisive, Janvier prolonged the discussion, consulting over the phone with Akashi, as well as with the Bosnian Serb general Zdravko Tolimir, who only one day before had denied the attack was even taking place. "As the discussion dragged on, a waiter in a red blazer began serving canapés and pouring red wine for each participant. The UN officers and officials had missed their dinner and Janvier or one of his staff had ordered refreshments. As Srebrenica's fate hung in the balance, Janvier's Crisis Action Team sipped wine and nibbled on gourmet sandwiches" (Rohde 1997:124). At last they came to a decision. Janvier agreed to night strikes; back in Srebrenica, however, Karremans opted against it, thinking it better to wait until the next morning. At 12:05 A.M., July 11, Karremans met with the civilian leaders in the enclave's post office. He assured them that if the Serbs did not withdraw, there would be massive strikes. " 'This area,' Karremans said, pointing at the wide swath of territory now held by the Serbs south of Srebrenica, 'will be a zone of death in the morning. NATO planes will destroy everything that moves' " (Rohde 1997:132). Those present at that meeting could not possibly have fathomed the tragic irony of his words. For indeed, beginning the next day, Srebrenica would become a "zone of death"—but not the kind of death and destruction Karremans, his troops, or any of the UN officials debating Srebrenica's fate had imagined.

Survivors of the genocide described to me how they peered up at the sky on the morning of July 11, and how they listened for the sound of the NATO planes. With each passing hour their panic grew, and the exodus began. People hastily packed up what they could carry, food and clothing for the next few days, and set off for the Dutch compound in Potočari. In the play *Priviđenja iz srebrenog vijeka*, the protagonist, Fatima, who survived the fall but lost both her husband and her son, moves from scene to scene pushing a wheelbarrow. I asked one of the Women of Srebrenica why this was significant, and she told me that wheelbarrows were the only functional "vehicle" in the enclave. When it came time to flee, some people placed their ailing or elderly relatives in wheelbarrows and pushed them the five kilometers to Potočari.

The story of the NATO planes that never arrived the morning of July 11 is a pathetic lesson in UN bureaucracy and, in particular, UN military bureaucracy. Expecting the aircraft to arrive at 7 A.M., the Dutch troops were prepared to guide the air strikes against the Serb positions south of the city. With no sign of the planes, at 8 A.M. the Dutch sent another request to Tuzla for air attacks. In the meantime, the Bosniak troops had followed Karremans's instruction to keep clear of the target area and thus had abandoned strategic strongholds. The Serbs were clearly preparing to attack the city, and at 9 A.M., still no planes appeared on the horizon. The Dutch called over to Tuzla to find out what was holding up the air attacks. A Pakistani colonel, chief of air operations in Tuzla, explained that they had filed the wrong form—that is, a form for air strikes rather than the form for Close Air Support. They needed to file the correct form and attach updated targets. The comedy of errors continued as the Tuzla command forwarded the now correct form to Sarajevo, but was required to resend it twice because it had not included the proper listing of targets. Delaying the request even further, apparently the Tuzla command center's secure fax was disabled for several minutes. By 10:45 A.M., Sarajevo had the complete, correct form for Close Air Support, but because of yet another miscommunication, the NATO planes that had been waiting over the Adriatic since 6 A.M. were sent back to refuel at 9 A.M. They would not be ready for another two hours. The request, originating from Srebrenica at 8 A.M., traveled from Tuzla to Sarajevo and then finally to Zagreb; General Janvier signed it at 12:05 P.M. and Akashi at 12:15 P.M. At the earliest, a new "package" of NATO planes would arrive at the enclave at 1:45 P.M. By then, the Bosnian Serbs had entered the city. Two NATO planes, F-16s from the Royal Dutch Air Force, arrived at 2:40 P.M.—having been in the area for twenty minutes but unable to make radio contact—and dropped a total of two bombs before flying off. Only one tank sustained damage in the strike, and no Serb soldiers were injured or killed because they had already left their vehicles and were in the city itself. Fifteen minutes later two American planes arrived in eastern Bosnia, but they failed to see the smoke flares lit by Dutch commando air controllers and so returned to base without dropping a single bomb. Finally, an A-10 heavy ground-attack aircraft was poised to strike, but the Bosnian Serbs issued an ultimatum: should the air strikes continue, they would kill the Dutch soldiers in their custody and shell the enclave—soldiers and refugees alike. The strikes were immediately called off (Honig and Both 1996:25–26; Rohde 1997:137–162).[32]

Video footage exists of the Bosnian Serbs' entrance into the city. It records General Mladić and his troops as they walk through Srebrenica's streets. He directs a subordinate to remove a street sign and orders his troops, "On to Potočari." He turns to the camera for an interview by Serbian television journalist Zoran Petrović: "Here we are in Srebrenica on July 11, 1995. On the eve of yet another great

Serbian holiday . . . We present this city to the Serbian people as a gift. Finally, after the rebellion of the Dahijas, the time has come to take revenge on the Turks in this region" (Rohde 1997:167).[33] Except for Mladić's entourage of soldiers, the city looks like a ghost town. This footage, recorded to document the Bosnian Serb military victory over not only the Bosniak defenses but also the United Nations' will and capability to defend their so-called safe haven, ironically now serves as evidence against the victors. The prosecution used it in the Krstić case because General Krstić appears with Mladić walking through the city. No doubt it will also be used against Mladić, should he ever appear before the ICTY at The Hague.

The Bosniaks had already fled the city, taking one of two routes. An estimated 15,000 Bosniak men and boys gathered in the villages of Jaglići and Šušnjari, located in the northwestern part of the enclave, where they prepared for the 50-kilometer trek through Serb-controlled land to free territory, specifically to the city of Tuzla. Fearing that they would be killed if they fell into the hands of the Bosnian Serb forces, the men felt they stood a better chance of survival if they tried to escape through the woods. They organized themselves according to brigades. At the head of the column were units of the 28th Division, followed next by civilians mixed with soldiers, and finally by the last section of the column, made up of the Independent Battalion of the 28th Division (ICTY Prosecutor v. Radislav Krstić 2001, par. 61). Approximately one third of the column was soldiers, but not all of them were armed. Because the men had to make their way through Serb minefields located at the periphery of the enclave, they were forced at points to walk in single file, forming a long column that spread out over miles. The last of the units left Šušnjari midday on July 12, twelve hours after the first men had set out (United Nations 1999, pt. vii, sec. F, par. 316). The other refugees—the women, children, elderly, and sick or injured—fled to Potočari, where they sought refuge at the Dutchbat compound. By early evening, the Dutch had allowed 4,000 to 5,000 refugees inside the perimeter, having cut a hole in the fence surrounding the enclosure. Eventually they decided there was not enough space to accommodate more, and blocked the entrance, leaving 15,000 to 20,000 people outside the compound in the adjacent buildings, parking lots, fields, and abandoned buses. Water was scarce, and there were no latrines. The summer heat only exacerbated the rapidly deteriorating conditions, as well as the exhaustion and panic felt by the refugees.

## DEPORTATION AND KILLINGS

With the fall of the enclave to the Bosnian Serb forces, General Mladić summoned Colonel Karremans to appear at the first of three meetings to take place over the next fourteen hours. At 8:00 P.M., flanked by a few of his officers, Karremans met Mladić and the Bosnian Serb Army delegation at the Hotel Fontana in Bratunac, where Mladić spent the better of forty-five minutes berating the Dutch commander for the NATO strikes (United Nations 1999, pt. vii, sec. F, par. 313). From Mladić's remarks, it appeared that at that time, he did not know the whereabouts of the 28th Division. They agreed on a second meeting later that evening, to which Karremans was to bring representatives from the refugee population.

At 11:30 P.M., the negotiations recommenced at the Hotel Fontana. This time Karremans was accompanied by the director of the Srebrenica high school, Nesib Mandžić, the sole civilian representative, who had been "plucked from the crowd in Potočari" (ICTY Prosecutor v. Radislav Krstić 2001, par. 128). The Serbs set an intimidating tone: the screams of a pig being slaughtered just outside the window interrupted the initial discussion, and shortly thereafter, Mladić set a broken sign from Srebrenica's city hall on the table. The Dutchbat leader tried to impress upon Mladić the plight of the refugees as well as the condition of the 100 wounded housed within the compound. Mladić in turn outlined his plan to transport the refugees out of the enclave, explaining that vehicles would be provided, but insisted that the Bosnian Army turn over all their weapons. If they did not, he would shell the Dutchbat compound. The two men agreed to a cease-fire until 10 A.M. the next morning, at which time Mladić, Karremans, and refugee representatives—people who could, in Mladić's terms, "secure the surrender of weapons and save [the] people of Srebrenica from destruction"—would meet for a final time (ICTY Prosecutor v. Radislav Krstić 2001, par. 130). Mladić asked for Naser Orić but was told that he had not been seen in the enclave since April. The meeting was videotaped; it captured Karremans and his fellow officers raising their glasses in a toast to Mladić's victory. "Although Karremans later explained that he had only been holding a glass of water, the effect of the images was to portray the UN and the Dutch army as legitimators of ethnic cleansing. The pictures have become a symbol of the UN's humiliation in Srebrenica" (Honig and Both 1996:31).

The third and final meeting took place the next morning at 10 A.M.

with Karremans, a delegation of three Bosniak civilian representatives (school director Mandžić, businessman Ibro Nuhanović, and economist Ćamila Omanović), Mladić, and other Bosnian Serb Army officers. Again in command of the meeting, which was also being videotaped, Mladić set out the choice that the Bosniak representatives should relay to the enclave's population: "You can either survive *[opstati]* or disappear *[nestati]*. . . . For your survival, I request: that all your armed men who attacked and committed crimes—and many did—against our people, hand over their weapons to the Army of the Republika Srpska. . . . On handing over weapons you may . . . choose to stay in the territory . . . or, if it suits you, go where you want. The wish of every individual will be observed, no matter how many of you there are" (ICTY Prosecutor v. Radislav Krstić 2001, par. 132; Bosnian words added).

As Karadžić had done during his remarks to the Bosnian Parliament back in 1992, Mladić explicitly mentioned the disappearance of the Bosniak population, in this case, the Bosniaks in the Srebrenica enclave. The notion of disappearing began to take on a more ominous meaning in light of his subsequent instructions. Mladić explained that all men of military age (which he specified as between seventeen and seventy) would be separated and screened for "war criminals."[34] Given the impossibility of disarming the men in the column who had already embarked on the trek through the forest (about whose activity and location Mladić was now aware), the refugee representatives were powerless to do Mladić's bidding. Thus, to survive, they and the rest of the refugees gathered at the UN compound had no choice but to leave the enclave. The Dutch and the Bosnian Serb officers then discussed the logistics of the refugees' transport. The Bosnian Serb Army would provide buses for all the refugees who "wished" to leave for Kladanj. Mladić asked Karremans to provide diesel for the transportation, but Karremans responded that he did not have the fuel. Finally, the Dutch commander requested that a Dutch soldier accompany each bus to oversee its proper transport to free territory. Mladić agreed to this request, and they determined that the evacuation would begin at 1:00 P.M. that day.

The so-called voluntary evacuation—in reality a forced expulsion—took place over the course of the next two days. By noon July 12, trucks and buses began arriving at the Dutch compound. Terrified by the sporadic shelling and the sight of houses set afire in the adjacent hills by the Bosnian Serb forces around the compound, people were clamoring to get on the buses. At the same time that the vehicles appeared, Bosnian Serb soldiers entered Potočari and began to walk among the refugees. Mladić himself made an appearance, again accompanied by the Serbian television journalist Petrović, as well as other media representatives. He oversaw the filming of his soldiers as they handed out loaves of bread and water to the refugees and candy to the children. In the now famous footage, women, children, and old men stand behind the thin strip of red-and-white tape separating them from the Serb soldiers—a pitiable symbol of the protection offered the panicked refugees. Mladić approaches them, gives a child an avuncular pat on his head, and tells the crowd, "Don't be afraid. Just take it easy, easy. Let women and children go first. Plenty of buses will come. We will transfer you towards Kladanj. From there you will cross to the territory controlled by Alija's [Izetbegović] forces. Just don't panic. Let women and children go first. Do not let any of the children get lost. Don't be afraid. Nobody will harm you" (United Nations 1999, pt. viii, sec. A, par. 322).

As soon as the video cameras stopped filming and the deportation began, the Bosnian Serbs began to show their true intentions. Quickly sidelining the Dutch soldiers as they tried to assist the refugees during the deportation procedures, the Bosnian Serbs asserted their control over the crowd. They dropped the façade adopted for the cameras and began hurling insults and hitting the refugees struggling to board the buses. They formed a column through which the refugees had to pass as they approached the convoy of vehicles. There they separated men and boys from the women and children, forcing the women onto the buses and the men to the left, toward what became known as the "white house," a residential property that stood immediately across the road from the Dutch compound. Mothers clung to their young sons even as the Serb soldiers wrested them from their grip. The men were forced to leave their belongings, including their identity cards, in a pile in the yard outside before entering the white house.

In contrast to the refugees' growing panic and the chaotic atmosphere that had descended over the compound, the Bosnian Serb forces appeared well prepared for their specific roles within a highly coordinated campaign. As a Dutch soldier later testified, "Everybody had been assigned a task, everybody knew his position. . . . It was indeed well organized" (ICTY Prosecutor v. Radislav Krstić 2001, par. 155). The troops were a collection of different military and paramilitary forces, each with its own commander. There were units from the Drina

Corps, including the Zvornik Brigade and the Bratunac Brigade, as well as paramilitary forces such as the Drina Wolves and irregular Serb forces, including members of Arkan's Tigers and the now infamous special police unit, the Scorpions. For their part, the Dutch troops displayed mixed reactions. Some attempted to intervene on the refugees' behalf, insisting on following the evacuation plan drawn up in Bratunac, whereby they were to accompany the convoys, and, in some cases, trying to gain the release of boys who looked too young or men who looked too old for the so-called screening. Others took part in the evacuation passively, standing aside as the Bosnian Serbs assumed control of the procedure. Bosniak witnesses later spoke of how some Dutch even assisted in the separation of men from women and children.

Throughout the afternoon and into the evening, the refugees continued to pack themselves onto the buses. Hours later they arrived at Tišća, where Bosnian Serb soldiers forced them to disembark and walk six kilometers to the Bosniak-controlled territory near Kladanj. Some wounded and elderly crawled on their hands and knees to safety. Of the ten locally recruited female staff members of Médicins Sans Frontières, three were held back by Bosnian Serb soldiers at Tišća. Apparently they were looking for Naser Orić's sister. Two were allowed to leave after an hour and a half of interrogation; the third, a nineteen-year-old nurse, returned several hours later after having been raped by the Serb interrogators. Military-age Bosniak men who had somehow managed to board the deportation buses were removed from the vehicles during stops along the journey or were separated and taken away when they arrived at Tišća. Back in Potočari, the white house rapidly filled with men, whose faces, according to the Dutch soldiers allowed to visit them briefly, registered sheer terror. The Bosnian Serbs held others in additional locations, such as near the zinc processing factory, and began loading them into trucks and driving them to detention sites in Bratunac.

By the evening of July 12, the Serbs had become even more aggressive in their persecution of the crowd around the compound. They picked out men, some of whom returned and others of whom were never seen again. They dragged off women as well. Two Bosnian Serbs raped a young woman in full view of several refugees, who were paralyzed by fear for their own lives, as other Serb soldiers stood by. Throughout the night screams, moans, and sporadic gunshots were heard, and by morning rumors abounded of killings and corpses being found in the proximity of the compound. As the next round of deportation buses arrived, people were desperate to leave.

During the initial twenty-four hours after the fall of the enclave, the international community struggled to respond to the unfolding debacle. On July 12, in Zagreb at the UN daily briefing, Akashi and Janvier defended the decision not to resist the Bosnian Serb takeover of the enclave. Ever concerned for his bureaucracy's reputation, Akashi recognized the potential public relations disaster and reportedly remarked, "It would help if we had some TV pictures showing the Dutch feeding refugees" (Rohde 1997:194). The Serbs, along with Petrović's camera crew, however, had already beaten them to it. The United Nations Security Council in New York convened for an emergency session, during which members drafted Resolution 1004, demanding that "the Bosnian Serb forces cease their offensive and withdraw from the safe area of Srebrenica immediately" (United Nations 1999, pt. viii, sec. B, par. 329). During the debate the representative of the Czech Republic warned against the failure to act, arguing that "if today we have adopted just another resolution full of demands that will not be underpinned by our determination to see them fulfilled, then we will be doing more harm than good, not only to the situation in Bosnia and Herzegovina but also to the position of the Security Council. The Bosnian Serbs will be reaffirmed in their belief that Security Council resolutions are just paper tigers. They will be tempted to repeat what they did in Srebrenica in Žepa, Goražde and other so-called safe areas, knowing that they can do so with impunity" (United Nations 1999, pt. viii, sec. B, par. 338). Caught in this crisis of the bureaucrat's "dual identity" (Barnett 1997:563), the representatives of the member states fretted not only about the fate of the Bosniaks in the enclave, but also the fate of the Security Council as a credible institution.

While the separation of men and boys and the deportations were taking place at Potočari, the men and boys in the column that had started out from Šušnjari came under attack. They made their way through the woods along a route parallel to the road running between Bratunac and Konjević Polje. At Konjević Polje the column had to cross over an asphalt road, leaving the cover of the forest. There the Bosnian Serb forces launched their most intense attacks and succeeded in cutting the column in two. Only a third of the Bosniak men made it across, while the others doubled back into the woods.

> By the afternoon of 12 July 1995, or the early evening hours at the latest, the Bosnian Serb forces were capturing large numbers of these men in the rear. Witnesses reported a variety of techniques used to trap prisoners. In some places, ambushes were set up and, in others, the Bosnian

Serbs shouted into the forest, urging the men to surrender and promising
that the Geneva Conventions would be complied with. In some places,
Bosnian Serb forces fired into the woods with anti-aircraft guns and other
weapons or used stolen UN equipment to deceive the Bosnian Muslim
men into believing that the UN or the Red Cross were present to monitor
the treatment accorded to them upon capture. In fact, Bosnian Serb forces
stripped the captured Muslim men of their personal belongings and, in
some cases, carried out random summary executions. (ICTY Prosecutor v.
Radislav Krstić 2001, par. 63)

An estimated 6,000 men from the column were captured along various
points on the Bratunac–Konjević Polje road on July 13. On that day,
some 1,000 to 4,000 Bosniak captives were held in the Sandići Meadow,
and an additional 1,000 to 3,000 men were detained in a soccer field
in Nova Kasaba, which the UN buses passed right by on their way to
Tišća.[35] Several of the deportees recalled seeing there hundreds of men
kneeling with their hands tied behind their backs. The Dutch soldiers
accompanying the deportation convoys later confirmed having seen the
captives in the field.[36] The Bosnian Serb forces proceeded to move the
men to various locations. From the Sandići Meadow, some traveled
by bus or were forced to walk to a warehouse in the nearby village of
Kravica. The remainder of the Sandići Meadow captives, in addition
to the Nova Kasaba detainees, were loaded into buses and trucks and
transported to Bratunac or other sites. General Mladić appeared at
many of these detention locations over the course of the next several
hours, promising the captives food and water, reassuring them of their
imminent reunion with their families, or explaining that they would
soon be exchanged for Bosnian Serb prisoners.

After passing yet another harrowing night in and around the Dutchbat compound in Potočari, the remaining refugees from the enclave
departed on the last of the buses for Tišća at 8:00 P.M. on July 13.
The deportation concluded with the refugees who had taken shelter
within the compound itself. Fearing for the safety of male members of
that group, the Dutch compiled a list of the Bosniak men among their
ranks between the ages of seventeen and sixty-five. Intended to document the individuals taken into custody by the Bosnian Serb Army—de
facto prisoners of war—the list recorded the names of 239 men. Major
Robert Franken promised the men and their families that he would
show a copy of the list to the Bosnian Serbs, telling them he had already
faxed it to The Netherlands and Geneva; in case the Bosnian Serbs confiscated the list, he would smuggle another copy in his underwear. He

hoped that the knowledge of this official record, submitted to international authorities, would prevent the Bosnian Serb forces from harming the men as known captives. As it turned out, however, none of them made it to Tuzla; they were last seen leaving the compound on that day. A tiny fraction of the refugee population within the compound was granted safe passage because they were employees of the Dutchbat or other international organizations working in the enclave. Although this group was to be limited to employees only, some family members of these workers managed to gain shelter with the UN troops.[37]

The men whom the Bosnian Serbs had separated at Potočari, approximately 300 from within the compound and 600 to 900 from outside the Dutchbat gates, had been transferred to various locations in Bratunac: an old school, a warehouse, a soccer field, and the buses and trucks used for their transport. By now the Dutch knew that some of the men separated at Potočari had been killed and that none of them had arrived at Tišća, where the Bosnian Army and aid workers met the women and children. Even as white house detainees were being deported from Potočari, they begged the Dutch for help. One officer testified at The Hague, "They were crying, you know, men—you can imagine men crying in front of you and seeking assistance from you, assistance which you cannot give—it had gone beyond my control" (ICTY Prosecutor v. Radislav Krstić 2001, par. 159). Furthermore, the Dutch soldiers knew that Mladić's insistence on screening the men for war criminals was merely a pretense.[38] The Bosnian Serb forces had stripped the men of their personal effects, including their identity cards, just outside the white house. "In the absence of personal documentation, these men could no longer be accurately identified" (ICTY Prosecutor v. Radislav Krstić 2001, par. 160).[39] After all the Bosniaks had departed from the compound, the Bosnian Serbs proceeded to burn their personal effects. At Bratunac the Potočari detainees were joined by thousands of men captured from the column (such as from Sandići Meadow and Nova Kasaba). The Bosnian Serbs did not keep these groups separate, again revealing that they had no intention of carrying out any legitimate screening procedures.

Over the course of the next five days, the Bosnian Serb forces executed and buried an estimated 7,000 to 8,000 Bosniak men from the enclave.[40] Some were killed individually, others in small groups, but the majority were "slaughtered in carefully orchestrated mass executions," which began on July 13 just north of Srebrenica (ICTY Prosecutor v. Radislav Krstić 2001, par. 67). Those who survived the first night of killings and detention were transported to execution sites north of Bratunac. The same buses and trucks used to deport the women and children now served as convoys for the men about to be slaughtered. From July 14 to July 17, Bosnian Serb forces executed the men en masse at various locations in the Bratunac and Zvornik regions.

> Most of the mass executions followed a well-established pattern. The men were first taken to empty schools or warehouses. After being detained there for some hours, they were loaded onto buses and trucks and taken to another site for execution. Usually, the execution fields were in isolated locations. The prisoners were unarmed and, in many cases, steps had been taken to minimize resistance, such as blindfolding them, binding their wrists behind their backs with ligatures or removing their shoes. Once at the killing fields, the men were taken off the trucks in small groups, lined up and shot. Those who survived the initial round of gunfire were individually shot with an extra round, though sometimes only after they had been left to suffer for a time. Immediately afterwards, and sometimes even during the executions, earth moving equipment arrived and the bodies were buried, either in the spot where they were killed or in another nearby location. (ICTY Prosecutor v. Radislav Krstić 2001, par. 68)

The judgment in the trial of Bosnian Serb general Radislav Krstić details the major execution sites as well as the burial locations connected to those sites (ICTY Prosecutor v. Radislav Krstić 2001, par. 201–253):[41]

- Cerska Valley (afternoon, July 13, 1995): The first of the large-scale executions occurred near Cerska along the road between Konjević Polje and Nova Kasaba. A mass grave was later found to the southwest of that road, from which 150 bodies were exhumed. Ligatures still bound the arms of the victims behind their backs.

- Kravica Warehouse (late afternoon, July 13, 1995): Bosnian Serb forces killed an estimated 1,000 to 1,500 men captured in the Sandići Meadow and transported to the warehouse in Kravica. Survivors testified that the Bosnian Serbs threw grenades and shot directly into the warehouse, packed with the Bosniak prisoners. ICTY investigators examined the site on September 30, 1996, and observed the "presence of bullet strikes, explosive residue, bullet and shell cases, as well as human blood, bones, and tissue adhering to the walls and floors of the building" (par. 208). Three gravesites are linked to the Kravica warehouse executions: two primary mass graves, Glogova 1 (at least 191 bodies recovered) and Glogova 2 (at least 139 bodies), and a secondary mass grave, Zeleni Jadar 5 (at least 145 bodies), which was linked to Glogova 2.

- Tišća (July 13–14, 1995): Bosniak men who had managed to board the buses deporting women and children were separated upon arrival at Tišća. Bosnian Serb soldiers took these men to a nearby school, after which they transported twenty-two men to a remote location and shot them.

- Grbavci School Detention Site and Orahovac Execution Site (July 14, 1995): A convoy of thirty buses transported 1,000 (though perhaps as many as 2,000–2,500) detainees from Bratunac to the Grbavci School in Orahovac on the morning of July 14. After spending several hours in the packed and sweltering confines of the school, the men were taken in trucks to nearby fields, lined up, and shot. Heavy machinery dug the graves even as people were being executed. Two primary mass graves were exhumed in that area, Lazete 1 (containing the remains of 130 individuals) and Lazete 2 (containing the remains of 243 individuals). Investigators found hundreds of blindfolds at each site. Bodies from both Lazete 1 and Lazete 2 were dug up and transferred to the secondary mass graves of Hodžići Road 3, 4, and 5, which collectively contained the remains of 184 individuals.

- Petkovci School Detention Site and Petkovci Dam (July 14–15, 1995): Approximately 1,500 to 2,000 detainees were transported from Bratunac to the Petkovci School on the afternoon of July 14. As at the Grbavci School, the men suffered for several hours in the crowded space of the school without food or water. During the night their captors called the prisoners out in small groups, ordering them to strip to the waist and remove their shoes. Their hands were tied behind their backs. They were then transported by truck to a field near the Petkovci Dam, where they were lined up and shot. ICTY personnel "exhumed a gravesite at the Petkovci Dam between 15 and 25 April 1998. Experts determined that this gravesite had been 'robbed,' using a mechanical excavator that resulted in 'grossly disarticulated body parts' throughout the grave" (par. 229). This primary grave contained at least 43 individuals. It is also linked to a secondary mass grave, Lipje 2, which contained at least 191 individuals.

- Pilića School Detention Site and Branjevo Military Farm (July 14–16, 1995): Between 1,000 and 2,000 detainees were transported from Bratunac to the village of Pilića, north of Zvornik. They were held at the Pilića School under deplorable conditions (no food, water, or latrines) for two nights. Some men died of dehydration during this period of captivity. On July 16, Bosnian Serbs called men out from the school in small groups, tied their hands behind their backs, and loaded them onto trucks. They were driven to the Branjevo Military Farm, where they were lined up in groups of ten and shot. "Sometimes the executioners were particularly cruel. When some of the soldiers recognized acquaintances from Srebrenica, they beat and humiliated them before killing them" (par. 234). Heavy machinery dug a grave while the executions were still taking place. The primary mass grave, known as the Pilića (or Branjevo Military Farm) gravesite, contained the remains of 13 individuals. A secondary mass grave, Čančari Road 12, contained the remains of 174 individuals. Ligatures and blindfolds were found at both sites.

- Kozluk: Approximately 500 prisoners were taken to the Kozluk site, located between the Petkovci Dam and the Branjevo Military Farm, where they were killed by an execution squad. The prisoners were forced to sing Serb songs while they were being driven to the site. The primary mass grave at Kozluk contained the remains of at least 340 individuals. It is linked to a secondary grave, Čančari Road 3.

In addition to forensic analyses of physical evidence such as soil, shell casings, and wheel tracks, aerial photographs taken by satellites slightly before, during, and after the period of July 13 to July 17 documented the presence of bodies and vehicles at many of the execution sites listed above, as well as the disturbance of earth associated with the initial digging and filling of the mass graves. These satellite images also provided evidence that Bosnian Serb forces attempted to conceal the primary mass graves during early autumn of 1995 by digging up and removing some or all of the bodies contained within them to a second location—hence the term "secondary mass gravesite." ICTY investigators estimated that "it would have taken at least two full nights and several trucks to move the bodies to the secondary gravesites," given that the longest distance between primary and secondary mass graves was 40 kilometers (ICTY Prosecutor v. Radislav Krstić 2001, par. 261).

In the late evening of July 16 and early morning of July 17, as the last of the Bosniak prisoners were being executed in locations such as Pilića and Kozluk, the column of men who journeyed through the forest broke through to free territory. Approximately 4,500 to 6,000 men had survived the 50-kilometer trek over six days, encountering intense attacks from Bosnian Serb forces along the way. Although Tuzla's 2nd Corps (Bosnian Army) did not launch any diversions to assist the incoming column, Naser Orić organized a band of volunteer soldiers that succeeded in weakening the Bosnians Serb lines enough to allow the men from the column to cross into the free territory near Sapna. An estimated 2,000 of the 10,000 to 15,000 men in the column had died during combat with the Bosnian Serb Army or when crossing over landmines. An unknown number of men had committed suicide in the forest. Approximately 6,000 of them had surrendered or been captured and were later executed at sites such as those listed above.

## THE AFTERMATH

The men who survived the trek immediately began searching for their own families among the women and children who had arrived at

Tišća on July 12 and 13. Of the 19,700 deportees registered with the International Committee of the Red Cross (ICRC, or Red Cross) by July 15, 5,670 took refuge at Dubrave, the airport outside of Tuzla, where a sprawling camp of white tents had been erected.[42] The Bosnian government struggled to provide accommodations for an additional 11,000 people. Many others found private housing among relatives and friends in the Tuzla area. Their arrival marked the start of the long and trying relationship between the displaced from Srebrenica (the refugees from the Podrinje region) and the Tuzla Canton—both its government and the local population.

The Dutchbat unit remained in Potočari at the UN compound until July 21, continuing to serve as Mladić's bargaining chip with the international community. On July 15, the Bosnian Serb general met in Belgrade with Serbian president Slobodan Milošević, EU mediator Carl Bildt, and UNPROFOR commander Lieutenant-General Rupert Smith. They negotiated the release of fifty-five Dutch soldiers being held hostage and agreed to the July 21 departure for the rest of the troops in Potočari. Mladić approved ICRC's request to access the Bosniak detainees. He promptly reneged on this pledge, blocking their attempts to reach the Bosniak prisoners—hundreds, if not thousands of whom were still alive at that point in time. In a final act of hubris, Mladić insisted that UNPROFOR compensate the Bosnian Serb Army for the fuel expended during the deportation of the Bosniaks from Potočari. Although Lieutenant-General Smith refused at the meeting, later that day the Dutch troops handed over 30,000 liters of fuel to the Bosnian Serbs in Bratunac (Honig and Both 1996:45).

When the Dutch troops did finally depart from Potočari on July 21, they traveled to Zagreb, Croatia. There on the afternoon of the following day, after having received a "heroes' welcome" by Crown Prince Willem Alexander of The Netherlands, Defense Minister Joris Voorhoeve, and other top military officials, they celebrated the end of the mission. "A party, complete with a forty-two-piece brass band playing Glenn Miller songs, cases of beer and drunken Dutch soldiers dancing in a chorus line, was thrown that afternoon" (Rohde 1997:325). Video footage of the party and the drunken soldiers appears in the BBC documentary *Cry from the Grave*. On the heels of the stark images of the refugees and captured men earlier in the film, their exuberance and laughter is painful to watch. In *Priviđenja iz srebrenog vijeka*, Almir Bašović (2003) parodies the Dutchbat soldiers' callous and self-indulgent celebration in a scene entitled "Potochari Party":[43]

*Music. UNPROFOR soldiers enter. They dance.*

*Lieutenant:* Good evening, welcome to the Potočari party. Here, with a little luck, we finally got some trucks with the necessary beer and cigarettes. I invite the Major to come up before us and officially open this party.

*Major Frank:* Thank you, lieutenant. So, Mladić outplayed us. But don't get upset about it because our honorable mission is drawing to an end. In the name of that, all those here are invited to join us in our modest celebration. Cheers!

*(The lieutenant pulls Major Frank off to the side. He speaks to him confidentially.)*

*Lieutenant:* Major, Sir, the translator, Hasan, claims that civilian observers saw bodies around the camp. What will happen to the people whom we threw outside?

*Major Frank:* Tell Hasan that his job is to translate and not to cause panic in the camp. Those are lies and rumors! I received a promise from General Mladić that nothing's going to happen to anyone. (He takes a sip.) Except for, of course, those who committed crimes. These people haven't had a taste of beer for two months. Don't let him spoil our party.

*(Major Frank shoves a beer into the lieutenant's hand. As the party goes on, the soldiers start to take off their clothes. When they are standing in their underpants and undershirts the party quiets down and the light goes off . . . )*

I attended the play on three separate occasions, twice in Sarajevo and once in Srebrenica, when the cast performed it free of charge at the city's cultural center on July 11, 2004, after the commemoration and mass burial of 282 identified persons at the memorial center in Potočari. It is uncomfortable to watch the party scene, especially in the presence of survivors of the genocide: the two Dutch soldiers gyrate to the sound of a pop song, taking swigs of beer and belting out the lyrics into the microphone. The character of Major Frank and the reference to Hasan remind the audience that the theatrical performance refers directly to painfully true stories. Major Franken had pledged to send to Holland and Geneva the list of 239 Bosniak men whom the Dutch had turned over to the Bosnian Serbs. Instead, on July 22, he submitted it to UN officials in Zagreb, who passed it along to the Red Cross. When given the opportunity in Zagreb to alert the world of what they had seen and what they suspected, Colonel Karremans and Major Franken chose instead to leave the storytelling to a handful of Dutchbat soldiers who had agreed to meet with reporters. Karremans read a short statement that failed to mention the beatings, rapes, and known executions (nine bodies found outside the compound, photographed by Dutch soldiers) at Potočari; the scene at Nova Kasaba and reports of gunshots nearby; the "Muslim hunting" incident, and the list of the 239 missing men.[44] Only in September, after the Dutchbat soldiers had returned from a month-long leave (during which time they were instructed not to speak to media representatives) did the Ministry of Defense initiate debriefing procedures. Rohde concludes, "In hindsight, the Dutch failure to speak out after they left the enclave was worse than their conduct during the Serb offensive" (1997:336).

Like tiles in a mosaic, the testimonies of the handful of Bosniak men who survived the executions, the men in the column, the deportees, and the Dutchbat soldiers slowly slid into place, and a picture of the Bosnian Serb capture of the enclave and disposal of its inhabitants became clear. The offensive and the ensuing violence had followed a well-orchestrated plan. Srebrenica's genocide was not a wanton act of violence, but a carefully crafted and executed operation whose success in part arose from the lack of planning and political will on the part of the very institution that had pledged to "deter" attacks on the so-called safe area. Given that in the Podrinje region buses and fuel were scarce, the Bosnian Serb Army's capacity to procure both and transport the entire population of refugees at the Dutchbat compound—an estimated 25,000 people—within a 48-hour period suggests that the operation must have been planned several days in advance (ICTY Prosecutor v. Radislav Krstić 2001, par. 140). The Bosnian Serb forces carried out mass executions of more than 7,000 men over the course of the following five days, digging mass graves to dispose of the bodies. The efficiency with which they accomplished the deportation and genocide revealed another aspect of the planning: outside troops—"efficient and experienced 'ethnic cleaners'"—were brought in and worked together with local police and militia (Honig and Both 1996:30). Moreover, the Bosnian Serbs' ability to occupy the enclave and then assume control of the situation at Potočari points to the strategic reduction of resistance from both the Dutch soldiers and the refugees. "The Dutch were intimidated by token aggression, but at the same time they were told that they would not be harmed if they cooperated. The Muslims were initially reassured by the distribution of some food and water and by promises that they would soon be free to go . . . but they were also subjected to outbursts of indiscriminate violence. Fearful and confused, both groups largely played into the hands of the Serbs" (Honig and Both 1996:30). In addition to reducing the refugees' resistance by offering morsels of food and reassuring words, some of the Bosnian Serb forces turned the aegis of UN protection on its head by using its promise of security to bait the men in the column. They stole vehicles and donned the peacekeepers' blue helmets and uniforms, using the age-old treachery of battle in which enemies pretend to be comrades.

The news of the genocide and the disgrace of the UN peacekeeping mission in Srebrenica finally began to affect the Western governments' political will. On August 10, in a closed session of the UN Security Council, US secretary of state Madeleine Albright showed CIA satellite photographs of the area of Novo Kasaba. The before and after shots of men lined up and subsequent mounds of freshly moved earth provided persuasive evidence that mass executions had taken place. President Clinton set aside the embargo policy and committed to the use of force in Bosnia. On August 30, 1995, NATO bombing began, and in three weeks its planes had flown 3,400 sorties and carried out 750 attacks against 56 targets. "They called the mission Operation Deliberate Force, as if to announce up front that what might have been called 'Operation Halfhearted Force' was a thing of the past" (Power 2002:440). By November, the bombs had succeeded in forcing the Bosnian Serbs to the negotiating table, and the Dayton Peace Agreement, reached in November 1995 and signed on December 14, 1995, officially ended the war. By establishing two entities—the Bosniak and Croat–controlled Federation and the Bosnian Serb–controlled Republika Srpska (RS)—the peace settlement divided Bosnia and Herzegovina among its three ethnic groups. The Serbs (31 percent of the population) received 49 percent of the land; the Croats (25 percent of the population) got 25 percent, and the Bosniaks (44 percent of the population) got the other 25 percent. The once predominantly Bosniak town of Srebrenica now lay in the Serb-controlled Republika Srpska.

## IDENTITY

When reading through the accounts of life in the enclave and the fall of Srebrenica, I am continually struck by the fundamental misreadings and manipulations of identity that lie at the heart of the loss of so many lives. Virulent nationalist rhetoric cast Bosniak refugees in the enclave as "Turks," whose expulsion from eastern Bosnia would avenge past injustices against the Serbian people. Morillon's UN flag became an empty promise of protection as the Dutchbat soldiers and their superiors in Zagreb and New York hesitated, paralyzed by their skepticism and mistrust of the enclave's population. More concerned about their own institution's reputation than the lives of thousands of Srebrenica's refugees, officials like Janvier and Akashi hid behind the language and protocols of the world's largest bureaucracy rather than face a crisis of UNPROFOR hostages. And when the air strikes never materialized, blue helmets and UN flak jackets tricked desperate men into surrendering. Finally, with the cameras rolling, General Mladić presented a façade of benevolence to the outside world only to turn around and direct the wholesale slaughter of thousands of prisoners of war.

The Bosnian Serb forces went beyond misreading and manipulating identity; they sought to annihilate it. They systematically eliminated the Bosniak presence from the enclave by expelling and executing its residents; then they dug up, moved, and reburied the remains, both to hide their work and to create the illusion that their victims had never existed. In an interview in his office, Amor Mašović, the head of the Federation Commission for Missing Persons, outlined the three ways the Bosnian Serbs deprived their captives of their individual identity:

> So through the recovery, the exhumation, the identification, the autopsy of the Srebrenica victims, it points to the fact that—I say this very often—the criminals took or snatched from them or stripped them of their identity. The first time they stripped them of their identity was when they took them prisoner, detained them, and when they took away from them what they had on themselves . . . their identity cards and passports and all those identity documents which could have testified to the first and last name of the victim. When they took away watches, when they took off their ring on which it is written their wedding day, which is also a strong identification document, perhaps even stronger than an identity card. If there's a wedding ring which bears February 21, 1965, that is a stronger document than an identity card. Why? An identity card can be my brother's or my father's or my son's, but a wedding ring on my finger is exclusively mine. For sure I didn't take the wedding ring from my son or my father and put it on my own finger. Therefore, at that point they stripped them of their identity, when they took the documents away from them while they were still living.
>
> They stripped many of them of their identity when they buried them with heavy machinery in mass graves, not separating body from body as would be expected. Even war goes according to rules, right? Even war. They kill people, people die, but after that the people they killed they bury in a civilized manner, one beside the other, and not in the manner in which Karadžić, Mladić, and the forces in Srebrenica did, burying them, throwing them away. That is the second deprivation of identity.

Finally, the third time when they took away their identity was when they came and removed them from the primary graves, tore up their bodies, and carried them off to secondary graves. And thus today we have the situation where we have the body of one man [found] in three different places which are kilometers and kilometers apart from one another. So those are the fundamental difficulties.

In explaining this three-step process by which the Bosnian Serbs destroyed their victims' identity, Mašović directs our attention to the social relations that form and bind together individual lives. The act of removing a wedding ring erases the material emblem of those ties, but traces of individual identity nevertheless endure. Bodies exhumed from mass and surface graves become a text to be read, yielding up clues that reconnect an individual to his web of social ties, to his family. Thus, it remains for people like Mašović, the forensic experts tasked with recovering and identifying the Srebrenica missing, to help surviving families reclaim what the Bosnian Serb forces sought so relentlessly to obliterate.

# CHAPTER 2

# The People and Place of Postwar Srebrenica

More than a decade after the fall of the enclave, Srebrenica remains a loaded term for Bosnians and for other people touched by the events of July 1995, including many who never set foot in the country, let alone the "Silver City,"[1] before the violence broke out in the spring of 1992. On one level, Srebrenica—the UN safe area—has come to represent the worst instance of the war's collective violence and the ineptitude of the international community to protect the vulnerable. On another, Srebrenica as a postwar place testifies to the splintering, devastating effects of loss. The challenge from an ethnographic standpoint is to tease out the relationship between the intertwined periods and populations of Srebrenica, studying its present state as the Bosnian city whose name has become synonymous with genocide. For just as my discussion of the identification process requires an understanding of the fall of the enclave and the ensuing violence, it also calls for an explanation of the context and people who gave rise to the innovative biotechnology used to identify its missing.

## THE CITY OF SREBRENICA

I spent the summer of 2002 in the large industrial city of Tuzla, in the northeastern corner of the Bosniak and Croat–controlled entity of the Federation. Tuzla is an urban center best known for its tolerant political climate and the towering smokestacks of the thermoelectric plant on the outskirts of town. In planning research on return communities in the Republika Srpska, I spoke with people on staff at the United Nations High Commissioner for Refugees and various NGOs about the process of minority return in the Podrinje region.[2] Describing the slow-paced return to parts of the RS, a friend from the Forum of Tuzla Citizens, one of the country's leading NGOs working on civil society strengthening and democratization, remarked, "Srebrenica is Bosnia's test." She was speaking about more than just returns—return is merely one yardstick the NGOs and international organizations use to measure postwar reconstruction. Given its recent past, the city, indeed, the entire municipality of Srebrenica, represents a testing ground for addressing the myriad social, political, and economic ills faced by the country, many of which are still perpetuated by unyielding nationalist politics.

Srebrenica's physical landscape mirrors the troubled circumstances surrounding the complex, shifting layers of its postwar community. Nestled in the mountains that rise up along the western valleys of the Drina River, the city is at once a beautiful and scarred place. The contrast between its natural surroundings and the depressing, battered feel of its streets reveals itself as you travel up the main road that runs along the north-south axis between Bratunac and Zeleni Jadar. At the base of the steady but steep climb to the city center from the northern entrance, a soccer field sits to the right. A collage of images and graffiti in Latin and Cyrillic lettering covers the chipped cement wall that separates the field from the road. Its bold and varied colors belie the run-down scenery that follows. Some of the phrases and scrawling, such as the symbol of the four *S*'s (*C* in Cyrillic)—Само слога Србина спашава/*Samo sloga Srbina spašava*/Only Unity Saves the Serbs—hint at the political tensions within the city above.

As you pass the collective housing for refugees (displaced Bosnian Serbs who came to Srebrenica after its fall in July 1995), the post office, the hospital, the bus stop, and various apartment buildings and houses, you sense the city's decayed, broken spirit. The scars of mortar shells and bullet holes still pock the sides of buildings. Around windows and on porch ceilings black streaks hint at the fires that once enveloped homes. A brightly lit, newly reconstructed *robna kuća* (department store) sits across the street from the city's main park, a perennially drab and ramshackle spot that volunteers—either youth groups or foreign activists—periodically try to spruce up with vigorous weeding and coats of fresh paint on the benches and walls. Around the corner to the

FIGURE 2. The city of Srebrenica in 2004. Photo by the author.

right, just beyond the boarded-up ruins of the Energoinvest building, stands the recently plastered and painted city hall, also home to the United Nations Development Programme (UNDP) office.

Farther up, past a series of small shops—among them some returnee businesses—and just beyond the open marketplace, the main road splits off into two parallel streets separated by a large hill. The road to the right, whose upper section is called Petrića, heads south to Zeleni Jadar and eventually to the border crossing with Serbia at Skelani; the other leads to Srebrenica's prewar tourist attraction, the spa resort Banja Guber. Taking its name from the two local streams, the Mali (little) Guber and Crni (black) Guber, the Banja billed itself as a homeopathic spa that drew from the city's natural spring waters, known for their medicinal properties. Several years before the war, a reporter describing Srebrenica as a tourist destination touted, "The Crni Guber is the only therapeutic water registered as a medicine, and that's not just in Yugoslavia, but in the world" (quoted in Salimović 2002:162). If one place in Srebrenica epitomizes the ardent nostalgia that its prewar residents feel toward their former community and former lives, it is the "Guber"—a place of social gathering and striking natural beauty. It was there in its cool shade that people came on lazy weekend afternoons to stroll alongside the streams that gushed down the hillside. In the evenings they would enjoy a meal and live music at the small restaurant at the top of the hill. And in the winter, they would brave the steep incline and hairpin turns to ski or sled down its snow-packed road.

At the base of that road, a narrow cobblestone track that winds alongside the water, still stands the Argentaria — the spa's former *"supermoderni medicinski centar."* For many years after the war, it served as alternative housing for Bosnian Serb refugees.[3] Their laundry would dry on lines strung out on the balcony and in the yard near the stream. Up the cobblestone road from Argentaria, there are wooden signs identifying the health benefits of the medicinal waters (erected by the local Srebrenica-Bratunac youth group and sponsored by UNDP): springs for healing skin ailments and sinus problems, enhancing beauty, strengthening lungs, combating anemia, and protecting eyes. The walk to the top is a peaceful, quiet journey; the sounds of the water and the fragrant, crisp air relieve the dismal scenes of the city below. Walking along the Guber, you catch yourself imagining what life in Srebrenica might have been like before.

## POSTWAR RESIDENTS, DIVIDED COMMUNITIES

Understanding postwar Srebrenica as a place populated by divided communities means recognizing the city's multiple layers and its three recent periods of inhabitants: residents of prewar Srebrenica, wartime Srebrenica, and postwar Srebrenica. Although there are people who can claim to have made their homes in the city or its surrounding villages during all three periods, its population has changed dramatically over the past fifteen years, as Bosniaks and Bosnian Serbs have moved in and out of its houses, apartments, and collective centers.[4] Since the early returns in 2000, the fork in the main road at the open-air market signals a demographic shift: from that point onward (on both streets), approximately 1,000 prewar, predominantly Bosniak residents have reclaimed their property and reinserted themselves into the postwar Srebrenica community. The houses that have received a donation for reconstruction are easy to spot, with their new windows and doors and bright orange ceramic roof tiles. Sometimes the reconstructed houses are empty; families living in Western European countries as refugees took advantage of the international aid agencies' zeal to support return and thus received a donation for a rebuilt house that they would use as a summer home. Others bear telltale signs of permanent occupancy, with flower boxes adorning windows and balconies, neatly tended vegetable gardens, or, in the winter, stacks of wood piled up beside the house.

The atmosphere on these two streets is quieter, more subdued than in the city below. Petrića, in particular, boasts a close-knit neighborhood. Old friends, mostly single, middle-aged or older women, have rebuilt a community for themselves. They visit one another, drink coffee together, and tend flowers or plants for a neighbor off visiting family in Tuzla or Sarajevo, much as they would have before the war. But they lament the fact that it seems like a "dead city," without any young people or the bustle of life. Except for the summer months, when former neighbors come back from places like Austria or The Netherlands, or on major religious holidays, Bosniak men, especially young men, and children are a clear minority in the city. As Senad, a young man whose family returned in 2001, explained, it is hard to be a young Bosniak in Srebrenica. So many hopes and expectations hang upon them. Too often when he walks down the street to the city center and greets his neighbors, some of whom are mothers with missing sons, he knows his presence is both welcome and saddening.

Religion is an important part of the returnee community life and its identity. Although not everyone attends the mosque, and many of the women do not wear headscarves as a part of their daily attire, most returnees are practicing Muslims. One of the five prewar mosques has been rebuilt through a donation by the Malaysian government. It stands between the two parallel roads with its minaret jutting out above the homes at the base of the hill. Five times a day loudspeakers mounted on top of the minaret project the recorded voice of the *muezzin*, calling the faithful to prayer. But few shoes are left at the entrance of the building during the worship services, as only a handful of people attend the mosque daily. The major religious holidays, *ramazan* and its three-day feast, *bajram,* as well as the *kurban-bajram,* however, swell the numbers of Bosniaks and infuse this upper section of the city with the bustle of traffic and visitors absent during the rest of the year.

Religion and ethno-religious identity also shape the other part (the majority) of the city's postwar population, the Bosnian Serbs. Most Serbs who live there now moved to Srebrenica after the fall of the enclave in July 1995. Many followed Radovan Karadžić's appeal to leave their homes in Muslim-controlled central Bosnia, such as Sarajevo's suburbs of Ilijaš and Ilidža, or in the cities of Hadžići, Glamoč, Vakuf, Ključ, and Olovo, and relocate to the Podrinje region of the Republika Srpska.[5] They were encouraged to take up residence in abandoned Bosniak houses and apartments on RS leaders' assurances that they would receive the title to the property and become its new, lawful owners. One friend described to me how Petrića used to be full of Serb families, many with small children. Mothers would sit outside for hours each day and talk as their children played in the streets. There was even a swimming pool in the summer months. But, as she wistfully remarked, most of those people moved on; either they were evicted when the Bosniak owners reclaimed their property or they bought or built a new house of their own in places like Bijelina or Zvornik. Even for the postwar relocated Serbs there is a nostalgic longing for a Srebrenica of the past.

The Bosniak returnees and Bosnian Serbs have forged an uneasy though relatively stable relationship as co-residents of the city. Tension arises with the occasional provocation. I saw this firsthand my second night in Srebrenica, July 12, 2003—one day after the commemoration and mass burial in Potočari. To the backdrop of nationalist songs, some inebriated Bosnian Serb attendees of a Petrovdan (St. Peter's Day) celebration held at the Orthodox Church began shooting off their guns.[6] Although firing guns at weddings and other religious festivals is a common practice in Serb villages, much of the nationalist folk music produced during the war invoked guns in a different context, celebrating military feats and encouraging animosity against opposing ethnic groups (Laušević 2000; Longinović 2001). Thus, many Bosniak returnees feared that the drunken bravado might escalate into something more threatening. Another manifestation of ethno-religious tension took place on a hill above the city near the remains of a medieval fortress. At the direction of the Orthodox Church, local Bosnian Serbs had erected a cross there to commemorate the site of a former church. An article in a local Serb newspaper explained the location's historical significance (a point hotly contested by prewar Bosniak residents and returnees): "The Serbian Orthodox *(pravoslav)* cross in the old town above Srebrenica disappeared the night before last from the place where more than eight hundred years ago a church . . . was raised in the once Orthodox seat of Srebrenica" (*Glas Srpske* 2004). During my sixteen months of fieldwork, Bosniaks clandestinely removed the cross three times; it was replaced each time. Finally, the Serbs mounted a much heavier, cast iron version set in a cement foundation. Too sturdy to remove, it stands in place, looming large above the predominantly Bosniak section of the city.

Apart from these infrequent though overt displays of ethno-religious politics, Bosniaks and Serbs manage to go about their daily lives without friction—shopping, visiting the post office or municipal buildings, walking along the Guber. And, although there are rare examples of enduring friendships between Bosniaks and Serbs, their social lives for the most part remain separate. Many returnees regard their Serb neighbors—in particular their former, prewar neighbors and colleagues—with distrust or a muted bitterness. On several occasions returnees pointed out to me men who had been present at Potočari during the deportation—a police officer, a factory worker, a former city official—men who walked freely about the streets of Srebrenica and Bratunac. To my own surprise, in video footage of the negotiations between Mladić and Karremans, I recognized the young man acting as Mladić's interpreter. When I first arrived in Srebrenica he was working at an international aid agency's office in Srebrenica and was responsible for overseeing the rebuilding of both Bosniak and Bosnian Serb houses in the region. I was present when one of the members of the Women of Srebrenica stood face to face with him in that same office, discussing the application process for a reconstruction package. Much later the woman told me she had been aware of the rumors that the young man had interpreted for Mladić at the fall of the enclave. Such direct reminders of the past increased some returnees' sense of insecurity, as well as the resentment they felt toward Bosnian Serbs for justifying or excusing the war crimes at Srebrenica while continuing to support their perpetrators.[7]

While divisions between Bosniaks and Bosnian Serbs in Srebrenica were obvious and understandable, after a few weeks of residence in the city I began to notice other tensions, ones specific to the returnee community. I had begun my fieldwork there volunteering with a Dutch NGO as a translator for their nursing outreach program.[8] Each day I accompanied a Dutch nurse who made house calls to vulnerable patients among both the returnee and Bosnian Serb populations. Through our interaction with these mostly elderly patients, their families, and neighbors, I noted the unspoken hierarchy that existed within the Bosniak community living in Srebrenica. Similarly, Adriana Petryna describes how the population of Chernobyl was "stratified in terms of categories of suffering," and those categories translated into social welfare benefits (2002:84). Srebrenica's Bosniak population had developed its own implicit categories and criteria of suffering and entitlement, some of which were tied to humanitarian aid and social welfare. On the one hand, there was an implicit ranking of entitlement to donations, specifically the donation of a reconstructed home. The Bosniaks judged one another according to implicit criteria about who was most deserving of aid—that is, who had lost the most. The loss of property and the extent of damage to a prewar home were offset by other factors such as whether the returnee had an independent source of money, for example, a substantial pension or prosperous relatives either living abroad or who had a good job in Sarajevo or Tuzla. Another unspoken criterion of entitlement to a reconstruction package involved the permanency of an individual or family's return. Community members who lived full time in their reconstructed homes considered those who spent only the weekdays in Srebrenica *"vikendaši,"* literally, "weekenders," because they left the city for their more comfortable family homes in Tuzla and Sarajevo on the weekends. Local government officials were the most commonly reviled *vikendaši;* their departure each weekend signaled their lack of commitment to the municipality they represented.[9] Life in Srebrenica was not easy, particularly in the bitter cold months of the winter, as not a single house in the city had central heating.

Two other important factors divided the Bosniak postwar community of Srebrenica along lines of suffering and entitlement. First, there was the distinction made between those who fled in the spring of 1992, before the violence engulfed the city, and the 365 residents who remained and suffered through three years in the enclave. One of my neighbors, an older man who often served as the point person for international visitors curious to meet a returnee and learn about life for Bosniaks in postwar Srebrenica, used to boast that he was among the very first to return. Another neighbor who had lived in Srebrenica up until its fall would remark resentfully that although the man was one of the first to return, he was also one of the first to flee. The same dichotomy plays out more generally as Bosnians criticize those who fled their country and praise those who stayed behind to defend it. Thus, in Srebrenica measures of loyalty and hardship privilege the handful of Bosniaks who stayed until the end, followed by those who left in 1992 and relocated to free territory within the country, and finally those who fled in 1992 and left the country altogether.

Loss of family members is by far the most consequential of the implicit measures of both entitlement and suffering among the Srebrenica community. Invariably when I met a surviving family member for the first time, shortly into the conversation the person told me how many relatives she was missing. This was part of her identity—her inescapable lived experience. *"Izgubila sam muža, dva sina, brata i oca"* (I lost my husband, my two sons, my brother and my father). Because of their sheer number, missing extended family members such as cousins and uncles did not even warrant mention. Such declarations were frequently made to strangers or as the preface to their statements to a print journalist or before a television camera. And, although survivors did not openly compare their losses, there was an unspoken "hierarchy of sufferers" (Petryna 2002:18) in which special status was reserved for mothers who lost their sons and, among them, for mothers who lost multiple sons. Nura, one of the leaders of the Women of Srebrenica, explained to me that she, having lost only her brother, was not in the same category as many of the association's other members. "Nothing," she said, "could compare to losing a child." In their coverage of Srebrenica-related stories, the media incorporated the same reverence for survivors who had lost children. Newspaper articles and political speeches regularly employed the phrase *"majke Srebrenice"* (the mothers of Srebrenica), and "mothers' tears" (as in the prayer on the memorial stone at Potočari) had become the catchphrase for the community's suffering.[10]

## WARTIME SREBRENICA AND THE WOMEN OF SREBRENICA

The wartime community of Srebrenica was distinct from that of its pre- and postwar days. Wartime families were residents of the enclave, a population that reached more than 50,000 people at its height, and in July 1995 was estimated to be 40,000. Apart from the small number of residents who stayed in the city until July 1995, this represents an entirely different group of inhabitants. To begin with, "Srebrenica" during the enclave years encompassed not only the city but also surrounding villages contained within the Bosniak-controlled and UN-protected "safe area." The socioeconomic demographics of the enclave differed significantly from those of the prosperous mining and resort town of prewar Srebrenica.[11] In great part because of their relative wealth, most of Srebrenica's urban and well-educated population was able to flee in 1992. The men, women, and children who sought refuge in the enclave afterward were predominantly (though not exclusively) from more rural backgrounds. Hailing from small towns, villages, and hamlets, many of them were more accustomed to the dress and practices of village life. It is these people, the 25,000 deported from the enclave, who in their grief, exhaustion, and anger became the enduring image of Srebrenica, recorded and broadcast throughout the world when the stories about the genocide began to surface.

The initial months I spent living and working in Srebrenica helped me to understand the disparate perspectives of Srebrenica's prewar and postwar residents, as well as to probe its complicated layers of interethnic social experience. It was my encounter with the association of the Women of Srebrenica in Tuzla, however, that taught me most about the community of survivors, the people who had called Srebrenica "home" for three years during the war. The association's members, women of all ages and from different villages and towns throughout the Podrinje region, also instructed me on the critical though problematic question of who belongs to and who speaks for Srebrenica.

My introduction to the Women of Srebrenica began with its two leaders, Hajra Ćatić and Nura Begović. As the public face of the organization, Hajra and Nura regularly appear in the newspapers and on television. Like their counterparts at the Association of the Mothers of the Srebrenica and Žepa Enclaves in Sarajevo, they are strong-willed, outspoken advocates for their members and, more generally, for the Srebrenica survivors.[12] From their inception, the two associations deployed gender strategically, mobilizing as "mothers" and "women" rather than around a more gender-neutral term such as *survivors*.[13] They understood the power of their status as mothers and women in drawing attention to their demands, just as the Bosniak leadership did in 1993 when they directed Naser Orić to use women and children to block General Morillon's vehicle from leaving the enclave. Nevertheless, Nura and Hajra, of the Tuzla-based Women of Srebrenica, were quick to point out that theirs was not a "feminist organization"; rather, it was an organization established in response to the loss of male family members (Delpla 2007: 222). Thus positioning themselves on morally secure and respectable ground within postwar Bosnian politics as mothers and wives (Helms 2007:237), the Tuzla and Sarajevo women waged campaigns of "truth and justice."

Through protests, press releases, and lawsuits the Srebrenica associations demanded accountability from the RS government, as well as from the international community, namely the Dutch and the United Nations. In doing so, the women thrust themselves into the political dialogue about issues ranging from the apprehension and indictment of war criminals to the identification process, the memorial center, and the recently drafted Missing Persons Law, adopted by the Bosnian Parliamentary Assembly in October 2004. Their input in the missing persons legislation in particular marked an important achievement: in representing the surviving families' needs, they forced the state to take into account the interests of the "mothers," who felt torn between accessing much-needed social security and declaring their missing sons to be dead. Their activism transformed the call for "truth and justice" into a codified right: Bosnia's Missing Persons Law officially established (and supposedly guaranteed) the "right to know" what happened to missing relatives and the whereabouts of their remains. By framing their concerns from the perspective of female relatives (primarily mothers) of the missing, they succeeded in shifting the political debate, making "legislation at least a triangular contest between state, community, and women's groups" (Das 1995:114).

Displaced by the violence in 1992 and 1995, surviving families and their representatives who founded the Srebrenica associations struggled to establish their sense of place and home during the years after the genocide. The association of the Women of Srebrenica was first formed in the camps of Dubrave and temporary shelters in Tuzla, as families began to demand answers from international authorities such as the International Committee of the Red Cross, UNHCR, and the UN peacekeeping mission in Bosnia. Tuzla had already become a destination of refuge for thousands of displaced persons from the Podrinje region. By late November 1995, its population had temporarily ballooned to an estimated 150,000. This number included the refugees from the Srebrenica enclave, and even eight years later, several thousand of them were still residing in collective centers or in private housing in and around the Tuzla area. Because of this concentration of the enclave's refugees, the Women of Srebrenica continued to maintain its office in Tuzla. Like many of the association's members, however, by 2003 Hajra and Nura had begun to split their time between their activities in Tuzla and their lives as returnees in Srebrenica and Potočari, respectively. They became what some permanent returnees might label reverse *vikendaši* because they traveled to their prewar homes primarily on weekends and extended holidays. I had met them just as they were settling into this pattern of weekday work in Tuzla and weekends in Srebrenica and Potočari.

In the context of their homes away from Tuzla, Hajra and Nura helped me to understand the important connection between their prewar lives and their work with the association. Located midway up Petrića, Hajra's white house, with its boxes of bright pink geraniums perched on the second-floor balcony, stands out as one of the few completely finished homes on the street. (It also signals to many that she is a much more prosperous survivor than others who have returned.)

The airy, light rooms of its interior served as the backdrop to count-less conversations Hajra and I had over the course of my fieldwork in Bosnia. In the first few weeks of our acquaintance, when I would visit her on a Saturday or Sunday morning in her living room, sipping coffee out of a *fildjan* (a small coffee cup with no handle), I learned the invaluable lesson of how to talk with a survivor of genocide about her missing relatives.

During these conversations, Hajra welcomed my questions about life in the enclave, the identification process, and the association's work. As I would learn when I got to know other family members of the missing, such discussions cannot exist in the abstract, but inevitably turn toward the circumstances of the individual person and the story of her miss-ing relatives. For some, this means describing the terrifying moments of their separation—the last time they saw their family members alive. For others, those memories remain unspoken, and instead they dwell on the details of their past life with their missing sons or husbands or brothers. In Hajra's case, her experience of the genocide is shaped above all by the loss of the younger of her two sons, Nihad ("Nino") Ćatić. By many accounts a gifted and passionate writer, Nino Ćatić was one of the few journalists who reported the plight of Srebrenica's refugees to the outside world.[14] The night before the fall of the enclave, he broadcast the warning that if the UN did not intervene, that recording would be his very last. It was. Although in poor health, he fled with the column of men through the forest, but never made it to Tuzla. His body has not been identi-fied, and Hajra fears that his mortal remains—like those of so many of the men who died in the forest—may never be recovered. During those first few conversations at her home, when she spoke of Nino, whose pencil-sketched portrait hangs on the wall in the adjacent room, and in particular about the circumstances of his certain death, Hajra had a tendency to look away, out the window or into the other room. She would move her fingers nervously along the fabric of the couch and often would cease talking altogether, leaving her thoughts to hang in the air. At first, I felt extremely uncomfortable with such abrupt silences but soon came to understand them as necessary periods of respite for her. Rather than pressing ahead with the discussion or saying something to ease the awkwardness of the situation, I learned to let those moments pass, to let Hajra pick up the conversation wherever she chose. Sometimes that meant she would circle back to the topic at hand; other times she would start in on another subject, pulling us away from the painful memories of her missing family members or life in the enclave.

Such conversations for Hajra, Nura, and the other members of the association were a regular part of their lives and an important means of developing and maintaining their visibility in the Bosnian and international public. They were frequently being asked by strangers to recall their missing relatives and recount their stories of survival and suffering. As evidence of those visits and conversations—not to mention a projection of the organization's political relevance—hundreds of business cards lie spread out underneath the plate glass covering the large table in the main room of the Women of Srebrenica office—from various news organizations, UN offices, NGOs working in Bosnia, military liaisons, VIPs from the Office of the High Representative and the International Criminal Tribunal for the former Yugoslavia, and even the occasional diplomat.

As I began to work with these women more extensively in Tuzla, my presence in the office changed from that of a visitor leaving behind a business card to a kind of associate whose skills counterbalanced the steady flow of questions. I became the association's amateur chauffeur, shuttling Hajra and Nura between their meetings and appearances in Srebrenica, the memorial center in Potočari, and occasionally Sarajevo. Having driven them to a given function, I was their guest and therefore frequently able to sit in and observe discussions to which otherwise I would never have gained access. Yet it was our travels to and from Srebrenica as *vikendaši* that most strengthened our friendship. On Friday afternoons the three of us would pack up the organization's car (a parting donation from Physicians for Human Rights) and head to Srebrenica for the weekend. Each ride would bring out stories, some of which I would hear repeated over the course of the year we spent together, about the fall of Srebrenica, the fate of the column of men, the detention and execution sites, and invariably the sites of exhumed as well as suspected mass graves. Then, each Sunday afternoon after a quiet weekend in Srebrenica, Hajra and I would load up the car once again, pick up Nura at her family's summer home in nearby Potočari, which she and her husband were rebuilding, and drive two hours back to the office in Tuzla.

REPRESENTATIONS OF THE MISSING

Located on a residential street directly behind the hulking brown apartment building of the *Dom penzionera* (retirement home), the office of the Women of Srebrenica takes up half of the ground-floor apartment

in a private house.¹⁵ It is easy to mistake it for a home rather than an
organization's headquarters because, just past the wooden gates, the
yard is filled with flowers, mostly roses, and well-trimmed shrubbery.
White lace curtains and several houseplants trim the large window just
beyond the garden. Only a poster, one announcing the July 11 commemorative ceremony, signals the presence of the office. Upon entering
the front door, you are immediately greeted by a collage of faces. There,
mounted on the upper half of the wall that runs lengthwise opposite the
front door, are the photographs of Srebrenica's victims. Because each is
a reproduction of a photograph provided by a surviving family member,
the images range in clarity and color. Some are faded and creased
black-and-white photos from identity documents or school pictures,
while others are color snapshots taken by family or friends. The serious
countenances of young soldiers in uniforms or middle-age men posing
for identity cards are mounted next to slightly fuzzy, color images of
teenagers smiling shyly and close-ups of men with arms draped over
each other's shoulders. The one that invariably catches my eye is that
of a young man smiling slyly out of the corner of his mouth as he turns
his head towards the camera. With a cigarette held to his lips, he looks
poised to make a joke or to tease the photographer. It always makes me
sad to see his playful expression and think of his fate.

Recently, as word has gotten out that the women are compiling an
album of all the victims' photographs, pictures of young boys have
been added.¹⁶ Seven- and eight-year olds with ears sticking out under
bowl-shaped haircuts—the kind of ears an older boy would hide in an
act of pubescent self-consciousness—now beam their innocent smiles
at you from across the wall. They were much older—probably six or
ten or twelve years older—when they were killed, but their families
have only these snapshots to provide.

The images of these men and boys immediately announce the primary object of the association's efforts. First and foremost, the women
who gather in the modest space of this two-room office seek the return
of their missing relatives. They point out their sons and husbands,
fathers and brothers to each other and to visitors, reciting the person's
name and gesturing to the spot on the wall. There is a bench covered in
long, faded yellow cushions that runs along the same wall as the photos.
When the office fills up with members and the women sit shoulder to
shoulder along the bench, the juxtaposition of their animated faces with
the collage of men and boys above is striking. Captured by the photographer's lens, the masculine visages remain frozen in time, a static and

FIGURE 3. Members of the Women of Srebrenica, with photographs of the victims. Photo by the author, courtesy of the Women of Srebrenica.

pathos-filled reminder of their absence. The women, older now, have had to push on with their lives, despite the disappearance of their closest family members and, in many cases, of their own children.

Throughout the main office, its corridor, and back room, more photographs, posters, and newspaper clippings adorn the white walls, providing a colorful and revealing testimony of the organization, its members, and its activities. In the back room the women have hung white sheets of poster board covered with photographs of their signature activity: the peaceful protest they carry out at 12 o'clock on the 11th of every month. The posters chronicle the protests over several months during one particular year, through the snowy streets of Tuzla and under the hot sun in midday August. In the corner to the right, there are stacks of folded-up, bright squares of fabric. Several of the same pieces of cloth are strung from the piping above and they hang like a valance across the length of the wall. These are the embroidered pillowcases, the markedly gendered symbol of the Women of Srebrenica's public campaign for the return of their missing family members. Each 11th of the month, the members of the association gather under a large chestnut tree across from one of Tuzla's bus stations and next to the newly developed recreation park. Another group heads out from the office laden with stacks of the pillowcases, which are sewn to one another in groups of ten, and they make the short trek across the center of town to join the assembly already gathered under the tree. In the minutes leading up to noon, the women begin to organize themselves into a long line. They swiftly unravel and dole out the sections of pillowcases, which are then tied to one another, forming a lengthy chain of fabric. The participants each take a section of the string of pillowcases and hold it up at waist level.

An evocative display of "women's work," each pillowcase bears the embroidered lettering that spells out the name, year of birth, and birth-place of a missing person from the Srebrenica genocide.[17] The Women of Srebrenica and the extended community painstakingly stitched these pillowcases for their missing relatives, friends, and neighbors in the years immediately following the genocide. A scene in Amir Bašović's play *Priviđenja iz srebrenog vijeka* captures the emotional force behind the handiwork. The scene takes place after the fall of the enclave at Fatima's home in one of the collective centers outside of Tuzla. Seated alone on the stage, she is struggling to finish the pillowcase's embroidery, and her failing health forces her to hand the task over to a neighbor, a young woman who also lost her husband in the genocide. The neigh-bor promises that she will complete the stitching for Fatima, thereby ensuring that the names of Fatima's son and husband are represented with those of the other missing. In total the Women of Srebrenica have more than 4,000 such pillowcases, each bearing the name of a dif-ferent victim. Stretched out along the line of women—some fifty or sixty members who regularly attend the protests—they form a colorful banner of names, yet another collage of the missing that the Women of Srebrenica hold up to the public as testimony to their relatives' unaccounted-for absence. At the head of the procession, there are two other large cloth banners. On the smaller one, printed in red block let-tering, is the phrase *"SREBRENICA 11.7.1995 NE ZABORAVIMO"* (Srebrenica 7/11/1995 Let Us Not Forget). The other, larger swath of material says in black lettering, *"TRAŽIMO NAŠE NESTALE"* (We Are Searching for Our Missing).

At noon the column of women begins their silent, peaceful protest. Proceeding single file on the sidewalk along one of the city's two main thoroughfares, they walk toward the major rotary intersection in the center of the city. There the chain of pillowcases borne by the surviving family members of Srebrenica's missing brings the midday traffic to

FIGURE 4. A pillowcase displayed at the Women of Srebrenica's protest. Photo by the author.

a stop, as the women cross the street and begin heading toward the center square, located beside one of the city's oldest mosques. Police officers stand in the rotary intersection overseeing the procession of women and ensuring their safe passage. Although Tuzla's drivers may have grown weary of the sight or annoyed by the inevitable blocked traffic, no one dares sound a horn in protest. Rather, a small entourage of journalists films and photographs the women from their point of departure to their assembly at the main square. As the line of women proceeds down the busy artery and alongside the cobblestone streets of the old city, people look on with a mixture of reactions. Some stare intently at the lettering embroidered on the pillowcases, reading the names and noting the birth years. I often wonder if they are from the region and are looking for someone's name in particular. Others focus on the spectacle of the women. They either avert their eyes, staring past them, or they look on with pity. On a rare occasion someone will address the women, expressing words of sympathy, or, conversely, frustration with the protest and the refugees' prolonged presence in Tuzla. But the vast majority of onlookers passing by in cars and buses or standing on the sidewalk appears inured to the colorful chain of pillowcases and the assembly of women. After so many years, the sight has become commonplace.

When the column of protesters reaches the main square, the women at the front begin forming a large circle by walking counterclockwise around the outer perimeter, all the while still holding up the chain of pillowcases. Once the entire procession has assembled in the square so that the line of women has sealed it off from pedestrian traffic, sometimes doubling up in concentric circles, the final stage of the protest commences. The women stand in silence as the journalists walk around the center of the square, filming and photographing the various protesters. Some conduct interviews with Hajra, Nura, and other members about their reactions to recent events related to Srebrenica. There are two women who regularly carry framed photographs of their missing family members during the protest. The pictures have been cut out and arranged in an overlapping collage with hand-drawn flowers encircling the faces. One of the women is quite old and extremely frail. Her hands tremble as she holds the frame up to her chest. The other woman is younger, in her mid-forties, and her framed collage bears the faces of her three sons and husband, all of whom are missing. She remains utterly silent throughout the protest, even as some of the other women whisper among themselves.

The dress and outward appearance of the women assembled in the square expose the cross section of social, religious, and economic backgrounds within the organization. The majority of women are older—forty years old and up—and most wear the traditional Bosnian Muslim dress of headscarves and long skirts. Many of these same women travel into the city on this day from the collective centers such as Mihatović and Simin Han and are arguably the most economically vulnerable group, having no permanent housing and severely limited incomes. The other women, a handful of younger members in their twenties and a collection of middle-aged women, including the leaders, Hajra and Nura, are more urban and secular in their appearance. They do not cover their heads, most wear pants or calf-length skirts and low heels, and a few wear makeup. Each month one or two small children accompany their mothers and stand along the line of pillowcases, their small hands clasped over the bright cloth. While others participate from time to time, there is only one man, nicknamed "Mustache," who regularly attends the protest. Always dressed formally in a dark blue suit, he stands in stark contrast to the rest of the assembly and yet manages to keep a low profile, as if careful to avoid drawing attention away from the women.

After several minutes of silence has passed, someone signals for the group to recite the *fatiha* (the opening chapter of the Koran), and the protesters slip their arms underneath the chain of pillowcases, raising their palms before their faces. They pray together for a few short moments and then the protest ends. The women untie the sections of the fabric and begin to fold them together. Some leave directly following this conclusion, but most gather in small groups in the square to talk with one another and catch up on recent news. Others draw close to a member who is speaking with a journalist, usually responding to a question before a camera or into a microphone. After the interviews are over, the core group of women heads back to the office with their arms full of the folded-up sections of pillowcases.

## A PLACE TO 'EMPTY OURSELVES OUT'

Whereas the women's protests presented the association's public message about their search for Srebrenica's missing, their informal gatherings afterward and on other quiet days in the office provided insight into how individual family members of the missing viewed and participated in the identification process. Upon their arrival after the protest, the women filled the two rooms of the office, taking seats around the large conference tables in the back room and on the benches and in the booth of the main room. Invariably Naza, an active member who often came to the office to spend afternoons with Hajra and Nura, would set to work preparing coffee and pouring soda into plastic cups. Some women would pull out their lunch, savory pastries wrapped in sheets of waxy paper, so that soon the office was filled with the pungent smells of a Bosnian kitchen. Naza would then distribute the *fildjani* (the small porcelain cups) filled with the steaming coffee. Saucers piled with sugar cubes were set out on the table, and most women would dip a corner of the cube into the black liquid, nibble off the soaked bit, and take a sip of the coffee. With their thirst now quenched, the women relaxed into easy yet animated conversation about a range of topics.

These monthly gatherings, which I attended regularly in 2003 and 2004, were an important opportunity for the members to learn about recent developments relating to Srebrenica and its wartime residents. They asked one another about their prewar property, their intentions about returning, and whether they had received a donation for rebuilding their houses. They talked about news from The Hague and the trials of Naser Orić, Slobodan Milošević, and indicted Bosnian Serb

Army officers involved in the genocide. Turning to Hajra or Nura, they peppered the leaders with questions about an ongoing lawsuit against the Dutch government, the recently adopted legislation for families of the missing, and the latest news regarding the identification process. They were eager to know about current exhumations and preparations for the next burial at Potočari. Not everyone listened raptly to the answers or engaged in these discussions—many fell into private conversations with the women seated next to them—but the information flowed back and forth throughout the two or three hours of these informal meetings.

On the few occasions when I observed visitors or members who came only infrequently to the office during these gatherings, I noticed some of the unspoken codes of behavior the women had adopted in the company of their own. While individuals spoke about their missing relatives when asked directly, they rarely lamented their personal losses to the other women. That is not to say they did not bemoan the tragedy that befell them as a group—the conditions in the enclave, the horrific sights and experiences of the deportation, the mass graves, and the conditions of recovered bodies. They might discuss among themselves any of these subjects—indeed they did, sometimes in graphic detail, eliciting from around the room the heavy sighs of *"Bože moj"* (my God)—but they avoided drawing particular attention to their individual grief. Among these regular members were women who had lost entire families, including multiple children; there were women who had been raped, and women who had witnessed their own family members being killed.

After one protest in the spring of 2004, a woman who was an infrequent participant in the protest joined the assembly back at the office. Seated at the foot of the long conference table, she engaged one of the more regular members in a conversation predominantly about her own troubles. The rest of the room fell silent, listening to her. Not long after she left (an hour or so before most of the women would begin to trickle out), they scoffed at her presumption that she was the only one with such concerns. If they spoke about personal problems, the regular members of the association tended to complain about health issues or burdensome trips to local governmental offices to procure necessary documents for their return or their benefits as family members of the missing. On the occasions when they did address questions of well-being, they often skirted the issue of mental health altogether and instead spoke in terms of emotional states—states of agitation to be avoided if possible and treated when necessary. They talked much more freely about taking medication prescribed by their family doctor than seeking counseling. Pills were always on hand in someone's purse, ready to be dispensed at the first sign of a member's distress. Indeed, the women were well practiced in self-administering such medication. They would swallow down the tablets before emotionally stressful events, such as a visit from ICMP staff, or when watching a documentary film about Srebrenica on television or participating in a commemorative activity.

The more intimate conversations among members about their grief and their missing family took place in the confines of the office on quieter days. There, in the main room, seated on the benches or around the glass-top table, two or three women would talk over coffee and lend each other support and sympathetic words. As one member explained, "We can come here and empty ourselves out *(da se ispraznimo),* mourn a little *(da malo oplačemo)*." One the most moving of such conversations that I witnessed took place between Hajra and another member, Hajrija. Hajrija had lost her husband and two sons in the genocide. The older of the two sons had married while living in the enclave, and he and his wife had a child in March 1994. When Srebrenica fell, Hajrija's husband and sons set off together in the column. She learned later that all three had survived a full month, hiding in the forest with a small band of other men. The Serbs discovered and attacked their position on August 13, at which point the group scattered, and none of her family has been seen since. Eventually her daughter-in-law left with the child to resettle in the United States. Hajrija cherishes her grandson, the flesh and blood of her own lost son. She often showed me photographs of him, a pudgy boy with crew-cut hair and a wide smile, and we spoke of his life in the United States on several occasions. I think it was reassuring for Hajrija to know that I came from the same country where he now lived and therefore understood the place in which he was growing up. But on this particular day, Hajrija was tearful.

The night before, her daughter-in-law had telephoned to tell her that she had remarried. Although the two women were on very good terms and the daughter-in-law made sure that her son remained in close contact with his grandmother, Hajrija was worried that this might change her relationship with her grandson. While she did not outright express the concern, all of us in the room understood that this event signaled a new chapter in the family's intertwined lives—the end of her daughter-in-law's status as her son's wife and the beginning of her existence as another person's spouse. Moreover, a different man than Hajrija's son would be father to her grandson. In fact, a few months later when I recorded an interview with Hajrija, she explained that the boy had defined for himself his relationship with his stepfather: "When she got [re]married she tried to convince him to call her husband, to address him like he was his father. 'I won't,' he says. 'He's not my father. So it's not for me to call him father.'" Nevertheless, on the day after Hajrija had learned her daughter-in-law's news, she felt the painful reminder of her missing son and the way in which life had moved on, leaving him further and further in the past. Hajra and Hajrija talked for a long time that afternoon, and in the end, when Hajrija got up to leave, it was apparent how important it had been for her to speak with another mother who was missing a son. Although Hajra openly acknowledged that she could not understand Hajrija's pain, she admitted that she herself sometimes wished her own son had married and had had children, if only so that she, too, could have such a living reminder of him.

## IDENTIFICATION

Spending time with the Women of Srebrenica eight, nine, and ten years after the genocide provided a limited view into the evolution of the organization's activism and its role in helping members such as Hajrija rebuild their lives. The pictures mounted on the office walls, the early issues of the organization's newsletter, *Bilten Srebrenica*, and the stories told by the women recreated a sense of the immediate postwar years; my view into the surviving family members' experiences and their involvement in the identification process, however, was framed by the emergence of the DNA technology. I arrived on the scene when the overwhelming majority of women had accepted the fact that their missing relatives were dead. They had already provided blood samples and were waiting for news of the recovery and identification of their relatives' mortal remains.

The Women of Srebrenica's search for their missing relatives was closely connected to the efforts of the other organization in Tuzla dedicated to the identification process: the International Commission on Missing Persons (ICMP). The directors and staff of both the blood and bone sample collection headquarters (Identification Coordination Division) and the Podrinje Identification Project in Tuzla had regular contact with the association's leaders and members. Indeed, ICMP was one of the association's major donors, funding among other things their office space and the publication costs of their newsletter.[18] Despite depending on ICMP for financial support, the Women of Srebrenica often acted as a watchdog organization for the identification process. When the association learned that Physicians for Human Rights (subcontracted by ICMP) had developed a pilot DNA-testing project in which samples were sent to a US laboratory, they demanded to know the results, the costs of the project, and why local resources could not be developed for such testing. In the second issue of *Bilten Srebrenica,* they wrote, "We still don't know the results of the pilot project, but we would also like to know why a closer laboratory isn't being used and why there are no efforts to create such a laboratory in Bosnia and Herzegovina" (Žene Srebrenice 1998a:9). Over the years, they voiced their disapproval of the slow pace of identifications, the lack of funding transparency, the presence of Serbian forensic experts at Srebrenica mass graves, and even the relationship between the Sarajevo ICMP staff and the Mothers of the Srebrenica and Žepa Enclaves.[19]

Beyond such concerns, however, ICMP could rely on the leaders and members of the Women of Srebrenica in Tuzla to communicate to Srebrenica's surviving family members the importance of providing blood samples for DNA analysis. For some people, the white lab coats and highfalutin scientific terminology bred distrust of the international organization, and it frequently fell to associations such as the Women of Srebrenica to convince family members of its worth. Hajra and Nura explained that in the early years they worked closely with ICMP (whose program was being carried out by Physicians for Human Rights) to provide contact information for relatives of the missing. When local DNA extraction capabilities were finally developed, they strove to educate their members about the process and encouraged them to give blood samples and to inform their own relatives. Later, after I had been working in the field with the case managers from the Podrinje Identification Project, I asked Hajra and Nura why some family members of the missing rejected the DNA and classical forensic evidence. They explained that such a response typically came from women, mothers, who were isolated—that is, from women who did not have the support of fellow survivors. If they were more connected to such a community, Hajra and Nura reasoned, they would see how others had scrutinized and eventually accepted the DNA technology. Moreover, they would have been able to witness the growing number of identifications as well as how other surviving families had reacted to the news. In this capacity, the association served as an important liaison for ICMP, relaying information about the identification process, its development and technology, and therefore reaching out to members of the community who might not otherwise embrace the DNA-based procedures. As both the leaders of the Women of Srebrenica and ICMP staff underscored, without those blood samples there would be fewer sets of identified mortal remains.

By 2003, identification had not only influenced the lives of the members of the Women in Srebrenica living in Tuzla, but it had significantly changed the postwar Bosniak community slowly returning to Srebrenica. As I will explore in subsequent chapters, many in the international community and the Bosniak nationalist leadership hoped that identification and the establishment of the memorial center in Potočari would encourage return. The numbers of minority returnees to the Srebrenica municipality did in fact increase beginning in 2001. By 2003, during the first year of mass burials of Srebrenica's missing, I watched the Bosniak returnee neighborhoods in Srebrenica grow; at the same time, members of the Women of Srebrenica begin to reclaim and restore their prewar houses in the Podrinje region. These movements also signaled changes in the Bosnian Serb population in Srebrenica, because reclaimed property entailed evictions of postwar Bosnian Serb inhabitants. The multiple layers of Srebrenica once again were shifting, in part due to progress made by advocates such as the Srebrenica family associations and the tangible results of the DNA-based identification process.

# CHAPTER 3

# A Technological Innovation

From the end of the war in December 1995 to November 2001, fewer than 1 percent of Srebrenica's missing were identified.[1] By the tenth anniversary of the genocide, the mortal remains of 1,938 individuals—nearly 25 percent of the total missing—had been identified and buried in the Srebrenica-Potočari Memorial Center.[2] The breakthrough in the identification process came on November 16, 2001, when DNA laboratory technicians at the International Commission on Missing Persons (ICMP) successfully extracted and matched the genetic profiles from the mortal remains of a sixteen-year-old boy and the blood samples of his surviving family members. Rijad Konjhodžić, ICMP's DNA lab coordinator at that time, had worked on the match: "It was quite amazing. . . . We had a mutation in our first case. And it had to be verified by Y-chromosome testing. So we can't believe our luck because mutations show up one in every 1,000 cases, and the first case we had one. I did the Y-chromosome testing on that one and it was done at 2 A.M. I woke everyone up. 'It's our guy.' . . . The preparations were really, really long. We invested a lot of time, a lot of patience, a lot of hours. We worked 14-hour shifts straight. We all know what we're working for but when the first ID dropped, you close the circle. You see that you're not working in vain, that it's working. If it worked for one case, it's going to work for another. So it was a big day, a big day for us" (Chipman 2005).

Science assumes a very powerful role in these unfolding events. But the story behind the development of the DNA-based technology used to identify missing persons of Srebrenica and, more generally, those of the conflicts of former Yugoslavia in the 1990s, is not one of reified science as deus ex machina, whose sophisticated instruments of genetic testing impart order in a disorderly postwar society. Rather, it is a story of knowledge production occurring within the specific sociopolitical context of postwar Bosnia and encompassing a range of sources of authority and expertise. Studying how this technology came into being entails assessing the network of actors both supporting and rejecting the knowledge it promised to produce, the political aims behind its creation, and the often competing claims of truth and objectivity underwriting its results. While media representations of the recovery process tend to credit DNA testing with the successful identification of nearly one quarter of Srebrenica's missing, there are other vital aspects of the process frequently overshadowed by the innovative application of this biotechnology. In particular, memory, imagination, and the capacity to comprehend and synthesize facts surrounding the events of the genocide and of the individual victims' lives are indispensable to identification. This and the two following chapters explore how the identification technology developed over time, focusing in particular on the social context and contingencies surrounding attempts to address the absence of knowledge created by the Srebrenica genocide.

## AN INNOVATION OF VIOLENCE

In order for us to identify the victims, we need first to find them. To this day we don't know where we stand with the recovery of the Srebrenica victims. If we take into account that there are somewhere around 8,500 missing from Srebrenica, today we have in the mortuary in Tuzla more than 7,000 bags, bags with mortal remains, but I wouldn't be able to say what number of bodies [that represents]. . . . *The problem namely with Srebrenica is the secondary mass graves as a kind of innovation that the Bosnian Serbs patented.* Nowhere in the world has it been recorded during the time of war that a people or a group of people who were in the battle of war did this—that is, after liquidation, after arbitrary execution, after the victims were buried in primary graves, in the most extreme,

uncivilized way with backhoes . . . a thousand victims
in one grave. . . . Thus, it remained for recorded history
of humanity that someone, after that, again came to the
graves and again entered with machines. Nowhere is
that recorded. Not even the Nazis in the Second World
War did such a thing. [Italics added]

> Amor Mašović, *head of the Federation Commission*
> *for Missing Persons*

The Srebrenica victims present a unique problem. According to Mr.
Mašović, they embody a new kind of atrocity, heretofore unknown
to humankind: the phenomenon of secondary mass graves. Invoking
world history, Mašović views this development beyond the parameters of Yugoslav or even Balkan violent conflict. He places it within
a broader European sociohistorical context and measures it according
to the indices of the Nazis' technology of mass killing.[3] The Bosnian
Serbs have surpassed even them, not in their mastery of execution, but
in their manner of defiling the initial burial sites. *"Čak i nacisti u toku
drugom svijetskom ratu nisu tako nešto radili"* (Not even the Nazis
in the Second World War did such a thing). Mašović recognizes the
mechanization of the crime, pointing out how the Bosnian Serbs "patented" *(patentirali)* an "innovation" *(izum)* when they returned to the
primary mass graves with their backhoes and heavy machinery. They
dug up the original sites and transported the contents (the decomposing
bodies of the victims) to secondary locations, sometimes depositing
them in multiple gravesites. Often bodies became disarticulated in this
transfer. Thus, it is possible for sections of an individual skeleton to be
exhumed from multiple secondary mass graves. In his public addresses,
Mašović often tells the grim story about how body parts from one
person have been exhumed from three different sites. The disturbing
example supports his claim that the technology used to cover up the war
crimes—not at all sophisticated in terms of its instrumentation—represents an innovation in violence. The secondary mass graves destroy
the physical integrity of human remains, not through cremation but by
the commingling and separating of bodies to the point that they are
indistinguishable as individual skeletal remains.

Mašović's description of Srebrenica's secondary mass graves as a
patented innovation implies a dehumanizing intent on behalf of the
innovators, the Bosnian Serbs who first deposited and later dug up,
transported, and reburied the victims' mortal remains. In Hannah

Arendt's discussion of the "objectivity" with which the S.S. regarded its concentration camps and extermination practices, she exposes how the language of science has been employed to recast violence. At the trial of Adolf Eichmann, Dr. Servatius was the defense witness who, according to Arendt, "was to carry off the prize for 'objectivity' ":

> The moment, one of the few great ones in the whole trial, occurred during the short oral *plaidoyer* of the defense, after which the court withdrew for four months to write its judgment. Servatius declared the accused innocent of charges bearing on his responsibility for "the collection of skeletons, sterilizations, killings by gas, and *similar medical matters*," whereupon Judge Halevi interrupted him: "Dr. Servatius, I assume you made a slip of the tongue when you said that killing by gas was a medical matter." To which Servatius replied: "It was indeed a medical matter, since it was prepared by physicians; *it was a matter of killing, and killing, too, is a medical matter*." (Italics in the original; Arendt 1994:69)

Servatius's depiction both professionalizes the act of extermination through the use of medical terms and dehumanizes the victims by pre-empting the consideration of them as anything other than objects of medical study, practice, or treatment. Mašović's terms, *innovation* and *patented*, likewise emphasize the dehumanizing technology employed by the Bosnian Serb forces. Rather than excusing the violence as clinical, he condemns its innovative form and, by association, its innovators for their inhuman treatment of human remains. Furthermore, by invoking the language of technology, he underscores the systematic, mechanized means by which the identity of thousands of men and boys was stripped away in the trenches of commingled bones. The heavy machinery used to dig up and scatter the remains fits within the larger scheme of the Bosnian Serbs' well-orchestrated plan to eradicate the Bosniak population from the Srebrenica enclave. It is from these notions of technology and innovation that my discussion of the identification of Srebrenica's missing begins.

## THE PROMISE OF A TECHNOLOGICAL INNOVATION: POSTWAR BOSNIAN STATE-BUILDING

In a world in which satellite images capture troops amassed on the border of a UN safe area, the ominous collection of prisoners of war in open fields, and the work of backhoes digging large craters in the earth, technology could have spared some of the Srebrenica victims' lives. But it was never employed to that end.[4] "The United States, which had some five spy satellites operating in space at all times, snapping some 5,000 images per day, did not even concentrate on tracking the fate of the men. Each time a satellite camera clicked, it captured a 100-square-mile chunk of territory. . . . They could depict foreign troop locations, additional buildings at suspect nuclear weapons sites, and even mass graves. But competition to secure images was fierce, as the satellites over Bosnia took pictures from an SMO, or support-to-military-operations, perspective" (Power 2002:408). Unfettered, the Bosnian Serb forces were thus able to put into practice a rudimentary though effective technology of violence, the results of which confounded early efforts to recover and identify the victims' mortal remains.[5]

The chaos of the commingled, disassociated, and partial skeletons that lay within the secondary mass graves eventually gave rise to another innovation: a forensic application of genetic science unique in scale and in method that finally offered a means of resolving the missing persons issue by matching blood samples of surviving family members with bone samples from recovered mortal remains. It was, however, an expensive endeavor. The DNA extraction and analysis procedures involved in identifying Bosnia's missing (including the Srebrenica victims) were costly, especially for a postwar country already dependent on foreign aid to rebuild its economy, its infrastructure, and its citizens' private property.[6]

Where did the money come from? How did such a costly technology come to be developed in Bosnia? What political forces enabled its creation? To appreciate the achievement, we must first consider the conditions foregrounding the identification efforts in the early postwar years. This entails sketching briefly the relations between the postwar state of Bosnia and its benefactors, the international protectorate presence that encompassed not only the cadre of advisors among the diplomatic corps but also the international organizations working in the country on the missing persons issue.

To begin with, the notion of identifying persons missing as a result of the war presented Bosnia's dual-entity government with a vexing political objective: to locate, recover, and identify the mortal remains of victims of all ethnic groups. The numbers of missing among the three ethno-national groups at the end of the war were significantly different: 87.8 percent Bosniaks, 2.8 percent Croats, 9 percent Serbs, and .4 percent others.[7] While recovering and identifying Srebrenica's victims were important goals for many Bosniak political and religious leaders, in particular those nationalist politicians from the Podrinje region eager to document claims of Serb aggression with concrete facts and numbers, Bosnian Serb officials were reluctant to support the identification initiatives, especially when it came to disclosing locations of suspected mass graves. Yet their cooperation was imperative—without Bosnian Serb authorities' participation, exhuming and identifying remains, especially those of the Srebrenica missing, would be extremely difficult if not impossible.

As with many aspects of its governance, the political structure of the postwar Bosnian state hampered its ability to undertake the task of identifying its missing citizens. The Dayton Peace Agreement had formally divided the Republic of Bosnia and Herzegovina into two entities—the Federation of Bosnia and Herzegovina and the Republika Srpska—and its federal government consisted of a convoluted equal-representation parliamentary assembly and a rotating tri-presidency.[8] Administratively divided along an ethnic key that reified and institutionalized the three ethno-national groups (Bosniaks, Bosnian Serbs, and Bosnian Croats), the postwar state encompassed parallel bureaucracies in the Federation and the Republika Srpska. The government of the Federation established its own entity-specific institution for identification, the Federation Commission for Missing Persons (Federalna komisija za traženje nestalih), and the Serb-controlled entity of the Republika Srpska created its equivalent organization, the State Commission for Exchanging of War Prisoners (Државна комисија за размјену ратних заробљеника), later renamed the RS Office for Tracing Detained and Missing Persons (Канцеларија за тражење несталих и заробљених лица Републике Српске).[9] Fundamentally, the two commissions were working on parallel but politically opposed projects—that is, recovering and identifying remains of people killed primarily by paramilitary and military forces belonging to or supporting the other entity. This division of labor underscored more than simply a lack of political cohesion around the issue of missing persons or distrust of entity-level institutional capacity; it laid bare the absence of a centralized power capable of responding to the crisis of identity provoked by the wartime violence. Rather, the government's divided structure ensured that institutional responses to missing persons would remain closely inscribed within entity boundaries. Thus, coupled with the disparity in respective numbers of missing persons and competing moral understandings of victimhood and aggression, the separate, entity-specific identification initiatives in the immediate postwar years precluded the kind of collaboration necessary to develop a centralized identification system, let alone one capable of marshaling the resources for DNA analysis.

Given that the divided government of Bosnia and Herzegovina was incapable of accounting for and recovering all of its missing citizens regardless of ethnicity, the task fell to the authority behind the postwar government—that is, the international presence intent on establishing a liberal democracy from the fractured polity of postwar Bosnia. Emerging from the negotiating tables of Dayton, Ohio, the government of Bosnia and Herzegovina was inextricably bound to an international protectorate, namely the High Representative, established in Annex 10 of the agreement to oversee the "implementation of the civilian aspects of the peace settlement."[10] The seemingly benign phrasing of its mandate belied the executive role the protectorate quickly assumed. The Office of the High Representative's (OHR) broad powers to "facilitate" and "monitor" the peace accord's implementation entailed removing elected officials, suspending judges, sanctioning municipalities and cantons, imposing laws, and even institutionalizing a separate territorial and political district (that of Brčko) (Coles 2007b:37–39).[11] In carrying out such drastic measures, the protectorate answered not to the Bosnian taxpayers but to foreign ministries who convened for the biennial gatherings of the Peace Implementation Council (Knaus and Martin 2003). OHR enlisted the support of other international organizations to carry out its mandate, chief among them NATO, the Organization for Security and Co-Operation in Europe (OSCE), and the United Nations. With its sovereignty thus encumbered, Bosnia became the site of sustained international intervention: "The peace treaty did not just usher in 'peace,' it also provided a liberal and neoliberal prescription for Bosnia's ills and a model for, and legitimization of, intensive interventions by international institutions" (Coles 2004:555).

A "state by international design and of international design" (Bose 2002:60), the dual-entity Republic of Bosnia and Herzegovina operated under the guardianship of Western governments, namely the United States, the United Kingdom, France, and Germany.[12] Their presence—from OHR to peacekeeping troops—was to be temporary, and their efforts were grounded in the concept of progress, movement along a linear trajectory away from past instability and irrationality toward a reformed and reconstructed state and society (Duffield 2002). Instituting comprehensive economic, political, and judicial reforms aimed at dismantling select residual socialist structures and repairing wartime damage, these governments' main objective was to usher

Bosnia into the "family of nations" and, more concretely, the European Union (Coles 2007a). As such, the international intervention into post-war Bosnia characterized by OHR and the cadre of international organizations fit within a broader trend that linked aid and development to issues of security and regional stability (Duffield 2002): global liberal governance driving projects of postconflict social reconstruction and political reform that draws its moral order not only from human rights and humanitarian intervention, but also from technoscientific ideologies of progress (Jasanoff 2006).

Identifying missing persons through the sophisticated instrumentation and presumably unassailable evidence of DNA testing provided yet another plane on which the invested Western governments could attempt social repair in postwar Bosnia. Two aspects of the technology made it an especially appealing form of intervention. First, cast as science in the service of "truth," it promised to transcend the politics of the region, counteracting the hyperbole, myth, and manipulation often associated with the task of recovering and identifying victims of ethno-national violence. Second, it was manifestly humanitarian. Who, aside from the perpetrators themselves, could object to returning the bones of a missing son to his grieving mother? Framed in this light, the work of identifying Srebrenica's missing, Bosnia's missing, and former Yugoslavia's missing became a dynamic project garnering support from a range of different actors, all of whom saw its potential results serving their own needs.

To begin with, exhuming and naming Srebrenica's unrecognizable remains allowed the Bosniak political and religious leadership—specifically the Bosniak political party SDA and the Islamic Community (Islamska zajednica)—and the international community a means of asserting authority. In the case of the latter, helping Bosnia acquire and implement this cutting-edge application of forensic science advanced the meta-narrative of progress through the transfer of technology and knowledge. It also demonstrated the international community's responsiveness to the surviving families, who held the UN responsible for failing to protect the enclave and who had demanded the technoscientific resource be made available to identify their missing relatives.

Beyond these more limited goals, the DNA-based identification technology provided the international protectorate presence and the Bosniak leadership a means to care for and control Bosnia's living citizens by accounting for the dead. The process of extracting and analyzing human genetic material presented a seemingly apolitical method of identification, "the formalized, codified, objectified systems of categorization developed by powerful, authoritative institutions" (Cooper 2005:72). Like other mechanisms of counting and categorizing, such as censuses and identity documents (Caplan and Torpey 2001; Scott, Tehranian, and Mathias 2002), DNA profiles enabled the individual identity of missing persons to be "codified and institutionalized in order to become *socially significant*" (italics added; Torpey 2000:13; see also Sankar 2001 and Lyon 2001), thus "making the dead count" by "making them socially legible" (Tate 2007:26). On the one hand, the mortal remains of Srebrenica's victims had to be codified and institutionalized for the state of Bosnia and Herzegovina to meet the families' needs, for example, to determine eligibility for monetary support as survivors of missing persons.[13] On the other hand, the identification technology developed to recognize those remains was instrumental in assessing wartime culpability by tabulating and "sorting out" (Bowker and Star 1999) the various victims. The simultaneous projects of individuating and collectivizing the missing thus worked to advance both Bosniak nationalist and international aims of repair—despite how differently each defined the path to such repair. As Drew Gilpin Faust writes in the context of the American Civil War, "Naming individualized the victims; counting aggregated them; the two impulses served opposite yet coexisting needs, marking the paradox inherent in coming to terms with [the war's] death" (2008:264). For the Bosniak leadership in particular, the recovery and reburial of its most emblematic group of victims, the Srebrenica missing, bolstered the ethno-national narrative of the incommensurability of Bosniak versus Bosnian Serb wartime losses, a point to which we will return in chapter 7.

   In response to the efforts and money spent on recovering the Srebrenica victims, the Bosnian Serb leadership had little recourse but to support, or at least reap the benefits of, the development of a DNA-based identification system operating in the country. Although there were significantly fewer Serbs missing at the end of the war, identification of their remains often required genetic testing. The RS government had its own grieving mothers to respond to and its own statistics to compile. Thus the project of identifying Srebrenica's missing, as it expanded into a region-wide effort to identify all of former Yugoslavia's missing, drew together opposing constituencies around the common goal of accounting for and commemorating the missing.

## LISTS OF THE MISSING:
## BUREAUCRACIES OF POSTMORTEM IDENTITY

The physical recovery of unnamed mortal remains from the Bosnian conflict began even as the war was still being waged, but it was not until after the signing of the Dayton Peace Agreement in December 1995 that identification efforts could begin in earnest. From the Bosniak side, the mass killings carried out in places such as Zvornik, Višegrad, Prijedor, and Srebrenica had dismantled and in some instances wiped out entire villages and families. One of the critical first steps in the identification process addressing their absence was to compile a list of the missing, a task undertaken by both local and international institutions. The international organization historically responsible for tracing persons missing as a result of armed conflict, the International Committee of the Red Cross (ICRC, or the Red Cross), took the lead in handling the initial reporting in Bosnia.[14] In the case of Srebrenica, the Red Cross received and processed claims made by family members, generating a list of those considered missing at the fall of the enclave. Confusion about the procedures for filing a claim, however, arose quickly during the first days at the temporary shelter in Dubrave. The Red Cross allowed only immediate family members to report a missing relative. Given the nature of the genocide at Srebrenica, such barriers hindered an accurate initial account of the missing. Neighbors, more distant relatives, and close friends who had crucial information to provide about a missing person were unable to do so, at least in this official context. In rare cases, their testimonies went unrecorded altogether, as thousands of the enclave's survivors left Bosnia to resettle in distant countries such as the United States, Canada, and Australia.[15]

In the weeks and months that followed, confusing restrictions surrounding the procedures of filing missing person claims compounded the refugees' frustration with the international organization's inaction and seeming indifference to the plight of their missing male relatives.[16] Furthermore, many family members became incensed by the Red Cross's decision (later reversed) to begin issuing a "death attestation" document for some of Srebrenica's missing about whom they had received information from Bosnian Serb authorities. The initiative was aimed at facilitating families' access to social welfare, but it also allowed the organization to remove individuals' names from the overall list of missing.[17] In February 1996, members of the Srebrenica community stormed the Red Cross office in Tuzla, demanding that the organization charged with tracing the missing do more to find their relatives, whom they still believed to be alive (Stover 1998:195; Stover and Shigekane 2002).

As time passed and the family members became more politically mobilized, forming their own advocacy associations, they too began to compile lists of the missing, based on information provided to them by their members. The lists generated by both the family associations and the Red Cross constituted the first attempts to disaggregate individual identity from the collective category of the missing and thereby force the public, both local and international, to recognize the specificity of their absence.[18] The family associations used Excel spreadsheets to record victims' names and other personal information—date of birth, place of birth, father's name, the place and date of disappearance, and so on. These collections of personal data also represented a formalized method of etching individual death into public memory by creating a bureaucratized catalogue of the victims of Srebrenica. Whereas some of the missing before the war had had little if any public record of existence (aside from a birth certificate), suddenly the opposite was true as the personal facts of their prewar lives began filling up reams of paper and computer screens. Synthesizing data for each missing person, these Excel spreadsheet records compelled action, their very form creating an "instrument, a tool, a means to an end—Action" (Riles 2001:156). The act of documenting their names formally recognized them as missing, and that state of absence demanded a public response.[19] Furthermore, the lists marked the first attempts to establish a central database for the victims—individual profiles a computer software program would one day sift through in its search for matches between the mortal remains of the missing and the blood of the surviving family members.

Ten years after the fall of Srebrenica, those involved in the identification process acknowledged that there would never be a complete list of Srebrenica's missing. Tellingly, the most successful effort to date to consolidate the various records occurred not for purposes of identification, but for commemoration.[20] Entrusted with compiling a complete list for a display (names of the missing etched into stone) at the Srebrenica-Potočari Memorial Center, the Federation Commission for Missing Persons published a document entitled "Preliminary List of the Missing Persons from the 1995 Srebrenica Genocide."[21] The list contained a total of 8,106 individuals, although Mašović, the commission head, emphasized that the number would inevitably increase as families reported names absent from the document.[22] The timing and the manner in which Mašović unveiled the list underscored its political significance: the announcement was made at a press conference at the Potočari Memorial Center Foundation headquarters one month before the tenth anniversary commemoration. The daily newspaper *Dnevni avaz,* backed by the leading Bosniak nationalist political party (SDA), printed the list as a special insert. Months later, however, Women of Srebrenica members complained that they never received an updated version from the Federation commission's office. Families kept coming to them with absent names, and yet the organization had no revised document to consult.

MISSING PERSONS NETWORK

Concerned with more than just listing the missing of Srebrenica, several institutions became involved in the recovery and identification of their mortal remains. In the initial postwar period, these included the Federation Commission for Missing Persons, the International Criminal Tribunal for the former Yugoslavia (ICTY), the International Committee of the Red Cross (ICRC), Physicians for Human Rights (PHR),[23] the University Clinical Centre in Tuzla (responsible for issuing death certificates), and an organization just being set up in the region, the International Commission on Missing Persons (ICMP). I began researching the topic of the Srebrenica missing in 2003, when the DNA-based identification system had already been in place for two years and the workload of identifying the victims' mortal remains was shared primarily among three of those institutions: ICMP, the Federation commission, and ICRC. There is a complicated history behind the current relationship among these organizations, one with several offshoots that concern evolving practice, consolidated authority and knowledge, and institutional rivalry.[24] While the following discussion outlines some of those issues, it does not trace the identification technology's evolution in full; rather, it details critical events as they were represented to me through my informants, primarily staff members of ICMP and members of the Women of Srebrenica in Tuzla. It is an important point to bear in mind that the circumstances of Srebrenica—its secondary mass graves, disarticulated skeletal remains, and the relative homogeneity, as well as relatedness, of the missing person population—were unprecedented, and responses to them necessarily developed over time, through trial and error. These responses involved institutional jockeying. They demanded revision and streamlining. And in the end, they produced a unique model for reattaching individual names to otherwise unrecognizable remains, a model that has become a resource in identification efforts far beyond the borders of former Yugoslavia.

Networks of actors develop from a controversy, an issue in dispute. In the introduction to the collection of essays *Making Things Public: Atmospheres of Democracy*, Bruno Latour (2005) interrogates our understanding of democracy through the idea of a public.[25] For Latour, a public is a temporary congregation of interested actors, people, institutions, and technologies, each vying to control the dispute and its outcome. The actors in the public want the issue to move beyond contestation and supposition, into the realm of the fact. Therefore, in order for a public to exist, there must arise a key issue, an unresolved question, whose potential resolution promises (or threatens) to impact the circumstances of the actors who have been drawn into the public dialogue surrounding the issue. Latour's interest is in more than just the form of the public; he also urges us to considers its methods of persuasion (of which science and technology often play an important role): "To assemble is one thing: to represent to the eyes and ears of those assembled what is at stake is another. An object-oriented democracy should be concerned as much by the procedure to detect relevant parties as to the methods to bring into the center of the debate the proof of what is to be debated" (2005:18). The difficulty, however, in this assembly of relevant parties is the epistemologically narrow insistence on facts. "Accurate facts are hard to come by and the harder they are, the more they entail some costly equipment, a longer set of mediations, more delicate proofs" (2005:21). In struggling to establish control over the public space of a controversy, the actors seek to master the facts surrounding the issue, transforming it from a question into a matter of fact. Organic in nature, the relationships between actors form out of overlapping and competing interests, and the actors themselves comprise both the animate and inanimate entities inextricably bound up in the issue at hand (Latour 1996).

In the aftermath of the war, Srebrenica's missing had become one such public, an unresolved controversy, and around it grew a network of actors that included the family members of the victims, the local and international organizations involved in identification, the people and institutions denying the genocide and the numbers of missing, and the media that covered various interpretations of the issue.[26] At the center of this public stood the missing themselves, the inanimate and nameless mortal remains that filled the yet-to-be-exhumed surface and mass graves littered about eastern Bosnia. On the one hand, their former state of animate existence—their lives as fathers, husbands, sons, brothers, uncles, and nephews—framed their significance within this network. On the other, through recovery and identification, their potential to yield evidence of Bosnian Serb crimes and Bosniak victim-hood, as well as to facilitate internationally backed processes of "truth and reconciliation," made them instrumental to the overall controversy of Srebrenica. As such, their absence demanded a response, spurring attempts at establishing the facts of their disappearance, such as a definitive record of their names.

The lists of the missing achieved a fairly accurate estimate of their numbers, but they did little to assuage the fear and pain felt by the family members. As Dr. Kešetović explained, the knowledge that their relative was missing, *somewhere,* was unsatisfactory for them. In the early years, the hope lingered among relatives that perhaps their loved one was still alive. Amor Mašović recalled, "I think that at that time more than 70 percent of the Srebrenica survivors believed that their relatives even up until 1997 were living in prisoner of war camps in Serbia. The military intelligence from the former Yugoslavia fed their illusions, consciously planting information."[27] Rumors propagated by the malicious and the criminal played on such emotions. "It went so far as that they would call people from Srebrenica, mothers, and pretend, 'I am your son, I am in this place, I'm well, everything will be OK,' so on and so forth. It was, I would say, a very ugly practice. But more than 70 percent of the people from Srebrenica believed it." Stories of survival also encouraged families' optimism. A handful of men had managed to survive three or four months in the woods and eventually escaped to free territory. Their testimonies fed the hope of those who could not bear the thought of their missing relatives' death.

At the same time, efforts had begun to identify the mortal remains of those victims already recovered. As with the lists of the missing, the competing interests of the network were reflected in the various approaches to these initial identification procedures. For the represen-tatives of the ICTY who were directly involved in the exhumation of graves, the emphasis was on mapping the grave as a crime site and on unearthing the *corpora delicti* as "articulate witness[es]" to the crimes committed (Lacquer 2002:77; Buchli and Lucas 2001). The exhuma-tions and autopsies were carried out with the primary goal of providing evidence about a crime, such as determining the cause of death or the presence of ligatures or blindfolds, rather than documentation of an individual identity (Delpla 2007:223).[28] Thus, these workers paid close attention to the manner of death and the features of the grave and less attention to the condition of the individual skeletal remains, which might have yielded information specific to identification. For example, at several of the early secondary gravesite exhumations directed by the ICTY, crucial information regarding the position of recovered body parts vis-à-vis other skeletal remains was not well documented, thus rendering the reassociation process more complicated and time-consuming than it would have been otherwise.

Less concerned with documenting war crimes, the Federation Commission for Missing Persons and the International Commission on Missing Persons (ICMP) were focused on identifying individual sets of recovered mortal remains. The Federation commission grew out of the wartime institution of the (Bosnian) State Commission for the Exchange of Prisoners, headed by Mašović, whereas ICMP was a postwar creation. Indeed, for an institution that has become so integral to recovering and identifying not only Srebrenica's missing but also missing persons from throughout former Yugoslavia, ICMP began as a modest endeavor, a Clinton administration afterthought. Well aware of the Srebrenica massacre and the existence of primary and presumably secondary mass graves, US president Bill Clinton announced its creation on June 29, 1996, at the G-7 Summit in Lyon, France:

> I am pleased to announce today the formation of an international blue ribbon commission on the missing in the former Yugoslavia, with former Secretary of State Cyrus Vance as its chairman. The commission will be made up of distinguished members of the international community.
>
> Uncertainty about the fate of the missing is a source of anguish for their families and a cause of tension between the parties to the Dayton peace agreement. Only a handful of the nearly 12,000 missing-person cases thus far certified by the International Committee of the Red Cross (ICRC) have been resolved to date. *This initiative will help to promote a full and timely accounting of the missing. . . .*
>
> The commission will encourage public involvement in its activities and will take firm steps to see that the parties devote the attention and resources necessary to produce early, significant progress on missing-person cases. It will also reinforce efforts to ensure that exhumations, when necessary to identify the fate of missing persons, are conducted under international supervision and in accordance with international standards. In addition, the commission will facilitate the development of an ante mortem database to support exhumation efforts.
>
> In the longer term, and with the help and guidance of affected families,

the commission will work to develop appropriate expressions of commemoration and tribute to the lost and the missing and to their loved ones.

Although the commission will be an international effort, the United
States will make a startup contribution of $2 million. (Italics added;
Clinton 1996)

By ensuring "international standards" and "international supervision," ICMP was to provide an unbiased, apolitical resource, addressing the needs of surviving family members, "regardless of their
ethnic or religious origin, in determining the fate" of their missing
relatives (ICMP 2003b). Begun as a small international organization
that contracted the services and expertise of Physicians for Human
Rights, ICMP would eventually become the lead international institution working on the identification process. As its efforts expanded,
so too did its financial support, especially from the US government,
to date its largest donor. With the exception of the Charles Stewart
Mott Foundation, ICMP's donors have been and continue to be state
governments: Canada, Denmark, Finland, Greece, Germany, the Holy
See, Iceland, Ireland, the Netherlands, Norway, Sweden, Switzerland,
United Kingdom, United States, and the European Union.[29]

By the time I arrived in the field to research the identification process
in 2003, ICMP's organizational structure reflected the multiple and
interconnected aims of scientifically grounded fact-finding and social
reconstruction (Huffine et al. 2001). Located in ICMP's Sarajevo headquarters, the Forensic Sciences Division encompassed both the exhumation and examination programs and the DNA extraction and analysis
programs. The Tuzla-based Podrinje Identification Project (PIP), whose
facilities and staff were dedicated specifically to the Srebrenica cases,
also belonged to the forensic sciences wing. The other major division
based in Sarajevo, the Civil Society Initiatives program, worked closely
with the families of the missing. Outlined on the organization's web
site, its objectives included the following: "To increase the capacity of
family associations; to advocate on the missing persons issue; to encourage regional networking and co-operation between family associations,
NGOs, and others; to address the rights of living family members of
the missing." Among its many activities, the Civil Society Initiatives
program gathered the various family associations from throughout
former Yugoslavia for workshops addressing concerns such as Bosnia's
Missing Persons Law, rights of surviving family members (especially
their right to know about their missing relatives' fate), and technical
training, including in media relations and grant writing. Furthermore,

it sought to engage family associations from the different ethnic groups in the discourse of social reconstruction. One such conference, entitled "Paths to Reconciliation," took up the topics of "truth, justice, and reconciliation," and "dealing with the past." In recent years, the Civil Society Initiatives division also began to explore the theme of transitional justice. In attempting to broker dialogues among family associations from different ethnic groups about reconciliation, its activities often invite reflection on common experiences of loss.

In the immediate postwar years, however, the primary objective of recovering and identifying the missing overshadowed the civil society–oriented agendas of social repair. Rather, staff from Physicians for Human Rights and the Federation Commission for Missing Persons focused their efforts on identifying the missing. They faced a gruesome and enormous task: to piece together partial remains scattered on the surface of the forest and lying within the primary graves, as well as to disentangle and then reassociate the commingled bones from the secondary and tertiary mass graves. Before they could begin this work, they first had to locate the unmarked gravesites and remains of men and boys who, as part of the column fleeing the enclave, died in the forest (Stover 1998:177–178). For information pertaining to these victims, they relied heavily on the ICTY investigators and the prosecutor's office. Detailed descriptions of the gravesites resulted from plea bargains and immunity deals at the tribunal, providing some of the most accurate and useful intelligence about the graves' locations. The most well known of those immunity deals was granted to Dražen Erdemović, a Bosnian Croat who had taken part in the executions at Pilića. His testimony, along with aerial photographs, confirmed the presence of bodies as well as a mass grave being dug on July 21 (Rohde 1997:345). Satellite images that had traced the movement of people, vehicles, and earth finally could be put to use, not to spare lives, but at least to reveal the whereabouts of the missing.[30]

During this immediate postwar period, teams of forensic pathologists and anthropologists (local and international) exhuming the Srebrenica-related gravesites, performing autopsies, and attempting to identify remains began to apply traditional forensic methodology, relying on physical evidence such as identity cards, clothing, and dental records. Given the task at hand, these efforts, especially the autopsy and identification procedures attempted by the Bosnian technicians, were sorely underfunded. In his account of the early forensic work, Eric Stover, former executive director of Physicians for Human Rights,

writes about visiting Dr. Zdenko Cihlarž, the director of the University
Clinical Centre in Tuzla, the institution responsible for conducting
autopsies and, when possible, issuing death certificates for recovered
Srebrenica missing:

> In the main laboratory of the institute, Cihlarz stopped and swept his arm
> around the room. "So, you see, it's all improvisation. Here you have one
> of the biggest forensic investigations of a war crime in European history
> and what have you got? Forensics on a shoe-string." In the dimly lit room
> I could make out boxes of bones stacked against the tiled walls. Here
> and there, bones had fallen out, collecting dust, on the floor. Makeshift
> examining tables had been fashioned out of planks and sheets of thick
> cardboard. Several medical and forensic textbooks lay strewn across table
> tops, their covers torn and dog-eared. (Stover 1998:179)

The nature of the executions and disposal of Srebrenica victims severely
hampered attempts to bring order to the chaotic scenes of the gravesites.
The forensic experts could not be certain that one body part belonged to
the rest of a given set of remains. Clothing proved deceptive because men
in captivity and flight had removed, exchanged, and picked up articles
of clothing along the way. Furthermore, the nature of the humanitarian
aid brought in to the enclave meant that the refugees were often wearing the same types and brands of clothing. Even identity cards found
on human remains could not guarantee the positive identification of a
missing person. Men who survived the flight through the forest to free
territory told of how they or others removed jackets from those already
dead and put them on themselves, or how the wounded asked other men
to take belongings such as identity cards and photos. Thus, traditionally useful sources of identification proved unreliable, even potentially
misleading. Nevertheless, in 2000 the Federation Red Cross funded
a project to compile photographs of clothing and personal possessions
recovered with bodies and print them as a book. It included eight hundred individual sets of such articles. Podrinje Identification Project staff
assembled the images and accompanying narrative descriptions of each
article. Two large volumes of the photographs were then circulated
throughout the Srebrenica survivor community so that families could
search through the pictures for their missing relatives' personal items.[31]

One day in the ICMP Podrinje Identification Project's administrative
office, Nedim, head of the case managers, showed me the poster-board
charts used by Physicians for Human Rights staff to track the early
identification efforts. These charts were the rudimentary antecedent
to ICMP's electronic databases. The heavy paper, yellowed and curled

from years of scrolled-up storage, revealed the faded attempts at hand recording the progress of individual cases. Nedim explained how frustrating the use of clothing and the photo books had been. Hunched over the chart spread on the conference table, I followed his finger as he traced across the multiple examples of unsuccessful identification attempts that had begun with a family member's recognition of an article of clothing. The dots of white-out covered over the ink jottings and lines of pink and green magic marker that filled the chart's rows and columns, mapping the truncated history of a handful of cases more vividly than anything I had seen in the database windows. In the upstairs office, I glanced through binders filled with hundreds of documents relating to the pre-DNA-based identification process, and Dr. Kešetović guided me through several examples we had spotted on the chart below.

Over and over, I saw how the recognition of an identifying item had led them down the wrong path, only to be corrected by the use of the outsourced DNA testing.[32] In most cases, rather than providing evidence of conclusive identification, the negative DNA results sent back from the foreign laboratory merely excluded that set of remains from belonging to the individual in question. In the end, as both Nedim and Dr. Kešetović affirmed, the photos yielded a very small number of identifications, a tiny fraction of those made prior to the advent of the DNA-based system: of the 800 sets of clothing and personal possessions included in the volumes, families "identified" 281 cases. Of those 281 cases, there were 72 instances in which the same personal effects were identified by different families. Following these leads, experienced anthropologists and pathologists conducted antemortem and postmortem comparisons, which in turn indicated 56 reasonable "presumptive identifications"—that is, cases where the information provided by the families concerning the missing person, his personal possessions and clothing, was consistent with postmortem data. Subsequent DNA testing on those cases, however, resulted in the exclusion of 25 out of the 56 presumptive identifications.

The sheer number of the Srebrenica victims, coupled with the severely degraded condition of the mortal remains, meant that conclusive identifications proceeded at an excruciatingly slow pace. From 1996 to 2000, approximately 70 individuals (of the estimated total missing, more than 8,000) were identified. ICMP later asserted that in the absence of DNA-based analysis, this rate would have continued unimproved: "It has been estimated that traditional forensic techniques

(i.e. autopsy by a pathologist), even when combined with solid antemortem data (i.e. physical dimensions, clothing, jewelry, etc.), will permit
identifications in only 5–8% of cases related to the fall of Srebrenica
in July 1995" (ICMP 2003a). Local and international officials charged
with the responsibility of recovering and identifying the remains found
themselves in a disturbing quandary. The number of remains shelved
in the Tuzla mortuary had so exceeded capacity that they had to begin
storing body bags in the city's abandoned salt mines. Aside from
being a less-than-ideal physical space for storing already decomposing
bodies, the makeshift mortuary in the salt mines' narrow tunnels was
in disarray. As Nedim explained to me, to pull out a single set of mortal
remains for examination required that the person assigned to the task
sort through the countless body bags stacked above and around it. The
slow and extremely uncomfortable work only further hindered the
overall process. It became obvious to everyone involved—families and
forensic technologists alike—that they were running out of space and
making little headway using the classical forensic techniques.

BLUEPRINT OF LIFE

DNA testing offered a glimmer of hope. In the first few years after the
war, the forensic pathologists of Physicians for Human Rights (contracted by ICMP), in cooperation with local experts, employed DNA
testing on what was termed "presumptive" cases—that is, cases for
which they had strong evidence that the remains belonged to a specific individual.[33] But soon people started calling for a more systematic
application of the technology. In particular, local and international
experts and advocates began to lobby for establishing a local DNA-
based identification system—not just for the occasional (and expensive) outsourcing of DNA extraction and analysis to labs in the United
States. Adnan Rizvić, deputy director of ICMP's Forensic Sciences
Division, explained, "ICMP saw that something had to change, so we
gathered and combined practically all the resources from the field, and
started this system." He credits Ed Huffine, an American DNA scientist
who joined ICMP in 1999, with the knowledge and expertise critical to
designing the initial DNA extraction and analysis model. Huffine had
spent the previous five years employed at the US government's Armed
Forces DNA Identification Laboratory (AFDIL), where he worked on
cases involving missing servicemen, including those from the Korean
War and the Vietnam War.[34]

The AFDIL scientists were just beginning to learn the potential of DNA testing for identifying multiple sets of human remains: over the period of five years Huffine worked there, the process became increasingly streamlined, as they went from staffing twenty scientists to test fifteen to twenty sets of remains per month down to one scientist fielding four to eight cases in the same period of time. Thus, with Huffine's expertise, along with other technologists recruited into the project, ICMP soon proposed a cutting-edge, wide-scale model of DNA testing. A systematic matching of genetic profiles provided the only viable solution to the long-term dilemma posed by the thousands of partial and disarticulated skeletal remains accumulating in the salt mines and mortuary in Tuzla.

What did DNA promise that the classical forensic techniques could not deliver? The technology of genetic science prioritized the seemingly indisputable specificity of human genetic material over all other potential clues into the identity of the recovered mortal remains. DNA analysis could determine the identity of major bones within a full or partial set of skeletal remains by matching them to the genetic profiles of the surviving family members. The task proposed by the local and international experts who lobbied for the development of a comprehensive bone-blood DNA matching system to identify former Yugoslavia's missing persons was enormous.[35] For the Srebrenica cases alone, ICMP would have to collect and process tens of thousands of blood samples from surviving family members, many of whom had already left the region to resettle in other countries, and at least one sample from each of the missing—provided they were recovered—in order to identify the 8,000-plus victims.[36]

The application of DNA analysis being proposed in Bosnia was unique; it broke from the conventional role of genetics in forensic pathology, which utilized the science in order to *confirm or exclude* an already presumed link or identification. In fact, the Bosnian system of postmortem analysis stood traditional DNA testing practice on its head. Here DNA analysis, the matching of genetic profiles, would act as the engine for the entire identification process. This was not to say that DNA analyses, specifically a positive DNA match, guaranteed a conclusive identification, but the technology could place the results of an individual case (the identity of a given set of mortal remains) within a statistical range of certainty.[37] At that point, classical forensic methods would again enter into the identification process, typically confirming or augmenting the statistical evidence of the DNA profile match.

FIGURE 5. Family member providing a blood sample at
ICMP's collection campaign in Linz, Austria, June 2004.
Photo by the author.

ICMP led this effort to transform the identification system. Relying
on the knowledge of local experts who understood the complexities
on the ground, including the problematic exhumations of secondary
mass graves as well as the dynamics within the community of surviving
family members, its staff set out to design the model for gathering and
processing DNA samples. They based the initial design of the DNA
matching computer software on a program used by the US Federal
Bureau of Investigation, tailoring it to the specific needs of the identification procedures. Bosnian experts were sent to the United States
for training, among them Dr. Rifat Kešetović, who would later become
the chief pathologist and director of the Podrinje Identification Project.
Anticipating the importance of having the Bosnian judiciary accept the
DNA-based identifications, ICMP staff members embarked on a public
relations campaign to convince officials of the scientific accuracy—and
thus legal weight in documenting individual identity—of the genetic
testing. As we will see in the following chapter, ICMP made similar
efforts to educate relatives of the missing, holding regular meetings
with family associations such as the Women of Srebrenica in Tuzla and
the Mothers of the Srebrenica and Žepa Enclaves in Sarajevo to discuss
the DNA-based system.

    In its promotional material, ICMP presents the science behind its
DNA identification program in lay terms: "Deoxyribonucleic acid

(DNA) is the blueprint of life." On the glossy pages of the pamphlet, photographs of the equipment, color-coded genetic profiles, bloodstain cards, and DNA strands guide the reader through the more technical language of nuclear and mitochondrial DNA properties. The accompanying narratives distinguish between the two types. A nuclear DNA profile, which contains half the DNA from the mother and half from the father, "normally points exclusively to a specific individual" (ICMP 2003a). Mitochondrial DNA, though more abundant and longer lasting than nuclear DNA, is inherited from, indeed identical to, the mother's DNA, and reveals the genetic material inherited from the maternal line. For the reader knowledgeable in the chronology of the DNA-based identification model created by ICMP, this distinction reflects lessons learned in the early phases of the identification efforts.

Before the initiative to establish local DNA laboratories, the forensics experts working on the Srebrenica cases used the outsourced samples of mitochondrial DNA as the primary means for genetic profiling and matching because it was more prolific in the bone and tooth specimens—that is, the hundreds of mitochondria present in each human cell are more easily extractable and, in cases where the bones samples were in poor condition (burned, chemically treated, or damaged by water), more durable than nuclear DNA. Family members recall that in the early years, PHR sought blood samples primarily from female relatives of the missing. With the postmortem identification system proposed by ICMP in 2000, however, mitochondrial DNA profiles were imprecise and, more importantly, ill-suited for a "blind" matching system. There were too many missing persons who shared the same maternally inherited genetic material, rendering it impossible to distinguish between certain sets of mortal remains. Thus, nuclear DNA became the preferred means of analysis as it could arrive at a more precise match between blood and bone samples.[38] But like the mitochondrial DNA, nuclear DNA had its own set of obstacles. The ideal combination of blood sample donors for a positive nuclear DNA match is that of both parents, a sibling, and, if existent, of the missing person's spouse and any children. The parents' DNA, strengthened by a sibling's sample, would provide the necessary profiles to determine whether the missing person is their child. The spouse's DNA means nothing on its own, but in combination with the children's, the missing person's genetic profile can be distinguished from that of any of his siblings.

Once again, the nature of the genocide at Srebrenica presented major complications for the nuclear DNA-based identification model.

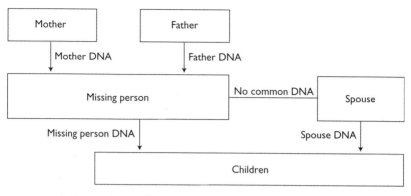

FIGURE 6. Relevant donors for nuclear DNA analysis.

To begin with, multiple members of families were missing, making it difficult for ICMP to collect the ideal blood sample combinations of parents, siblings, spouses, and children. This also meant that in cases where multiple sons of the same parents were missing, it became much harder to distinguish between them as brothers. Finally, many of the family members whose blood samples were critical to an identification had resettled in other countries. Even if they had survived the genocide, ICMP could not collect their samples unless they returned to Bosnia.[39]

The design and strategy of ICMP's DNA identification program, specifically its blood collection program, is an exercise in mapping genealogies. The blood collection teams and data entry staff at the Identification Coordination Division apply their understanding of genetic inheritance when assessing the availability of relevant blood samples. They question potential donors about family members, their precise relationship to missing persons, and their whereabouts. These staff members work along a genealogical script, and with each question seek out the possibility of a relevant, existent potential donor that might yield the critical genetic material to "close the circle" of a nuclear DNA match. Such interviews take place with each donor (surviving family member) at ICMP facilities or at the person's residence. The mobile blood collection teams are made up of a pair of staff, working in tandem to gather not only the necessary blood samples but also the pertinent data. They collect the blood samples by lightly pricking the donor's finger and pressing four drops onto a bloodstain card. The card is then sealed and they place a matching barcode on it and on the accompanying paperwork (the donor blood sample form). The data entry staff then transfers the information recorded on this form into the database set up for the donor blood samples. The database assigns each donor a numerical value according to the relevancy of the sample in relation to nuclear DNA analysis: 5 points are given to the mother, father, and spouse; sisters, brothers, and children are awarded 2.5 points. For each missing person, a window in the database indicates the total number of points accrued through the collection of blood samples. A missing person with 10 points is considered a strong case. If the body is recovered and DNA successfully extracted, ICMP should be able to generate the necessary genetic profile matches to identify the person. As ICMP staff showed me, however, there are still hundreds of Srebrenica cases with total values of only 0 or 2.5 points.

The use of barcode technology in the identification process meets two overt goals: to safeguard the identity of the donor and thereby remove bias, particularly based on ethnic identity, and to catalogue the data in a streamlined manner, protecting against human error as much as possible. The barcodes are scanned into the computer, allowing the information now tied to it, such as the genetic coding of the bloodstain card, to be catalogued without reference to individual identity. ICMP staff describes this procedure as "blinding" the sample. Aside from the obvious issue of confidentiality of personal genetic information, the barcodes serve as a preemptive response to criticism of ethnic bias. All samples (blood and bone) collected throughout former Yugoslavia travel to the facility in Tuzla for processing. The program's designers understood the political climate that surrounded the missing persons issue within the region and anticipated the skepticism that their work—carried out in a facility in the Bosniak and Croat–controlled entity of Bosnia and Herzegovina—might meet from authorities in Serbia and Macedonia, Kosovo, the Republika Srpska, and Croatia. By removing all traces of individual identity and location, ICMP staff hoped to eliminate the possibility that human knowledge, with its subjectivity and biases, would interfere with the processing of the samples. The "blinding" technique implied an apolitical agenda. Furthermore, given the estimate that ICMP would process up to 100,000 samples over a period of five to seven years, barcodes provided a means of cataloguing the physical material for easy referencing and sorting, a method vital to the overall structure of the computer software that conducted DNA match searches, as well as to the organization of such vast amounts of information.

On a more metaphorical level, the barcodes, along with the case numbers assigned to each person entered into ICMP's master database strip away identity in order to achieve the final aim of restoring it. The barcode becomes a temporary and superficial means of recognizing the human being or set of mortal remains behind the sample. Through this step the physical material enters into an entirely new pattern and sphere of recognition: its synecdoche, the barcode, now signals new information to a new set of eyes—that of the computer scanner, the lab technicians, and the data entry staff. The missing person, within the network of identification technologists, also enters into a different phase of absence, one running along a track that is parallel to, though separate from, that of his absence from the lives of his missing family members. While his relatives maintain a sense of his personhood in their memories, imaginings, and even fears, for the identification technologists, he appears on the monitor. The details of his life and physical attributes fill up the windows of the computer program designed to reattach his name to his mortal remains. Thus, his state of absence transmuted his identity from a person whose life and physical being held meaning for those around him to a purely empirical entity. In this state, he has become a set of data ordered by software and called up on the monitor by the fingertips of a technician for whom his name holds no meaning.[40] Just as his relative's dried blood is stamped out of the stain card and placed into tiny vials for extraction in the DNA lab, so his physical material—bones or a tooth—becomes an object of scientific scrutiny.

## RECOVERY, REASSOCIATION, AND RECOGNITION

In fact, this distanced recognition begins much earlier in the process than at the moment when a barcode is attached to a bone sample vial. ICMP describes the trajectory of an identification as a "grave-to-grave" process: from the anonymity of the mass or surface grave all the way through to the reburial of the identified mortal remains in a place of meaning, which, for the overwhelming majority of Srebrenica victims, is in the cemetery at Potočari. The remains of a missing person thus follow a path that leads them out of the disorder imposed by the violence of genocide back into the social order that had once shaped their lives and their relationships to their families. To arrive there, these remains undergo a series of transformations in which the technology of the identification process superimposes seemingly arbitrary signposts upon the physical matter exhumed from the gravesite.

To grasp the complexity of the identification process, one must understand the conditions in which the majority of the Srebrenica victims' mortal remains are recovered—that is, a jumble of bones, sometimes tissue or clothing, and earth from a secondary mass grave. During the late summer of 2003, when I was living and working in Srebrenica, exhumations began at one of the largest mass graves from the 1990s found in Bosnia, indeed all of former Yugoslavia, in the Podrinje region at a place called Crni vrh. Initial reports in the media indicated that the grave might contain remains of victims from both the 1992 massacre in Zvornik and the Srebrenica 1995 genocide.[41] I obtained permission from ICMP to visit the site in September as the final stages of the exhumation were taking place. I arrived at midday just a few minutes before the exhumation crew would break for lunch. Standing at the end of the trench, which was approximately thirty yards in length and fifteen to twenty yards in width, I was struck by the powerful stench of decomposing bodies and the marbled colors of the soil. Forensic anthropologists and archaeologists were working at one end of the grave, where the earth was muddy and clung to the skeletons being extracted. I could make out sets of bones (a ribcage and skulls), but it was difficult to distinguish the bones as sections belonging to an individual body. They jutted out from the earth, overlapping at awkward angles. I watched a forensic anthropologist lift up a pant leg as she probed the clothing to discern its skeletal contents. Shortly thereafter she began to prepare the set of bones—what looked to be a relatively complete body—for its initial stage of identification.

The first task was to demarcate the area in which she found the remains. This is done by stretching a thin tape around the space that encompasses the body, the clothing, and any personal possessions that seem to belong to that set of bones. Next, a piece of white paper bearing the handwritten combination of letters and numbers that will serve as the reference code for the body or body parts is placed with the remains. This code stays with the recovered remains throughout the course of the identification process. To a trained eye, the letters at the beginning of the reference indicate the grave from which the body was exhumed; the final set of numbers signifies the body or body part within the overall set of skeletal remains exhumed from that particular grave, for example, 007 of 150. The remains, encircled with tape and identified by the reference code, are then photographed. Finally, the individual exhumation site is dismantled, as the body parts are placed in a plastic body bag that also bears the reference number just assigned to the remains. On that day I watched the anthropologist discard chunks of mud caught between the skeleton and clothing and transfer the bones into the white bag. With her torso bent close to the bones, her footing slipped slightly, and she nearly fell into the muddy, gruesome mess. She straightened up, seemingly unaffected, and continued to place the skeletal remains in the plastic bag. Unlike the visitors, perched at the grave's edge with hands held over their mouths in horror or covering their noses, she appeared at ease standing among the decomposed bodies, sifting through earth and bones for clues to individual identity.

In the case of the Srebrenica-related exhumations, the remains are usually transported to the Podrinje Identification Project (PIP), the ICMP facility specifically dedicated to the genocide. Since 2004, however, many of the Srebrenica remains recovered from secondary mass graves have traveled first to an intermediate facility where teams of forensic anthropologists attempt to reassociate the violently disrupted sets of skeletal remains. There they try to piece together upper bodies with lower bodies, skulls with torsos—in essence, complete the human jigsaw puzzle created by what Mašović has termed the Bosnian Serbs' patented innovation. The creation of the reassociation centers, first in Visoko, near Sarajevo, and then in Lukavac, near Tuzla, marks a later, though highly significant, development in the identification process, one that streamlined the use of DNA testing for the Srebrenica victims.

I visited the facility in Visoko in the summer of 2004, accompanying the head forensic anthropologist and her assistant from the ICMP office in Sarajevo. Inside the well-lit, spacious warehouse, the hands-on, gritty work of reordering the victims' bodies was taking place. On that day hundreds of skeletal remains lay side by side, neatly arranged throughout the room, filling up the floor space like a quilt of human bones. Each set of remains rested on a meter-long strip of brown packing paper, with the bones carefully reconfigured into their proper positions. Some, though not all, of the skeletal remains included skulls. As if resting upon pillows, they tilted gently back against the plastic body bags that had transported the remains from the exhumation site. While the forensic anthropologists began their day's work, I wandered about through the vast room, taking notes on the different sets of bones and their relative states of reassociation. The sheer volume of skeletal remains, several hundred, brought home the magnitude of the Srebrenica genocide in a more visceral and graphic way than I had experienced attending the mass burials at Potočari or viewing the abstract screens of the ICD databases. Toward the back of the room I caught wind of the same pungent smell that had hovered above the pit at Crni vrh. In a side chamber there were several body bags stacked atop one another. A Bosnian worker explained to me that these remains had already undergone reassociation and were now ready for transport to the storage spaces to await the results of DNA testing. The vast majority of the remains in the facility, however, were still incomplete or contained too many of the same bones—three femurs or two skulls. With one set of remains I spotted a clump of long dark hair, no longer attached to the skull but resting above a reassembled ribcage. Handwritten sheets of paper gave instructions for future testing or reassociation: "M-6—No connection between skull and rest of skeleton. 2 DNA samples—skull and femur. Before identification check on bone-to-bone match." Some sets of remains had a color-coded diagram of a skeleton lying next to them. The coloring indicated what was missing and present, and where samples had already been taken. Later, when I had the chance to examine the PIP case files, I would see that the same type of colored diagram existed for each identified body.

After surveying the room full of skeletal remains, I turned to watch the anthropologists at work. They sat on small stools bent over a set of remains, each picking up various bones and turning them over in their hands. One was handling pieces of vertebrae. She took two in her hands, examined their edges and contours, and tried fitting them together to see if the articulation was correct. It appeared so. She held those pieces together and tried a third. The painstaking work of reassociation proceeded one bone at a time—yet the room was filled with hundreds of skeletal remains. Within several months of that visit, the ICMP forensic leadership decided that the Visoko facility approach to reassociation was inefficient. To extend the jigsaw analogy, at Visoko the anthropologists and staff had laid out too many pieces of the puzzle; there were too many sets of skeletal remains being processed at one time. By 2005 a new facility, located closer to Tuzla, had picked up where Visoko left off.

This time a different team of forensic anthropologists worked on much more limited sets of mortal remains, typically a subset of remains exhumed from the same secondary grave or other secondary graves linked to the same primary grave. Rather than relying primarily on forensic anthropological examinations, as the staff at Visoko had, the Lukavac team began with forensic anthropology in order to narrow the field of subsequent DNA testing. For example, if an anthropologist finds two sets of remains—body parts, for example, the bones of an upper body and the bones of a lower body—to be highly compatible in age, bone quality, and perhaps articulation, he or she will order samples cut from each set, if possible from the femur and humerus, and send them to the lab for a limited series of DNA testing.[42] If the match is conclusive, the body is then reassociated and treated as a (relatively) complete set of skeletal remains.

Eventually, the reassociated skeletons and more complete remains from the Srebrenica graves arrive at the Podrinje Identification Project mortuary facility in Tuzla. There, the more complete remains are cleaned and returned to the exhumation body bags. The clothing and personal articles are separated from the remains, washed, dried, and placed into individual brown paper bags (bearing the same reference label assigned at the gravesite). If a bone sample for DNA testing has not already been taken, the staff members cut away a small segment, when possible using the femur or humerus because of their relative density, which is best suited for DNA extraction. They may also use a tooth as a specimen.[43] The samples are then sent to the ICD bone department for cleaning and cataloguing. Just as with the bloodstain cards, the bone samples receive a barcode before being transferred to Sarajevo for DNA extraction and analysis.

By the time the samples leave the ICD bone department, the transformation is well under way—this section of bone has left behind the grim smells and tainted earth of the gravesite and entered into the next stage of recognition, safely contained in the sterile packaging of its clear plastic vial and discrete barcode. The missing person has lost yet again a part of his body, but this time the violence—the sawing away of a tiny section of the bone sample—works to counter the brutality that the missing person experienced at the hands of the Bosnian Serb forces.

The next and most technologically advanced procedure of the identification process occurs in ICMP's DNA laboratory in Sarajevo.[44] There, the technicians attempt to extract DNA from each sample submitted, producing a genetic profile by reading (measuring) sixteen sites, or loci, found along the DNA strand. Each locus contains the genetic coding for that particular site on the strand, represented by two numerical values, one from each parent. Therefore, each locus has two numbers, such as 9.0/12.3. The complete profile for any given sample is a map of the series of sixteen loci. This numerical representation, a distillation of the sample's genetic material, provides the identification process with its most valuable and powerful tool. These numbers can now be fed into the computer software program, which searches through more than 84,000 samples in order to find their match—to reunite the missing person with his genetic kin.

The successful processing of these genetic profiles does not depend exclusively on the software, but also requires the trained eye and vast knowledge of the ICMP staff members who implement the DNA matching programs. On a daily basis, the DNA matching department, located in the Tuzla ICD facility, receives and inputs the numeric representations of DNA profiles from recently collected blood and bone samples. The software then locates candidate matches from among the entire pool of samples, seeking the profiles that exhibit enough overlap to be a potential match with the newly entered data. The results of this initial screen are not definitive; rather, they simply direct the technicians toward potential matches. The technicians must then screen the profiles to determine whether there is in fact an appropriate match.

Given the large number of missing persons, there exists the possibility that genetically unrelated individuals appear to the software as potential matches. The technicians perform a kind of genetic detective work, flipping through both the missing person and donor databases to assess the probability that the two profiles match. Certain details may signal a false match, such as when the location of the mass grave from which the bone sample derived does not match the logical origination of the donor blood sample.[45] If the bone came from a mass grave that is known to contain only victims from Srebrenica 1995 and the blood sample donor is from Priština (in Kosovo) or Prijedor (in western Bosnia), the technicians will tentatively rule out that match and proceed down the list. When they spot what seems to be a viable match, such as between a missing person (bone sample) and a relative listed in the donor database whose information is electronically tied to that of the missing person in the separate missing person database, they explore it. Evaluating the compilation of potential matching profiles according to ICMP case numbers assigned to both the donor and the missing person, the technicians can quickly determine who among the software-generated list of potential matches are relatives of the missing person. Often the computer may match up only one or two of the donor relatives to the newly entered data. The technicians build upon these initial matches, comparing the genetic codes (the series of sixteen dual-digit loci) to determine if the match holds with other members of the family who have donated blood samples. In some cases, samples

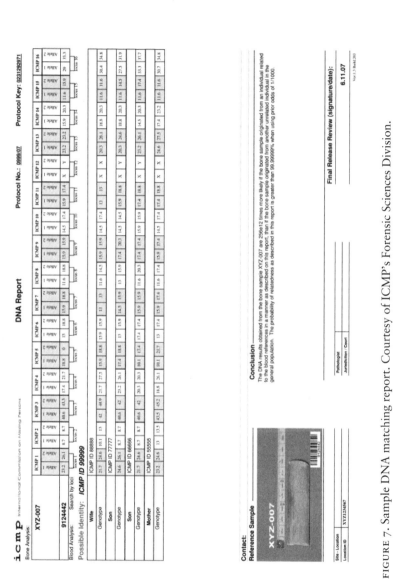

FIGURE 7. Sample DNA matching report. Courtesy of ICMP's Forensic Sciences Division.

are missing, for example, when a parent is deceased (buried in a known place) or a missing person himself, and the technician must recreate his or her genetic profile based on the combination of available data from the other living parent, child, and/or sibling. As with the mobile blood collection teams, the DNA matching department staff mentally maps the genetic relations of the given family and, when possible, strengthens the initial "hit" by compiling additional matches within the missing person's network of donors.

In the end, after the easily identifiable false potential matches have been culled, remaining candidate missing persons are evaluated computationally through full genetic kinship analysis. ICMP staff members perform this task using the software program DNAView. The genetic profiles for all family reference samples for the missing person are imported together with the profile from the bone sample. The program calculates the complex mathematics that produce the final statistics indicating the strength of the genetic evidence that links the bone profile to that specific family.[46]

The genocide at Srebrenica has so devastated families across generations that often there are multiple missing persons from one immediate family, and this presents significant problems for producing successful DNA matches. The technicians' capacity to recognize potential links and follow slim leads epitomizes the innovation of this technology: its success lies in more than simply the technologically sophisticated instruments of DNA extraction machines, software programs, and databases. The human capacity to think creatively and analytically is key to the endeavor. The first time I sat down with the DNA matching department staff to watch them at work, I was baffled by the speed with which they moved from computer window to window, drawing grids and recording genetic codes. I was hard-pressed to follow their explanations.

Several months later, after I had been working with ICMP at the ICD facility, I decided to try again. More familiar with the various screens of the respective donor and missing person databases, I was able to follow their movements and understand their process of evaluation. I learned that matching also takes place between bone samples—again, in the cases where multiple family members are missing, such as both a father and son. One of the department's most dramatic achievements was the identification of an entire family that was missing: a husband, wife, son, and daughter, along with both of the husband's parents. Identification through the successful matching of nuclear

DNA appeared almost impossible. With only the blood samples from the wife's sister and brother, however, ICD staff were able to work along the chain of genetic material, from blood to bone, then bone to bone, until they had matched the remains of all family members. The wife's siblings' blood samples identified the wife; the profile from her bone sample identified the children, and from the combination of the children's and wife's DNA, they could identify the husband's remains. Finally, his DNA led them to both of his parents' remains. This chain of discovery derived from the positive identification of one bone sample. In telling this story, the four technicians stopped their work and joined in the narration. One woman drew me a picture of the family tree, pointing out the path that the identification process followed in matching the various samples. They clearly took pride in the accomplishment and their contributions to the DNA-based technology's success.

Because the blood collection and DNA matching procedures are carried out by ICMP staff members and thus depend on their careful notations and cognitive abilities, there exists, of course, the possibility of error. ICMP implemented a strenuous review process to safeguard against mistakes. By the time the matching report is finalized, five signatures at the bottom of the page attest to the veracity of the DNA matches and the accompanying statistical analysis. A complex series of calculations that evaluate the probability of the match occurring within the given parameters of the particular set of missing persons, the statistical analysis provides ICMP with a means of quantifying the precision of its work.[47] As the case managers at the Podrinje Identification Project put it, "The statistics have to be good"—that is, they have to pass the 99.95 percent threshold in order for the match to advance the case into the final stages of identification. If the statistical review shows that the match falls below the threshold, ICD resends a sample (blood or bone, depending on where the imprecision lies) for a second round of DNA analysis. They may also request an additional sample from the missing person's family, from a relative who has not yet given one.

The statistical analysis does more than provide the "experts" with a means of gauging the precision of a given identification. It also gives them an invaluable linguistic tool when they are communicating with the family members. Although they never say that a DNA match is 100 percent accurate, the articulation of the percentage as 99.95 and upward fortifies the already established aura of scientific infallibility. How could one refute a truth claim whose veracity has been calculated down to the hundredth of a percentile? It is not, "we are very confident that this body is your son's," but "we are 99.998 percent sure that this is your son's body, meaning it's statistically impossible that it is another person." As a concrete and unassailably convincing number, the percentage is a dramatic distillation of the science behind the identification. The final report, summed up in a single percentage indicating strong statistical probability, is the logical end to a process suffused with the authority of science, including the white lab coats and the plastic gloves worn by the blood collection teams.

Despite the trust that the overwhelming majority of the families place in the technology of identification, the concept of DNA analysis remains abstract and intangible for many. Indeed, ICMP faced a significant challenge when first introducing the technology to the relatives of the missing, as PIP chief pathologist Dr. Kešetović explained:

> Perhaps now it looks easy, right? But at that time [start of the DNA-based identifications] it wasn't easy to convince the families to accept such a way. There was an enormous task—that is, the collection of the relatives' blood. There is always that certain factor of people who refuse to give their blood sample. . . . It was only in the beginning that they did not understand entirely well what it was about. It wasn't clear to them why the family had to provide blood in order to carry out the analysis. Fundamentally they didn't understand what DNA was, how DNA is inherited, and with what probability DNA can help identifications. The majority of people at that time knew that through blood types you could determine identity—not identity but the category of a particular group of people. And a majority of people, laymen, knew that that method didn't have great probability, for example, if you find blood type A, you recover it, it's clear to you that around 20 to 30 percent of the population could belong to that type. They didn't know about DNA.

I heard the same sentiment expressed by members of the Women of Srebrenica in Tuzla. They were reluctant at first, wary of the unfamiliar and esoteric language of "deoxyribonucleic acid." Some explained that they would have preferred to gain access to the clothing and personal possessions—not just looking at the photographs in the Red Cross book, but, as one woman put it, walking through a warehouse of personal articles laid out for viewing. The directors of the Women of Srebrenica understood, however, that this was an ineffective method, and one prone to misidentification. Thus, their organization eventually had pushed hard for the creation of DNA labs in Bosnia and Herzegovina and for the testing of all recovered remains.

As Dr. Kešetović implied, however, not everyone among the family members accepted the technology of DNA analysis. Indeed, many were reluctant to provide blood samples to ICMP. Among a population that had been utterly betrayed by authorities, foreign and local, survivors of Srebrenica were skeptical about why ICMP required blood samples. Moreover, before there was more widespread public awareness about the ideal donor combinations for nuclear DNA analysis, it was even more puzzling why a spouse would need to provide a blood sample, having no direct blood link to the missing person.

Beyond their wartime experiences, families' confusion and skepticism about genetic testing often arose from socioeconomic and cultural factors. Many of the Bosniak refugees in the enclave had come from villages where education levels were significantly lower than in urban centers, especially among women. Bringa notes that even though "in recent years rural families increasingly encouraged and wanted their [Bosnian Muslim] daughters to continue with school after the compulsory eight years," household demands and religious values often limited girls' education to primary school (1995:109, 110). Because the majority of immediate surviving family members were women, the burden of providing blood samples fell to them and depended on their understanding its necessity within the identification process. Furthermore, conducting mitochondrial and later nuclear DNA analysis—thus requiring samples from female family members, both parents of the missing, and, when applicable, *spouses* of the missing—may have seemed incongruous with Bosnian Muslims' kinship reckoning, which is primarily agnatic (Bringa 1995:144; Lockwood 1975:70–74). Nevertheless, as Adnan Rizvić, deputy director of ICMP's Forensic Sciences Division, pointed out, Bosniaks' fundamental belief in blood links has proven helpful in the long term. In his view, the use of bloodstain cards rather than buccal swabs, which take samples from the inside cheek or mouth cavity, was instrumental to the successful collection of DNA samples from families of the missing. The symbol of blood helped translate the technology into the tangible logic of kinship (Strathern 2005:26).

Despite ICMP's attempts to explain the science in more familiar terms of kinship and bloodlines, skepticism nevertheless persists, making the news of identification based upon DNA analysis unacceptable to some families. This is especially true when the more obvious links between the missing person and the relative's memory of that person are absent or unrecognizable. I witnessed such a reaction when accompanying two PIP case managers in the field as they visited a mother who was missing three sons and her husband from the Srebrenica enclave. It had taken them several months to track her down, for she had moved without providing ICMP a forwarding address. We arrived unexpectedly, three young women dressed in city clothes, climbing out of an SUV with diplomatic plates. The woman had been sitting on her front steps, and as she got up to greet us, she brushed off her skirt and smoothed back her hair. The lead case manager for the file, Jasmina, explained that we had come from the International Commission on Missing Persons; the woman quickly ushered us into the house, away from her neighbors' curious stares.

Once we were all seated in the living room, Jasmina began to explain the reasons for our visit. She reminded the woman first of the fact that she had given a blood sample, then shifted course to the results—the statistics that pointed toward a conclusive match between her blood sample and the remains of one of her sons. The woman looked down at the floor, her lips pressed into a thin line and her brow deep with furrows. With the mention of the DNA results she shook her head and said in a low whisper, "I don't believe in that" *(Ne vjerujem u to)*. Jasmina pressed her, asking why not. Again, "I don't believe in it." The conversation continued between the two, but it was mostly Jasmina who spoke, trying to explain the nature and accuracy of the technology. She eventually pulled out photographs of the clothing exhumed with the body, but the woman recognized very few of the articles. In the end, she signed the papers that confirmed the identification, but everyone in the room sensed the awkward resignation with which she pressed her ink-stained finger on the signature line. She had accepted officially what emotionally and rationally she denied: her son's death. At the meeting's conclusion, as we climbed back into the car to leave, her stoic expression finally cracked and, as if in slow motion, her face began to melt with the anguish of the news, her chin quivering as she fought back tears. Jasmina got out of the car and went to her. They spoke for a few moments and she returned. The woman did not want help. She wanted to be alone. We watched her figure recede behind the house. For her, all the sophistication and precision of DNA analysis could not make sense of her loss or reorder her life. In that moment the technology offered few consolations, despite its impressive statistics.

## THE SYNECDOCHE OF DNA

Among the many pictures and posters on the wall in the office of the Women of Srebrenica there is a black-and-white photograph of a scene at the temporary refugee shelter in Dubrave from July 1995. In it, a few women are seated on the floor, facing an old woman as she stretches out her hand before her. One day I asked about the photo and Nura, one of the association leaders, told me the story of how, in those first chaotic days, some people had sought out fortune tellers, old women from the villages who were thought to know how to decipher fates in the traces of coffee grounds and the lines of a palm. Getting few if any concrete answers from local and international officials about the aftermath of the enclave's fall, the women in the camp were desperate for information, signs, any sort of clue as to the fate of their loved ones. They were desperate for hope. So they went to these village *gatare ili vračare* (fortune-tellers or witch doctors) in hopes of learning more. Word spread of this practice, and not long afterward a woman in Tuzla began offering her services—to tell the fortune of the missing—by reading signs from beads of lead as they were poured into boiling water. Apparently the reading took place in three stages, three separate visits for which the fortune-teller charged one mark. I was surprised to learn that Hajra, the no-nonsense director of the Women of Srebrenica, had herself gone to such a reading. She shrugged her shoulders and told me that she paid her three marks like everyone else. These were the same women who years later would learn the news of their missing sons and husbands' fate through the language of genetics and its statistics. This is not to say they have blindly accepted knowledge from whatever was the most promising source of the moment. But they have traveled a long road of varied truth claims, and along that journey have watched their hope turn into resignation.

DNA technology played a significant role in this transition. The ominous promise it held out was to resolve the fate of the missing by returning sets of mortal remains to families, and, in doing so, it shaped the way people on both sides of the process (experts and families) conceptualized a posthumous state of human existence. DNA became the critical, entrusted, indeed indispensable proof of individual identity for the thousands of sets of nameless mortal remains. In attempting to recognize those remains, the technology developed by ICMP equated the body with the person, relying upon an invisible, intangible synecdoche of sixteen dual digits to stand in for a human being (Rabinow 1999; Foucault 1981). Matching genetic profiles promised to reattach personhood (signposted by a name) to physical remains and, thereby, to reconstitute the identified person as a social—and political—subject. This act of identification hinges on an implicit faith in the production of scientific knowledge—a complex social process camouflaged by the "metonymic genius of language that converts DNA into a stark signifier of truth" (Jasanoff 1998:718).[48] The danger in conceptualizing DNA both as an emblem for individual being and as the vehicle for knowledge production lies in what disappears from the picture. To begin with, such a framing underestimates the indispensability of subjective knowledge and social experience within the identification process. Paul Brodwin writes about the problematic reliance on the "general cachet of science as the ultimate guarantor of truth" in the example of tracing one's ancestry through genetics: "It also involves judging the worth of genetic knowledge against other kinds of claims to authentic identity and group membership" (2000:324). In the Srebrenica case, other claims or proofs of identity often fall within the more subjective field of memory; yet the success of the DNA-based system in thrusting science into the forefront has relegated this kind of knowledge to a secondary, less valued position within the overall process. "Knowledge of identification is arrived at not intuitively through the eye or through feelings or senses, but through procedures delayed and mediated through the giving of intimate bodily fluids, such as blood" (Sant Cassia 2005:181). This, in turn, affects how we conceive of the missing person. In representing an individual as a series of numbers, the technology reduces the missing person's existence, which travels during this state of prolonged absence along a trajectory of recognition, to too narrow a plane. In short, it prioritizes the missing person's genetic profile over his social being. While the synecdoche of DNA enables computer software to recognize a set of mortal remains by translating and distilling them into a digital genetic code, that same series of numbers lacks the humanism inherent in surviving families' memories and the knowledge of the identification experts.

The identification process for the Srebrenica victims demonstrates the difficulty of trying to draw lines between the fields of science and humanism. Rather, from start to finish, we see their interconnection and mutual dependence. If the blood collection teams did not explore the possibility of relevant donors and the matching department staff did not cull the list of genetic profiles generated by the computer software, they would arrive at a mere fraction of the DNA-based matches they have found thus far. Similarly, the authority of the "facts" of DNA profiles and positive matches depends on families participating in and trusting the identification process. Neither ICMP nor the Federation Commission for Missing Persons will ever insist that families accept the news of an identification if they do not accept the grounds upon which it is based, primarily DNA evidence. In the end, identification means recognition on the most intimate of levels—that of the surviving relatives. The results of the DNA analysis will remain static numbers on a sheet of paper without the family's recognition, not only of their significance, but also of the other information they reveal, including where and how the person was killed and buried. In the end, it is precisely the subjective nature of human knowledge that has made this application of DNA technology both innovative and successful.

## DNA AND THE DISCOURSE OF FACTICITY

Just as families accept or reject identification based on the strength of its evidence, so too does the public assembled around the Srebrenica missing. "To provide undisputable proof has become a rather messy, pesky, risky business" (Latour 2005:19). The identification technology developed to counter Srebrenica's mass graves and number of missing required significant political and financial support in order that its "facts" of recovered and identified sets of mortal remains could become undisputable evidence. ICMP casts its work as apolitical, "blinded" like its barcodes; it calculates individual identity down to the hundredth percentile. In emphasizing the facticity of the identification technology, ICMP and its closest partner in the Srebrenica cases, the Federation Commission for Missing Persons, implicitly acknowledge the multiple audiences involved in identification. One of those audience members is the Bosnian Serb public.

The controversy around the Srebrenica genocide has engendered an insistence on facts regarding the historiography of the event and the means of recovering and naming its victims. In a sense, the language of facticity, epitomized by results grounded in genetic science, has transformed the local discourse used to assess wartime losses and culpability. The "objectification" (Keane 2005:81–82) implicit in these heightened standards of proof reveals not only how the DNA-based identification technology has penetrated the discourse, but also how people have, in turn, reinforced its authority. Facts become meaningful and powerful, not simply because of the authority of their source, but because of the ways in which they are then deployed in the controversy at hand. For example, in an editorial published for the daily newspaper *Dnevni avaz* the day after the Federation Commission for Missing Persons released its Preliminary List of the Missing Persons from the 1995 Srebrenica Genocide, longtime correspondent Almasa Hadžić (2005) wrote about the importance of the language of facts. *"Jučerašnje objavljivanje podatka o broju ubijenih Srebreničana, prikupljenih na način kako to savremeni svijet i njegova tehnologija zahtijevaju, najbolji je put da se istina o ratnim događajima u BiH prezentira jezikom činjenica"* (Yesterday's publication of the information about the number of people from Srebrenica killed, collected in the manner required by the present world and its technology, is the best way to present the truth about the wartime events in Bosnia, in the language of facts). She contrasted the list's precise documentation of names, birth dates, places of birth, and parental names with the "statistical lies from the smaller Bosnian entity" (the RS), whose lists of missing imprecisely catalog "the hair-dresser from Nedžarić," "Jela—the officer's wife," or "an unknown engineer from Breka." As if echoing Latour, Hadžić illustrates how the controversy has evolved: the "truth" surrounding the events of Srebrenica in July 1995 represents a hard-fought battle of competing claims—including the names and numbers of its missing. As she points out, the language of facts, couched in statistics and empirical evidence, forces the competing parties to enter into the same dialogue. It raises the stakes by raising the standards of proof, including lists, names, and numbers of missing persons. In order to arrive at those highly prized kernels of truth, however, the facts must be recognized and accepted by more than simply those who claim them.

# CHAPTER 4

# Memory at Work

In the July 2000 issue of *Bilten Srebrenica,* the Women of Srebrenica's publication, there is a black-and-white photograph of a woman holding up what look to be the tattered remains of a jacket and pants. The caption reads, "Mother Đemila Recently Found the Mortal Remains of Her Two Sons Sulja and Sadik."[1] Đemila's story was an unusual one. Neighbors of hers had returned to their prewar property and in the process of clearing the neglected land, they came across the remains of eighteen victims from the enclave, including those of two of Đemila's three missing sons. While it was common enough that people found skeletal remains upon returning home, the fact that Đemila was able to travel to the site of the illicit grave and recognize articles of clothing was remarkable. "As soon as I saw the remains of the body and the clothing, I recognized Sulja's jacket and pants that he had bought from a Canadian. . . . Three days later we went out again and near a beech tree we found my son Sadik. You could see that animals had carried off some of the remains, but there were more bones than there had been with Sulja. But God willed it that there was recognizable clothing. They even found a letter of his, and, though damaged, his handwriting was still legible" (Žene Srebrenice 2000:9). Although it is not mentioned in the article, doubtless the Federation Commission for Missing Persons later exhumed the bodies and ICMP performed DNA tests to confirm the presumptive identification of Đemila's sons.

The picture of Đemila holding up the clothing embodies one of the most important moments in the identification process for surviving family members: the tangible, material connection between the missing person's recovered remains and the image of the missing person in the relative's mind. Although the advent of DNA technology as the driving force behind the identification process privileges the invisible and nontactile proof of genetics, the recollections of the missing (memories of clothing, personal possessions, and physical appearance) have their place in recovering and recognizing the Srebrenica victims. In this chapter, I explore how such recollections are gathered together and ordered as antemortem data, another bureaucratic strategy to synthesize the personal information relevant to the identification process. I examine moments when family members' memories of the missing offer clarification, as well as when they cause confusion. These same moments reveal how, in the final stages of identification, when classical forensic techniques are brought to bear on individual cases, the relationship between the missing, their families, and the technologists becomes more intertwined. The parallel tracks of the missing person's existence—as memory and as object of study—begin to turn in toward each other when individual identity becomes reattached to mortal remains.

## MOUNTING THE SLOPE OF THEIR PAST

When they sat together in the office, the members of the Women of Srebrenica often spoke of memory, either sharing recollections of July 1995, related events or people, or examining how their memories alternately sustained and betrayed them. In the summer of 2004, I began to record conversations with some of the women at the office, and many of our discussions centered on the powerful role memory plays in surviving family members' lives. In one such conversation, Rejha, a middle-aged mother of three, described what happened when the memories themselves were absent. Her husband, father, brother-in-law, and several cousins and uncles were missing:

> R: It is difficult, you know, it's difficult for you after nine years.
> I can remember a little bit of the details, say, of what I remembered before. After nine years it's difficult to go through everything. All of a sudden you return to 1995, to Srebrenica when there was such a crowd, when we were leaving, my husband on one side, I on the other. And then they come to you, those images, the details of the frightened faces come to you. I think it's a harrowing experience.

S. W.: Did you succeed in recognizing anything from the book of the clothing, the one with the photographs?

R: No. I didn't recognize anything, anything at all.

S. W.: But do you think that now, if someone were identified, like your father or husband, it would be possible for you to recognize the clothing?

R: I would recognize the clothing. I would recognize them.

S. W.: So you still have—

R: I still have everything in my mind, in my mind every-thing—which clothing, what kind of clothing it was.

S. W.: How is it for the children? When they gave blood samples, did they understand why it was necessary? How old were they?

R: Well, when we left Srebrenica my eldest daughter was in the first year of high school, maybe sixteen years old. The younger one was fifteen. They were all young, but my son, the little one, even more so. He was two years old then. He only knows his father in a picture, when he points out that that is his father. Through pictures. We constantly tell him stories and through pictures we tell stories that he knows. He was small and he doesn't remember, he doesn't remember anything. Although when they came—they came recently to collect blood samples—I explained to him. He went with me down there and gave blood. I say, "Son, you have to give blood for your daddy, so that we can see that your father is found." He says, "I will, Mom." He said, "It doesn't hurt." He says, "If it hurts, it will pass, but I'm giving blood so that I see that they find my daddy." The child thinks that his father is living. I think that I can't . . .

S. W.: He thinks that he's still living?

R: Yeah, even now he thinks this. . . . He asks me everything—how it was, how we left, where we came, why we didn't go together. "Why," he asks, "didn't we go together?" I said, "Son, we couldn't, the men went through the forest, something we couldn't do. You were small, you—I had to carry you." And you see that he'd gotten a little angry, you know. He asked, "What happened?" I said, "I don't know, son." He thinks that he [his father] will contact us. Maybe there'll be some-thing someday . . . we'll see. And then in this way, when in Srebrenica, when there is a burial, he follows it intently on television. He watches television, asks me, "Is our daddy dead? Will we bury daddy in Srebrenica?" I said to him, "We will, son (Hoćemo, sine)."

There is such a soulful resignation to the final two words Rejha utters in this quotation, "Hoćemo, sine." She and her youngest child, too young to recall his father, each battle the consequences of memory. The same memories that offer a means of recovering her husband's mortal remains—the final image of him standing opposite her at Potočari, each article of his clothing etched into her mind—also bring back the emotional trauma of their separation. "And then they come to you, those images, the details of the frightened faces come to you." She describes this as *"jedno veliko preživljavanje"*—a harrowing experience. Her language evokes a mental journey, in which her mind travels across the years, to land suddenly back among the mass of people assembled at the UN peacekeepers' compound in Potočari. It is a kind of perceptual movement, the action elicited by a memory-image, which Henri Bergson explores in *Matter and Memory*. "By this memory is made possible the intelligent, or rather intellectual, recognition of perception already experienced; in it we take refuge every time that, in search for a particular image, we remount the slope of our past" (1991:81). For Rejha, remounting the slope of her past is an extremely emotional, not just intellectual, endeavor, and the "survival of images" (Bergson 1991; Ricoeur 2004:433) for her entails a latent terror: "the details of the frightened faces" that are ever present, on the cusp of her recollection. That same immediacy of images resonates in her insistence that she would remember the clothing of her father and her husband. She repeats herself, "I would recognize the clothing. I would recognize them." Her tone of absolute certainty is unmistakable.

Her son struggles with an entirely different dilemma of memory. He has none to speak of, literally. Instead, he assembles the images of his father vicariously culled from the recollections of his older siblings and mother. He grafts onto those half-formed traces his father's likeness once captured by a camera lens. The man in the photograph becomes the person he builds up in his mind as his father. When gaps arise in this narrative, he presses his family for details and they willingly oblige. Rejha's final description of her son watching the Srebrenica commemorative ceremony and collective burials on television reveals how his notion of his father wavers between childlike hope and adult reason. A part of him still holds out for the possibility that his father is alive; another part knows that the prospect of his father's death is real, indeed, inevitable. He has already participated in the process that might bring about that conclusion when he provided ICMP with his blood sample.

Rejha's memories and her son's imagination illustrate how family members of the missing maintain the individual identity of their loved ones during the prolonged state of absence before their mortal remains are recovered and identified. This is the intimate, private side of such memories. But those same recollections may also serve a more public role in the identification process: just as Rejha and her older children feed details to her son about his missing father in order to attach meaning to the face in the photograph, so the information families recall and provide to ICMP and the International Committee of the Red Cross (ICRC, or Red Cross) about missing relatives lends strength to DNA profile matches. In some cases, information provided by the family becomes the decisive factor in finalizing the identification; in much rarer instances, as with Đemila's sons, memory initiates or determines the identification.

## COLLECTING AND ORDERING MEMORIES

In their more public function within the identification process, memories are translated into quantitative and qualitative data. Recorded onto the sheets of a questionnaire, these details serve as signposts in the process of evaluating a possible identification. They help the experts and the families recognize the missing person. Antemortem data encompass not only descriptions of the clothing that the missing person was last seen wearing or any personal possessions he had with him, but also physiological details, such as his height, the condition of his teeth, the color and length of his hair, and any injuries, such as broken bones, he sustained before death. These data also map the final moments of the missing person's life as recalled by family and friends. Did he go through the forest or to Potočari? If the former, where was he last seen alive? Who saw him? The details and descriptions provided by the family create a narrative profile of the missing relative that forensic experts and case managers will utilize in assessing the identity of a given set of mortal remains.

In the current design of ICMP's identification procedures, the importance of antemortem data is relative. The capacity of these data to confirm or distinguish the identity of a missing person depends on their significance relative to postmortem data and DNA evidence. In most cases, they become relevant in the final stages of identification, after DNA testing has matched blood samples from surviving family members with bones samples extracted from recovered remains. When compared with postmortem data, antemortem data tend to support the statistically certain genetic evidence documenting individual identity.

As we saw in the previous chapter, however, the contribution of antemortem data to identification has not always been limited to this role of comparison in the final stage of the process. Rather, when local and international experts first applied classical forensic techniques to the Srebrenica cases, they hoped clothing, personal possessions, and information about the missing person's physical characteristics and medical history would prove more successful, yield more results. Significant time and effort were expended attempting to gather such information from surviving family members. Although genetic testing eventually became the driving force behind the identification process, the correspondence between postmortem data and recollections as antemortem data continues to influence families' responses to the news of identification.

The system of collecting, cataloguing, and utilizing antemortem data evolved with the changes in international intervention in the identification process. This work began with the Boltzman Institute, a small NGO from Austria.[2] The responsibility for gathering antemortem data then passed to Physicians for Human Rights (contracted by ICMP) and, in 2000, to the Red Cross.[3] Physicians for Human Rights staff developed a standard questionnaire that they filled out during interviews with families of the missing. They sought informants who could give the most accurate and detailed accounts, ideally individuals who could describe not only the missing person's physical characteristics, but also what he was wearing immediately before his disappearance and where and when he was last seen. Unlike the more open-ended form used by the Boltzman Institute, the Physicians for Human Rights questionnaire was more complicated and structured.[4] A database was created to match antemortem and postmortem data. The idea was not to arrive at perfect matches as much as to narrow significantly the field of possible identity (Komar 2003). Therefore, rather than searching through 1,500 potential missing person profiles, the forensic experts could consider a case within the scope of a mere thirty or forty similar profiles.

As with the personal information entered into the missing persons and donor databases at ICMP, the antemortem database required synthesized factual snapshots of the missing persons immediately before they disappeared. Through the bureaucratic forms of the standard questionnaire and database, information gathered could be easily categorized and read. Problems, however, have arisen with the form's rigidity and the multiple layers of translation involved in collecting, storing, and eventually reinterpreting the data provided by families.

Building on the already existent antemortem data form, the Red Cross recently expanded the scope of the interview so that it now comprises 150 questions. To streamline the data processing, they modified the coding system that Physicians for Human Rights had implemented when it first took over the collection phase. The interviewers recording each piece of information, such as the type and color of the missing person's jacket, translate the description into a numerical code that is later entered into a database. In theory, this coding system should facilitate the Red Cross's ability to conduct antemortem-postmortem comparisons, but in practice, the numerical representation of family members' recollections often strips away the specificity that makes antemortem data so vital to the final stages of identification. Furthermore, as a case manager at the Podrinje Identification Project (PIP) observed, implementing the coded antemortem data collection system requires that the information—the family members' recollections—pass through five different hands: the informant to the interviewer, the interviewer who records and codes the data, the data entry staff member who types the coded responses into the database, the person searching the database, and finally the case manager back at PIP reading the printed-out data. The case manager argued that such a convoluted process practically guaranteed distortions and dilutions of the original recollections and descriptions provided by family members.

Another complicating factor in collecting data for missing persons several years after their disappearance is that recollections are variable. The passage of time inevitably influences surviving relatives' memories of July 1995. While Rejha has a very strong sense of her recollections and is sure she will be able to recognize her husband's clothing, other family members feel less certain when asked to recall very specific details, such as colors, patterns, brand names, and logos. What remains vivid for one person has become blurred for another. Among the many attempts to explain such variability and complex peculiarities of memory—particularly the relationships between its emotive and cognitive properties—the approach taken by Henri Bergson in *Matter and Memory* is especially useful for understanding the remembering required of Srebrenica's surviving families.[5] Bergson sets the following scenario: in attempting to learn a lesson (a text) by heart, he reads it repeatedly and commits it to memory after several readings. Having learned it by heart, he now has a fixed memory of the lesson as a whole. But he also has the memory of each distinct and successive reading. In Bergson's terms, the former (the memory of the lesson learned by heart) is a "representation . . . an intuition of the mind which I may lengthen or shorten at will"; the other (the memory of each reading) is an "action"—"it is lived and acted, rather than represented" (1991:80–81). Mediated through the individual's body, through an intellectual movement, the memory of the *act* of reading is "as capricious in reproducing as it is faithful in preserving" (1991:88). Bergson's example suggests that the Srebrenica families' recollections of their missing relatives are "lived and acted," because as memories, "they bear upon events and details of our life of which the essence is to have a date, and, consequently, to be incapable of being repeated" (1991:83).

But what if the very act of recollecting, of remembering a specific image or set of words, has occurred repeatedly? Bergson does not mean to say that this second type of memory is static. On the contrary, "time can add nothing to its image without disfiguring it," and "if it still deserves the name of memory, it is not because it conserves bygone images, but because it prolongs their useful effect into the present moment" (1991:83, 82). The family members completing antemortem questionnaires recall the images of their missing relative as best they can, but because those recollections are, as Bergson says, "lived" and not merely "learned memories," their specificity has faded over time. Lacking the cohesion of a lesson learned by heart, these recollections come to families in bits and pieces; the details of some images—a look of fear or a reassuring embrace at the moment of separation—may remain vivid, while others, such as the texture or pattern of fabric, can disappear altogether. Mary Ellen Keough, a former Physicians for Human Rights staff member, explained that such interviews "test people's memories," and frequently relatives feel pressure, even guilt, when they cannot recall details that they think will be critical in identifying their missing family members. Antemortem data questionnaires completed in the immediate postwar years often provide more in-depth descriptions of clothing or personal possessions. The wife of one missing man remarked in reference to her own ability to recall details, "It's been nine years, not nine days."

## MEMORIES, TIME, AND DISCREPANCIES

When I began to work with the PIP case managers, accompanying them into the field for family visits, I understood better the complicated nature of the antemortem database and the clumsy collaboration that existed between the Red Cross and ICMP concerning how best to collect antemortem data. In addition to inaccuracies or imprecision stemming from the questionnaires, PIP case managers were bothered by the two organizations' overlapping work. For example, when they open a file for a missing person—that is, when a DNA matching report has prompted the transfer of the file to the PIP office—they request a copy of the antemortem questionnaire from the Red Cross. In many instances, because these data have not yet been collected (or, though collected, not yet processed), case managers contact families to set up their own antemortem interviews. They have to: before they can reveal anything about the potential identification of the relative, they must have compiled basic information regarding the missing person's clothing, physical characteristics, and his disappearance. On at least three different occasions in the field, I witnessed the embarrassment of the PIP case managers when they embarked on such an interview, pulling out the sheets of paper, only to learn that a Red Cross team had already posed the same set of question weeks, if not days, before. In all three instances, the case managers proceeded to duplicate the work, running through the entire form and recording the specific details about the missing person's clothing.

As they explained to me later, they felt safer collecting the information themselves rather than waiting for the Red Cross data, which might not be as detailed or accurate as the subsequent antemortem-postmortem comparison would require. The bureaucratic method of collecting these data and the awkward division of labor between the two rival organizations have thus increased the emotional toll on family members in these situations. Relatives are needlessly compelled to recall twice over the images of their missing relatives and the events leading up to their disappearance.

Unlike the Red Cross staff, PIP case managers have the advantage of both extended field experience and access to information from the postmortem examinations (the autopsy report, the forensic anthropologist's examination, photographs, and detailed descriptions of personal articles found with the mortal remains). Although PIP case managers do not disclose postmortem information to informants (family members) at the time of the interview, the knowledge contained in those reports nevertheless often guides their questioning. For example, I was present for an interview in which the case managers, Enver and Senad, had very specific information about the missing person's prior injuries and physical characteristics. Before we arrived at the house, they explained to me that the case's DNA statistics were very strong, but there was no antemortem questionnaire in the file. Senad had been unable to reach the missing person's mother, with whom the missing son had lived in the enclave, and so had contacted the sister. She had returned to her prewar house in a village on the road between Konjević Polje and Bratunac. We met her there and they conducted the interview in the small living room of her recently reconstructed house. Because she had not been living in the same household as her brother during the war and had not seen him in the final few days leading up to the fall of Srebrenica, she could not provide any information about his clothing. She did, however, describe his hair—distinctively long, dark hair that he usually tied back in a ponytail. Although Enver and Senad said nothing at the time, this description matched the hair found on the skull exhumed with the mortal remains of the person in question. They then went on to ask the woman about any injuries her brother might have sustained before July 11, 1995. From the pathologist's report, they knew the man had suffered some kind of wound to both legs, inflicted by heavy artillery.

Their questions began around the general topic of injuries, but as she could not recall his condition with much specificity, they turned to a more leading line of inquiry: was her brother injured in the leg? When did this happen? A few months before the fall of the enclave, in the spring of 1995? To their disappointment, even the suggestive nature of their questions could not prompt the sister's recollection. She remembered he had been limping but did not know the extent of his injury, whether he went to the hospital, whether it was his right, left, or both legs. When we returned to the car, the case managers explained that they would need to try again to locate the mother and ask her about the injuries. The sister's interview was too inconclusive. I was puzzled—if the DNA analysis statistics were so strong and her description of the hair so close, why could they not proceed with the identification rather than seeking out another informant? Their response was grim but followed the imperative logic of the Srebrenica cases: they could not be sure that the recovered head belonged to the other skeletal remains in the body bag. They needed more information.

Senad and Enver, along with other PIP staff, spent months helping me understand the nature of their work and the delicate relationship among the DNA evidence, the antemortem data, and the postmortem data. They taught me some of the tricks of the trade with the antemortem data interviews. One of the points they repeatedly stressed was that memory, though enduring, was rarely constant and often associative. Each person remembered and described details—colors, fabrics, styles, sizes, teeth, builds—in different ways. Part of their job in the antemortem interviews was to help the person put those images into descriptive language. The more they knew about the types of clothing, personal possessions, routes of flight, and patterns of behavior among the refugees in the enclave, the better they could help the family members articulate their memories.

For many relatives of the missing, recollections were often influenced by their own changing circumstances. The PIP case managers needed to bear this variability in mind when pressing people for detailed descriptions. Their classic example involved getting the informant to provide an accurate estimate of the missing person's height. Having worked several years with Mercy Corps, an international aid organization involved in the reconstruction of prewar homes, Senad had a particular theory about people's estimates of height. Often close relatives, especially mothers, did not know the missing person's exact height, so they estimated based upon their recollection of how high he stood relative to the doorframe in their home. They relied on what William James termed a "network of associations"—facts linked with other facts that help secure a memory (1983:622–623). The problem for the family members was that the reconstructed houses invariably had higher ceilings and doorframes than the prewar homes, especially those found in the villages of eastern Bosnia. Yet the mother would describe her son's height relative to these taller doorframes, thus, providing a skewed estimation. The "lived and acted" memory shifted with the changing circumstances (points of reference) in the person's life. When an informant was unsure of the missing person's height, both Senad and Enver used the same method of calculation. They would rise up, asking the family member to stand beside them and indicate how high she had stood against the missing relative—up to his chest, shoulders, jaw, and so on. They then estimated the missing person's height relative to both their own height and where she reached next to them.

Emina, another of the case managers, told a poignant story about how memory can play tricks on the informant as he or she tries to recall certain details of the missing person's physical characteristics. She was working on a case in which the father of a missing person had witnessed his son's capture by Bosnian Serb soldiers when they were attempting to flee through the forest. Having escaped the soldiers himself, he hid in the nearby brush and watched as the Serbs beat his son and forced him to strip. Ten years later he was still tormented by guilt. He had witnessed but was unable to stop his son's aggressors, paralyzed by his own fear. Moreover, he had survived, while his son had been tortured and killed. The man was, as Emina put it, a shell of a person. Nevertheless, during their conversation, as she asked him about his son's physical characteristics and clothing, he tried valiantly to recall the minute details. Emina had already reviewed the postmortem file and knew that the young boy had had his right front tooth extracted. When she asked the father about his son's teeth, the man described him as missing his left front tooth. Emina pressed him on this detail, and, after a moment of reflection, he realized that he had been envisioning his son's smile as if in a mirror—mistaking left for right and vice versa. Again, a "lived and acted" recollection, the memory image appeared to him as his son would have before his own eyes.

Sometimes in their visits to families for antemortem interviews, the PIP case managers would ask to see a photograph of the missing person. In particular, they hoped to find an image that showed the missing person's hair color and teeth. I was present for one such visit. The surviving relative lived in a small village about thirty minutes from Srebrenica, off the main road to Sučeska. It took us several stops to locate the village, a cluster of twenty or so houses at the top of a steep and narrow track. The approach of the large vehicle attracted the attention of the village residents. At the first house three women appeared from behind the thin sheath of lace curtain hung from the doorframe. The family member whom we sought was standing among them and indicated her house on the other side of the village. We offered her a ride but she set out to walk the short distance, and soon all eyes were following our strange procession. Once inside the house and out of earshot from her inquisitive neighbors, Enver and Senad introduced themselves as staff of the International Commission on Missing Persons. In a gentle tone, Enver explained that they had come in order to get information about her missing son. He was careful not to say anything specific regarding a possible identification. But I already knew their plan: if the circumstances were right—that is, if the woman seemed emotionally able to bear the conversation well and if the information she provided about her son's clothing and personal possessions was close to the postmortem data—they were prepared to proceed with the identification. They had all the material necessary to complete the case both in the file and in the car. They had brought along a sealed plastic envelope containing the personal possessions exhumed with the body. The course of the conversation would dictate their on-site decision.

When Enver and Senad began the interview, pulling out the paperwork from the file folder, a neighbor appeared at the door. The mother of the missing person invited the woman to take a seat and the conversation resumed. As soon as the mother realized what questions Enver and Senad were about to ask, she explained that she had visited the Red Cross office in Srebrenica a few days before to provide the antemortem data. Enver paused for a moment. What should he do? Leave the interview and wait for the Red Cross results? When would he be able to return to this remote village? Would the roads still be accessible by then? He pressed ahead, asking the woman if she would mind giving him some of the same information. She agreed. Soon after, a second neighbor, along with her daughter, arrived and took a seat on the couch next to the mother of the missing person. The interview proceeded, with both Enver and Senad taking careful notes—one on the regular antemortem questionnaire, the other recording each article of clothing described by the mother on separate sheets of paper. Within another five minutes, three more neighbors appeared. As seats had run out, they stood to the side or knelt on the floor. One woman was seated immediately to the left of Senad. She had spotted the file and stared openly at its contents, craning her neck to get a better view. Enver noticed this as Senad leafed through the papers, at one point pausing on the color photocopy of the clothing exhumed with the body. He subtly reached his hand across the file and pushed it closed. Senad understood the signal and shielded the papers more carefully.

After going through the descriptions of the missing son's clothing, they turned to his physical characteristics. Enver asked whether the mother had a photograph of her son. By now, the room was full. Two old men had joined the gathering, the older of whom sat immediately across the room from Enver and Senad. With the interview paused as the mother searched for the photograph, this man asked if they had come with news about anyone else missing from the village. Dressed in soiled work pants and a tattered wool sweater, with a black beret and thick glasses, he looked like the archetypical Bosniak villager. The other women explained that this man had lost all four of his sons. Indeed, the two old men seated before us were the only men living in the village. The rest had been killed or had fled and resettled elsewhere. Enver explained that, regrettably, they had only come regarding this case.

The mother soon returned with a faded black-and-white photograph of four young men standing shoulder to shoulder, smiling broadly into the camera. She pointed to her son and both Enver and Senad examined the photograph carefully. Someone among those gathered asked to see the picture, and it was passed around the room. The old man in the beret held it in his hand for a moment. He told us that one of his own missing sons was also in the photograph. The room grew silent and, for that instant, the memory of those four men filled its space. All of us—relative, neighbor, total stranger alike—felt their absence. I could not help but think of the very different sort of photograph that lay tucked in the sheets of the case file resting on the coffee table. Those images of clothing and personal possessions, taken by an identification technologist with no connection to the missing person, held out a critical means of bridging the gap in identification, of drawing together these two parallel states of absence.

But in the end, Enver and Senad, without consulting with each other openly before the assembly of villagers, decided it was not right to continue with the identification. As they informed me in the car later, the circumstances were less than ideal. The woman's description of the clothing and the personal possessions was too different from what they knew was found with the remains. Furthermore, the meeting had become too public, and it would have been impossible for them to safeguard the conversation (or to prevent upsetting comments or questions from her other guests), as they might have done in a more private setting. Enver pulled out the case file and handed me the color photocopy of the personal possessions exhumed with the body. Among the articles pictured there was a *džezva* (a small pot for preparing coffee), a cigarette box, keys, and a document that bore the insignia of the Red Cross. There was also a copy of a faded Polaroid photograph whose colors had so blurred and run together that you could hardly make out the image. But the figure of a woman wearing a headscarf, sitting beside a young boy was still discernible. It looked like it might be the woman we had just visited. Staring at this image, I wondered at the irony of the case photographs, of the picture of a picture that connected the missing with the living and yet sat in the folder of complete strangers.

Withholding knowledge, as Enver and Senad did in this case, is a disconcerting though understandably necessary practice. A mistake in the identification process could prove exceedingly painful for the relatives of the missing involved in the particular case. What if the case managers proceeded with the family's confirmation of an identification based on an on-site antemortem interview that contained such discrepancies? What if those discrepancies later pointed to the identification of only a body part rather than the full body? In addition to causing the family much anguish, such hasty decisions could jeopardize the trust ICMP relied on within the community of surviving family members. For this reason, case managers unfailingly return to the office and consult with Dr. Kešetović about incongruities arising from antemortem-postmortem comparisons. Because most family members do not know the precise steps of the exhumation and identification process, they may never pick up on the delay. After I had spent several months working with ICMP case managers, Hajra and Nura of the Women of Srebrenica asked me whether an antemortem data interview conducted by a case manager (as opposed to a Red Cross staff member) meant that the remains of a missing person had already been identified. It was a difficult question to answer because, all of a sudden, I too felt the burdensome responsibility of knowledge. If I said yes, then perhaps a member would someday recognize the antemortem questions of the case manager visiting her home as a direct signal of identification, a premature conclusion that could prove extremely problematic and distressing for both the family member and the case manager. In the end, I explained the various scenarios and underscored the inconclusive nature of the antemortem data interview, especially when there are multiple male relatives missing from the same family.

Existing on a separate track altogether from the memories of the missing person maintained by surviving relatives, the PIP staff members' knowledge of a missing person pertains to a case, a problem to be solved. As such, the case files generated for the Srebrenica victims represent a different state of absence, one organized into columns of data that, in most instances, eventually slide into place to produce a match—through genetic profiles, but also through antemortem data. For a period of time between the issuance of the DNA matching report (which indicates that the bone sample belongs to a particular individual) and family notification, the knowledge of the missing person's identity remains in the hands of strangers. These strangers piece together both his skeletal remains and the final moments of his life. They open up the memories of the missing person, provided to them in descriptive chunks of antemortem data by the surviving family members, and compare those recollections with the physical remains of the person—from his bones laid out on the anthropologist's examination table to the personal possessions stored on a shelf in the PIP mortuary.[6] For many of the Srebrenica victims, that period of absence is especially prolonged. The Bosnian Serb "innovation" of the secondary mass grave so disrupted the physical remains of the individual victims that identification can take years. The process of exhuming and reassociating different body parts, identifying them through DNA testing, and finally completing antemortem-postmortem data comparisons may span well over a decade, as is the case with the most recently identified sets of mortal remains, buried at the memorial center in Potočari on July 11, 2007.

## ANTEMORTEM-POSTMORTEM COMPARISON

In following ICMP's work and, in particular, the Podrinje Identification Project's role in the identification of the Srebrenica victims, I was struck by the points of intersection between these two different tracks of absence—that is, the memory of the missing person and his existence as a yet unresolved case. One of the most interesting examples of this overlap occurs during the examination of the clothing and personal possessions exhumed with the bodies or body parts. In order to understand better this stage in the antemortem-postmortem data comparison, I spent several days observing the work of Amir, the PIP staff member responsible for photographing, examining, and writing detailed descriptions of articles recovered with each body or body part. A criminologist also trained in social anthropology, Amir has a gifted eye for detail and a curiosity that pushes him to imagine the lives and circumstances of the people who once wore or carried the objects that he studies. His position within ICMP is unique: although he has some contact with family members who wish to view personal articles recovered with their relatives' remains, for the most part he engages with the identity of missing persons through their material possessions.

While the forensic anthropologists can glean something of the missing person's life by examining his skeletal remains—his relative age, some of his medical history, or his cause of death—it is Amir among the PIP technologists who gains the most intimate, albeit indirect, knowledge of the missing person's life and death. Along with his own observations, he has access to both postmortem reports and the family members' memories as recorded in the antemortem questionnaires. Furthermore, he has the DNA matches upon which to base his own reflections on the missing person's identity. In his efforts to advance the process of recognition, he supplements "objective" DNA evidence and autopsy reports with the vital, though inherently subjective, recollections contained in the antemortem data.

With a case file open on his desk, Amir begins his antemortem-postmortem comparison by emptying a brown paper sack onto the floor of his office, a small room in the PIP mortuary. The clothing contained in the bag belongs to a missing person for whom a DNA match at the International Coordination Division facility has generated a potential identification. The bag bears the same reference code as the body with which it was exhumed. Once the articles lie spilled out on the floor, he gently disentangles the material, sorting out the various layers of clothing, footwear, belts, straps, and threads into discrete piles. Clad in medical scrubs and rubber gloves, Amir proceeds undaunted by the smells and condition of the clothing. Depending on how much clothing is contained in the paper sack, he orders the articles in the right-hand corner of the office, within the space designated for photographing. A red-and-white strip of plastic tape sets off the left side of the space, indicating to-scale measurements for each article. The trick, he tells me, is to capture in the photograph as many significant features of the clothing as physically possible.

Once he has arranged each article within the space and photographed the collection, Amir examines the pieces of clothing in greater depth. He pats down trousers, feeling along the upper stitching and pockets to see if there is anything inside that the initial examiner, who washed and dried the pants, might have missed.[7] He looks carefully along the inside of the waistband for any hidden pouches. He examines the shirt collar to see how worn the fibers are. Turning to me, he explains that shirts worn by the missing person day in and day out during the three years in the enclave will show significant fraying along that area. He points out the woolen socks and their distinctive stitching, the patchwork on pants and underwear. Such details may help family members identify the clothing more readily, as their handiwork is often immediately recognizable. Amir tells me that usually a woman, such as the missing person's mother, wife, or sister, washed and darned the clothing during their refuge in the enclave. While some of the outer clothing may not look familiar, relatives' socks or underwear may be more easily recognized than a jacket or a shirt.

During his examination, Amir consults the antemortem data recorded in the questionnaire to see how (if at all) the information provided by the informant fits with what lies before him on the floor. I observed him with one case in which the informant, the missing person's daughter, had recalled that her father was wearing a short-sleeved shirt. Amir bent down over the long-sleeved shirt recovered with the body and pointed out the multiple creases on each sleeve, indicating that they

FIGURE 8. Amir examines articles recovered with a set of mortal remains. Photo by the author, used with permission.

had been rolled up. This might account for the discrepancy, especially as the daughter had provided the information five or six years after the fall of the enclave. As Amir remarked, however, the accuracy of the antemortem data can vary depending on who conducts the interviews. In this same case, the interviewer had failed to ask about personal possessions, but two articles (prayer beads and a silver spoon without a handle) had been exhumed with the remains.

In another case, I watched Amir work through the belongings of a body recovered from a primary grave. Two paper sacks contained several different articles of clothing: two pairs of pants, a tweed jacket, a brightly colored hand-knit sweater, an undershirt, and a long-sleeved button-down shirt. The file indicated that the missing person was an old man who probably dressed warmly in anticipation of the cold nights. Amir immediately noticed that the blazer had a hole in the upper right breast, near the pocket just below the collarbone. So too did the sweater. He lined them up to show how they were in the same place, suggesting that the hole was most likely from a bullet. He then consulted the file, but unfortunately, there was no antemortem data questionnaire. In the autopsy report, Amir read that the person was found with blindfolds and ligatures. He then placed the contents from the second bag, an undershirt and long-sleeved shirt, on top of the jacket and sweater. They, too, had holes in the same spot. With four pieces of clothing bearing holes in the same location, Amir surmised that all four articles belonged to the same person and that the victim had sustained a gunshot wound to his upper chest.

The clothes, shoes, and personal possessions Amir examines often tell a story about life in the enclave at the same time that they provide clues about the identity of the missing person or his manner of death. The quantity and quality of the humanitarian aid delivered to the enclave meant that people frequently had identical pieces of clothing. Flipping through the Red Cross book of photographs of clothing exhumed with mortal remains, you see multiple examples of the same silkscreen-logo sweatshirts and T-shirts. From my discussions with PIP staff, one item struck me as a particularly pitiful and ironic emblem of the Srebrenica victims' fate: the prototypical generic shoes shipped to the enclave as humanitarian aid. Their cheap rubber soles and flimsy fabric had led the refugees to dub them "*mrtvare*," dead man's shoes. According to some of the women at the office of the Women of Srebrenica, the name referred to the Serb custom in which the deceased is laid to rest wearing a new (but apparently low-quality) pair of shoes. I wondered how many people in the enclave considered the irony behind the name or thought that they might someday be buried in those same cheap shoes provided to them by the international community. Because they were so common, the *mrtvare* became a standard term in the PIP case managers' vocabulary and Amir's descriptions. Distinguished only by color—dark or light—or distinctive repairs made to the fabric or soles, the *mrtvare* served as yet another manifestation of how individual identity in the enclave tended to blur into a more collective category.

## BIOGRAPHICAL OBJECTS

The remnants of clothing and personal articles yielded up stories to Amir's careful eye about the lives of the individual missing persons. During one of my first few visits to his office, he pulled down from the shelf filled with distinctive personal possessions exhumed from the Srebrenica graves a pale yellow *džezva,* a small coffee pot, whose handle was broken. He posed the question: What does such an object recovered with the body of a missing person tell you about what he had been thinking at the time of his flight? It spoke to his intentions, maybe in that instance the absence of urgency. Perhaps the person thought the Bosnian Serb siege was merely a ruse and that the UN peacekeeping

FIGURE 9. Personal articles recovered with the mortal remains of Srebrenica victims. Photo by the author, courtesy of the ICMP Podrinje Identification Project.

forces would turn the aggressors back after a day or two.[8] In the meantime, he would set out for the forest with the column of men, ready to prepare some coffee for himself along the way. He had little sense, Amir ventured, of the horrors to come. Or take the other objects lining the shelves of his office: letters and photographs extracted from pockets, a small leather-bound Koran, an army water bottle with a name etched into its side, an old-fashioned alarm clock, tobacco tins and cigarette holders. Having discarded all other personal possessions, why did the missing person cling to such articles? What personal significance does each represent to the missing person, and, in turn, his family? A biographical object may be "a prop, a storytelling device, and also a mnemonic for certain experiences" (Hoskins 1998:4). For Amir, these objects embodied the lives of the missing, their personal histories, and their relationships with their families, their faith, and their understanding of the circumstances in which they found themselves in those last few days of their lives. He cannot know the meanings of these objects; he can only try to represent their likenesses as accurately as possible, through photographs and narrative descriptions, so that the meanings may reveal themselves to the eyes and ears of the people who possess the intimate knowledge of the missing person.

The photographs he takes offer the surviving family members an indirect means of recognizing their missing relative from the personal articles recovered with his remains. Despite the high quality of the color photocopy that the case managers show to the families during the notification meetings, often they find it difficult to be certain. Colors are invariably faded or distorted from decomposition and the flash of the camera. The contours and distinctive stitching may not be visible in the photograph. For these reasons, the case managers encourage the families whenever possible to visit the office and view firsthand the clothing and personal possessions. One of the members of the Women of Srebrenica, Ešefa, described her experience examining the articles recovered with her husband's and her father's remains:

> E:  ... My brothers-in-law were first [to be identified], and my husband was identified on the 8th of January [2003].
>
> S. W.: And did they say where they were? Where they were found?
>
> E:  Yes. My father was dug up from grave to grave. He was killed and buried in Pilića, and from there he was removed and in Hodžići near Zvornik was tossed somewhere. He was found there in a grave. The same thing happened with my brother-in-law.
>
> S. W.: The same—
>
> E:  Yes, but my husband was found in a grave in Nova Kasaba. Apparently he wasn't dug up ... And then later they came to me to confirm—with the blood that we had given—to confirm that it was they ...
>
> S. W.: In the beginning did they show you pictures, and after that—
>
> E:  First they bring you a photograph, a picture of clothing on paper. They bring this to your home. It's a little tough to recognize them in the pictures because you see ... when the photo's a little dark, it's more difficult for you to recognize. When we went there to look [at the clothing], and you see it in person, it's easier for you to recognize. So they brought me my husband's things on paper, but I knew his [things]. Even though a lot of the clothing [in the enclave] was the same ... because there was nothing there, and so you'd sew those parachutes, the ones that fell with the packets.[9] Then I went to view his clothing, and it was his things, it wasn't torn up.
>
> S. W.: Had he sewn it?
>
> E:  No. A tailor there sewed the pants for him, but I knew which ones they were, and what kind of clothing he was wearing

underneath. The only thing was the socks, but, hey, they
changed their socks . . . Everything was new, well preserved
as if he had just put it on, not at all torn. . . . My father's clothing
wasn't torn, nothing on the pants, nothing. Above they were
just a little decayed. My father's socks had been new woolen
ones, and the new wool wasn't destroyed. But what my husband
had—Nura was with me—he put on the pants as if he knew that
he wouldn't return that day, with an extra pair of sweatpants
underneath. Everything was new. Everything, the shirt as well,
so that when the shirt wasn't capable of being damaged, then
you know . . . On [my husband's] shirt here [indicates location]
there was only a tear as if by a knife, where the bullet pierced.
Somewhere next to it there was a box that held tobacco. . . .
Someone had made flint and steel, so that the stone would light
a fire. We found a cigarette holder with it. And it appears that
the box was pierced from when he was shot in this area [indi-
cates location] and because the tobacco box had a hole. I brought
it back home so that the three kids would have a memento. For a
long time I didn't dare tell the children that I went.

S. W.: How old were they when—

E: Well, that was before the first burial. They identified my husband in January, and that March he was buried. They were
grown. My son was sick and I didn't dare tell him. When I told
him that they found his father, he asked whether there was
anything of his that remained that would serve as a reminder
of him. I said, "I'm going to show you children something,
but don't get upset." . . . When I opened the envelope and my
son, immediately my son—he was in the third grade when
Srebrenica fell—he immediately recognized it because he knew
what it was. Because his father had made a cigarette holder with
his own hands. He had made the tobacco box. We all did that
there. So he recognized it. For the girls it was a bit like they
didn't know. They were young. They don't remember anything.
The youngest doesn't even know [her father], just from photos
and stories. She doesn't remember her father at all. Now she's
in the eighth grade. It's difficult . . . difficult.

Ešefa's narrative walks us through her reactions to the experience of
viewing the clothing in person. She reflects on life in the enclave—how
and why they would sew pants from parachute material—and on the
practices of the men who fled through the forest, for example, that they
changed their socks along the way. In describing her husband's articles
(pants, sweatpants, a shirt, and socks), she automatically compares them
to those found with her father's body. Moreover, the clothing leads her
to speculate about her husband's manner of death. The clothes did not

bear traces of brutal violence, but the slit of the bullet hole in the area of his upper chest and the damage to the tobacco box suggest an execution by shooting. Seeing the clothing in a photocopy of a photograph alone would not have given her such a tactile sense of its condition.

An accomplished seamstress herself, Ešefa pays close attention to the state of the fabric, and her language highlights the way in which she interprets the condition of the various articles. Repeatedly she expresses her surprise about what has escaped damage and decay: *to nije ni satrovala* (it [the clothing] wasn't torn up); *uopšte satrglo nije* (not at all torn); *ima malo im istruho* (they were just a little decayed); *ona nije istrala* (it wasn't rotten). Furthermore, her husband's clothes help her understand his behavior and state of mind in those last hours. "He put on the pants as if he knew that he wouldn't return that day, with an extra pair of sweatpants underneath." These details reinforce her own recollections at the same time that they lend support to the other evidence of her husband's identified remains.

Ešefa's narrative also reveals the powerful connection that many surviving family members feel toward the personal articles that are exhumed with the bodies of their missing relatives. Viewing the skeletal remains—something PIP case managers always discourage families from doing—offers no visible link to the image that family members have of the person in the final moments at the fall of the enclave. Indeed, the irreconcilable difference between the memory and the bones on the examination table (or more indirectly, the images in the ubiquitous video footage and newspaper photographs of exhumation sites) makes it harder for some family members to accept the news of identification. For those such as Ešefa and her son, however, a personal possession recovered and returned to the family forges a new connection between memories of the missing person and the knowledge of his death. Something as singular as a hand-carved tobacco box serves as a posthumous "biographical object" (Hoskins 1998), one capable of telling, or at least prompting the telling, of the missing person's life story. Furthermore, as a crucial part of the identification process, this object imparts a finality to the news that the abstract statistics of the DNA analysis cannot always provide. The son recognizes his father's hand-carved tobacco box and understands the implications of its homecoming.

Under Amir's tutelage, I began to grasp the critical role antemortem data could play in confirming or determining an identification. Aside from the photographs he takes of the clothing, he also writes detailed descriptions of each article, noting the color, type of fabric, brand

and size (when possible), stitching, and any distinctive features such as pockets, zippers, and buttons. These descriptions are placed in the case file along with the color photocopy of the photograph of the clothing and personal possessions, what Ešefa meant when she said, "They brought me my husband's things on paper." When the case managers set out to notify the family of the potential identification, they have already reviewed both the photocopy of the personal articles and the written descriptions. Often the latter helps them guide the family members as they look at the pictures. In many cases, families are unable to travel to Tuzla in order to view the articles in person. Thus, they rely on the written descriptions to provide vital information about the various articles recovered with the body that they cannot discern from merely viewing the photocopy.

I accompanied Enver and Senad in the field for one such visit. The missing person's wife and recently married son had returned to their prewar home in a village on the banks of Perućac Lake, a reservoir off the Drina River. The dirt road leading down to the village was in poor condition, adding to the isolation of the already remote community of returnees. We found the wife and son after a couple of stops for directions, and the five of us took our seats at a makeshift picnic table looking down at the lake below. It was early October and a beautiful, warm autumn day. Listening intently, the wife and son took in the news of the potential identification with calm, resigned expressions. Senad and Enver proceeded to show them the pictures of the clothing and the actual personal possessions recovered with the body. They had brought the latter with them, in a plastic envelope, which they now opened up to extract the contents—a small plastic bank credit folder and a silver tablespoon. The mother and son examined the articles closely, straining to read the print on the inside of the credit folder. They discussed whether the missing man had owned such a document. Perhaps—he had taken out a loan for a tractor before the war. The wife could not definitively recognize the spoon, a response that drew harsh criticism from her son. "How could you not know a spoon from your own house?"

They then turned to the picture of the clothing. The case was unusual in that three different jackets had been recovered in the vicinity of the missing person's body. Because it was unclear which of the three jackets (if any of them) belonged to this particular set of mortal remains, the jackets were photographed together to allow the family to view each. The wife and son looked carefully at the picture and discussed what they remembered of the man's jacket. Unfortunately, the colors had faded or been distorted, and, at first glance, they did not recognize any of the three. When Senad began reading the description of each jacket provided by Amir, however, they were able to recognize distinctive features, in particular the zipper and waistband. On a second review, they identified one of the jackets as that of the missing man. A second picture showed the other articles recovered specifically with the body—pants, underwear, socks, and a shirt. Again, the detailed written description offered information essential to recognizing the articles. As Senad read aloud the notes pertaining to the pair of swim trunks used as underwear, the woman cut in excitedly. She knew precisely what Amir had meant when noting that there was an alteration to the waistband. She explained that she had sewn a band of elastic into the edge of the waistband of her husband's shorts. Amir's description matched her own. The photograph, which captured only the clothing's exterior, would not have revealed this telltale detail.

In that instant, her memory-image of the jacket connected not with the photocopied photograph on the table but with the words of Amir's description. Recollections and bits of information slid into place, enabling the woman to recognize what had been unrecognizable in the two-dimensional reproduced image of the jacket. Toni Morrison writes about just such a moment—evoking an almost physical movement, a sound, within the mind that aligns perception and memory—when the mother, Sethe, recognizes her daughter Beloved:

> When the click came Sethe didn't know what it was. Afterward it was clear as daylight that the click came at the very beginning—a beat, almost, before it started; before she had heard three notes; before the melody was even clear. Leaning forward, Beloved was humming softly.
>
> It was then, when Beloved finished humming, that Sethe recalled the click—the settling of pieces into places designed and made especially for them. (1988:175)

Family members who viewed the objects or photographs, or who read or listened to Amir's narrative descriptions of articles recovered, related to me this visceral sensation of recognizing their missing relatives' personal possessions, of memory falling into place with the sight or feel of those objects.

## MEMORIES AS DEFINITIVE PROOF

There are some Srebrenica cases for which DNA profile matches alone do not provide sufficient evidence to identify remains. In these instances, the antemortem data, including the clothing and personal possessions recovered with the mortal remains, do more than confirm identification. They play a crucial role in determining it. I saw this most clearly with the example of two young men, brothers aged seventeen and twenty-two. They were very close in height and had no notable injuries or illnesses whose traces the forensic anthropologist might have detected when examining the recovered remains. Neither man had married or had children, and the DNA matches between their respective bone samples and the blood sample from their mother could not distinguish between the two bodies. More precisely, the exhumation teams had recovered a nearly complete body for one brother, but only the lower half of the second brother. Nevertheless, Amir was to conduct an antemortem-postmortem comparison for both cases to see if the antemortem data provided by the mother could help determine which son belonged to which body or body part.

An assistant brought two different brown paper sacks to Amir's office—one was marked as a body, the other as a body part. Amir shook out the contents of the first bag (exhumed with the body part): a pair of camouflage pants, a belt, and a pair of underwear. The second bag (exhumed with the more complete body) contained dark-colored high-tops, which Amir thought might have come from UNPROFOR, a ball of threads attached to a silver button engraved with the word "Levis," dark socks made of a synthetic material, and a bit of a shoulder strap, a felt band, and scraps of material presumably all from a rucksack. Amir explained that synthetic material decomposes at a much slower rate than cotton; hence, the socks were intact while nothing but threads remained of the denim jeans. With the shoulder strap and miscellaneous material, he ventured that the man had carried a rucksack, possibly with food, which animals later destroyed or carried off. Having already consulted the file's autopsy report, he noted that the articles in the second bag (from the more complete body) were recovered on the surface of the forest, a fact borne out by the condition of the clothing. He then reviewed the antemortem data questionnaire. The mother reported that both sons went through the forest, as a part of the column. The younger son was wearing army pants, while the older had on "Texas" jeans. She had heard that while they were in the forest, the younger son left searching for water and came back wounded. He was later seen captured and held as a prisoner in a school. According to Amir, her information corresponded with the location of the grave from which he (more precisely, a part of him) was exhumed. He was most probably taken to Kravica, the Serb village where Bosniak men who had been captured in the woods near Bratunac were held and later executed. Their bodies were in turn dug up and reburied in secondary mass graves. The combination of the locations of the respective grave-sites and the mother's precise descriptions of her sons' clothing helped to determine the identity of the two sets of mortal remains.

A month and a half later, by sheer coincidence, I ended up accompanying Enver and Senad when they visited the mother of these two young men to notify her of the identification of the older son, the one who had died in the forest. Before our arrival, Enver and Senad explained that it was a very sensitive case because the woman, now the sole survivor of her family, had lost both her sons and her husband. This was the first identification. She had returned to her prewar house in a village on the road between Bratunac and Skelani. We arrived to find her sitting on a little stool on the steps outside her door, sorting beans that were drying in the sun. After brief introductions, she brought out three plastic white chairs and we each took our seats. With the glare of the midday sun in our eyes, we squinted at one another and down at her fingers, still running across the shiny white and liver-colored beans.

Enver and Senad began the conversation carefully, first asking her about when she gave the blood sample and then explaining that a result had come back. There was a possibility that her older son had been found. They needed, however, to confirm some information. They began with the clothing—did she recall what he was wearing? Yes. They pulled out the pictures, as well as the written descriptions from Amir, and I immediately recognized the items as belonging to the case that I had watched Amir photograph. I remembered seeing both sets of clothing lying on the office floor. Now I found myself face to face with the missing person's relative, the informant, and was witnessing firsthand as she recognized the clothing and recounted the same story about each son's flight and the younger son's injury and capture. Again I was struck by the fact that we three strangers had more knowledge of her sons' current condition—indeed, that both were dead and that only part of her younger son's body had been recovered—than did she, the person to whom that knowledge meant the most.

Looking at the picture of the clothing, they discussed each article: the jeans, the synthetic socks—here Enver explained the difference between the decomposition rates of cotton and synthetic fabric—the belt, the shoes, and the rucksack. The woman said that the jeans had been a gift, a donation, from some doctor during the war. The rucksack

had contained another pair of pants, but Enver explained that only bits
of material remained of it. They talked about the shoes at length. She
said that although her son had received them through humanitarian aid,
they were not *mrtvare*. Reading from Amir's notes, Enver mentioned
that the shoes seemed to have undergone some repair. The woman confirmed this, recalling that a shoemaker had indeed fixed them for her
son. The meeting ended after she signed the papers acknowledging the
identification, and we left shortly thereafter.

Once we had climbed back into the car, I told Enver and Senad about
having seen the second son's clothing in Amir's office. They explained
that it would have been inappropriate to mention anything about the
second case, especially because only the lower half of the younger son
had been recovered. The woman lived alone, and the news of her older
son's identification was already stressful enough. While they would await
Dr Kešetović's instructions about how best to proceed with the case,
presumably they would not contact her again until the upper half of the
other son's body was identified. Enver predicted that he would visit her
at least two more times with news about her two other missing relatives.
The parallel tracks of the missing persons as memory and object would
draw these two people, the expert and the family member, together for
at least two more meetings, as they shared and exchanged knowledge
about the victims, their lives, and their postmortem profiles.

The experiences of accompanying the PIP case managers in the field
and watching Amir at work in the mortuary significantly broadened my
understanding of the interdependent relationships among antemortem
data, postmortem data, and the DNA evidence. Furthermore, I now saw
how fruitless, indeed, mistaken, it was to draw value distinctions between
the perceived objectivity and subjectivity of the forms of knowledge that
bring about an identification. Certainly, the DNA-based technology
of extracting and analyzing genetic profiles has become the primary
and most effective means for resolving the dilemma of absence—the
ambiguous status of a missing person—by reattaching personal identity
to physical remains. The success of this technology, however, relies on
other critical sources of knowledge, including family members' recollections of the missing person, from his physical characteristics to the
clothes on his back at the fall of the enclave. Memory, imagination, and
supposition, therefore, do not exist on the opposite side of some verti-
cal line drawn between their subjectivity and the objectivity of DNA
science. Rather, these different kinds of knowledge gain significance
within the process of identification in relation to one another.

# CHAPTER 5

# Where Memory and Imagination Meet

But never should I be able to wipe out of my memory that
contradiction of her face, that anguish of her heart, or rather
of my own: for as the dead exist only in us, it is ourselves
that we strike without ceasing when we persist in recalling
the blows that we have dealt them. To these griefs, cruel as
they were, I clung with all my might and main, for I realized
that they were the effect of my memory of my grandmother,
the proof that this memory which I had of her was really
present within me. I felt that I did not really recall her save
by grief and should have liked to feel driven yet deeper into
me these nails which fastened the memory of her to my
consciousness.

> Marcel Proust, *Remembrance of Things Past,*
> *Cities of the Plain*

On August 2, 2001, the International Criminal Tribunal for the former
Yugoslavia convicted Bosnian Serb Army general Radislav Krstić of
genocide. The first (and only, to date) such conviction in the history of
the international court, the successful prosecution of the Drina Corps
general finally recognized through legal instruments the level and nature
of the crimes committed against the people of the Srebrenica enclave.[1]
The decision officially legitimized the application of the term *genocide*
to the Srebrenica case, and thus became a major impetus for Bosnian
Serb officials to confront the charge and, albeit in piecemeal public
statements, begin to recognize the crimes.[2] The conviction depended
in part on moving and detailed testimony by survivors. Some of their
words addressed the dilemma of missing persons, bearing witness to

the irrevocable consequence of the crimes—that is, the crisis provoked by anonymous death and the absence of loved ones. This testimony moved outside the court's realm of direct concern and reflected the relatives' personal hopes and fears. The following excerpts from the testimony of a Bosniak woman, Witness DD, about her son's separation from her at Potočari illuminate some of the contradictory needs of the court and the surviving family members:

> *[Witness DD]:* We walked for about 50 metres, and then from the left column one of their soldiers jumped out, and he spoke to my child. He told us to move to the right side, and he told my son, "Young man, you should go to the left side." And then he said, "Why me? I was born in 1981." But he repeated what he had said, "You people should go to the right-hand side." He had some kind of bags in his hand, and the soldier told him to throw the bag to the right side and to go to the left, but I grabbed him by his hand and I—he kept repeating, "I was born in 1981. What will you do with me? What do you want me to do?" And then I begged them, I pleaded with them. Why are you taking him? He was born in 1981. But he repeated his order. And I held him so hard, but he grabbed him. And then my son threw out that bag, and the soldier picked up the bag and threw it on a pile on the right-hand side, and he took my son's hand, and he dragged him to the left side. And he turned around, and then he told me, "Mommy, please, can you get that bag for me? Could you please get it for me?"

> *Judge Rodrigues:* [Interpretation] Madam, please, take your time. Take your time to calm down. We are here with you; we're listening to you. Take your time.

> *[Witness DD]:* That was the last time I heard his voice. . . .

> *[Ms. Karagiannakis]:* What do you think has happened to your husband and your two sons?

> *[Witness DD]:* How do I know? As a mother, I still have hope. I just can't believe that this is true. How is it possible that a human being could do something like this, could destroy everything, could kill so many people? Just imagine this youngest boy I had, those little hands of his, how could they be dead? I imagine those hands picking strawberries, reading books, going to school, going on excursions. . . .

> *Judge Wald:* I have no questions for the witness except to thank you for coming and sharing your very

sad story with the Tribunal. I think it will help
us in making our decision. Thank you.

*Judge Rodrigues:* [Interpretation] Me too, madam, I have a very
small question for you. Do you have anything
that you would like to say and that has not been
asked of you?

*[Witness DD]:* [Interpretation] I do. I wanted to say if I had
known these people would betray us the way
they did, those who had sworn to protect us
and signed documents to that effect, I would
have saved my family, my husband and my
children. We could have sought shelter somewhere and at least we would have died together
and our bones would be together. I would have
stayed in front of our house together with my
whole family and let them all kill us together
if I had known what would happen.

*Judge Rodrigues:* [Interpretation] So, madam, I wish to repeat that
you are an extremely brave woman. You have said
that the body lives, but perhaps the soul needs to
gain strength from the little hands of your son.
You must continue living, at least if for no other
reason than to testify about all those events that
you have shared with us and to avoid, as you have
said, that fools may appear again in the future.
So that is a very good reason to continue living.
We thank you very much for coming here and we
would like to wish a better life for you and for all
your loved ones. So you may now leave.

*[Witness DD]:* [Interpretation] May I say one more thing,
please? May I?

*Judge Rodrigues:* [Interpretation] Yes, go ahead.

*[Witness DD]:* [Interpretation] I would like to appeal to you
to ask Mr. Krstic, if you can, whether there is
any hope for at least that little child that they
snatched away from me, because I keep dreaming
about him. I dream of him bringing flowers and
saying, "Mother, I've come." I hug him and say,
"Where have you been, my son?" and he says,
"I've been in Vlasenica all this time." So I beg
you, if Mr. Krstic knows anything about it, about
him surviving some place . . .

*Judge Rodrigues:* [Interpretation] Yes, madam, I think all of us
have heard your plea, and I think that all the
people who are here and who can do something
will do it. But I repeat, you have good reasons

> to continue living. All the people here present
> and all those listening to us will do whatever is
> possible to do. We understand and feel for your
> suffering. I will ask the usher to lead you out
> now. Thank you once again for coming.
>
> [*Witness DD*]: [Interpretation] Thank you too. (ICTY Prosecu-
> tor v. Radislav Krstić 2000b: 5754–5755; 5761;
> 5768–5769)

The disjunction between the two parties in this discussion arises from their understandably disparate points of reference. The court, specifically Judge Rodrigues, conceives of this woman and her personal history within the context of the trial of General Krstić. No doubt he spoke sincerely when he told her that they, those in the court, "feel for your suffering." But whether he *understood* her, as he so claimed, is less apparent. Witness DD described to a courtroom full of strangers the painful separation from her son. She gave voice to the sentiment that she and her family had been betrayed by those sworn to protect them. She expressed her wish to have died together with her family on their own soil rather than to have suffered the pain of her sons' and husband's disappearance and the utter lack of knowledge concerning their deaths. Grounded in the "contingencies of home and of domesticity" (Ross 2001:268), her testimony revealed the powerful significance of the event of death, more specifically, of dying among one's family and in one's home.[3] In response to her dark wish, the judge tries to comfort the woman with a reason to live—if nothing else, to bear witness to the events that she and her family experienced.

With that remark, Judge Rodrigues has placed her life in relation to something much more distanced from her already articulated framework. According to him, her knowledge of genocide and her ability to share it with the outside world in order to prevent its future enactment should provide her with reason to live. This consolation ignores one of the most charged aspects of her testimony: that she lives in a present suspended between the memories of her son and her family before the genocide, the imaginings of a different end, and, finally, the sliver of hope that her young son is still alive. As with so many of the surviving family members, the past overshadows both the present and the future—regardless of the role they, as survivors and witnesses, might play in documenting the genocide at Srebrenica and preventing its repetition. This moment of public disjunction exemplifies what Ricoeur means by the phrase, the "crisis of testimony" (2004:175). Oral testimonies such as those of people who survived the extermination camps of the Holocaust pose a "problem of reception" because the audience has only limited shared comprehension from which to draw when encountering the testimonies: "This comprehension is built on the basis of a sense of human resemblance at the level of situations, feelings, thoughts, and actions. But the experience to be transmitted is that of an inhumanity with no common measure with the experience of an average person" (2004:175). "To be received, a testimony must be appropriated, that is, divested as much as possible of the absolute foreignness that horror engenders. This drastic condition is not satisfied in the case of survivors' testimonies" (2004:176). The "absolute foreignness" of the mother's testimony prompts Judge Rodrigues to place her words within the context of the tribunal's shared comprehension—that is, to divest it of the horrifying void in her knowledge of her family's whereabouts, and place her testimony safely within the bounds of its present-day function as supplementing the court's record of the Srebrenica genocide.

The oft-quoted testimony of Witness DD speaks not just to the divergent perspectives of the witness and the court but, more important to understanding what identification means to surviving family members, it illustrates the overlap between memory and imagination. Witness DD opens up her mind's eye to the outside world, describing how she envisions her son's hands, "those little hands of his . . . I imagine those hands picking strawberries, reading books, going to school, going on excursions." The synecdochical image appears in action, in motion, in the midst of the everyday life of her missing son. She tells the court of how he comes to her in dreams, explaining where he has been all this time. The emphasis on place is unmistakable: her imagination has created an alternate narrative about her son's absence in which he has been living in a Serb-controlled city in the Republika Srpska. She confronts the court with her need to unseat this imagination and replace it with more concrete knowledge. Thus, she poses the question to Krstić: Can he tell her if this boy still lives?

In a parallel moment of testimony in the same case, Witness O, a young man who was seventeen years old in July 1995, describes his escape from execution. Amid the graphic details of the mass killings, he seizes upon his fear at the instant he is called from the truck to lie down and be shot among the piles of other corpses:

> So when I reached my spot, at that point we were watching those dead
> people. You could tell that those were dead people there. There were

several Serb soldiers there. I don't know how many there were, five or ten, but they were standing behind our backs. But it all happened very quickly, in a matter of seconds. And then I thought that I would die very fast, that I would not suffer. *And I just thought that my mother would never know where I had ended up.* This is what I was thinking as I was getting out of the truck. And when we reached the spot, somebody said, "Lie down." And when we started to fall down to the front, they were behind our backs, the shooting started. (Italics added; ICTY Prosecutor v. Radislav Krstić 2000a:2912)

Though relieved by the thought that his death would be swift and he would not suffer, the young man nevertheless is pained by the prospect of such an anonymous end. His mother would not know where or how he died. She would not know where his body would lie. Just as for the other mother, Witness DD, the question of place is inextricably bound to the experience of death. This absence of knowledge—not knowing where their missing lie—plagues the surviving families. Witness O anticipates this in the very instant in which he is about to join the stacks of nameless corpses.

## DREAMS, IMAGININGS, AND THE POSSIBILITY OF RESOLUTION

Both witnesses' testimonies underscore the problematic absence of knowledge inherent in that festering "somewhere" described by Dr. Kešetović—the unknown place of death and unmarked gravesite where the missing relatives' mortal remains now lie. Their words also touch on the prickly thorns of imagination that create alternative, sometimes hopeful and other times horrific, narratives about the missing person's prolonged state of absence. As I have written earlier, to be absent is to be missing both in time and in space. It is natural, therefore, for the surviving families to seek out the where, the how, and the when (if not also the why) of their relatives' final moments of life and death. In doing so, they attempt to link their lived experiences of the present with those of the past—that is, to recognize each missing person's traces, be they memory-images or physical remnants of his material being. "Now the concrete process by which we grasp the past in the present is *recognition*" (Bergson 1991:90).

There was of course a time when the absence of these men and boys did not automatically signal death. Before the truth of the massacre had become firmly rooted in the survivors' minds, during those early years when mothers such as Witness DD still held out for the miraculous return of their sons, dreams and imaginings sustained hope. But because "the shadow of death hangs over all disappearances" (Ricoeur 2005: 64), eventually those dreams of return took on a different significance, forging a new connection with the missing. In the Islamic tradition, it is held that interaction between the living and dead occurs through the medium of dreams (Smith and Haddad 2002:50–54).

One of my earliest encounters with this realm of spiritual connection—with survivors' dreams—was in Srebrenica during a conversation with a woman, a returnee, who had lost both her sons in the genocide. She was one of the patients of the Dutch NGO's nursing outreach program, and we had come to check her blood pressure and blood sugar level. It was an extremely hot afternoon in July, and the woman's face was noticeably flushed. After taking the readings, the nurse began to ask her about her recent health. The woman described her state of agitation. A few days before, she had dreamt about one of her sons, whose birthday had just passed. I remember fumbling with my translation for the nurse. There was a word I could not understand, at least not in the context of the woman's narrative. In the dream she looked down into a grave and heard his voice saying "*uči, uči.*" At the time I could only think of two meanings, the imperative form for either the verb *učiti* (to learn or study) or *ući* (to enter). Several days later I recounted the incident to a Bosnian friend back in Tuzla, who in turn explained that the woman most likely meant another verb altogether, "*učiti,*" to pray.[4] The son was imploring the mother to pray before his grave. He came to her in the dream as dead, not alive, and spoke to her about her obligations to his soul.

As I would come to learn, such experiences also entailed conscious imaginings of an impossible present. On a glorious spring day in 2004, when driving back from Srebrenica to Tuzla, Hajra of the Women of Srebrenica remarked how sad the season of spring had become for her. In Bosnia, spring's arrival brings people out into the streets to stroll arm in arm and to linger over coffee at outdoor cafes. She saw these young people, full of bloom and life, and thought of how her son Nino would have enjoyed sitting at those same tables, drinking a cold beer with friends. For many of the mothers, fond memories would jump across the span of time like a spark, kindling new yet familiar images in the endless stream of possibilities that began with phrases such as "what if" and "what would." They were the type of imaginings that conjured up little hands picking strawberries and young people enjoying a round of cold beers on a perfect spring day. And for those who had returned to their prewar homes, the melding of memories and imagination gave the fleeting sensation that their children were right there, just around the corner. *Na trenutak momentalno nestada ih. Isto kao ti nabereš jabuku i nestala je.* In the words of a mother missing all three of her sons, who has returned to her small village outside of Srebrenica, "In a moment, instantly, they disappeared. It's just as if you pick an apple and it disappeared."

But what of those instances when the mind desperately but fruitlessly searches for either memories or secondhand knowledge to fill in the troubling gaps amid the narrative of their missing relatives' tragic fate? Unfortunately, a darker imagination plays an equally powerful role in the lives of Srebrenica's survivors. Without recourse to their own memories or access to a complete account of the event, they are left to picture it in all its terrible detail. As Bergson asserts, "to picture is not to remember" (1991:135); indeed for the families of the missing, picturing or imagining their relatives' suffering becomes an act of suffering in and of itself. One need only look to the example of the now infamous Scorpions tape. Whereas the stories that emerged from the handful of survivors of the mass executions and the men who succeeded in walking through the forest were oral testimonies, the videotape broadcast repeatedly during the month leading up to the tenth anniversary of the genocide provided vivid, unfiltered images of torture and death.

I accompanied *Dnevni avaz* reporter Almasa Hadžić on her visit to interview one of the families whose members had recognized their father (husband) in the footage. A young woman in her early twenties, the daughter recounted her reaction to seeing the tape for the first time. Immediately she recognized her father, the man whom one of the Scorpions repeatedly kicks in the head while he crouches on the floor of the truck transporting them to their execution site. It felt like she herself was being kicked in the stomach, she said. She recognized him again as one of the two men who were spared long enough to carry the four other bodies into a house near the field where they had been gunned down. His movements, his shoulders, the way he turned his head all confirmed for her that she was watching her father in the last few moments of his life. The family members of those six individuals have been granted a perverse reprieve from the absence of knowledge that surrounds the deaths of the remaining victims of Srebrenica; they now know, indeed have viewed, their sons' and fathers' execution. For the rest of the Srebrenica families who watched the ghastly scenes of those few minutes of footage, the tape has fed into the half-formed images of their mind's eye, adding to the already fertile ground of their imagination.

I argue throughout this study that identification of mortal remains presents the single abiding resolution to this absence of knowledge. It bridges the enormous and dreadful chasm between surviving family members' memories of the missing and their imaginings about the nature of their relatives' death and the place of their bones. The news is not always welcome because not every family member can accept the dismantling of his or her imagined narrative. For some, identifying a recovered body signifies a new death—that of the lingering hope that somehow the missing relative survived. Given how sensitive these moments of reckoning are, the final stage of identification, in which the families reenter the process to verify the identity of their missing, is by far the most challenging for all involved.

My insight into the encounter with the news of identification comes from both sides of the experience: from the PIP case managers responsible for communicating the information and the family members who receive it. In these instances, I examine the critical moments of recognition, strategies employed by the case managers to negotiate the conversation, reactions of family members to the news, and ensuing discussions between the two parties. The encounter represents the metaphorical transfer of authority over the missing person's identity—from the more distanced expert to the close relative. Through that act, the details surrounding the missing person's absence shift away from conjecture and imagination into the realm of data and statistical certainty. The news of identification produces knowledge and elicits responses, as families reconcile what they have remembered, imagined, hoped, and dreaded with the contents of a case file spread out before them.

## TRUST

Nedim, the head of the PIP case managers, told me an important story about trust. On March 31, 2003, on the occasion of the first mass burial at the memorial center in Potočari, two families appeared at the gravesite for one man. Though unrelated, apparently both families had a missing relative with the same first and last name, and, as fate would have it, the same father's first name. The family whose relative had been identified (through DNA analysis) had already met with PIP case managers, authorized the identification, and signed the papers pertaining to the burial. The other family learned of the man's identification only on arrival at Potočari that day. Mistakenly thinking that the man to be buried was their relative, the second family was outraged that they had not been notified of the identification. Confusion and frustration arose at the gravesite as both families claimed the identified remains to be those of their relative. After some debate, they struck a compromise and agreed to bury the coffin together. The following day, however, the second family stormed into the PIP office and demanded an explanation. Fortunately, the case managers could verify the proper identity of the buried man and rectify the misunderstanding. The incident laid bare for the PIP staff the painful consequences of mistakes and miscommunication. It also revealed two levels of trust involved in this final stage of identification: first, the vital trust between the families and the case managers who convey the identification process's results; and second, the trust that the overwhelming majority of families now place in the DNA-based identification technology.

Consider for a moment the idea of social reconstruction that the identification technology is supposed to effect—be it on the more intimate, familial level or the community or societal level. In order for identification to serve as a means for rebuilding something, it must be accepted as true and its evidence seen as verifiable and trustworthy. The latter term refers to an essential feature of the entire process. Although reactions vary according to individuals, family members' responses to the news fundamentally hinge on a sense of trust. They must trust the source of knowledge, indeed, the entire network of actors dedicated to resolving the fate of their missing relatives. The trust they place in the various organizations and their representatives has developed over time and through direct engagement with specific individuals.

For example, Amor Mašović, head of the Federation Commission for Missing Persons, enjoys widespread popularity among Bosniak and especially the Srebrenica surviving families because he has established himself as their most visible public advocate on the issue of missing persons.[5] He appears regularly on national television and in newsprint, giving updates on exhumation sites and the number of bodies identified, and is often photographed taking part in the exhumations and in the company of surviving families of the missing. More importantly, he offers his personal opinion on a range of topics related to Srebrenica, the genocide, its perpetrators, and the victims, both the missing and the surviving families. *"Amor nam je jedina nada"* (Amor Is Our Only Hope) reads the headline for an article in the daily newspaper *Dnevni avaz* about the Mothers of the Srebrenica and Žepa Enclaves' Islamic holiday gathering, to which Mašović was invited. Mr. Mašović tells the women assembled in the office, "We are far from our final goal. The process of searching [for the missing] takes a long time. I believe that we will find your missing and I promise that we won't give up." The reporter then quotes one of the mothers as saying, "I lost two sons and my husband. I have been waiting years for them to find them. Amor is our only hope" (*Dnevni avaz* 2004a). Most members of the two leading family associations (the Women of Srebrenica, based in Tuzla, and the Mothers of the Srebrenica and Žepa Enclaves, based in Sarajevo) trust that the Federation commission led by Mašović will not cease its efforts until it has uncovered all of the Srebrenica mass graves. As further evidence of their faith in his leadership, in July 2007, Mašović received the Potočari Charter award (*Potočarska povelja*) for his contributions to the identification efforts, an award given jointly by the family associations and the Institute for Research of Crimes against Humanity and International Law, headed by the SDA-affiliated academic Smail Čekić.

The International Commission on Missing Persons likewise has sought to establish trust between itself as the lead international organization for the identification process and the families of the Srebrenica victims. Overlap between ICMP and the Red Cross, in particular concerning the collection of antemortem data, and the work of Physicians for Human Rights initially left some family members confused about ICMP's precise role in the process.[6] Despite the many meetings ICMP staff has held with the family associations over the years, its proper name still eludes the general membership of the Women of Srebrenica. I rarely heard family members refer to ICMP by its name or even its acronym when discussing identification; rather, they simply used the pronoun *they*, for example, Ešefa's remark: "And then later they came to me to confirm," or, "First they bring you a photograph, a picture of clothing on paper. They bring this to your home." The PIP case managers are frustrated by the imprecision and often feel that they are fighting a losing battle to distinguish their organization from the Red Cross. On an almost daily basis, families mistake PIP staffers as being from Crveni krst (Red Cross).[7]

Regardless of such confusion, most families of the Srebrenica missing do know ICMP's local and, in some cases, international staff members who have been working on identification for several years. Based first in Tuzla and now in Sarajevo, Adnan Rizvić is well known and trusted as the local head of the organization's Forensic Sciences

Division. Dr. Rifat Kešetović is arguably ICMP's and specifically PIP's most trusted figure among the Srebrenica community in Tuzla because of his role as the chief pathologist and director of the PIP facility. It is there that the final results of the identification process emerge, and, under his supervision, the case managers proceed to notify the families of the news. Like his staff, Dr. Kešetović appreciates the delicate work of building and maintaining a relationship of trust between his program and the family members. He recognizes, however, that the technology of DNA analysis has effectively distanced the families from the identification process even as it promises better end results. Wary of allowing the esoteric language of genetic science to dictate the family members' understanding and involvement in the identification of their missing relatives, he stresses the need for them to be included in the overall process in order for them to respect its results:

> Many of the forensic specialists who are involved in the process of iden-tification do not like to have much contact with the families. They wish to show their work only through science and in that way they just present the identity of the particular person, arrived at only through scientific methods, dry facts, etc. To begin with I don't have that sort of approach. I'm not saying that I don't use science—I use it an extraordinary amount and I respect only facts, but, from the onset I believe that the family must be actively involved in the identification. This means that the family must be shown the entire analysis, everything that we have done in the uncover-ing of the identity so that they understand from the beginning everything that has been done. . . . But for them it is a much better feeling when they know that they themselves were actively involved in it, that they were not just passive observers of that which for years they have sought, since the end of the war.
>     On the other hand, since the beginning of my work in those gatherings [with the families] . . . I have clearly, loudly, and publicly told the families that I will never sign an identification if I am not certain. There have been situations when families have insisted that [the identification] be finished, but I have had doubts. I explained to them that there are uncertainties, that we need to double check, and after that I will finish the case. But again we did it together. I think that it is fundamental that the families have an extraordinary respect [for the work]. Of course it is only proper that it be respected when you involve someone in something that is of extraordinary concern, because it [identification] concerns them most of all. At the end of the day, they are the ones who are affected.

A soft-spoken and reserved man, Dr. Kešetović interacts with the families differently from the forensic specialists he described above or the media-savvy Mašović. He has developed his relationship with the community of survivors by engaging them on very personal terms, but also terms well removed from the intrusive and at times manipulative public spotlight. Notoriously camera-shy, even at the height of the media frenzy in the days leading up to the tenth anniversary, "the doctor" as he is called by his staff and the family members, was reluctant to grant any interviews. Undoubtedly his presence in Tuzla (rather than Sarajevo) and his interaction with the displaced Srebrenica community in that city have further improved his standing among the concentration of displaced persons who made their homes there in the years after the war. Through his early outreach efforts, he succeeded in gaining the families' trust by making the procedures, the science of DNA analysis, as transparent as possible for them. Members of the Women of Srebrenica in Tuzla described how he came to them on several occasions to speak directly about the advent of the comprehensive DNA testing program. Contributing to an issue of *Bilten Srebrenica*, Kešetović framed the success of the technology in relation to the families' participation, specifically in the context of their blood samples: "There is no doubt that this program applied in the last two years has drastically increased the number of identified persons in enormous part because of the great response of the families to give blood for analysis" (Žene Srebrenice 2004:8). His emphasis on family involvement, coupled with his own pledge never to sign an identification for which he is not absolutely certain, has made him an esteemed and trusted ally in the families' search for their missing.

Following their director's lead, the PIP case managers strive to maintain the same level of trust throughout their interactions with families both in the field and in the office. As with the antemortem-postmortem comparisons, they employ certain strategies to protect family members from undue stress. For example, in some instances, this means that during their initial encounter with the contact person they do not uphold the standard of transparency described by Dr. Kešetović. Instead, they take their cues from the contact person—the member of the family who has been appointed to receive news concerning the recovery and identification of the missing relative. Because the burden of informing the entire family about the identification will fall to this person, the case managers encourage him or her to evaluate how and when to relate the news to the rest of the family.

Another key tactic for building trust and facilitating communication with families is the case managers' insistence on using their first names—Emina, Jasmina, Enver, and Senad. They are all young, well-educated Bosniaks, residents of Tuzla, and, in this sense, are of a different socioeconomic background than many of the surviving relatives, the majority of whom lived in small villages in eastern Bosnia prior to the war. Introducing themselves by their first names and giving the families business cards listing only their first names and the office telephone numbers (rather than e-mail or postal addresses), they attempt to establish a familiarity that will not only ease the tension surrounding the conversation but also encourage families to communicate openly with them even after the notification meeting has concluded. Because most families are missing more than one member, the case managers often visit the same household or close relatives of that household on multiple occasions. By developing a good rapport during the initial contact, they set the pattern for future visits. Furthermore, given the dynamics of the Srebrenica survivor community, positive interaction with families through which trust is both built and maintained naturally enhances the success of the overall process. Confusion or suspicion concerning PIP staff, their expertise, or their professionalism would significantly undermine their work, indeed the work of the entire organization, including the results of the DNA testing.

As much as ICMP would like to maintain its reputation for having a multiethnic staff and an ethnicity-blind approach to identification procedures, PIP case managers present an important exception to the rule. The case managers' ethnicity plays an integral role in their ability to engage with the families. Simply put, the Srebrenica community would never countenance Bosnian Serbs working in this capacity. In the fall of 2004, behind closed doors, the Women of Srebrenica protested the presence of two Serbian forensic anthropologists working as ICMP staff at Srebrenica mass gravesites. Bosnian Serb case managers would be entirely unacceptable for them.[8] Immediately obvious from their first names, the case managers' ethnicity signals an unstated partisanship. In their presence and knowing their ethnicity, survivors often grieve openly and some express unguarded anger and bitterness directed at Bosnian Serb war criminals, nationalist politics, even general society.

And although these young staff members are not strict in the practice of their religion, their Bosnian Muslim identity provides them with both the linguistic tools and the knowledge of cultural, specifically ethno-religious, practices vital to conversations between strangers about death and burial. After several trips into the field in the Republika Srpska with Enver and Senad, I realized that they used certain colloquialisms to tailor their speech to the relevant audience.

They alternately hid and played to ethnicity as the situation required. When it was obvious that they were approaching a Bosniak (usually tipped off by dress, such as men wearing dark berets or women in *dimije* and headscarves), they would use traditional Muslim greetings such as *"salam alejk" or "merhaba."* When they thought the person a Serb, they would say, *"dobar dan"* (good day), and if they could not tell either way, they simply asked, *"kako je?"* (How is it going?).[9] Senad joked that if you said the wrong thing (mistook the person's ethnicity), you would get the wrong directions.[10]

Just as with the antemortem data interview visits, the case managers prepare themselves for the encounter with the family by reviewing the contents of the case file carefully before they contact the family by phone to arrange the meeting. Whenever possible, they ask the family contact person to come to the office. Whether returned to their prewar homes or newly constructed houses in the Federation, or still residing in collective centers, most families live outside of Tuzla; therefore, the case managers spend a significant portion of their time in the field. If they are able to reach the contact person on the phone, they arrange the details of the meeting beforehand. The more they can anticipate about the visit's setting, the better they will be able to guide the conversation. Thus, both their administrative strategies for notifying families and their own demeanor during the discussions help to establish a relationship of trust between themselves and relatives of the missing persons.

INFORMING AND RESPONDING

The conversation transferring the knowledge of identification—and therefore definitive knowledge of death—from the case manager to the family member is by far the most sensitive interaction of the entire process. Up until this point, this knowledge has rested disproportionately with the experts, from the moment that the DNA matching report is generated to the antemortem-postmortem data comparison conducted by the PIP staff. The identification technologists are more privy to information regarding the missing person's posthumous state than his own family, and it is they, not the relatives, who first "recognize" the missing. This reversal of roles makes for an especially delicate discussion. According to Enver, the PIP case manager who has worked in this position since its creation, the passage of time and the advent of the DNA technology have succeeded in preparing most family members for this conversation. The majority of the surviving relatives have steeled themselves for the telephone call; indeed they now expect and long for it. As one woman, a mother of two missing sons, remarked about her expectations regarding the recovering of her sons' remains, *"Živiš u nadi i u nadi umreš"* (You live in hope and in hope you die). She has yet to hear from ICMP and has become resigned to the wait.

Despite such intellectual preparation for the news, emotional responses inevitably vary across individuals. For this reason, both the families and the case managers try to prevent certain relatives, typically the mother of a missing son, from hearing the news directly from a stranger. I was present for several such meetings. In a case with Enver and Senad, the brother of the missing person warned that his mother was in very poor health and would not be able physically to bear the news of her other son's death. Thus, when we pulled up to the hamlet nestled in the hills of the southern region of the Srebrenica municipality, Senad asked neighbors picnicking under the shade of a tree to alert the son that we had arrived. He cautioned the old man who volunteered to act as the messenger not to say anything in front of the ailing mother. Once the brother appeared, we sat down at a table in the neighbors' yard, well hidden from the mother's sight, and they slowly reviewed the contents of the case file.

Sometimes, however, it is impossible for the case managers or the contact person to shield more vulnerable family members from the painful encounter with the news of identification. This happened in a case of a missing man whose wife, the contact person, was estranged from her husband's family. After learning of his identification, the wife deferred to her mother-in-law regarding the final signature of identification papers and decisions about the man's burial. Enver and Senad planned to visit the house when the other son (the missing person's brother) was also at home. Unfortunately, work had delayed him, and this left only the mother. Once seated across the room from her three guests, the old woman looked up anxiously from beneath her headscarf at Enver, who had begun a cautious introduction of ICMP. Although he said nothing concrete about her son's identification, it was clear that she understood the visit's import. With her hands trembling even as they rested on her lap, the old woman began to cry softly. Moments passed and Enver filled the silence of the room with idle talk, none of which neared the subject of her son's identification. Gradually he turned the conversation to her other son, asking when she expected him home from work. It was quickly decided that Enver and Senad would come back in two hours' time.

When we returned to the house later that afternoon, the brother greeted us at the door. In a hushed voice, Enver quickly explained that they had come about the identification of his missing brother and, seeing his mother's condition, decided that it was best to conduct the discussion in his presence. Moments later, with the mother, the son, and the three of us again seated in the living room, Enver embarked on an elaborate explanation of the identification procedures. He was trying to ease the old woman into the news of her son's death and subsequent identification. The brother and mother confirmed certain physical features of the missing man, such as his teeth and a childhood injury. On the subject of the clothing, Enver used very vague language, explaining that nothing recognizable had been recovered. For a split second the implications of this detail seemed to hang in the air. Was it that the man had no clothes on him when he died? That perhaps his captors forced him to strip? That they tortured him? The dreadful, unspoken possibilities loomed behind the fact that they could show her no clothing. Perhaps in response to this awkward omission, Senad offered clarification. He explained that lightweight cotton decomposes more quickly than synthetic fibers. The misplaced logic of this explanation, however, caught the mother's attention. She whispered something about his clothing not being cotton. Enver gave Senad a meaningful look and pushed the conversation ahead onto the next topic.

The brother had several questions. He wanted to know where the body had been recovered, whether it was complete, and how his brother had died. Enver and Senad read from the reports contained in the file and showed him the diagram of the skeleton that indicated the missing bones and the sample extraction points. On the subject of the manner of death, again Enver spoke in vague terms. This time he made a subtle gesture toward the mother, and the brother nodded his head. When we finally left the house, accompanied by the brother, Enver apologized for cutting off his questions. He was worried about how the mother might bear such information. He then told the brother more specific details from the autopsy report and promised that a copy of the report would be sent to him along with other follow-up paperwork. With those in hand, the brother could then speak with his mother as he saw fit about the details pertaining to her other son's death.

The visit epitomizes many of the challenges confronting both the experts and family members when navigating such conversations.

Gestures, facial expressions, even words left unsaid dictate the path of the discussion as much as the verbal exchange between the two parties. During the summer and fall of 2004, I accompanied Enver, Senad, Emina, and Jasmina on several notification visits and gradually became familiar with the pace and course of these meetings. I began to recognize the signs that cued the unfolding of information about the missing person's manner of death, the condition of his mortal remains, and the location of the grave from which he was exhumed. The case managers crafted certain impressions to fit the circumstances of the particular cases and families involved, a social performance akin to acting (Goffman 1959). I also picked up on the subtle strategies that they employed to make the encounter easier on the families. Sometimes this meant disclosing the information slowly. Other times they would lay the groundwork with a brief visit in which they reviewed ante-mortem data; they would then follow up several weeks later, hoping that the first visit had helped the contact person prepare herself for the actual evidence of identification and, therefore, death. Some cases took years. That summer Enver had completed a case he had been working on for five years. He had adopted the strategy of visiting the reluctant parents every so often when he was in the region. Sometimes he brought up the case; other times he simply stopped in on a "social call." Finally, one day the mother told him she was ready to sign the papers—five years after he had first come to them with the news of their son's identification.

Through these visits and my discussions with the Women of Srebrenica, I also gained insight into the range of initial emotional responses families had to the news of identification. Many of the women described to me the experience of learning the news as if the event—the terror of those days at Potočari and the moment of separation from their loved ones—was happening all over again. Although the passage of time had prepared them in some ways, it did not diminish the emotionally wrenching experience of simultaneously recognizing and remembering.

From the more distanced view as a silent observer during the case managers' home visits, I witnessed the mixture of resignation and grief, reactions invariably tempered by the setting of the conversation among strangers. First and foremost, following the rules of Bosniak hospitality, the families were concerned with the comfort of their guests. Thus, at the very moment they were learning the details of their relatives' death and the recovery of mortal remains, they were obliged to act as hosts, preparing coffee, pouring juice, and offering sweets. Many family members seemed to anticipate the visit and appeared relatively composed when viewing the photographs and diagrams and eventually signing the identification papers.

But in the presence of the Women of Srebrenica, I saw less guarded reactions. I accompanied Hajra and Nura on visits to association members whose missing relatives had recently been identified. An informal social visit, the meeting allowed the individual member a chance to discuss the experience with her peers. In expressing the association's condolences for the woman's loss, Hajra and Nura, along with other members, would bring coffee, sugar, and other foodstuffs to her home, and they would spend the afternoon together. On one such occasion, the mother, Emina, whose son had recently been identified, had prepared an elaborate lunch for her guests. In between the many courses, she spoke of her encounter with the PIP case manager, her trip to the PIP facility to view her son's personal articles, and the emotional instability that prohibited her from traveling to Potočari for the actual burial. She kept the color photocopy of the clothing recovered with her son's body in a plastic sleeve on the bureau in her living room, a practice so distressing to her young daughter that the girl reportedly threatened to tear up the morbid image to keep her mother from looking at it each day.[11] Passing it around for the women to view, Emina described in detail the condition of the clothing and her memories associated with the various articles.

This opened the door for another woman in the party of guests, Ešefa, to share her own experience of viewing her father's and husband's clothing. Periodically Emina broke into tears, and the women assembled in her living room patiently waited for her to regain her composure, uttering words of consolation and encouragement. In that same meeting, Ešefa produced from her purse a tattered piece of notebook paper whose creases were so worn that holes ran along their edges. An acquaintance had given it to her to pass along to Hajra. It had belonged to Hajra's son, Nino. We all watched silently as Hajra carefully unfolded the fragile paper with trembling hands. Pausing to read it over, her eyes began to well up with tears and she explained that it was his handwriting, one of his poems. The page was handed around the room for each woman to read and just for that moment the focus on Emina's lost son expanded to include another of Srebrenica's victims, one whose remains had yet to be found.

'THAT IS NOTHING TO ME'

Not everyone among the surviving relatives is able to accept the news of an identification. Typically, these family members are not as involved in the network of support associations such as the women in Tuzla. For a variety of reasons, they reject the science of DNA or the fact that their relatives' mortal remains—usually their sons'—have been recovered. They spurn the suggestion of death. In one such case that I witnessed, a woman whom Enver and Senad visited grew noticeably hostile once she learned the purpose of their house call. She had lost three sons in the enclave, the oldest in 1993 (already buried) and the two younger boys in July 1995. The antemortem-postmortem data comparison for the recovered remains pointed to one of the two sons missing after the fall of Srebrenica. The DNA analysis, though statistically sound, could not distinguish between the younger brothers. The visit necessitated the case managers' on-site decision: if the mother confirmed her earlier rec-ollections, recorded in an antemortem data interview from 1997, and recognized any of the clothing, Enver and Senad would tell her about the identification. If not, they would stop short of revealing the DNA statis-tics and wait to consult with Dr. Kešetović about how best to proceed.

We entered the property by walking up the steep driveway that led to her house. There, at the end of the dirt track we found the woman tending a cow. We quickly made our introductions while the animal finished up its pail of pumpkin rinds. From the moment Enver uttered the name of ICMP, the woman was on edge. She immediately made it clear to them that she was not about to accept their news. She nei-ther invited us into the house nor brought out chairs or stools for her guests—a telling disregard for Bosniak customs of hospitality. Instead, the four of us stood awkwardly facing one another. With arms folded across our chests, and she with her hands on her hips, our body lan-guage reflected the tension among us. Enver began by confirming that both she and her husband had given blood samples, subtly remind-ing her that she had participated in the process that had led them to her doorstep that day. He did not mention that she had filled out an antemortem questionnaire—a critical omission whose significance I understood only after the meeting had concluded. He then told her that they had reason to believe that the remains of one of her sons had been found. She shook her head. She had heard her sons were in Serbia. Unphased by this claim, Enver and Senad pressed on by explaining the identification process, trying to chip away at her defensiveness.

Finally the woman agreed to take a look at the color photocopy of the clothing recovered with the remains. At Senad's suggestion, she retrieved two chairs from her house, but even then, as she placed them before us, she would not sit down. For an uncomfortable few moments all four of us continued to stand in a circle around the empty chairs. At last, Senad took a seat in order to open the file and extract the photocopy. The woman sat down opposite him. He handed her the paper. Without even allowing herself pause to look at the clothing pictured, she spat out, *"To mi je ništa"* (That is nothing to me), dismissively flicking the back of her hand against the sheet. Her son had left with only a T-shirt on his back, she insisted. "He never had any such sweatshirt," she said jabbing her finger at a dark blue jersey with a light gray circular pattern on the chest. He never had such a sock; he was wearing different pants, darker in color. One by one she rejected each article displayed in the photo, save for the underwear, about which she was uncertain. Senad asked if her son had taken a rucksack, perhaps with clothing inside. No. He persisted: if her son decided to head through the forest, he probably would have had more than just a T-shirt. She snapped back, "I know what I pulled out of the armoire in the rush that day." Sensing her growing frustration, Enver interjected, explaining that clothing recovered with a body can prove deceptive because many of the men changed or picked up different articles along the way. This might be the case given that her sons were said to have survived several days after the fall. She rejected even this notion, saying that she had specifically taught her children that it was wrong to take anything off a dead person.

Enver and Senad saw the futility of continuing along this vein and so changed tack, inquiring about the details of her sons' disappearance. She recounted in full the story of each: one was last seen alive about ten days after the fall; the other allegedly survived three months in the forest, traveling to Žepa and back. Enver and Senad were keen to hear about the first son because the antemortem-postmortem data comparison appeared to match the recovered remains with his profile. Was the person who last saw him alive still in the area? Would he be able to recall the son's clothing? What about her husband? She dismissed both possibilities.

Finally Enver and Senad circled back to a topic that they had hinted at very briefly in the beginning of the meeting. Had the son ever sustained an injury to his forehead? Here, as I learned later, they were working from both the antemortem data that she had provided several years earlier and the pathologist's report. In the questionnaire, she had reported that as a young boy this son had been in an accident and had hurt his head badly enough that they had taken him to the hospital. The forensic examination bore out this story: there was evidence of an injury, trauma sustained to the skull that had occurred well before the man's death. But when asked specifically about the possibility of such an injury, she said that her son had never hurt his head. Rather than calling her on this apparent misrepresentation or omission, Enver moved on to the teeth. She had reported in the antemortem data questionnaire that he had had teeth extracted; again, the forensic report corroborated her earlier recollection. Now she told Enver and Senad that his teeth had been perfect—as perfect as her own dentures, she said with a broad smile.

The entire experience of witnessing this woman's utter rejection of the possibility of her son's death, coupled with Enver and Senad's patient and at times cunning attempts to reconcile her current recollections with her previous testimony, reveals the obstacle that memory sometimes presents in the identification process. For whatever reason, this woman could not or would not recall the details of her son's life that would confirm the identity of his mortal remains. Well schooled in the art of these conversations, Enver knew that by introducing either the DNA evidence or the antemortem data questionnaire, they would further alienate this woman—perhaps to the point that she might never accept the identification of either son. After we had driven off, we began to pick apart the conversation. I noted that I had never seen a family member answer the question about teeth so definitively. Most people pause and think for a moment, especially about the back molars, for which they have no ready image to call up in their minds. But this woman did not miss a beat—her son's teeth were perfect. Senad thought that she was lying in that instant, and Enver understood his frustration.

It was Senad's first such case, where the family member totally denied the possibility of something they as case managers knew to be at least 99.95 percent true. Enver said that this kind of case, this kind of reaction, used to be much more prevalent in the early years of the DNA-based identifications and before the burials at the memorial center in Potočari. I asked him why this woman did not want to accept the news. He responded simply by saying, "It is not that she doesn't want to; it's that she can't. She is not ready to accept it." He ventured that perhaps by the next visit, after she had had some time to absorb the information, to look over the photocopy they left with her, she might feel differently. "Or maybe," he added, "we will have to wait until the other son is identified, and then go to her with both cases. Whatever the situation, this will be a very difficult case." And it may become a case that ICMP cannot complete. For in the end, it is the family's verification—acceptance—of the identification that finalizes the process. Without that acceptance, the case remains indefinitely unresolved.

Though a rare example, the mother's reaction vividly illustrates the problematic relationship between memory and imagination for many of the Srebrenica victims' surviving families. In her imagination, this particular woman clings to an alternative narrative in which her sons live in Serbia, a hope most likely fed by immediate postwar propaganda and rumors about the enclave's men working as slave laborers in Serbian mines. The absence of the person has created an absence of knowledge for his family members. They have only the final images of the person either as he fled with the column or at the separation at Potočari from which to construct a conclusion to his personal history. The tension between those images and the images of the mass executions is enormous. For example, some of the women and children on the convoy of buses glimpsed hundreds of men with their hands behind their heads kneeling in the Nova Kasaba soccer field. Almost all of the survivors have seen the gruesome pictures from exhumation sites that appear regularly on television and in the newspapers. The twin absences prompt the families to seek not only the physical return of the missing person's remains, but also an account of his final moments of life. Imagination can torment them in this search, depending on which narrative they graft onto their own memories and experiences.

## FILLING THE GAPS OF KNOWLEDGE

For most of the Srebrenica cases, resolving absence—both absence of knowledge and absence of physical remains—depends on the intersection between memory and the results of genetic testing. In *Memory, History, Forgetting,* Ricoeur interrogates the "constitutive weakness" (2004:181) of testimony (memory) by juxtaposing it with documentary proofs, or what he calls "clues." The DNA-based identification process used to recover the Srebrenica victims' mortal remains operates along a similar dialectic: the family members' recollections represent testimony, while DNA profiles serve as documentary proof. I have argued that the identification process often succeeds because of the mutual dependence between the two. But at the moment of the family's encounter with the news of identification, the two sources of evidence are often an imperfect fit. Nor do they provide a *complete* account of the missing person's fate. As Bergson demonstrated, memory is neither a constant nor an all-encompassing representation of the past, and DNA evidence cannot bridge the gaps in knowledge about the missing person's experience of death.

Without a body and in the face of this crisis (absence) of knowledge, imagination has filled in where memory left off. This is the tragic conundrum of the Srebrenica missing. Despite the efforts of all those bound up in the identification network, there will always be gaps in knowledge. There will never be a complete rendering of those final moments of life and death that the victims experienced. The families have heard the survivors' stories, have seen over and over photographs of mass graves and even video footage of executions. Yet absence leaves crevices, which imagination fills. "The act of imagination . . . is an incantation destined to produce the object of one's thoughts, the thing one desires, in a manner that one can take possession of it" (Sartre 1961:177). While the surviving family members do not desire the violent ends they imagine for their relative, nevertheless, through imagination, they attempt to "take possession" of the missing person's fate, wresting it from the vacuum of knowledge forced on them by his absence.

That memory and imagination pave the way for the return and recognition of a person long absent from family and friends is a recurring theme in Western literature, and one that sheds light on how family members encounter the news of identification for the first time. The function of memory in such moments is perhaps most famously illustrated in Homer's *Odyssey,* when the hero tries to conceal his identity from Euryclea, the housekeeper, as she washes his feet. But Euryclea is not fooled by his disguise; she recognizes the scar on her master's leg. Her recognition leads to a long flashback, recounting how Odysseus received the scar as a child. In his analysis of this passage, Erich Auerbach focuses on how the phenomena are represented in a "fully externalized form, visible and palpable in all their parts, and completely fixed in their spatial and temporal relations" (2003:6). The "genius of the Homeric style" according to Auerbach lies in the poet's casting these phenomena (of both past and present) in a "uniformly illuminated, uniformly objective present" (2003:7). The housekeeper's memory of the scar, the story of the past injury, and the moment of recognition that passes between the two people all appear suspended in this present. Similarly, recognizing missing relatives through clothing or teeth or skeletal traces of injury triggers other recollections, which although fixed in time and space in the surviving family member's mind, nevertheless are experienced in the present moment. As one Srebrenica mother once told me, "Ten years passed and it's the same as if it was yesterday. But it wasn't ten years. *It was but an instant.*" She is certain that she will recognize her sons' clothes; their image will appear as if she saw them a mere moment ago.

Another famous (and true-life) story of return that helps us to understand how imagination, alongside memory, might act as a catalyst for recognizing the missing person's remains—and in turn, his death—is the tale of the sixteenth-century French peasant Martin Guerre.[12] In fact, the story is one of false return and false recognition, for it is not Martin who comes home after eight years to the wife and child he had previously abandoned, but another man assuming his identity, Arnaud du Tilh. With none of the modern methods of identification at hand to confirm or disprove his claim, Martin's family, friends, and neighbors in Artigat had to rely on their memories to judge whether this person was in fact Martin Guerre. But as Natalie Zemon Davis points out, the residents of Artigat had already prepared the way in their imaginations. "First of all, he was wanted in Artigat—wanted with ambivalence perhaps, for returning persons always dash some hopes and disturb power relations, but wanted more than not. Second, he came announced, predisposing people to perceive him as Martin Guerre" (1983:43).

In a similar manner, the families of Srebrenica's missing desire with obvious and extreme ambivalence the return of their missing relatives' mortal remains, and they are predisposed to believe in that return and to recognize those remains. As I described in chapter 4, often families feel an unspoken pressure to recognize recovered articles of clothing and personal possessions depicted in the color photocopies presented to them by the case managers. The family members' anticipation is aroused not only by the telephone call placed by the case managers about their upcoming visit to the family's home, but also by the images of mass graves that regularly appear in the Bosnian media.

The way in which family members react to the news of identification depends in part on what they have previously remembered and imagined. The documentary proof of DNA matches contends with different kinds of narratives—some built on memory and others supplemented by imagination. For some relatives, the sight of clothes on the color photocopy sheet leads to recognition, or more precisely, to "mnemonic recognition," consisting in the "exact superimposition of the image present to the mind and the physical trace, also called an image, left by the initial impression" (Ricoeur 2004: 430).[13] But is the superimposition of those images always correct?

> Upon this converge the presumptions of reliability or unreliability directed to memories. Perhaps we have placed a foot in the wrong imprint or grabbed the wrong ring dove in the coop. Perhaps we were the victims of false recognition, as when from afar we take a tree to be a person we know. And yet, who, by casting suspicions from outside, could shake the certainty attached to the pleasure of the sort of recognition we know in our hearts to be indubitable? Who could claim never to have trusted memory's finds in this way? (Ricoeur 2004:430)

Ricoeur refers to the pleasurable certainty inherent in recognition, but, in the case of the Srebrenica families, their responses to that certitude are much more complicated. Stripped of the context, the image of a recognized personal item might evoke fond memories, but given the significance of its recovery, the experience of viewing it only adds to the evidence of the missing person's death. Like the act of providing a blood sample, recognizing an article or recalling a specific physical characteristic makes the family members complicit in the identification process and, more specifically, in the acknowledgment of their relative's death.

Given that absence signifies both a spatial and temporal void, remembering, piecing together the imprint with an image, involves notions of place and time. Delaying a discussion of collective remembrances until the following two chapters, I wish to focus here on the individual act of recognition as one step in documenting the missing person's identification and personal history. Consider the recovered articles of clothing and personal possessions from the perspective not of the expert comparing antemortem and postmortem data, but from that of the family member who is trying to recognize her relative and, in doing so, discover the details of his death. Whether on paper or in person, viewing the personal possessions and clothing recovered with the remains often helps connect those remains—now entirely unrecognizable as bones without flesh—to the image of the missing person that the individual family member has harbored in her mind for the past several years.

Likewise, recollecting physical characteristics that match details found in the postmortem report helps link the story of missing relatives' disappearance and the story of their recovery. The two narratives begin to merge. For example, someone like Ešefa knows the pair of pants that she washed for her husband within the context of their life together in the enclave; when she recognizes them either in the color photocopy or at the PIP facility, she can connect the physical material exhumed from the mass grave as being the same cloth that her husband wore in the enclave and on the day of their separation in July 1995. The clothing thus acts as more than simply a "documentary proof" within the overall identification but as one piece of material remains that reappears along the disjointed time line of the missing person's life in the enclave, his flight or capture, and finally his execution.

During this same discussion, in which the family member begins to piece together the chronology of her relative's death, she also learns important information about the recovery of his remains from a particular gravesite, be it a surface grave in the forest or a primary or secondary mass grave. The officials working on the gravesite (representatives from the Federation Commission for Missing Persons, ICTY, and ICMP) have reconstructed certain aspects of the crime, as well as the events leading up to it. They have evidence to suggest, for example, the manner of death; whether the grave is secondary, and, if so, where the primary grave was located; and whether the men in the grave were captured in the forest or seized at Potočari. In most cases they are able to sketch chronologically and spatially the journey the victim made while still living and the journey his body made after his execution. Much of this information is new to families and, in the cases of the secondary mass graves, is highly disturbing as they learn the extent to which their relatives' mortal remains were mutilated and separated during the reburial process. Most family members ask about when the body was exhumed; often the date is disconcertingly distant, sometimes as far back as 1996. The case managers attempt to explain the long interval between the exhumation and this meeting by referring to the complex and time-consuming nature of the DNA analysis, but it is an awkward moment for both parties.

Although the information relayed during these meetings succeeds in removing at least some sense of the anonymity surrounding the relatives' execution and burial, it is limited in its capacity to displace the lingering fears (imaginings) that families have about their missing relatives' last moments of life. Some family members ask the case managers pointed questions about the condition of the recovered remains, the type of mass grave from which the victim was exhumed, or signs of torture, all in an effort to complete their relative's personal history. On a family visit with Emina, I looked on as the sister of the missing person sobbed uncontrollably upon learning the news of his identification. When she regained her composure, she expressed how deeply troubled she was by not knowing about her brother's final moments of life. While Emina recounted the details surrounding the exhumation of his remains, the young woman listened attentively.

She was, however, anxious to discuss one particular topic and with some trepidation sought Emina's permission to ask a question. She wanted to know if her brother had suffered in his death. She wanted to know if there was evidence that his hands had been bound or his eyes blind-folded. In this case, neither ligatures nor a blindfold had been exhumed with the body, and upon learning this, the young woman appeared visibly relieved. He was her younger brother, and they had been very close. The idea of his suffering had tormented her. Although the information disclosed in the conversation with Emina could never fill all the gaps in her knowledge of his final moments of life, it had relieved some of the devastation wrought by her imagined narrative of his suffering. When Emina broached the subject of bones missing from the skeleton, the sister immediately asked whether his head had been found. Emina and the other case managers told me later that this is a chief concern for family members—the presence of the skull among the skeletal remains. Case managers dread cases where the skull is missing because they know how disturbing that piece of information is for family members to hear and for them, in turn, to disclose.

## QUESTIONS OF ABSENCE

The absence of major bones implies brutality in either the manner of death or the conditions of the grave. In the case of a surface grave, it points to the possibility that an animal carried off parts of the remains or that the body lay exposed to the elements for months, even years. With the secondary mass graves, the practice of digging up and transferring the bodies with heavy machinery reminds family members of the Bosnian Serb "innovation" of violence. Either situation is especially distressing in light of Bosnian Muslim burial practices. The ritual handling of the bodies of the deceased and the timing and manner of burial have been egregiously violated.[14] Such desecrations throw into disarray the surviving families' responses to the death and, in turn, to the soul of the missing relative. In the Islamic tradition, Smith and Haddad observe,

> not only are the dead usually understood to be cognizant of the degree to which they are missed and of the ways in which their personal affairs are being carried out, but the carelessness of the washers and those who prepare and wrap the body in its shroud has been seen by some to cause anguish to the departed. Many anecdotes indicate that disrespect for the area in which a body is buried . . . as well as failure to care for the grave itself properly can cause extreme discomfort to its occupant. (2002:59)

Moreover, it becomes even more difficult for family members to ignore the implications of violation and desecration when they are faced with the absence of body parts, especially the skull. Witness DD described imagining her young son's hands, but a person's head and all that it entails—his face, his eyes, the full range of emotions expressed on these features—more than any other part of the physical remains, embody the character of the missing person. Absence of a skull makes the identification extremely traumatic if not impossible for some family members to accept.

The issue of partially recovered bodies has posed difficult questions for both family members and those seeking to identify the missing. In November 2004, representatives from the family associations and the institutions involved in recovering and identifying Srebrenica's missing convened to discuss the growing dilemma posed by the backlog of cases with DNA-identified partial bodies, the majority of which had been exhumed from secondary mass gravesites. This meeting represented a milestone within the overall process. ICMP and the Federation Commission for Missing Persons had succeeded in identifying most of the (relatively) complete bodies exhumed to date and thus faced a choice: should the partial bodies remain "on ice," as PIP staff figuratively termed it? That is, these remains could be held indefinitely while exhumations of the remaining mass graves continued. Or, should the organizations notify the families and allow them to decide whether to proceed with the burial or wait for the recovery of the remaining segments of the skeleton? It was a decision with important consequences. On the one hand, moving on to the partial body cases would accelerate the identification process; more families would learn the fate of their loved ones, even if that meant they gained only partial knowledge and incomplete remains. On the other hand, taking those incomplete sets of remains "off ice" would complicate the process in significant ways, particularly from a forensic standpoint.

The discussion had already begun several years earlier, when the members of the identification network attempted to define what constituted a (relatively) complete body. Drawing from commonly accepted forensic guidelines and theological advice from the Bosnian Islamic Community (Islamska zajednica), the forensic technologists at ICMP and the Federation Commission for Missing Persons established the threshold of 70 percent: if 70 percent of the skeletal remains had been recovered, they would contact family members with the news of identification. Three years after the advent of the DNA-based identification system, the time had come to consider how best to approach the growing number of identified partial remains.

Thus, the November 2004 meeting with the family associations revisited the 70 percent criterion. The family representatives unanimously voiced their preference for being notified when "even one bone" of their missing relatives had been recovered. The forensic experts expressed concern that burying partial sets of remains might hamper the identification of additional remains found afterward. This scenario was especially problematic for remains exhumed from separate mass graves, which were likely candidates for reassociation—a common occurrence among the Srebrenica cases. The more skeletal remains present and available for DNA testing, forensic anthropological examination, and antemortem-postmortem data comparison, the more certain the forensic technologists could be that all the bones belonged to the same individual. Uncertainty might require that remains already buried in the Potočari memorial center cemetery be re-exhumed for comparison and further testing. Dr. Kešetović voiced his concern that such procedures would only compound the distress already experienced by families of the missing.

In the end, the family representatives won out in their insistence on being notified of the identification of partial bodies, and shortly thereafter PIP case managers began to pull those cases off the shelves and to contact the families. However, because not all of the families were privy to this discussion and its resolution, in the early weeks and months of handling these new files, the case managers met with shock and sometimes anger. Enver likened this phase to the early days of DNA-based identification, when families were not as well prepared for the news or the evidence and therefore reacted to PIP case managers with hostility and mistrust, sometimes even blaming them for the news they brought. In the case of the partial bodies, one problem was that the diagram that case managers showed to family members depicted the *missing* (rather than the recovered) bones of the identified mortal remains. Senad recounted that family members turned to him in horror and asked, "Why have you even come to me?" It would have been easier, he explained, to inform the family about which bones had been found rather than which ones were still missing.

The phenomenon of an identified partial body raises several questions central to the notions of absence and identification within the context of the Srebrenica victims. What does "even one bone" of the missing relative's skeleton signify for the family? Does it help them respond to the dilemma posed by their missing relative's absence? How does it affect the way they conceive of his whereabouts? The location of the missing person's remains has extraordinary significance for surviving family members. Repeatedly I heard families of the missing say that they just wanted to know where their relatives' bones were and thus to have a place to visit and care for their souls. But what might this mean in the case of a partial body? Does discovering the whereabouts of a missing person's torso or skull mean that the person himself is no longer absent? Does a grave containing a mere fraction of the man's skeletal remains signify an absence or a presence within that space? "A gravestone is a sign whose silent presence marks an absence" (Ho 2006:20). The secondary mass graves and incomplete bodies of the Srebrenica victims, however, challenge the notions of marked absence and presence. Indeed, can one be partially found, therefore present, and yet, at the same time, partially missing, and still absent? Incomplete bodies complicate rather than distill our understanding of what constitutes presence (and absence) after the crush of annihilating violence.

The issue of partially recovered bodies also requires that we consider how the science behind the identification procedures frames the materiality of a human body. To what extent has a genetic profile, the microcosmic readings taken along the DNA strand—the "biological signature of the living" that "'testif[ies]' through [its] muteness" (Ricoeur 2004:174)—come to represent the missing person? As Mark Skinner, former director of ICMP's Forensic Sciences Division, once asked me, "How do we define identification?" Is it merely through technology's rubber stamp, which asserts its authority in reattaching an individual name to a set of mortal remains? Or is it the official acceptance on the part of the family of that technologically based claim—that is, when the mother of the missing son signs her name on the identification confirmation papers? Or, finally, is it when she watches his coffin being lowered into the grave at the cemetery in Potočari and can now, at least more fully, complete the temporal and spatial narrative of his final moments of life and death? As I learned from the families of the missing, answers to such questions come on an individual basis and sometimes not at all.

## DECISIONS OF BURIAL AND
## THE RETURN OF GUARDIANSHIP

The social experience of recognizing missing persons' remains through witnessed, sanctified burial begins with surviving families. Upon learning the news of identification, relatives of the missing find themselves in a position finally to determine the whereabouts of the recovered remains. Thus, the meetings between the case managers and victims' families end with a discussion about where they wish to bury their relatives. The families have the choice either to bury the body as a part of the collective funeral ceremony at the memorial center or to bury the body independently.

The vast majority of families wish their relatives to be buried with the "others" *(sa ostalima)*—that is, the other victims of the genocide—in Potočari. If there are multiple missing persons within the same family, the case manager explains the possibility of having relatives buried alongside or within close proximity to one another in the memorial center's cemetery. They instruct the family's contact person about the necessary paperwork that he or she must submit to the Federation Commission for Missing Persons, the local entity responsible for coordinating the burials at the Potočari cemetery. The families submit their requests even when a missing relative's remains have yet to be recovered and identified, thereby ensuring that a place, an empty plot next to or nearby other identified relatives, will be available for the person. Thus, families can ensure that brothers, fathers, sons, uncles, nephews, and cousins will eventually rest in the same general area, if not immediately beside one another, as the male side of the Srebrenica families is gradually reconstituted in the memorial center cemetery.

By ending the meeting on this point of discussion, the case managers initiate the transfer of authority over the missing persons' identification and the fate of their mortal remains to the families. This act reverses the flow of power that had initially made the refugees in the enclave subject to UN protection and, when the Dutchbat abdicated its responsibility to safeguard them, the victims of the Bosnian Serb aggression.

It reverses the flow of power that had reduced the victims' remains to nameless bodies and forced upon their surviving families the crisis of their absence.

After years of having no knowledge of or control over their missing relatives' remains, let alone access to their final moments of life and death, families can once again assume their rightful status as the most intimate guardians of the missing persons' remains and individual identity. The careful planning of the memorial center's cemetery counteracts the disorder of the mass and unmarked graves, and families participate directly in this final stage by imposing their own mark of order on the arrangement of plots. Concluding the meeting with the topic of reburial also causes a shift in perspective: although the news of the identification will invariably force family members' minds back to the horrific events of the genocide, they at least are able to envision the missing person's future existence within the context of his individual gravesite. Furthermore, the decision about where to bury their identified relative sets them along the path of finally being able to fulfill spiritual obligations to the deceased. A grave provides families with a space through which they can now interact with the souls of their dead through prayer, ritual, and remembering.

Establishing a place for the gravesite grants families new, though still incomplete, knowledge about their missing—now identified—relatives. The decision shifts the mode of the missing person's presence from the indefinite realm of hopeful imaginings and resigned conjecture to the fixed facts of place and statistical certainty of identity. The known gravesite provides families with a means to connect their memories of the missing relatives to the circumstances of their present lives. The memorial center and cemetery are the final home for the missing. Developing a relationship with this space constitutes the next step in this mode of presencing the missing, which I will consider in more depth in the following two chapters, about the commemorative ceremonies and mass burials that take place at Potočari.

But a grave still cannot answer all their questions, and although the troubling "somewhere" mentioned by Dr. Kešetović has been replaced by a specific location—a plot in a cemetery—the knowledge produced by identification will never entirely erase the family members' imaginings about the missing persons. Even though their remains have been physically restored through identification and sanctified reburial, the dearth of knowledge may continue to provoke families' imaginings, such as Witness DD's visions of her young son's hands picking strawberries.

There are, however, some moments in the families' lives when memory and imagination combine to ease them into this new period, which begins with the news of identification. I once accompanied a friend, a woman who had lost both her husband and younger son at the fall of the enclave, to visit her prewar home. She was in the process of reclaiming it, having already evicted the Bosnian Serb occupants. She gave me a tour of the inside. We walked through its empty, stripped spaces and paused in her missing son's room, where a vine had poked its way through the broken glass of the windowpane. We walked out onto the porch, whose painted wall still bore the outline of a cross, a marked vestige of the previous occupants' ethnicity, and she pointed to the picnic table in the overgrown garden below us. There, she explained, her family would sit in the summer afternoons.

As she locked the back door and we proceeded along the path around to the front yard, I heard her call out to someone. I turned my head in time to glimpse her waving good-bye. I asked her, *"Ima li nekoga tamo?"* (Is someone there?) Wiping tears from her eyes, she replied, *"Nema nikoga, sine"* (There's no one, child). In the windows both in front and in back of the house, she had placed the traditional Bosnian Islamic death notice, neatly trimmed with bright green paper. It announced the death of her husband, whose remains had been identified and buried in the memorial center a mere half a kilometer down the road. Despite the finality of his identification and burial, she invokes his and her son's absence each time she waves good-bye to them at her back steps.

CHAPTER 6

# Return to Potočari

Over dinner one evening in Sarajevo I spoke with a former classmate and some of his international friends about the July 11 commemoration ceremony at the Srebrenica-Potočari Memorial Center. One person present at the dinner was working at that time as a high-ranking administrator in a large international aid organization's headquarters in Sarajevo. Hearing that I was conducting research on the identification of Srebrenica's missing, he asked me if I didn't think the whole ceremony was a "circus." In his view, the families were being used and, as far as he could tell, they appeared to be conscious, willing participants in the manipulation.

Several months later, during the run-up to the tenth anniversary, I accompanied Hajra, Nura, and another member of the Women of Srebrenica to a commemoration organizational meeting at the memorial center foundation office. The room was packed with members of the organizational committee and reporters. At the head of the long conference table, several politicians sitting on the committee—including the SDA mayor of Srebrenica, Abdulrahman Malkić, and the head of the Federation Commission for Missing Persons, Amor Mašović—were discussing when to show a newly released documentary film on the Srebrenica genocide. Should it be screened the day before or the day of the commemoration? In the battery factory or elsewhere?[1] Who should view it? After several minutes, Nura stood up and said, "Speaking for the families, I would say it's not so important when or how this film is shown. The most important 'film' people can see is the sight of the coffins being buried in the cemetery that day. That's the best film for people to watch."

Nura's remarks paint a picture of the July 11 commemoration that is very different from the "circus" characterization offered by the aid administrator. He sees the families as willing pawns and the ceremony as spectacle; Nura acknowledges the performance aspect of the ceremony when she refers to the burial as a "film," but her statement is a compelling reflection of the seriousness with which the Srebrenica families approach the day and in particular the interring of the coffins. Far from being a "circus," the July 11 commemoration and mass burials are for them a meaningful and important occasion. How can one event elicit such divergent perspectives? And how has the act of identifying Srebrenica's missing contributed to this divergence?

The answers to these questions rest in the dual nature of the families' participation in the process of identification, which is both individualized and collective. In discussing the advent of the DNA-based technology and families' experiences of identification in the previous three chapters, I have stressed the individualized aspect. Having worked closely with families of the missing and the case managers of the Podrinje Identification Project, I have emphasized the routine, day-to-day procedures of DNA match reports and antemortem-postmortem data comparison, as well as the intimate encounters between case managers and family members. I have underscored the roles played by memory and imagination in producing identifications and in the families' reception of the news that their loved ones' remains have been recovered. Thus, the perspective I have presented so far is one primarily of individual experience. But as the remarks above demonstrate, the conclusion of the identification process—burying the recovered and identified mortal remains—for the overwhelming majority of families occurs in a collective setting and in a highly charged political atmosphere. Indeed, as we will see, the commemoration ceremonies and burials at the memorial center are massive events, involving tens of thousands of attendees, including top international and Bosniak officials, countless cameras and microphones, and, most importantly, hundreds of coffins interred on the same day. Why do almost all of the families choose to forego a more individualized, quiet event in a more familiar place for this collective funeral at a common burial site?

Their decision reflects a fundamental idea: the victims of the Srebrenica genocide were both individual and social beings. This is a defining concept for the identification process and one that shapes the social import of its results. These missing persons have names, birth dates, and hometowns; they belong to families, neighborhoods, schools, firms, and factories; they had different religious beliefs and politics; in their free time, they may have played soccer or gone fishing or played music with friends. Yet, on that fateful day in Srebrenica on July 11, 1995, such traces of their individual identity were effectively effaced by collective violence. Indeed, those men and boys were separated from the crowd at Potočari or captured from among the column fleeing through the forest because they were *identified* not as individuals but as part of a collectivity—that is, members of the perceived ethno-religious group of Bosnian Muslims. And they were killed, their bodies dumped into mass graves, for that same reason (Komar 2008).

In large part this accounts for why the overwhelming majority of the surviving families have chosen to mark the successful restoration of their missing relatives' remains not by individual graves scattered throughout eastern Bosnia but by a communal, commemorative space. There, they memorialize the tragic event of collective violence as much as individual lives lost. Plot by plot, they slowly reconstitute the male side of their families, creating a space that diminishes—if only for one day each year—the decimating effects of collective violence, namely death and dispersal. The specific location of the memorial center is significant, too. By establishing it at the former Dutchbat compound in Potočari and burying the remains of identified victims in its collective cemetery, families mark the space—*"the place where it all began"*—as the locus of the international community's abrogated pledge of protection.

As illustrated by the international aid worker's characterization of the ceremony as a "circus," however, the expectations of those involved—from the families of the missing to Bosniak political leaders and the international community—diverge widely. For the families, the identification process culminates in sanctified, witnessed burial of their individual loved ones. However, the place where this occurs, a public memorial complex dedicated to "martyrs" (a term I will explore in the following chapter) and containing a centralized cemetery, also provides a discursive space in which Bosniak political leaders attempt to forge a new nationalism, one based on blood spilled as much as on blood inherited.[2] These political narratives, in turn, confound international aims of social reconstruction and reconciliation.

Through an examination of the commemorative ceremonies and

mass burials that have been taking place at the memorial center, I explore those often conflicting assumptions about and responses to the results of the DNA technology. Much of this discussion centers on memory. However, whereas in previous chapters I have emphasized the individualized nature of such recollections (manifestations of Henri Bergson's notion of memory as action), here I will focus more on collective remembering. This shift requires a conceptual reorientation, seeing memory—its production, performance, and consumption—as communal commemoration. Dependent on social milieus, the "collective memory" (Halbwachs 1980) emerging from the Srebrenica-Potočari Memorial Center is profoundly shaped by religious and political discourses, some of which interpret recovery and burial in unexpected and at times contested ways. Such memory conforms to an increasingly standardized template of commemorating missing persons and mass fatalities that situates the individual victim within a collective category of national (or in this case, ethno-national) loss.

## SREBRENICA AND THE LEGACY OF YUGOSLAVIA'S MASS GRAVES

Burying the identified remains of Srebrenica's victims belongs to a long legacy.[3] Regardless of how families or international onlookers view the events of July 11, the politics of memory play an enormous role in the narratives cultivated in that space, and that memory extends well beyond the three and a half years of the Bosnian war. Amor Mašović's assertion that the Bosnian Serbs patented an innovation of violence that even the Nazis did not attempt overlooks an important and indeed parallel segment of Balkan history: the ethnic violence that occurred in Yugoslavia during World War II and its concomitant unmarked mass gravesites. Those graves provide an essential historical backdrop for understanding the Srebrenica-Potočari Memorial Center, its space and design, and, in particular, the mass burials of recovered mortal remains.

In her collection of essays *The Culture of Lies,* the Croatian writer Dubravka Ugrešić discusses the parallel strategies of memory used in nation-building:

> Terror by remembering is a parallel process to terror by forgetting. Both processes have the function of building a new state, a new truth. Terror by remembering is a strategy by which the continuity (apparently uninterrupted) of national identity is established, terror by forgetting is the strat-

egy whereby a "Yugoslav" identity and any remote prospect of its being re-established is wiped out. . . . The terror of remembering is, of course, also a war strategy of setting up frontiers, establishing differences: we are different from them (Serbs), our history, faith, customs and language are different from theirs. (1998:80–81)

In addition to drawing boundaries and establishing differences, another phenomenon falls within Ugrešić's description of the war strategy of remembering: namely, unearthing mass graves and reburying bones.[4] Obviously, forgetting and remembering mass killings and mass graves were not practices begun in the territories of former Yugoslavia in the 1990s—they already spanned centuries and continents. From the *Iliad* to Abraham Lincoln's Gettysburg Address, as classicist James Tatum writes, "mourning inspires the poetry of war as surely as its monuments" (2003:1). This is especially true of responses to the mass fatalities that characterized twentieth-century warfare (Winter and Sivan 1999; Winter 1995). One need only recall the Battle of the Somme, Bergen-Belsen, or Hiroshima to know that marking mass, anonymous death, including the very place of death (Hayden 1999), has become integral to processes of remembering and forgetting. But in trying to appreciate the social meaning of identifying Srebrenica's missing, we need to limit our scope and contextualize its most visible end result—that is, the memorial center and its collective cemetery—within former Yugoslavia's recent history. The period of World War II and socialist Yugoslavia through the 1980s relates most directly and critically to the ethno-national violence that brought about the Srebrenica genocide and the ethno-national discourse that dominates the way in which its victims are remembered.

The terror of remembering, as Ugrešić notes, was a war strategy utilized predominantly by Serbian and Croat leaders in the late 1980s and early 1990s as Yugoslavia began to unravel.[5] The classic and often cited example of the Serbian discourse of remembering is Slobodan Milošević's speech on June 28, 1989, at Kosovo Polje, in which he commemorated the six hundredth anniversary of the Ottoman defeat of the Serbian Army.[6] " 'Slobo' was revered by the masses as a hero and a saint. . . . His portrait could be seen on thousands of buses, next to images of Serbia's older heroes from the past (such as Karadjordje and Lazar). . . . Milošević had a clear message for other Yugoslav nations: 'Six centuries after the battle of Kosovo Polje we are again engaged in battles and quarrels. These are not armed battles, but the latter cannot be ruled out' " (Duijzings 2000:198).

Milošević understood the rhetorical power of the battle at Kosovo Polje: through it he could reference memories (what Robert Hayden has labeled "secret or hidden histories" [1994:167]) of much more recent violence—that of World War II.[7] From the Axis occupation in April 1941 to the Partisan (Yugoslav Communist resistance forces led by Josip Broz Tito) liberation of Zagreb in May 1945, Yugoslavia experienced widespread violence in which ethno-national, political, and religious identity often defined perpetrators and victims.[8] Croatian fascists (Ustaša) massacred Serbs, Jews, and Gypsies, and their Muslim collaborators in eastern Herzegovina and southeastern Bosnia carried out atrocities against Serbs. Serb royalists (Četniks), led by Draža Mihailović, killed Partisans and Muslims. And when the tide of power finally turned, the Partisans exacted retribution on the Croatian Ustaša, the ethnic Italians, and the remaining armed forces aligned with the Axis powers. By either executing them or forcing them to flee the country, the Communist-led Partisans effectively eradicated opposition to the revolutionary new state they envisioned for Yugoslavia.

Thus, rather than opening up dialogue about atrocities experienced by different segments of the population during the war, the Communist Party's successful consolidation of power in post–World War II Yugoslavia depended on silencing certain memories and selectively embracing others (Ballinger 2003:106). Under the banner of "brotherhood and unity" *(bratstvo i jedinstvo),* Tito cultivated a policy of national equality that nevertheless required a carefully controlled historiography of wartime events, for which he set the tone in his 1948 report to the Fifth Congress of the Communist Party of Yugoslavia (Komunistička partija Jugoslavije, or KPJ). In it, he dismissed the scourge of "Great Serbian hegemony" and bourgeois Yugoslav social order, instead lifting up the KPJ for its role in bringing about the "new Yugoslavia" and the "realization of brotherhood and unity of our peoples" (Banac 1992b:1085–1086). That realization entailed a strategy of forgetting: "As Communist rule entailed ideological control over the representation of the past, those horrifying events that would disrupt interethnic cooperation were not to be mentioned, except in collective categories, all 'victims of fascism' on one side, and all 'foreign occupiers and domestic traitors' on the other side" (Denich 1994:370). As Duijzings notes, in eastern Bosnia, this meant that monuments erected after 1945 to commemorate human loss, namely victims of fascism, would be located predominately in Serb villages, as well as in mixed Bosnian Muslim and Serb towns, including Srebrenica and Bratunac;

notably, none were placed in Muslim villages. When names of victims were listed, they were Serb names. Thus, the " 'ethnic' subtext" of the monuments clearly delineated which ethnic group (Serbs) had fought on the right side, and which group's victims (Muslims) merited no public acknowledgment (Duijzings 2007:148–149).[9]

But even as the Communist Party's institutional historiography attempted to banish certain events from the public eye and thereby diminish ethno-national claims to suffering or triumph, the very structure of the "Titoist compromise" of a socialist federation ensured that the country's organization according to territories would reinforce "national identities by making them the basis for the federal republics" (Verdery 1999:97; see also Hayden 1992b). Rising "inter-republican polemics" in the late 1960s and early 1970s, fueled by contentions over how the federal government should distribute economic resources to the various republics, fed into escalating nationalist movements (Banac 1992a; Donia and Fine 1994:180–183). Beginning in the late 1960s and especially after Tito's death in 1980, scholars and politicians in the different republics sought to revisit the KPJ-sanctioned history of World War II.

Memories of violence that targeted ethnic groups and debates over numbers of victims became increasingly instrumental in the years following Tito's death, especially concerning the "Ustaša-Četnik rivalry" (Ballinger 2003:111). During that decade of growing instability and the decentralization of state power, these debates became fodder for the political manipulations of nationalist leaders, who sought territorial as well as historical revisions in their efforts to forge new nation-states (Verdery 1999:95–97). Fear played a significant role in nationalist rhetorical strategy and, as anthropologists of former Yugoslavia have demonstrated, so too did dead bodies. "One of the most potent weapons for building nationalism seems to be the uncovering of (semi)hidden massacres" (Hayden 1994:172).

Arguments arose concerning the number of dead from World War II—particularly Serbs and Croats—and historiographers on each side struggled to establish, inflate, or minimize the number of victims on each side.[10] The Ustaša-run concentration camp of Jasenovac served as an especially contentious site of wartime history (Denich 1994; Hayden 1994, 1992a; Banac 1992a; Boban 1990). Croatian nationalists, including the future president Franjo Tudjman, downplayed the official Yugoslav historians' calculation of 600,000 Serbs killed there.[11] Tudjman claimed the number to be approximately 60,000, while Serbian estimates placed it as high as 1.1 million (Donia and Fine 1994:141). Hayden writes that for the Serbs the camp became a "metonym for the entire Ustaša campaign to eliminate the Serbs from Croatia. Arguments that attempt to minimize the number of victims at Jasenovac and to deny the ultimate evilness of the Ustaša campaign against Serbs ignore this metonym and are thus both offensive and ominous to Serbs, especially those living in Croatia now" (1994:177).

Fixing the number of victims of the World War II ethnic violence (such as those killed at Jasenovac) provided one plane for debate and contestation; physical remains offered up yet another, more visceral, means of reinforcing and recasting the victim-perpetrator narrative so vital to the political strategies of the nationalist leaders in the late 1980s and early 1990s. For example, in 1991 the exhumation of caves and ossuaries containing the remains of thousands of Serb victims of the Ustaša was broadcast on radio and television. The recovered bones took on a nationalist political meaning: "In August, a huge public funeral was held for what Radio Belgrade described as 'three thousand victims of the Ustaša genocide, whose bones were recently removed from ten caves in Herzegovina.' . . . The line of coffins stretched for one and a half kilo- meters; the liturgy was sung by the patriarch of the Serbian Orthodox Church, and speakers included Serbian politicians from Bosnia and Herzegovina, politicians from Serbia, and leading Serbian nationalist intellectuals" (Hayden 1994:179). Although the bodies remained name- less, the public and politically infused mass burial ensured that their presumed ethnicity was reascribed to them, becoming the primary focus of the commemoration and thereby reinforcing the narrative of Croats as perpetrators of genocide and Serbs as victims.

These debates and public commemorations form the historical back- drop of the Srebrenica-Potočari Memorial Center, whose collective cem- etery joined a practice of remembering and forgetting, and indeed strat- egies of nation-building, already well established in former Yugoslavia. In her book *The Political Lives of Dead Bodies*, Katherine Verdery writes, "Burials and reburials serve both to create and to reorder com- munity. . . . A (re)burial creates an audience of 'mourners,' all of whom think that they have some relation to the dead person" (1999:108). With the reburials of the late 1980s and early 1990s, "new, narrower, national communities" were formed, "as the group of participants has come to be monoethnic. . . . Burials bring people together, remind them of the reason for their collective presence—relatedness—but that relat- edness has now become ethnically exclusive" (1999:108).

In the case of Srebrenica, however, relatedness—what Jay Winter (1999) calls the "fictive kinship" that has characterized war's "agents of remembrance" since 1914—reflects the mixed, rather than exclusive, audience that convenes at the memorial center at Potočari each July 11. Because the genocide implicated not only Bosnian Serb and Serbian forces but also the UN, NATO, and Western governments, the intended audience at Potočari encompasses a pointedly multi- (rather than mono-) ethnic assembly. The fictive kinship that forms in the vast field of the Srebrenica-Potočari Memorial Center develops out of a complex intertwining of motives and responses—from grief to guilt, anger to empathy. And the Bosniak political and religious leadership uses the opportunity of the commemoration not only to address their Bosnian Serb and Serbian neighbors, but also to speak directly to the international community present among the diplomatic corps, aid agencies, and media representatives. As we will see, it appears to be an effective message: by participating in the events at Potočari, representatives from the UN community of states locate their position in the Srebrenica controversy safely on the side of the victims (Duijzings 2007:165). Thus, the diverse audience members gathered at the Srebrenica-Potočari Memorial Center for the annual commemoration and mass burials are connected not just through their support for and participation in the identification process, but also through the manner in which they relate to the genocide itself.

Foregrounding the memorial center events with the nationalist debates about World War II victims and perpetrators runs the risk of viewing the culmination of the identification process strictly in terms of political instrumentality. Certainly—as I will demonstrate at different moments in my description of the preparations for and events of July 11—nationalist and international political agendas help shape the commemorative activities and the very atmosphere of collectivity among the crowd of people at the ceremony. But nationalist politics are not the only, or the primary, impetus of meaning-making that follows from identification. While "dead bodies have posthumous political lives in the service of creating a newly meaningful universe" (Verdery 1999:127), these same dead bodies have personal, familial, religious, and communal lives that intersect and diverge at varying points in the experience of the mass funeral and burial ceremonies on July 11. It is because of such social ties that the identification of the missing elicits the wide range of responses from the people gathered at the memorial center on these occasions.

EARLY EXPECTATIONS: POTOČARI AND
ESTABLISHING THE MEMORIAL CENTER

On the road between Bratunac and Srebrenica, just past a cluster of
newly rebuilt houses on the right and across from the dilapidated factory buildings on the left, a stretch of land is cordoned off by a tall
iron fence with a stone entrance. Near the main gates, the bright blue
and yellow national flag of Bosnia and Herzegovina billows in the
wind—an unusual sight in the Bosnian Serb entity of the Republika
Srpska. Slowing down to look beyond the fence, you see a field half full
of earthen mounds capped with identical slender white tombstones.
This is the cemetery within the complex of the Srebrenica-Potočari
Memorial Center. It is the burial grounds for the victims of the genocide, the place to which the mortal remains of thousands of missing
persons will eventually return.

The creation of the Srebrenica-Potočari Memorial Center represents
a hard-won battle on the part of the surviving family members. Its
space also embodies the odd amalgamation of aesthetic tastes, impro-
vised religious practice, and the need for order imposed on a social and
physical landscape deeply scarred by genocide. The memorial center
is remarkable, first and foremost, as a spatial monument: it is a commemorative place established at the site where the crimes against the
enclave's inhabitants began and where the international community,
represented by UN peacekeeping forces, abrogated its pledge to deter
attacks against the safe area. Moreover, it was created in direct response
to the painful lack of knowledge about where and how missing family
members died, as well as where their mortal remains have lain while
still unrecovered. In this sense, the center's cemetery has become the
locus for the final stage of the identification process, providing a space
for the proper burial of recovered and identified remains.

In the years immediately following the end of the war, the notion
that surviving families could return to their homes, let alone bury the
remains of their relatives killed in the genocide, *in* or *near* Srebrenica,
was unthinkable. The political environment beyond the entity border
ensured that their only hope of even visiting the former enclave was on
a police-escorted and UNHCR-sponsored bus. Hajra Ćatić recounted
her first trip back to Srebrenica in 1999 in an article for her association's publication, *Bilten Srebrenica:* At the bus station, "several Serb
policemen were waiting for us. They informed us that we couldn't visit
our houses, but just walk around the city and maybe get copies of offi-

cial documents [personal documents such as birth certificates] from the city hall. . . . En route [to my street] the new inhabitants of my city cursed our Muslim mothers *(dobacivali i psovali balijsku majku)*, but we didn't pay them any attention" (Žene Srebrenice 1999:9). Despite such hostility, when plans began to surface for establishing a memorial center within the Federation in Sarajevo or in Kladanj (a city on the road between Tuzla and Sarajevo, far from the Drina River valley), leaders of the family associations began to voice both their objections and their demands.[12] They insisted that any memorial center must be located in the Srebrenica area. In the words of one family member, "My son was born in Srebrenica, not Sarajevo."

In a rare instance of consensus, the Tuzla-based Women of Srebrenica and the Sarajevo-based Mothers of the Srebrenica and Žepa Enclaves lobbied against the Kladanj site. The latter group conducted a survey of its members, reportedly collecting 2,000 completed questionnaires about the location and design of a memorial center for Srebrenica (Duijzings 2007:158; Nettelfield 2006:111; Pollack 2003a:189; Pollack 2003b:795), and the former group concentrated its efforts on winning over the support of the international community, specifically the Office of the High Representative (OHR), then led by Wolfgang Petritsch. In my conversations with members of the Women of Srebrenica, many also emphasized the integral role played by the Islamic Community in lobbying OHR on behalf of relatives of the missing. At a time when the surviving family members struggled against the conventional wisdom that the monument must be located in the Bosniak and Croat–controlled territory, representatives of the Islamic Community took their case to the international decision makers within the country.[13] The head Islamic leader in Tuzla, Mufti Husejn ef. Kavazović, recalled his first appearance before the assembly of American and other diplomats at a meeting about the location of the memorial center:

> They thought that a cemetery in Srebrenica would not be safe. I said to them, actually, I asked them a question—whether the United States would be able to guarantee that the cemetery in Kladanj would be secure, that nothing would happen, that no one would ever desecrate it. Naturally they said that they could not guarantee anything, and then I said that it is entirely logical for us that we seek that it be in the region of Srebrenica. And then the women from the associations—naturally they had probably already a developed position on that question—I think they preferred that it be there. . . . I think that in the discussion the decision was made to wait until the political situation in Bosnia and Herzegovina stabilized. And it was, I think, in that meeting in some way that the position was adopted

both by the families of the victims and the Islamic Community, and even, we can say, by the political structure of the Bosniak people.

At a June 2000 meeting, the Srebrenica Municipal Council took up the location of the memorial and cemetery. With its Bosnian Serb representatives walking out on the actual vote, the council unanimously agreed that the memorial and cemetery should be located in the Srebrenica municipality, but disagreement persisted about the exact place. Breaking the stalemate, Wolfgang Petritsch issued a resolution on October 25, 2000, to establish the memorial center and its governing foundation. Couched in the terms of authority derived from the Dayton Peace Agreement, the language of the resolution's preliminary clauses reflects the Office of the High Representative's intention not only to provide a site for burial, but also to extend the purpose of the space to fulfilling other political goals:

> Respecting the fact that the recognition of the inherent dignity and of the equal and inalienable rights of each and every human being is the foundation of freedom, justice and peace in the world;

> Out of the respect further for the solemn duty which falls upon the living to ensure the dignity and proper burial of the dead, and respecting the rights of the families of the deceased to bury their dead in accordance with their religious beliefs, a right which flows from Article 9 of the European Convention for the Protection of Human Rights and Fundamental Freedoms;

> Acknowledging with deep regret that the bodies of approximately four thousand of those who met their deaths as aforesaid and who were left without proper burial have now been exhumed yet still await burial in a proper and final place of rest, and that the bodies of an unknown number of further victims of the slaughter at Srebrenica remain to be recovered and exhumed from places still unknown;

> Concluding that further delay in determining the final resting place and a site for a memorial for those who perished in the aforesaid slaughter would be an affront to humanity;

> Conscious of the importance of establishing such a cemetery and memorial as a means of bringing reconciliation to the peoples of Bosnia and Herzegovina, which reconciliation will in turn promote the return of displaced persons and refugees and permanent peace . . . (Office of the High Representative 2000)

The resolution repeatedly emphasizes the memorial center's capacity to enable proper burial, and, as with many of the governmental structures born from the Dayton Peace Agreement, its justification is couched in the discourse of Western liberalism. The first paragraph cited ("Respecting the fact . . . ") invokes the ideals of "inherent dignity" and "equal and inalienable" individual rights. The reference to the right of families to bury their dead according to their religious traditions has no foundation in a specifically Bosnian text, law, or religious dictate; rather, it "flows from Article 9 of the European Convention for the Protection of Human Rights and Fundamental Freedoms." No mention is made of Bosnian Islamic practice. According to the resolution, proper burial (as a direct result of identification) will foster reconciliation—a term that even ten years after the genocide, many of the families of the missing utterly rejected—as well as return, and, even more hopeful, permanent peace.[14] Thus, from the first moment the memorial center was created, the international community, embodied by the Office of the High Representative, infused it with expectations of peace-building and social reconstruction. On March 31, 2003, when the first remains were buried at the memorial center cemetery, High Representative Paddy Ashdown echoed these hopes in his address: "For those who we bury, this marks a final resting place. For those who mourn, I hope this marks a milestone on the long road from grief to peace. And for those who watch, let this be a moment to re-dedicate ourselves to the ongoing struggle for truth, justice, reconciliation and recovery" (Office of the High Representative 2003b).

The funding of the memorial center also illustrates the vested interests of foreign governments eager to see progress indexed by terms such as *reconciliation* and *recovery*. A foundation brochure, published in March 2004, lists the top donor as "embassies," with a contribution of 5,054,730 KM, followed by "BiH governments/institutions," with 3,284,000 KM, and finally "private companies/personal donations," with 2,037,363 KM.[15] Many personal contributions came from a fund-raising campaign that took place during the summer of 2003.[16] The RS government contributed 2 million KM as the result of a suit filed by family members. The Human Rights Chamber for Bosnia and Herzegovina decided in favor of forty-nine family members of the missing in claims filed against the Bosnian Serb government. Brokered by the Office of the High Representative, the chamber's award for reparations entailed a lump sum payment—not to the families who filed the initial claims, but to the foundation of the Srebrenica-Potočari Memorial Center.[17]

In the October 2001 issue of *Bilten Srebrenica,* the Women of Srebrenica dedicated a page to the question *"Šta mislite o Memorijalnom kompleksu?"* (What do you think about the memorial complex?)[18] Members expressed a range of concerns and expectations:

> Džemila Delalić—The mortal remains should not be buried until the battery factory becomes a component of this complex.

> Nura Alispahić—A religious monument must be provided for in the composition of the complex.

> Rufejda Buhić—If they were killed, I want a grave for my son and husband in Potočari, and I think that the other mothers are of the same opinion, regardless of whether they [their relatives] are identified or not.

> Abida Omerović—In the composition of the memorial complex there should be several structures such as the following: a space where there will be displayed articles from our missing, a projection room, an archival room and library building, an office, restrooms, parking lot, lawns, souvenir shops, shops for books, audio- and videotapes, a religious monument, a central market, a main area for assemblies and longer-lasting visits.

> Nura Mustafić—The building of the memorial complex in Potočari is also connected to our return to those places. If there's no building [of it], there's no return. (Žene Srebrenice 2001:6)

The women's comments addressed several pressing issues concerning the memorial center about to be built at Potočari. Chief among them were the cemetery's design and the complex's facilities. Rufejda touched on a question that had especially troubled families of the missing: what would happen to those individuals for whom remains were never recovered and identified? As we will see in the subsequent chapter, the identification experts, the Islamic Community, and family representatives eventually determined that gravestones would be placed for all victims, regardless of whether their remains were recovered. Džemila's concern addressed not the individual plots in the cemetery, but the commemorative significance behind the center itself. For her, including the battery factory (the UN peacekeeping forces' compound) in the complex was crucial: without it, the story of international involvement would become conveniently excised from the physical plant and thus from explicit commemoration. The other women touched on the socio-

economic function and impact of the center, including return, as well
as its religious aspects. Though merely a sampling of the Srebrenica
families' opinions, these remarks illustrate how closely intertwined the
political, personal, religious, and social meanings of the space were
from the onset.

In conversations with returnees, members of the Women of Srebrenica, and families of the missing whom I met when researching the
identification process, repeatedly I heard the comment that the memorial center was to provide an enduring monument documenting the
scale and nature of the genocide. Mufti Kavazović explained how the
space was to help distinguish facts from myths:

> It is to show what happened. Thus, to show oneself, to show others,
> that someone is responsible for what happened. . . . I have said that
> for us it is very important that as soon as possible the truth is asserted
> and those graves should be opened up immediately. . . . This is very
> important because man is a creature who sometimes knows to create
> myths, to create myths from everything. Sometimes, naturally, a myth
> can be positive, right? But sometimes it can be very negative, such as
> the myth about Kosovo, about Kosovo Polje, and so on. For Bosniaks
> it is extremely important that it is *documented*, that they know the
> *facts* here, so that later one cannot make up any sort of negative myth.
> Rather, it is extremely important that we do it now, while we are living,
> and, as witnesses of all this, over generations we can transmit the right
> picture *(pravu sliku)*, so that later they will not imagine *(zamišljaju)* this
> picture, what happened, in what manner it happened, and so on. Because
> of this, indeed, perhaps because of *this,* it is important that it be exactly
> in Srebrenica.

The mufti fears that the human propensity to create myths around
certain events might distort what he considers to be the facts of the
Srebrenica genocide. Acknowledging that there are positive examples,
he nevertheless cites the Serb "myth" of Kosovo Polje (where Milošević
made his famous speech about the Serbs' defeat by the Ottomans) to
illustrate his point.[19] Through the memorial center, the swift exhumations of mass graves and identification of victims, and the testimonies
of witnesses, future generations will not be left to *imagine* the events
and how they occurred. Kavazović asserts that they will know the
facts; they will have the memorial center, with its 8,000 tombstones as
a physical testament to the events of July 1995.

Gradually developed over the following two years through collaboration between Bosnian and international consultants and architectural
planners, the basic layout and design of the memorial center satisfied

the families' requirements (as articulated by the leaders of the family associations such as the Tuzla and Sarajevo groups), as well as their advocates among Bosniak political and religious leaders.[20] The Office of the High Representative secured the property of the battery factory for inclusion in the compound, thus ensuring that the site of refuge and eventual deportation and separation would remain intact and accessible to the public, including the Dutchbat graffiti and UN insignia painted on the entrance of the driveway to the battery factory (Office of the High Representative 2003a). Within the gated compound on the eastern side of the road between Bratunac and Potočari, the cemetery was laid out so that the individual plots would slowly fill petal-shaped sections of land extending out from the center religious structure, the *musala*.

Just as the language of the Office of the High Representative's resolution called upon international ideals of human rights, so the complex's design reflected an already well-established tradition of monuments commemorating mass death: "In fact tens of millions of names came to stand as memorials, first in the hundreds of nineteenth century memorial parks that followed the founding of Père Lachaise in Paris in 1804, then on the battlefields of the American Civil War, and most dramatically on the millions of gravestones and vast commemorative walls of the Great War. Maya Lin's Vietnam memorial of names was, of course, born at Thiepval in the Somme" (Lacquer 2002:90).[21] From the cemetery full of individual graves to the series of stone panels bearing the names of each victim, the space would simultaneously memorialize individual lives lost and collective suffering. In the case of the stone panels, the Srebrenica memorial center would echo the stark, evocative tribute to mortality of other such war monuments, including the Vietnam Veterans Memorial, whose official list of dead structures its very design. The memorial's designer, Maya Lin, explained the power of the individual name in its capacity to remind and engage the onlooker:

> What then would bring back the memory of a person? A specific object or image would be limiting. A realistic sculpture would be only one interpretation of that time. I wanted something that all people could relate to on a personal level . . .
>
> The use of names was a way to bring back everything someone could remember about a person. The strength of a name is something that has always made me wonder at the "abstraction" of the design; the ability of a name to bring back every single memory you have of that person is far more realistic and specific and much more comprehensive than a still

photograph, which captures a specific moment in time or a single event or a generalized image that may or may not be moving for all who have connections to that time. (Quoted in Tatum 2003:4)

As with the Vietnam Veterans Memorial, passing row upon row of individual names creates the effect that "no single death is now any more or any less significant than any other. . . . visitors who come looking for one name are made witnesses to the sum total of all the deaths recorded there" (Tatum 2003:5; see also Sturken 1997:58–63). Furthermore, beyond personalizing the scale of mass fatality at Srebrenica, the list of the more than 8,000 names etched onto the stone panels would provide a direct, visual response to Bosnian Serb attempts to minimize, downplay, and even deny the killings that took place in July 1995. Like the Vietnam memorial, it would proclaim "that each one of its inscriptions is one too many" (Harrison 2003:139).

Surrounded by the stone panels listing the Srebrenica dead, the *musala* itself, an open-air prayer space, stands out architecturally, with its pyramid-shaped roof and striking mixture of materials (wood, marble, glass, and metal). It is there, in the *musala,* that the religious ceremonies take place. Nearby is a rose bed where a collective ossuary will someday contain the remaining unidentified bones of Srebrenica victims. Adjacent to the *musala* stands a smaller structure, a mausoleum *(turbe)* that shelters one of the many memorial stones bearing inscriptions paying tribute to the victims and the event. The compound also includes several fountains *(šadrvani)* and a place for ritual washing *(abdesthana).* When construction was complete, the foundation hired a grounds crew and guards to maintain the property. By the early spring of 2003, the center was opened to the public, and on March 31 of that year, the first mass burial took place in the memorial center cemetery. The coffins of six hundred identified victims were interred.

At the annual commemoration on July 11, 2007, a memorial room *(spomen soba)* was officially opened, creating the first installment of what will someday become the center's museum. Located in one of the empty battery factory buildings across the road from the cemetery, the memorial room houses a permanent exhibition displaying several profiles of missing persons. Black-and-white photographs of the missing accompany brief narratives about each person. In each glass case there is also a personal possession, an article recovered with the individual's remains, which the family donated to the exhibit.[22] Discussions about the museum's design and especially this exhibit brought together a mix of Srebrenica survivors and foreign advisors. The Dutch interfaith organization Interkerkelijk Vredesberaad (IKV) facilitated meetings between representatives of family associations and a delegation from the Dutch Herinneringscentrum Kamp Westerbork, a memorial and museum established at the site of the World War II concentration camp. Commemorative monuments (existing and planned) thus provided a forum in which Dutch activists and Srebrenica surviving families could engage in dialogue beyond that of the Dutchbat's role in July 1995.

PREPARATIONS

Four years and seven mass burials later, by July 11, 2007, a total of 2,908 individual sets of remains had been interred in the Srebrenica-Potočari Memorial Center.[23] The remains of an additional 166 individuals were buried in private plots by the victims' families, many of whom had returned to their prewar residences. All future mass burials for the Srebrenica victims will take place at the memorial center annually in conjunction with the July 11 commemorative ceremonies.

In the weeks and days leading up to these burials, both families and the staff of the various institutions involved in the identification and burial processes are caught up in a flurry of preparatory activities. For ICMP's Podrinje Identification Project (PIP) staff, this stage marks the conclusion of their direct involvement with the individual missing person cases for which families have officially confirmed the identification. While case managers remain available for families to answer questions regarding ICMP-related work on the cases, the Federation Commission for Missing Persons, in collaboration with the Islamic Community and the Foundation of the Srebrenica-Potočari Memorial Center, assumes responsibility for the funeral and burial arrangements. On the day of the commemoration, ICMP's staff members are present as observers rather than direct participants in the events at Potočari.

With the burial preparations under way, for the first time in the entire series of identification procedures, spanning almost ten years, the mortal remains of each individual are physically reunited with that human being's name: PIP staff members, consulting lists matching the name of the individual to the exhumation site number, now write in permanent marker the name of the missing person directly onto the white plastic body bag that contains his mortal remains. They then transfer the body bags to the custody of the Federation Commission for Missing Persons and the subcontracted private mortuary facility in Visoko, near Sarajevo, where the coffins are prepared. The mortuary staff assembles the *tabuti*—simple, unfinished pine boxes no more than five feet in length—in the open space of one of the facility's buildings.[24] In another workshop in the mortuary facility, they create small rectangular placards to be mounted on the foot of each coffin. As the body bags arrive from Tuzla, the Visoko staff empties the contents into the pine boxes. The first external Islamic marking of the *tabuti* occurs when green cloth is draped over and secured to the individual coffins.

Shortly thereafter, the individual identity of each set of remains is physically attached to the coffin itself. Etched in white lettering on the surface of the black plastic tag and typed onto a certificate mounted on the end of the coffin, this documentation represents the convergence of the two parallel tracks of the missing person's identity—as object of biotechnological scrutiny and as individual, social being:

JKP City Cemetery Visoko
Number: 1016
Visoko: 6/23/2005                         Bag number: GL3–002BP GL3–001BP
First and last name: XXX (YYY) ZZZ        ICRC: BAZ 912206–01
Date of burial: 7/11/2004
Place of burial: Potočari-Srebrenica Memorial Center
Parcel: M 5, row 14, gravesite 16
Time of burial: 1 pm
                                         Administrator for the interment

The numeric codes of the International Committee of the Red Cross (ICRC) and ICMP (as the "bag number") refer to the missing person's official existence while in the custody of the identification technologists. The Red Cross number has tracked the missing person from the very first day that his absence was recorded. In initial months following the end of the war, that number intimated the possibility that the person was traceable—that he might still be alive. When DNA technology became the driving force behind the identification process, the ICRC number came to represent another means of cataloguing an individual within the comprehensive list of the dead. The ICMP number (the bag number) indicates the place of recovery, the starting point of the physical journey traveled by the unrecognizable set of skeletal remains: from the exhumation site, to the shelves in the PIP mortuary or Tuzla salt mines, to the DNA extraction lab, to the pine box assembly in Visoko, and finally to the hollowed-out section of earth (parcel 5, row 14, gravesite 16) in the cemetery at Potočari. In this particular case, the ICMP number also tells a story about the missing person *before* his recovery. There are two numbers listed under "designation" or "bag number," each ending with BP, the abbreviation for "body part." The tag and the sheet both indicate that these two sets of mortal remains were exhumed separately though within the same mass grave (GL3).

Although both documents list the date of burial, the paper certificate provides a more detailed chronology of when the mortal remains arrived at Visoko as well as the precise time of burial. Taken together, these notations work to offset the utter lack of documentation of the missing person's death and the whereabouts of his remains for the past several years, superimposing a posthumous state of order that counters the physical decimation rendered by the secondary mass graves. Even the place of burial appears in a language of heightened structure: parcel, row, gravesite. The missing person's absence and identification are now conjoined through the explicit marking of time and space. Because these elements have been brought together in this manner (and are subsequently visible to family members), ICMP policy dictates that photojournalists must not capture images bearing the identification code numbers, such as those on the body bags. Eventually, the families will learn of these numbers—be it through identification paperwork or labels on the *tabut*—and ICMP wishes to avoid the possibility of upsetting families should they happen across an image of their missing relatives' remains laid out on an examination table or in a body bag on a mortuary shelf.

Of the two documents mounted on the *tabuti*, only one piece of information announces the missing person's identity as a human being rather than just a set of remains: the inscription of the person's last name, his father's first name next in parenthesis, followed by his own first name. These three words evoke the social, familial context of the individual's life at the same time that they reinsert the individual into the public spheres of documentation and commemoration (Scott, Tehranian, and Mathias 2002). To a person from the Podrinje region, the family name often provides a rough idea of the missing person's hometown. A quick scan of the list of the 600 individuals interred at the first mass burial at Potočari in March 2003 lays bare the insularity of the Podrinje villages, with rows of the same last name—nineteen men are listed with the last name Alić, seventeen with Mehmedović (three of whom are brothers, sons of the same father); and twenty-five with Salihović (including two sets of two brothers).[25] Many of these men would have lived in the same villages, perhaps even the same homes, as their fathers. Although changes in labor patterns and education had resulted in the decline of the practice, up until World War II, Bosnian Muslim villages were organized primarily according to patrilineal-based households (Bringa 1995:41–43; Lockwood 1975:59–64).[26]

The annihilation and displacement of the Podrinje region's Bosniak men further altered the face of this order. Indeed, many of the fathers listed on the black plastic tags may well have been victims of the same massacre and will find their resting place alongside their sons, grandsons, and nephews in the Srebrenica-Potočari Memorial Center. As the victims tried to escape, some anticipated this very danger. The men who fled the enclave through the forest were often traveling with members of their own villages. Survivor Mevludin Orić started out together with his family and neighbors. "The entire male population of his village marched together. . . . Each family faced a dilemma. If they walked together, one shell could wipe out every male member of the bloodline. After a few miles, Mevludin let his father and [half-brother] drift away. He thought it was better if they walked in separate groups" (Rohde 1997:190). The lists of the identified, as well as the names attached to the coffins, attest to the fact that indeed many families from the Srebrenica enclave lost multiple male relatives in the massacre.

The two spheres of existence—the missing person's identity as an object for technological resolution and its meaning for the family members—collectively become the external signposts for the remains housed within the coffin. These identifying markers distinguish each coffin from its counterparts—the identical wooden boxes draped in bright green cloth and awaiting transport to the memorial center at Potočari. The transformation is under way; the *tabuti* have replaced the anonymous confines of both the unmarked graves and the white plastic body bags, wrapping each set of mortal remains in the mantle of ethno-religious practice.

## JULY 9: TRANSPORT AND TRANSFER

On Friday, July 9, 2004, two days before the mass burial, the Visoko City Cemetery staff loaded the 338 coffins onto several trucks, and the column of vehicles embarked on the daylong trip to the Srebrenica-Potočari Memorial Center. This journey was the final stretch of the circuitous homecoming that the remains had traveled since being unearthed from their respective unmarked graves, transferring their custody from the experts to the Srebrenica community and its individual families. Relatives of the missing and others gathered at the facility to bid the convoy farewell. It then wound its way through the capital city of Sarajevo, stopping briefly before the building of the presidency, where officials, including then chairman of the presidency Suljeman Tihić, emerged to pay their respects to the identified victims of the genocide. Even before arriving at the memorial center, the remains had thus become objects of political discourse, and, more cynically, political gain, among the Bosniak leadership within the Federation. With the scenes before the presidency recorded by the media, the convoy, flanked by security escort vehicles and personnel, continued on the road to Kladanj, where it would finally leave Federation territory and enter the Republika Srpska.

At this juncture in the journey, place—the coffins' destination and how they were temporarily stored—became the signature feature of their return to Potočari. Once the convoy arrived at the memorial center, the trucks pulled in behind one of the buildings of the battery factory, and the official transfer of the bodies into the hands of the Srebrenica community began. The moment was at once intimate and public, with families of the victims, returnees, members of the family associations, members of the Islamic community, and an entourage of media representatives all present for the convoy's arrival at the memorial center. A group of men and boys began to unload the coffins from the three trucks into the warehouse. Shortly thereafter, an informal religious ceremony began. Back against the far wall of the empty gray warehouse, which was slowly filling up with the coffins, the young imam of Srebrenica had gathered family members—almost entirely women—together for *tevhid*. Bringa explains that "*tevhid* is the most formalized ritual in which congregational prayers are said on behalf of the dead. . . . [It] is held five times following the death of any individual, male or female, usually in the house of the deceased" (1995:187, 188).[27] The first *tevhid*, thus, would traditionally take place in a private space, rather than in a physically nondescript, public building such as this warehouse. But the transport to and storage of the coffins in the battery factory compelled a change in religious practice. There, the women and a few small children knelt on the concrete floor in a circle around the imam, reciting aloud the prayers with upturned palms. Photojournalists drew close to capture the image of their figures bent in prayer, documenting the impromptu service inside the dimly lit warehouse.

To the backdrop of the hushed voices reciting the prayers, the silent procession of coffins continued. With one person on each end, individual *tabuti* proceeded at a steady but unhurried pace into the warehouse and were set gently on the floor in line with those already resting there. Two young men then worked their way through the rows, adjusting the coffins' positions on the floor so that they stood in perfect symmetry, making sure that the newly established physical order was unblemished. Outside at the trucks, the ease with which the men pulled the coffins off the vehicles' shelving and handed them to the outstretched arms below did not escape the onlookers' notice. Women remarked wistfully about how the coffins were so light, too light, in fact, because they contained only bones. Given the modest weight of each coffin, the men and boys worked without pause. Gradually the right-hand side of the building began to fill up with evenly spaced rows of the green *tabuti*.

The orderly placement of the coffins and the explicit, external identification mounted on each allowed the families to undertake their own search for their recovered relatives in a systematic fashion. Once the *tevhid* prayer had concluded, some people began to look among the coffins for their relatives, friends, and neighbors. Many present had come specifically to receive their relatives' mortal remains finally returned to them. People stooped over the ends of the coffins as they walked, straining to read the names written on the black plastic placards mounted on each. Unlike the scenes at the exhumation sites, where mothers standing at the grave's edge tried to discern the colors and material of clothing that could be their sons', here the families relied not on their own recollections but on the official labels. Those coordinating the unloading of the trucks asked the family members to wait, to keep clear of their path, promising that they would have ample time to search more completely when all the coffins had been removed from the trucks.

When a coffin of a relative was recognized, the entire assembly of people in the warehouse turned their eyes, if only for an instant, to the emotional reunion. The most poignant example of this occurred when one of the men carrying the coffins gestured to an older woman standing nearby; she rushed over, placing her hands on the green cloth of the *tabut* and crying out in anguish. In her wake, several other family members, including some small children, followed. Once the coffin was placed on the floor, the family members gathered around it and wept. The body was that of the woman's husband, and the man who had gestured to the woman was their son. I was standing among a small cluster of women at the time, and, watching the scene unfold, most

FIGURE 10. The return of the coffins *(tabuti)* to the former UN peacekeepers' compound, July 9, 2004. Photo by the author.

of us began to cry—even a veteran journalist who had been covering Srebrenica since the war began. The wailing made others look away uncomfortably. Bringa notes that loud crying in the presence of the deceased is seen as a kind of emotional pollutant (1995:185).[28] Again, the unusual circumstances under which these men and boys had been killed, and their delayed recovery, profoundly affected how families reacted to the sight of the coffins. The scene also grabbed the attention of media representatives. A local reporter and returnee to Srebrenica recorded the sounds for a piece he would broadcast on a Radio Free Europe program that afternoon in which the disembodied wail (like the emblematic images of grief-stricken women in *dimije* and head-scarves) would foreshadow representations of the emotionally charged commemoration ceremony two days later.

The political significance of the event continued to be well documented by the media. A local Stranka demokratske akcije (SDA) politician bent close to one of the coffins, which contained his father's remains. Even though he had sought refuge in the corner of the building to cry in solitude, a color photograph of him crouched low with

FIGURE 11. Media coverage of the coffins' arrival at Potočari. Photo by the author.

his hands covering his face would appear the next day in the newspaper *Dnevi avaz* (Hadžić 2004b). The personal encounter with his father's remains—the moment in which his father's body was physically returned to him—fed into a larger political objective on the part of the SDA-backed publication to portray him for a public audience as both victim of and advocate for Srebrenica. With the municipal elections only three months away, his personal grief made for good publicity—regardless of whether he had intended the exposure.

Amid the religious, political, and communal responses, that afternoon in the cool, dark space of the warehouse, individual identity recovered from among tens of thousands of blood and bone samples found its most powerful, immediate meaning among the family members, friends, and neighbors. At long last, they read the names on the coffins and remembered the people whom they once knew. Thus, the fastidiously maintained structure of anonymity guiding the DNA-based identification procedures finally succeeded in restoring personal identity and rendering nameless remains recognizable to those most intimately connected to the process. With relatives' hands resting on the *tabuti*, the missing persons' memory and remains once again occupied a recognized social and physical space among the community of Srebrenica survivors.

## JULY 10: ANTICIPATION AND DISAPPOINTMENT

This first encounter between the victims' remains and the small gathering of surviving relatives and returnee community members was only the beginning of the communal activities of remembrance that would take place over the next forty-eight hours. As the number of participants grew, the scope of the events shifted, reflecting the converging interests involved in commemorating the genocide and its victims. On July 10, however, the main focus of the activities still centered primarily on Srebrenica's surviving families and the returnees to the region, rather than on politicians or representatives of the international community.

In the early evening, people once again assembled at the memorial center—this time across the street, inside the gated complex—for final preparations, as well as for a more formal evening prayer service with readings from the Koran, followed by the screening of a film produced by the Federation Commission for Missing Persons, *Marš smrti* (March of Death). As people began collecting near the covered prayer space, the *musala*, the Visoko mortuary crew continued to work in the cemetery off in the distance. The holes of the empty graves pocked the field's surface, and shovels lay on top of the mounds of soil piled high beside the open pits, ready for the next day's burials. As dusk fell, a warm breeze sharpened the already pungent smell of the freshly dug earth, and the odor filled the air around the *musala*. Transporting the 338 coffins from the battery factory warehouse across the street, the reloaded trucks backed in through the main gates, where once again men lined up to carry the green *tabuti* to the covered space beneath the *musala*. Three small boys rushed up to the truck, excitedly awaiting their chance to carry one of the coffins. Too young to understand the contents of those pine boxes or what had happened to the people whose remains were now housed inside them, they rejoiced in completing the task, in demonstrating their strength and maturity. When I later mentioned this scene to Nura, she said that the boys' families had probably told them what an honor it was to carry a coffin. Once all 338 *tabuti* were lined up in symmetrical rows under the *musala*, the religious ceremony began. In contrast to the day before in the battery factory, men and women prayed in the same space, ordered in two concentric semicircles around the clerics.

The peaceful, reflective mood that filled the memorial center that evening gave no hint of the emotionally charged atmosphere that would pervade the space a mere eighteen hours later, when more than 20,000 people would gather inside its walls. The night before the July 11 commemoration, the Srebrenica community assembled in relative isolation in the memorial center, participating in a religious ceremony and contemplating the fate of their missing relatives. Most members of the media had already left, as there was little newsworthy in the quiet scenes of the prayers. In contrast, the intensity of the next day's events would sweep up participants and onlookers in the official ceremony, one guided primarily by public acts of commemoration rather than the more private rituals of remembrance that marked the evening of July 10.

Later that evening in Srebrenica, I sat with a group of women who were struggling with a keen sense of disappointment and loss. Drinking coffee on the back terrace of a returnee's house, the women drifted into a long discussion about life in the enclave and the events of July 1995. I listened to Rufejda, a woman in her late fifties who had recently returned to her prewar home outside of Milići, talk about her missing family. Her head covered with a scarf tied snugly beneath her chin, Rufejda looked older than her years. She held a cigarette in her left hand, propped up on the plastic lawn chair's armrest, and would move it, as if tapping lightly against a wall, to underscore whatever point she was making. She lingered over the cigarette while she talked, letting the smoke waft up from her raised arm, as if she were more interested in watching it burn down to the filter than actually smoking it. Her calm expression stood in stark contrast to the stories she was telling.

Rufejda spoke of her home, the house that she had begun to reconstruct. She reflected on its relative emptiness and the solitary life she now led. As with many of the widowed women survivors, one of the disheartening facts of her postwar life is that she has no one to cook for. Her labors in her recently reclaimed home—the piecemeal improvements she attempts, having been repeatedly denied a donation to reconstruct her house—were a constant reminder of the irreparable void in her life: she is missing both her husband and son, who was in his early twenties when the enclave fell.[29] She explained that everything she and her husband had had in their house (plundered after their flight) and everything that she now worked so hard to fill it with would have been for her only child, her son. She last saw him at the fall of the enclave, in the panicky, uncertain moments of flight. He had wanted to stay with her. Recounting these last minutes together, she lingered over the description of their parting and his words to her.

Prompted by the circumstances and events of the day, sitting there on the terrace of her friend's home in Srebrenica, Rufejda pored over her memories of her son. But she also circled back to the topic of his and his father's absence and the ways in which she tried to commemorate their lives through her religious practices. Rufejda described how she gives money each year to the Islamic community so that at *kurban-bajram* they will sacrifice sheep in the name of her son and her husband. She also gives money so that they will be named in prayer by the members of her mosque. Pausing a moment, she then said, *"Šta će biti kad umrem? Niko ih neće spomenuti"* (What will happen when I die? No one will mention them.) No one will remember them or remember to say prayers for them. Rufejda understood that with her death, the specific, intimate memory of her family—her husband and only child—will also die because, despite her attempts to make them shared through her participation in her religious community, they exist primarily in her individual recollections. Thus, she consoled herself with the notion that at least through their eventual burial, they will endure within a collective setting, souls remembered by the Srebrenica community and its descendants.

# CHAPTER 7

# 'That you see, that you know, that you remember'

While tombstones are mostly signs of absence, and mostly silent, at times of pilgrimage they are noisy with the sounds of many presences. Movement makes all the difference. We cannot understand the grave, the destination, without paying attention to the journey beyond it.

Engseng Ho, *The Graves of Tarim*

Strictly speaking, the graves at Potočari are not destinations of pilgrimage, but the journey behind and beyond them helps us to understand why identifying Srebrenica's missing is so meaningful to so many people. In examining the processes of innovation and recognition in the past several chapters, I have attempted to unfold the journey leading up to this final place, the graves in the cemetery at the Srebrenica-Potočari Memorial Center. In this chapter I turn to the events of commemoration and burial to explore how names etched onto wooden and stone markers remind the present of those absent, drawing people into expressions of remembrance that have multiple meanings and audiences.

As with the tombstones described by Engseng Ho, "many presences" are assembled at the Srebrenica-Potočari Memorial Center on July 11. They come to partake of and witness the creation of new graves alongside recently dug ones. It is the largest postwar annual commemorative event held in the country: tens of thousands of people convene in the fields in and around the memorial center to remember the crimes and their victims. At once an occasion for ritualized and impromptu remembrance, the July 11 activities have evolved with the advances in the identification technology. DNA analysis has successfully identified more than 3,000 of Srebrenica's missing, and the ceremony now centers on the mass funeral and burial of the most recently identified sets of mortal remains. In this sense, each July 11 commemoration frames its message of remembrance—*Ne Zaboravimo* (Let Us Not Forget)—with the names of individuals recovered and reburied. The message is also profoundly shaped by Bosnian Islamic theology and practice, whose rituals guide people through the funeral and burial events at Potočari. The families of the identified victims travel from all over Bosnia and, in some cases, from far corners of the world to witness the consecrated interment of their relatives' bodies. They are joined by Srebrenica's extended community and by visitors from postwar Bosnia's different religious, political, and social spheres. The convergence of Bosniaks, international representatives, and the media for these occasions also elicits responses from the Bosnian Serb public. And, as I will demonstrate, some of those responses directly challenge the narrative of Serb criminality and Bosniak victimhood articulated through the prayers, speeches, and, above all, the mass burials at the memorial center.

The July 11 ceremonies held at Potočari are collective events that seek to build order from the chaotic experiences of the war and the genocide at Srebrenica. But order is an elusive idea in a place such as Srebrenica, whose shifting layers of community and hierarchies of suffering and entitlement preclude a uniform response to the absence of more than 8,000 individuals. Earlier, I emphasized how identification technology has gradually reordered sets of mortal remains and pieced together details of the missing persons' final moments of life and death. Here, in my descriptions of July 11, I mean to contrast the notions of restoration and knowledge production with the "movement" filling the memorial center and its cemetery. For although a physical order emerges with the carefully marked *tabuti*, the mixing of people, words, and actions at Potočari on this day suggests that the "newly meaningful universe" (Verdery 1999:127) actually encompasses a rather messy, and at times awkward, confluence of responses to Srebrenica's missing.

The first July 11 funerals *(dženaze)* for the Srebrenica victims—in absentia—took place in the Federation. On that day in 1998, people gathered in Kladanj, and in 1999 services were held both in Federation territory (in Vogošća) and in the Republika Srpska at Potočari. At the latter site, approximately 300 people assembled for the service, defying the threats and insults of hostile Bosnian Serbs whom they encountered along the roadside as they traveled through the entity and past Bratunac. From that year on, the commemorations were held in Potočari. On July 11, 2001, the marker stone for the Srebrenica-Potočari Memorial Center, a three-ton block of white marble inscribed on all four sides with the words *"Srebrenica juli 1995"* was laid at the site. The following year, foreshadowing the identifications and mass burials of 2003, a model headstone (*nišan*) was unveiled at the annual ceremony. The seven commemorative ceremonies and mass burials (March 31, 2003; July 11, 2003; September 20, 2003; July 11, 2004; July 11, 2005, July 11, 2006, and July 11, 2007) have followed a similar format, combining public addresses with religious ritual and musical performance. Each concluded with the interment of the coffins by individual gatherings of families, friends, and clerics at the gravesites.

In the analysis that follows, I draw on experiences of these commemorations and burials, emphasizing the July 11, 2004, annual ceremony to extend the discussion begun in chapter 6 about the preparations leading up to the day's events. Periodically, however, I also focus on the tenth annual commemoration because of its heightened meaning for Srebrenica's survivors and the ways in which it differed from other July 11 ceremonies. Throughout this analysis of the past commemorative events, examples of political discourse, religious practice, and intimate encounters help portray the dynamic space of the memorial center and illuminate the graves themselves as important sites of meaning-making for the extended community of Srebrenica.

## BOSNIAN ISLAM AND SREBRENICA'S MASS FUNERALS AND BURIALS

The acts of commemorating and interring Srebrenica's victims both follow and improvise on Bosnian Muslim burial practices. They attempt to reconcile the circumstances of the genocide—anonymous death, sacrilegious burial, and the defilement of both individual identity and physical being—with the return of mortal remains through a consecrated and witnessed funeral service. On the one hand, much of the improvisation involves the individual families: their decisions about whether to bury their relatives in the memorial center cemetery, who will be (is able to be) present at the graveside, and whether, where, or how they will conduct the subsequent *tevhid*. On the other hand, the Bosnian Islamic Community (Islamska zajednica) has responded to the devastation of genocide through more than just counsel and prayer: it has been asked to consult Islamic law to make sense of Srebrenica's aftermath—that is, the chaos of the secondary mass graves and the disturbing truth that many of the missing will never be recovered.

In developing a theological response to Srebrenica, the leading

Bosnian Islamic clerics have advised the memorial center foundation, surviving family members, and the identification commissions regarding how Sharia law applies in the extraordinary conditions of the Srebrenica victims' mortal remains. At the only public forum to have taken up the issue formally, the March 2003 roundtable discussion entitled "Srebrenica, between Truth and Justice—Memory and Hope," the Tuzla mufti Husejn ef. Kavazović set forth the Islamic Community's conclusions based on Sharia texts. At the core of this set of doctrinal guidelines lies an important claim for social membership that applies to the general category of Bosniak victims of the Srebrenica massacre: "It is an undoubted fact that those who were killed violently were Muslims, whose faith was Islam."[1] In this religious position, the victims' ethnicity as Bosniak signified their religious faith (Islam), even though some individuals may not have actively practiced the religion. Indeed, some may have considered themselves—brought up during the Yugoslav era of *bratstvo i jedinstvo* (brotherhood and unity)—communists and, therefore, atheists. In their posthumous life, however, according to the Islamic Community, they are Muslims and their mortal remains require proper funeral and burial services as such.

But in order to carry out those proper rites, the Islamic Community first had to address the definition of *missing person* and its religious implications: Kavazović explained that "Sharia law considers a missing person as a person who went missing for some reason and for whom we do not know the current whereabouts or their status: whether they are alive or dead. . . . Bearing in mind the circumstances leading to mass executions of Muslims from Srebrenica and Žepa, which are confirmed by the verdicts of [the] ICTY, as well as the discovery of mass graves, it is assumed that the victims who are still missing are presumed to be dead" (Kavazović 2003). The Tuzla mufti thus supported this particular position through a striking amalgam of judicial precedents (from an extraterritorial, international court) and Islamic law. Finally, according to the Islamic Community's reading of the Hanbali legal school, persons who go missing during circumstances of war "would be considered dead if more than four years had passed after their disappearance."

The Islamic Community also had to craft a theological response to the *physical anomaly* presented by the Srebrenica remains—their location in mass and surface graves, the process of exhumation and subsequent storage in body bags in the Tuzla salt mines and mortuary, and so on. This meant first interpreting their posthumous significance in relation to the violence of July 1995. At the roundtable discussion, Mufti Kavazović explained that the victims of the Srebrenica genocide would have the status of *šehid* (martyr), and therefore the "whole Muslim community has a permanent obligation toward them."[2] Applying the term *šehid* to the Srebrenica victims was by no means an anomaly; rather, both during and after the war, Bosniak political, religious, and military leaders used this word to refer to an expansive category of Muslim dead—from soldiers to civilians, men and women, heroes and victims—a practice that over time effectively diluted its religious meaning and dismantled hierachies of victimhood (Bougarel 2007:175–180).

Yet in the Tuzla mufti's presentation at the 2003 roundtable discussion, the religious meaning behind the term was explicit and, as such, it determined the religious practice to be accorded both recovered and unrecovered remains of the Srebrenica missing. To begin with, by designating them *šehidi*, the Islamic Community supported the position that funeral and burial costs should fall to the entire community rather than the individual families.[3] Furthermore, according to Kavazović, their bodies are not required to undergo the "usual cleansing ritual nor will the remaining clothing be removed from them," because they (the victims as martyrs) are themselves considered clean. This claim resolved the dilemma posed by the conditions of the skeletal remains as objects of exhumation and identification. The remains are washed by identification technologists but not according to religious practice, and clothing recovered with the bodies or body parts is likewise washed and dried, but stored separately from the remains during identification procedures.

Mufti Kavazović then turned to the material and spiritual quandaries presented by the secondary mass graves. He posed three questions: How should the burial of unidentified recovered remains be approached? How should the burial of small, commingled body parts incapable of reassociation be handled? Should there be gravesites for victims whose bodies will never be recovered? In each instance, Kavazović emphasized the importance of ritual burial—be it a grave marked by an individual tombstone or bones of multiple persons buried within a collective tomb. In the case of both *identified* complete and incomplete bodies, the Bosnian Islamic tradition requires that the remains be interred and marked. "In the tradition of Bosnian Muslims, the grave should be marked by a *'nišan'* tombstone on which is written the identity of the dead person. . . . The same treatment should be used for incomplete body parts for which the identity is known. They should be treated as complete bodies even when the funeral prayer is conducted as well as for marking their grave."

Kavazović justified these instructions by reminding his listeners of the commemorative—rather than strictly religious—obligations they have toward the victims, obligations that stem not only from Srebrenica's recent past but, more generally, from Balkan history:

> Muslims in BiH were several times victims of crimes committed by neighboring people. The majority of those victims remained unmarked and were successfully covered in the last two centuries. . . . For the first time in Bosniak history, by the verdict of an international court, the acts of the crime of genocide committed against Muslims in BiH were confirmed. This fact gives the right to take a step forward, showing the world the centuries-long killing in those areas. Putting a tombstone for each victim of the Srebrenica tragedy is an issue of our debt toward him or her. If the world couldn't or didn't want to protect the victims, we should not allow them to be forgotten. In the act of placing tombstones, I don't see any obstacle from the religious side, bearing in mind the intention to prevent the [forgetting] of the victims, as well as on the side of the crimes. (Kavazović 2003)

In the final words of his presentation, Mufti Kavazović emphasizes the need to identify and remember the victims through physical gravestones and the rituals of funeral and burial services. In doing so, he claims, the Bosniak community addresses crimes and omissions not only of the recent violence, but also of violence from the past two centuries, including, presumably, Muslims killed in World War II who were not recognized through public monuments because they did not belong to the category of "victims of fascism."

The theological guidance provided by the Islamic Community has determined important aspects of the cemetery's design and the burial procedures on July 11. First, the position articulated by the Tuzla mufti supported the longer-term resolution for recovered remains incapable of reassociation (with the rightful set of mortal remains) or of identification: the collective ossuary that now serves as a rose bed in the memorial center. Second, according to Kavazović's presentation at the roundtable, the identification of the victims as Bosnian Muslims has determined the material religious marking of the coffins and both the temporary and permanent grave markers. As I indicated in the previous chapter, a sheet of green cloth covers each of the coffins to be buried at Potočari. Furthermore, all temporary wooden markers (bašluci) placed at the head of the individual gravesites were green in color, and etched above the black plastic placard listing the person's name, birth date, and place of birth were the Islamic symbols of the star and crescent.

According to Bosnian Muslim practice, the wooden marker is replaced by the stone *nišan* (gravestone) after one year; in the case of the memorial center cemetery, the *nišani* were not placed until July 2006, three years after the first burials at Potočari. Like the temporary markers, the *nišani* are identical: slender white gravestones bearing the same personal data, as well as a line from the Koran: *"I ne recite za one koji su na Allahovom putu poginuli: 'Mrtvi su!' Ne, oni su živi, ali vi to ne osjećate"* (And call not those who are slain in the way of Allah "dead." Nay, they are living, only ye perceive not).[4] During my fieldwork among families of the missing, returnees to Srebrenica, and members of the Women of Srebrenica, I heard no objections raised against the use of the green cloth or the design of the grave markers. In the case of the temporary wooden markers, it appeared that several individual families reinforced the explicitly Islamic symbols of the star and crescent by draping prayer beads *(tespih)* over the marker itself.

In a conspicuous reversal of the DNA technology's primary thrust throughout the identification procedures, the uniformity and overtly religious design of both the *tabut* and grave markers reascribe the recovered remains not with individual identity per se but with the very ethno-religious identity that had been the target of the Bosnian Serbs' collective violence. It is a purposeful, revealing shift in the overall process of recognizing Srebrenica's missing. The identification procedures carried out by the International Commission on Missing Persons began by removing all traces of ethno-religious identity. Once matched by the computer software, the "blinded" samples of the missing person and his family members (their blood) eventually helped identify the mortal remains as belonging to a specific individual. That person's full name was then attached to the coffin and the grave marker. The list of the identified was printed in the newspaper and on programs available at the memorial center that day.

Throughout these procedures, restoring individual identity has been the principal aim, and the hundreds of coffins laid out in perfect symmetry beneath the *musala* attest to the technology's success. Yet the very nature of the memorial center's centralized cemetery, its mass burials, and the uniform religious markings on each coffin and grave have the effect of reinserting the individual whose remains have been recovered and identified into the collective category of Bosnian Muslims, and, according to the Islamic Community, Bosnian Muslim martyrs. From a distance you cannot read the writing on the grave markers and thus cannot distinguish one from the other, except for the occasional offering such as flowers or *tespih* (prayer beads) placed on the grave. Thus, driving past the memorial center, you see a field full of mounds and identical white gravestones. Ethno-religious identity that had impelled the violence against these men and boys now physically dominates the cemetery's appearance. Blood spilt—as much as blood transmitted—defines the collective identity emerging from this space.

## CEREMONY, SPEECHES, AND PRAYERS

As with the previous three mass burials at Potočari, on the morning of July 11, 2004, an estimated 20,000 people converged on the space of the memorial center. While some drove in private vehicles, most attendees arrived by buses that had departed from cities through-out the country very early that morning. Free of charge, this public transportation was provided by the memorial center foundation. The buses and several hundred private cars filled the parking lots to the side of the run-down factory buildings of the memorial center and the adjacent fields. Despite the numbers, people moved with ease toward the main gates. Once at the threshold, the foot traffic slowed and for a brief moment as the stream of bodies bottlenecked between the entrance walls, the enormity of the crowd was almost oppressive. This was especially true at the tenth anniversary, one year later, where metal detectors manned by RS police officers had been set up at the main entrance. As I made my way through the gate, past the police-woman monitoring the flow of people, I saw from the corner of my eye a handful of attendees who gingerly sidestepped the contraption and entered the complex undeterred. The security check that day was more for show than effect, it seemed.

In 2004, once inside, people moved about the center, seeking out family and friends, graves, a spot on the grass or among those stand-ing who had already secured a clear view of the upcoming ceremony. Given the main emphasis of the day—the burial of the identified vic-tims—there was an ironic inversion of prioritized guests: the members of the international community (mostly from the diplomatic ranks), national political leaders, and the press corps congregated in the VIP section cordoned off around the *musala,* where they would enjoy the closest view of the speakers. The rest of the crowd, mostly Bosniak members of the extended Srebrenica community, milled about the cem-etery, hovered at the periphery of the VIP section, or took seats on the sloping hill facing the *musala.* I watched as people stopped mid-stride to greet one another, friends, former colleagues or classmates back from Europe or further abroad for the occasion of a relative's burial. Foreign (non-Bosnian) attendees skirted the edges of the cemetery, trying to catch a glimpse of the empty graves. Photojournalists snapped pictures of faces already bathed in tears.

From the hillside looking down, you could see how the crowd spanned generations and gathered both rural and urban populations. Women in *dimije* and headscarves stood beside men in blue jeans and T-shirts. While some people captured the scenes with camcorders and digital cameras, others whispered prayers beside graves. Having spent so much time in Srebrenica and with the Women of Srebrenica, I was surprised, as I had been at the previous ceremonies at Potočari, to see so many men present, especially young men. Since the fall of the enclave, women have been the public face of the survivors' community and its most vocal activists: from the politically mobilized "Mothers" and "Women" of Srebrenica to the single women returnees who are the backbone of the Bosniak population in the city.[5] I usually thought of Srebrenica's men in terms of those who were missing—that is, dead.

The sight of so many people underscored the collective nature of the event about to take place, yet the coffins neatly ordered in rows beneath the *musala,* the physical center of the ceremony, reminded the onlookers of the individuals being commemorated and buried that day. When the moment came to begin the ceremony, people drew in closer, taking seats on the grass or squeezing in among the crowd gathered behind the VIP section. All faces turned toward the *musala* for the now familiar series of addresses that began with presiding politicians' introductions and brief statements and concluded with a longer speech by the head Bosnian Muslim cleric, Reis ul-ulema Mustafa Cerić. Each address was made in Bosnian and translated into English (for the benefit of a tiny fraction of the attendees), an act underscoring not only the formal, public aspect of the event, but also the obvious orientation toward the international members of the audience.

The arrangement of speakers, moving from the political to the religious, illustrated how closely intertwined the Bosniak nationalist and Islamic leadership was in their responses to the genocide and its commemoration. Sulejman Tihić, the leader of the SDA political party and then chairman of the presidency of Bosnia and Herzegovina, spoke predominantly about the genocide, its perpetrators, and the political climate in the RS that continues to protect and revere those war criminals. A subdued, even tepid speaker, Tihić directed his commemorative speech as much to the families assembled before him as to an absent audience—but one that would learn of his address in the subsequent media coverage: the Bosnian Serb government and public, and their counterparts in Serbia. His speech invoked a narrative of Serb criminality (and by implication, Bosniak victimhood), echoing the language of the "new totalizing histories" deployed in the early 1990s by Croat and Serb nationalists (Hayden 1994:181). "War crimes" he said, "cannot by any means be justified, especially not through the protection of so-called national interests, or the pretext that others committed crimes. A criminal cannot be a national hero because he has neither a people nor a religion" *(Ratni zločini ne mogu se ničim pravdati, posebno ne zaštitom tzv. nacionalnih interesa, ili izgovorom da su zločine činili i drugi. Zločinac ne može biti nacionalni heroj, jer on nema ni nacije, ni vjere) (Dnevni avaz* 2004b).

The Muslim cleric Reis Cerić, taking his place at the podium near the *musala,* shifted the tone of the ceremony toward a subtler though equally pointed message. His style was radically different from that of President Tihić. A gifted orator, he knew how to use language and cadence, volume and tone, to draw out his ideas and capture his audience. He also speaks English and thus did not require a translator, but rather read his text first in Bosnian and then in English. In this speech, an effective rhetorical device was the repetition of a particular phrase, which opened each of his paragraphs, *"Nema odgovora na pitanje zašto . . . ali* ima *odgovora na pitanje zašto . . ."* (There is no answer to the question why . . . but *there is* an answer to the question why . . . ). In one of the most powerful segments of the speech, he defined what Srebrenica meant for Bosnia:

> There is no answer to the question of why they do not want to listen to the voice of [their] conscience, but there is an answer to the question of why our voice is not one of revenge.[6] Because revenge is not our religion, because revenge is not our fate, because revenge is not the Bosnian way.
>
> Truth is our religion, justice is our fate, Bosnia is our way of living together. Srebrenica is our sea and our shore of salvation. In it we can all be drowned, but in it we can also all be saved.

> *Nema odgovora na pitanje zašto neće da čuju glas savjesti, ali ima odgovora na pitanje zašto je naš glas da nema osvete. Zato što osveta nije naša vjera, zato što osveta nije naša sudbina, zato što osveta nije bosanska mjera.*
> *Istina je naša vjera, pravda je naša sudbina, Bosna je naša mjera suživota. Srebrenica je naše more i naša obala spasa. U njoj se svi možemo utopiti, ali u njoj se svi možemo i spasiti. (Dnevni avaz* 2004c)

Reis Cerić invoked Srebrenica as a *Bosnian* (not exclusively Bosniak) experience. Yet as the head of the Bosnian Islamic Community, he spoke of *"naša vjera"* (our faith) and *"naš glas"* (our voice), which implied the Bosnian Muslim religion and Bosniak voice, given the context of the gathering. Demonstrating his political savvy, Cerić nevertheless recognized his international audience, among whom stood the High Representative, Paddy Ashdown. By inviting Bosnians to view Srebrenica as both their "sea" and "shore of salvation," Cerić gestured toward the international community's expectation of a tolerant, inclusive national ideology.

It is difficult to separate out the political overtones from the religious messages in this first segment of the ceremony. In part, this is because the Bosniak nationalist political leadership (Tihić, SDA, their representatives and appointees, including the Federation Commission for Missing Persons' president Amor Mašović) and the Islamic Community leadership have such close ties. Much of SDA's rhetoric is couched in terms of ethno-religious identity, and thus its prominent role at Potočari creates the perception that the July 11 commemorative and burial services entail a melding of the Bosniak religious and nationalist political worlds. Two photographs in the daily newspaper *Dnevni avaz* (often seen as a mouthpiece of SDA) capture the inseparability of the two organs of Bosniak leadership: in one photograph, their respective representatives stand, with palms raised in prayer, before the *tabuti* under the *musala*. The caption reads, *"Reis ef. Cerić predvodio dovu za duše žrtava srebreničkog masakra"* (Reis ef. Cerić led the prayer for the souls of the victims of the Srebrenica massacre); a second photograph depicts Cerić flanked by President Tihić and Bosniak minister of foreign affairs Adnan Terzić, with other clergy standing behind and to Cerić's right and left (*Dnevni avaz* 2004c).

The musical performance of a piece from the choral composition *Srebreničko inferno* followed the formal addresses. Clad in ankle-length shimmering white robes, a choir stepped off to the side of the *musala* into a grassy clearing. Nothing about their clothing reflected Bosnian Muslim traditional dress; as with the *musala*'s design, the choir seemed more about artistic, as opposed to ethno-religious, expression. Performed in several cities throughout the country, the music has become quite familiar to the Srebrenica families. Its signature refrain is the voice of a child who calls out plaintively, "Mother, sister, where are you? I can't find you," to the surrounding chorus of young adults. It is a mournful melody and a powerful interlude between the speeches and prayers that follow.

FIGURE 12. Prayers before the *musala*, July 11, 2004. Photo by the author.

Once the music concluded and the choir had filed back into the crowd, the ceremony turned to the event's religious rites, the *dženaza*, and Reis Cerić urged people sitting on the sloping hill and on the periphery to fill in the ranks of those already gathered to pray. Here, more than at any point in the ceremony, gender divisions were apparent as the women arranged themselves in rows behind the men, who were closer to the *musala*. In the VIP section, women left the immediate area at the request of the Muslim men about to pray. The only exceptions were the female media representatives, who remained within their ranks, operating cameras and microphones to capture the sights and sounds of the religious service. Bringa explains that the separation of men and women during prayer was common within traditional mosques in rural Bosnia, as well as in the larger mosques in urban centers, and that the "lack of any clearly defined physical segregation causes women to be that much more careful not to trespass. Thus, men always make up the front rows closest to the *mihrab* (a niche in the wall at the front of the mosque, facing the *kibla*, from which the *hodža* leads the prayers), while women sit in the back rows towards the entrance" (1995:201).

The same configuration and separation existed in front of the *musala.* Over the course of the next several minutes, following the words of the cleric leading them in the *dženaze-namaz* prayer, the long lines of men and women rose and sank in a collective motion, a sea of backs facing the attendees who did not join in the religious rites being enacted. Some of the women had brought prayer mats upon which they now knelt. The light or brightly colored cloth of their long skirts, or *dimije,* and headscarves stuck out against the darker dress of the rows of men that wrapped around the *musala* in an arch. Some of those who chose not to join the rows of people praying below followed the service, reciting the words softly and gesturing in accordance with the prayer. Others, mostly foreigners or young Bosniaks, looked on in silence or chatted quietly among themselves.

## THE COFFINS' FINAL JOURNEY

With the funeral service completed, the final and most important part of the ceremony began: transferring and burying the 338 individual coffins. Once the last prayer was recited, family members began to walk toward the cemetery, seeking out the gravesites where they would receive their relatives' coffins. From the hillside, the sight of the vast crowd—thousands of people making their way to the opposite side of the center—recalled the circumstances of July 11, 1995. A Dutch man, the only former soldier of the 1995 Dutchbat to attend the ceremony, afterward contrasted the orderly, calm procession that day with the chaotic, panicked atmosphere surrounding the compound at the fall of the enclave.[7]

One by one, the bright green coffins were picked up and carried over to a column of men who had assembled to the right of the *musala* in the direction of the cemetery. Lifted above the men's heads, the coffins began to travel across the bridge of upheld hands, slowly and gently, toward the cemetery. Young and old men stood side by side, two and three deep, to assist with this transfer. Capturing the scene from their perches on the grassy embankments near the *musala,* local and international photographers recorded the images of the coffins being borne across the crowd.

Even as it entered into the spontaneous assembly of supporting hands, the procession of coffins maintained a prescribed order. On both ends of each coffin, a number had been attached that corresponded to the number of the gravesite to which it now traveled. The Visoko City Cemetery staff responsible for the layout of the cemetery and the indi-

FIGURE 13. The procession of coffins, July 11, 2004. Photo by the author.

vidual plots had designated the location of the empty graves according
to where other family members were or would in the future be buried,
as well as to the limits of space. Thus, by the fourth mass burial, the
northern-most corner of the center's cemetery was almost entirely filled
up with plots. In order to help families find gravesites on that day, posters with a diagram of the cemetery and a list of the individual identified
persons, along with their gravesite and row number, had been placed
in strategic locations around the center. Small wooden signs mounted
on stakes marked the various parcels (sections of the cemetery) for the
families' orientation.

    Spreading out into the cemetery, the extended community of Sre-
brenica organized itself for the final burial rites of the day. While the
coffins passed slowly and steadily through the crowd, people sought
out the gravesites, threading their way through the streams of bodies
heading in the same general direction but to different corners of the
cemetery. It was a confusing scene. Once surrounded by the enormous
crowd and standing on the level ground, you could easily lose your sense
of orientation within the vast cemetery. The signposts marking parcels
were only shoulder-high, so that they became invisible as soon as people
filled the cemetery's space. The Muslim clerics, dressed in long black

robes *(džube)* and white and maroon headdresses *(ahmedije),* had also left the inner circle near the *musala* and proceeded to individual grave-sites, where they would conduct the burial rites *(učenje na kabura).* As had become the custom with each of the previous mass burials, the national and local officials, along with the high-profile international guests, in this case, High Representative Paddy Ashdown, were led to specific graves to assist with the burial. Inevitably, a photograph of the diplomat with shovel in hand would appear in the next day's paper.

If any one moment at the memorial center on July 11 most epito-mized the convergence of people and their responses to the identifica-tion of Srebrenica's missing, it was the physical passage of the coffins across the crowd, into the cemetery, and finally to the individual plots. The act involved everyone present in some manner of commemora-tion, a shared and social remembering that is a part of collective memory (Halbwachs 1980). Unlike his early mentor, Henri Bergson, Halbwachs believed that individual memories depend on and gain significance through other people. For him, memories are public and shareable, closely connected to social influences and milieus: "Our memories remain collective, however, and are recalled to us through others even though only we were participants in the events or saw things concerned" (1980:23). At Potočari that day, there was a mix of witnesses, extended community members, and others who had no recollections of Srebrenica during the war but nevertheless joined in the commemoration. For the Bosniak population—the overwhelming majority of those attending—the space, the number of people, even the summer heat recalled the events of July 11, 1995. Attendees who had no such memories were participating in a communal act of remembrance, either as observers of or participants in the passing of the coffins. "A remembrance is gained not merely by reconstituting the image of a past event a piece at a time. That reconstruction must start from shared data or conceptions" (Halbwachs 1980:31). In the case of Srebrenica, the reconstruction also derived from a shared experience: witnessing the carrying of the coffins, whose contents were individual sets of mortal remains yet whose design and movement intimated a collectivity. Some bore the coffins, others photographed them; still others awaited them at the graveside. Most stood in silence and watched them pass over the bridge of hands.

Now part of a long, slow train of motion that had concentrated the crowd and its attention, each *tabut* bore the insignia of individuality: the person's name and corresponding identification numbers, as well as the number of the specific gravesite. The sight was at once jarring in the way it dramatically revealed the number of victims, and ordering because of the identical appearance of the coffins and the smooth transferal across the crowd. The focus of the ceremony had shifted away from the *musala*, the nerve center of the complex's physical space, and had dispersed through the crowd into the separate, private sites of the individual graves. The coffins left the hands of the community and passed into those of the waiting family members.

The actual burial of the coffins happened swiftly, with little pause for ceremony other than prayers recited over the graves. Once the *tabut* arrived, the relatives, close friends, and neighbors placed it directly into the grave and began to shovel the loose earth from the mound at the side of the pit. Five or six men labored in silence over each gravesite, while the female attendees stood apart on the opposite side. The cemetery had come alive with exertion, movement, and emotion, all directed toward the men and boys whose remains were being laid to rest. The air was soon thick with the noise of the burials: the low wailing of mothers and sisters and the metallic scrape of the shovels biting into the mounds of earth. Within minutes, the constant muffled thud of the soil hitting the wooden boxes began to resonate throughout the field, a muted drumbeat to the voice calling out over the loudspeaker in alphabetical order the names of the 338 persons being buried that day. As the sun shone brightly overhead and temperatures peaked, beads of sweat appeared on the brows of the men shoveling the earth; periodically they would hand off the tool to another relative or neighbor who stood nearby. Gradually the landscape of the cemetery changed as the mounds of earth filled in and topped off the empty spaces above the coffins. With each shovel of earth, the field was regaining its level plane and the discrete physical boundaries between each gravesite began to melt away, opening up a view to the field now full of smaller, fresh mounds and a community exhausted by its efforts.

The individual burial rites took place at different paces and according to the families' varied sense of ritual. Beside some gravesites large groups of family members and friends had gathered, while others had more modest attendance.[8] Often the graveside assembly prayed together as a group, and though they had convened around an individual plot, they were enveloped within a community of fellow mourners and survivors. After the prayers were concluded at a gravesite, friends and neighbors who had attended the burial would search out other graves to visit. Gradually people began to make their way toward the

exit and to their cars or the buses on which they traveled in the morning. Trucks bearing tanks filled with potable water now served the
parched attendees as they exited the center. Within another hour the
gradual exodus of people and vehicles would empty out the center and
its adjacent parking lots and fields. Some visitors would drive south to
Srebrenica or nearby villages to visit their prewar homes or neighbors
who had returned. In some cases, they left to perform the *tevhid* (the
formal funeral prayers) in their prewar homes with the rare gathering
of extended family and friends.

CHANGES IN PRACTICE AND PLACE

In some regards, the funeral ceremony and mass burial of the 338
victims followed Bosnian Islamic tradition closely. With clerics and
families attending, the bodies were interred according to Islamic ritual.
But in other ways, the cemetery at Potočari and the collective funerals held there diverged considerably from Bosnian Muslim practice. To
begin with, the presence of women at the gravesite signaled a significant change from prewar religious practice. As Bringa notes, Bosnian
Muslim women were traditionally expected to remain at home rather
than witness the burial: "The local *hodža* gave a beautifully argued
explanation: 'Women never go to the graveyard, only men do. . . . The
moment which is the most difficult is when the body is carried away
from the house. And when the journey towards the graveyard starts
the women remain. In that most difficult of moments the women are
together in the house where they recite prayers for the dead person's
soul, and it becomes easier for them to cope. Women do not go to the
grave because they cry a lot'" (1995:186). The mass funeral and burial
at Potočari directly broke with this tradition; indeed, as the coffins are
picked up and borne through the crowd, the presiding cleric instructs
the gathering that women are allowed to proceed to the gravesites. For
just as the genocide has interrupted families, reduced their numbers,
and transformed their structure, so too has it forced a modification
upon this particular aspect of the community's religious practices.[9]

Likewise, the composition and location of the cemetery are markedly different from the traditional Bosniak gravesites. In the predominantly rural communities of the Podrinje region, the villages from
which the refugees fled to the enclave in 1992, most families had their
own private cemeteries, family plots located on their own land. In the
Srebrenica area, although there were communal cemeteries, they usu-

ally contained the plots of extended families, people related through marriage or connected as neighbors. For example, Nura's husband's father, who was buried on July 11, 2004, could just as easily have been buried within the family cemetery in Potočari. Indeed, Nura and her husband had recently reclaimed their prewar summer home in Potočari and cleaned up the land, including that of the family cemetery. They could have chosen to bury the father at home with his other relatives. But they decided his grave should be in the memorial center cemetery.

The same was true for another victim, whose parents, a frail older couple, had returned to their prewar house up in the hills above the road leading from Srebrenica to Potočari. The couple was missing several of their male relatives, including their son and two grandsons, who had lived with them in the cluster of stone houses that once made up their hamlet. Their daughter-in-law had survived and moved abroad. When the remains of their son were identified, another member of the family, most likely one of their daughters living in the Federation, served as the contact person. Because the father was in particularly bad health, often exacerbated by emotional stress, presumably the daughters and daughter-in-law decided on the location of the grave without consulting with the parents. But the old couple acknowledged that they would have welcomed the return of their son's body to their own land. A small fenced-in cemetery containing two or three headstones stood in a field to the left of the path leading up to their house. According to their own sense of tradition and their desire to be close to their son's remains, they would have wished to bury him in that family cemetery rather than in the memorial center.

Improvisations and modifications of Bosniak burial practices for the refugees living in the enclave, however, had begun well before the establishment of the memorial center in Potočari. Hundreds of people died during the three years of isolation in the UN enclave, and many of the dead were refugees who had come from neighboring municipalities such as Vlasenica or Zvornik. There was no opportunity to bury bodies in family plots. A walk along paths that climb the steep hills surrounding the city reveals the occasional makeshift grave, whose rudimentary and worn marker barely designates its presence.

While the circumstances of the war and the harsh conditions of life in the enclave had inured its residents to hasty funerals and makeshift plots, the genocide profoundly influenced the survivors' desires concerning the burial of its victims. Many survivors felt that those who died together should be buried together, a symbolic gesture toward their collective suffering and the indignity of the secondary mass graves. Families spoke about the victims in terms of solidarity when they said that they wanted their relative to be buried with "the others," or "the rest of them" *(sa drugima, sa ostalima)*. Community leaders, in particular the family associations in Tuzla and Sarajevo, understood the importance—the visceral, tangible testimony—of a cemetery with 8,000 headstones, as opposed to the victims being buried in private graves scattered throughout both the Federation and the Republika Srpska (Pollack 2003b, 2003c).

Nevertheless, some families have decided to bury their relatives privately, outside Potočari. According to ICMP's records, by December 2007, 166 such individual burials had taken place since the identification process first began. Some of those identifications occurred well before the establishment of the memorial center, and the families decided not to wait. Enver, the PIP case manager, explained that following the opening of the memorial center, individual burials became much less frequent. In those rare instances, families usually chose to inter their relatives in local cemeteries, places where the missing person had been born or had lived before 1995. "The main reason," he explained, "was that the identified person had indicated before the war, 'if anything should happen' that he wished to be buried in the place where he was born or had been living." In other cases, families have decided against Potočari because they wished to bury the relative in the same cemetery as his other family members, who died before the war. But as Enver put it, "There are very, very few such individual cases."

The memorial center, thus, had become the final destination for the vast majority of Srebrenica's identified victims, and their return was the primary focus of the commemoration activities. The day's events ended with the collective interment the 338 coffins, witnessed by thousands of people. Shortly thereafter, the crowd dispersed and the fields around the memorial center emptied out. In those deflated moments afterward, as in the succeeding days, when small groups and individuals returned to the graves to pay their respects to a relative or friend, the center and its cemetery assumed a more subdued, intimate atmosphere. The crush of people and cameras had faded into the distance, and it belonged once again to the quiet surroundings of Potočari's run-down industrial zone. Returnees who lived in the nearby villages, Bratunac, and Srebrenica would come to tend their sons' and husbands' graves and pray for their souls, fulfilling their responsibility to the dead as well as to themselves (Bringa 1995:194–196).[10] As an old woman, the mother of a man identified and buried there, explained, "You go there, you commemorate, you caress the earth [of the grave] the same as if he [the person buried there] were alive. . . . We pray for them, say prayers for the bodies that are buried, and then we head home." In similar words, Mufti Kavazović emphasized to me the importance of Muslim cemeteries being nearby, close to the villages, where people could easily visit their deceased relatives. The proximity reflects the connection between the living and the dead. "Our concern is the spiritual *(duhovni, spiritualni)* life, and in some way it is connected to our dearest. For us, they are not dead. We believe, especially the martyr . . . for us he never dies. Thus, he remains. From generation to generation *(sa koljena koljeno)*, he lives, as long as he is living, as long as he is living in our memories in some way."

TENTH ANNIVERSARY

July 11, 2005, was the first commemoration and mass burial at the memorial center where the sun did not scorch people's faces or turn the clay-colored earth into dusty clouds stirred up by the throngs of visitors. Instead, it was a day wrapped in cold, damp air. Rain that had fallen through the night and early morning left the cemetery a muddy field and filled the 611 open graves with shallow pools of water. As anticipated, the crowd was significantly larger than for any of the previous commemorations. Estimates afterward would place it around 50,000 people. Everything seemed doubled in intensity, from the number of people and vehicles to the media coverage and security personnel. Even Christiane Amanpour had returned to broadcast a special CNN report from Potočari.

Preparations and logistical planning had begun well before the journalists descended on the Podrinje valley. The groups involved faced different pressures. As the case managers at the Podrinje Identification Project informed me, they had been scrambling to meet with families and finish cases for the past several weeks. Sitting in their office during the days leading up to July 11, I heard the phone ringing continuously and watched the constant traffic of families stopping in to ask questions. For just as PIP staff hoped to complete as many cases as possible, so families were anxious to hear news—especially those who had traveled back to the country specifically for the tenth anniversary. The same frenzied atmosphere had also overtaken the office of the Women of Srebrenica. For at least a month prior to the commemoration, Hajra and Nura fielded the daily barrage of journalists' questions and families' inquiries. Because the two of them lived in the front room of the office space, transforming the slender benches into beds each night, they rarely escaped the late evening telephone calls or unannounced visits from reporters seeking interviews. Some of the reporters were callous in their demands for the most pathos-filled photograph or tearful soundbite. The classic pose became that of a member sitting or standing in front of the collage of photographs of missing men and boys that now completely covered the office wall. Indeed, an article that appeared in the *Economist* opened with just such a shot of Hajra, looking as exhausted and sad as I have ever seen her (2005). Yet Hajra and Nura obliged, as if they felt this was their last chance to shake the outside world into recognizing their community's losses.

The tenth anniversary commemoration activities spanned continents, growing in frequency and scale as July 11 approached.[11] Conferences, book and film releases, art exhibits, theater and musical performances, lectures, newspaper and magazine articles, and political talk shows all took up the theme of the Srebrenica genocide, many touching on the identification process and the success of the DNA testing. More than at any point during the previous commemorations, the tendency to commercialize and consume the event became apparent. Like the American yellow "Support Our Troops" sticker, there was a *"Ne Zaboravimo"* (Let Us Not Forget) green, ribbon-shaped bumper sticker being circulated, an example of the "ethno-marketing" prevalent during the conflicts of former Yugoslavia in the 1990s (Petrović 2000:173). A diaspora group organized a reverse "March of Death—To Freedom" that retraced in part the trek made by the men trying to escape the enclave to Tuzla. After three long days of hiking through the hills and forests—and not before stopping at a mass grave just outside of Potočari whose exhumation had been strategically timed to coincide with the anniversary—the column of weary men and a handful of women (mostly international) arrived at Potočari on July 10.[12] With the nonstop media attention, several of ICMP's staff and even some members of the Women of Srebrenica told me they just wanted the day to pass.

Although the commemoration followed the same format as the previous ceremonies and mass burials held at the memorial center, the political significance of the tenth anniversary and the differing interpretations stemming from that milestone became immediately apparent. I arrived with several returnee neighbors from Srebrenica, and just as we tried to enter the center, we got caught up in a large, unscheduled (at least officially unscheduled) demonstration, led by one of Srebrenica's most strident nationalist activists. He had gathered together a crowd of men who held an enormous banner displaying the Bosnian flag. Bearing the banner through the main gates, they yelled in unison, *"Živjela Republika Bosna i Herzegovina!"* (Long Live the Republic of Bosnia and Herzegovina!) Many of these same men were also wearing T-shirts emblazoned with the image of Naser Orić in protest of his indictment at The Hague. As we passed them by Hajra snapped, "You should be ashamed of yourselves. This won't help him at all." She was angry because she felt the protest would be bad publicity for Orić as he stood trial at the tribunal.

The assembly of international representatives surpassed even the opening of the memorial center on September 20, 2003, when former US president Bill Clinton gave the keynote address. For this tenth anniversary, Serbia sent its highest official, President Boris Tadić, as a part of the first Serbian delegation of statesmen to attend a commemorative ceremony at Potočari. The lineup of American and Western European speakers represented the various political organs either implicated in the fall of the enclave or invested in the notion that its commemoration would lead to reconciliation, including, among others, Britain's foreign secretary, Jack Straw; UN Secretary General Kofi Annan's chief of staff, Mark Malloch Brown; head of the US delegation, Pierre-Richard Prosper; and president of the World Bank, Paul Wolfowitz. Wolfowitz charmed the crowd with his brief opening words, a greeting spoken in Arabic. The irony of both that rhetorical gesture and his presence at an event commemorating genocide against Bosnian Muslims seemed to pass unnoticed by most members of the audience, despite how strongly Bosniaks disapprove of the war in Iraq.[13]

Hajra was burying her husband that day. After the speeches and prayers, her surviving son and daughter-in-law and her closest friends, the women who had struggled alongside her to reclaim and rebuild their cluster of houses in Srebrenica, assembled at the graveside. I, too, was among them, standing with my landlady and her daughters as they encircled Hajra. We waited for what seemed like at least an hour for the coffin to arrive. It was number 282, almost at the half-way point of the total number of *tabuti* crossing the bridge of upheld hands through the crowd and into the cemetery. I remember very clearly when it finally arrived. I saw the number on the end of the coffin as it approached, and within another moment the men who stood at the side and ends of the grave began to lower it in. Hajra's son climbed down into the grave itself to receive and position the coffin. Then they began to shovel the earth and Hajra wept. All of us standing with her wept.

What remains in my mind about those minutes is the sense of shared grief. I struggle to recall the words uttered by the speakers who mounted the podium earlier that afternoon, but I can see the young woman's face, her eyes red with tears, as she knelt beside a nearby grave, reaching out her hand toward its green marker. I recall with clarity the look on my landlady's face as she leaned in to support her best friend, who was watching her husband's coffin disappear under the shovels of earth. I remember how we stood at the washbasins outside the restrooms afterward and tried in vain to clean the mud off our shoes. Someone had said that it was wrong to leave with the cemetery's mud still stuck to our feet, and so we lined up with others to scrap off the clay dirt from the soles of our shoes. The clumps of earth began to clog the basins; they were meant for washing hands and bare feet, not muddy shoes.

## BOSNIAN SERB RESPONSES

The atmosphere of collective grief present in the cemetery that afternoon, as on the other July 11 commemorations, was limited in its reach. However much the Srebrenica families and Bosniak political and religious leaders intended to compel absent Bosnian Serb audiences to appreciate their message, the events at Potočari tended to polarize and silence dialogue within the region. Early on in my fieldwork in Srebrenica I heard a Bosnian Serb man refer to the memorial center in Potočari as "their Mecca." His phrase captured a sense of resentment felt by many of the Bosnian Serb inhabitants of the city, most of whom had come as displaced persons to the region after the fall of the enclave. Each year, during the days surrounding the Srebrenica commemorative ceremonies and mass burials, I watched members of the city's two ethnic groups subtly distance themselves from each other. The predominantly Bosniak streets stretching up from the city center filled with cars bearing European license plates and visitors lingering in the streets. The Bosnian Serb neighborhoods seemed more subdued, even withdrawn, during the day before and on the day of the commemoration.

The occasion of the tenth anniversary exacerbated tensions among Bosniaks and Bosnian Serbs in the eastern part of the country, especially with the influx of diaspora and local and international media coverage. Throughout the month prior to the commemoration, news reports about Srebrenica appeared daily on television, radio, and in print. The Scorpion tape had surfaced in early June, and the images of the young men being abused and later executed became disturbingly familiar sights on the evening news in the Federation. One week before the tenth anniversary ceremony, the RS police found explosives in a warehouse near the memorial center. It was rumored that the police might have planted the bomb material themselves, but in any case its discovery unnerved many people planning to attend the July 11 ceremonies. Among the several local and international artists who undertook commemorative projects for the occasion, photographer Tarik Samarah had run a giant billboard campaign in several cities throughout Serbia, as well as in Zagreb, Croatia, displaying some of his most provocative photographs relating to the Srebrenica genocide. To the right of each photograph were the following words:

| SREBRENICA | SREBRENICA |
|------------|------------|
| 1995–2005  | 1995–2005  |
| Da vidiš,  | That you see, |
| da znaš,   | that you know, |
| da pamtiš  | that you remember |

Vandals destroyed the majority of the twenty-seven billboards by spray-painting across the images taunts such as the infamous phrase "*Nož, žica, Srebrenica*" (Knife, Wire, Srebrenica), "Ratko Mladić" (the name of the Bosnian Serb general who directed the takeover of the enclave and deportation and execution of its inhabitants), and "*Biće reprize*" (There will payback) (Handžić 2005a, 2005b). Samarah said that the vandalized billboards would be replaced immediately. But he also understood that the graffiti made his message that much more visible to an international audience: "I know that today many reporters are walking around the places in Belgrade where the billboards are displayed. Everything will be photographed and published afterwards. . . . I think that tension is rising. And that doesn't surprise me at all. Several million people have seen the billboards which have to remind citizens of the fate of Srebrenica's civilians" (Handžić 2005b).

On the day of the commemoration itself, a combination of Bosnian Serb official obstructionism and private citizens' protest significantly delayed or even prevented hundreds of people from attending the event, and later, from leaving the memorial center in a timely manner.

For example, several buses coming from Sandžak, a predominantly Muslim region of Serbia, were turned back at the border between the two countries, and others were delayed en route from more distant Bosnian cities, so that their passengers were unable to reach Potočari. When the burials finally concluded and the buses and private vehicles began to exit the memorial center, traffic slowed to a standstill. Nothing moved for hours because further down the road some Bosnian Serbs had set tires on fire, succeeding in blocking the kilometers-long column of traffic.

For their part, Bosnian Serb residents of Srebrenica tried to clear out of the city for the tenth anniversary, staying with relatives or friends in places like Bijelina or across the border in Serbia. It was an awkward period for them—regardless of their own views on the fall of Srebrenica—as residents of the city so marked by violence carried out in the name of their ethnic group. It was impossible to ignore the reporters, prewar Bosniak residents, and foreign activists, artists, and attendees of the commemoration who were staying in the city. In earlier years, most would have remained at home to celebrate Petrovdan (St. Peter's Day), an Orthodox Serbian religious holiday on July 12. Each year I was present in the town on Petrovdan (2003, 2004, 2005, and 2007), a large gathering took place at the Orthodox church just above the city center.[14] Following a religious service, other celebrations commenced, some more menacing than festive in tone. For example, on July 12, 2007, after the ceremony at the Orthodox church, a group of Bosnian Serb men, clad in black uniforms and bearing *četnik* (Serbian royalist World War II) flags, gathered in the city center to commemorate Serbs killed in Srebrenica and Bratunac during the war. Several of them were wearing T-shirts emblazoned with the pictures and names of Ratko Mladić, Radovan Karadžić, and World War II leader Draža Mihailović, as well as with the year 1389 on the upper sleeves. Bosniaks in the city were angry that neither the local police nor international security forces attempted to prevent or disperse the gathering (Mustafić 2007).

Thus, beyond its religious significance, July 12 has also become an occasion for Bosnian Serbs to memorialize their own wartime losses and thereby provide a counternarrative to the events taking place at the Srebrenica-Potočari Memorial Center. In fact, the July 12 memorial indexes an important change in Bosnian Serb historiography of the 1992–1995 war. In the immediate postwar years, many openly celebrated July 11 as the day of Srebrenica's "liberation," a euphemism for General Mladić's campaign eradicating the enclave of its Bosniak population. But as Duijzings notes, this eventually became an untenable practice: "Apart from growing embarrassment about celebrating Srebrenica's 'liberation' on the same day as the commemorations in Potočari, the shift in the Serb ceremonial calendar from 11 to 12 July, and more generally the growing emphasis put on Serb victimhood, are not only ways to counter the Muslim discourse and raise international awareness. They also serve to neutralise divisions within the local Serb community about how (not) to commemorate the Srebrenica massacre" (2007:162).

Rather than engaging the Bosniak narrative directly—as RS officials had done in previous years by minimizing the number of Srebrenica missing and categorizing them as strictly military casualties—Bosnian Serb political leaders and activists turned attention away from the Srebrenica missing and toward their own victims.[15] By 2001, theirs had become a discourse of tabulating losses rather than celebrating "liberation." This shift in rhetoric meant expanding the scope of events being publicly remembered: rather than limiting commemorations of Serb losses to July 12, 1992, when Bosniak forces killed several Bosnian Serbs in villages within the Srebrenica municipality, the day would also mark the killing of Serbs by Naser Orić's forces in Kravica on January 7, 1993. Eventually, the number commemorated would expand to include all Serbs killed in the region during the three-and-a-half-year war.

In addition to public rhetoric, changes in Bosnian Serb modes of commemoration entailed establishing physical memorials to the slain. Several kilometers down the road from the Srebrenica-Potočari Memorial Center, Bosnian Serbs built a monument memorializing an alternative narrative of victims and perpetrators in the wartime enclave of Srebrenica. In the village of Kravica in the months leading up to the tenth anniversary commemoration at Potočari, a concrete structure—something between a small amphitheater and roofless church—arose next to the main road running through the village.[16] Its most dominant feature was a thick, seven-meter-high Orthodox cross built into the structure at the center of one end. In the days before July 11 someone had mounted a Serbian flag on top of the cross, and its colors—red, blue, and white—stood in stark contrast to the gray concrete of the monument. On July 12, 2005, Bosnian Serbs in Kravica, Srebrenica, Bratunac, and other villages in the region held memorial ceremonies for the Bosnian Serb people killed in the region from the period of 1992 to 1995. Their decision to remember publicly those dead on the day after the Srebrenica commemoration was an obvious retort to the Bosniak narrative of the genocide.

The Bosnian Serb and Serbian media coverage emphasized the emotional responses of those gathered: "Bratunac—The day after the commemoration in Potočari, Serbs in Srebrenica, Bratunac, and in the surrounding villages yesterday grieved and cried for their wartime victims. The day before yesterday the whole world was with the Bosniaks, yesterday the Serbs were alone." They "wailed over the victims of the 1992 bloody Petrovdan, 1993 bloody Christmas, the bloody Kravica, bloody Bjelovac" (Šaponjić 2005). In Bratunac, Dragan Čavić, then president of the RS, addressed the crowd, challenging the way in which numbers of victims served as criteria for recognizing war crimes. Even as the dominant Bosnian Serb rhetoric had embraced tabulating wartime losses to emphasize parity, he was indirectly attacking Bosniaks' insistence on recognizing the disproportionality of the war crimes committed by Bosnian Serbs versus those by Bosniaks: "The crime of Srebrenica is a tragedy of great proportions, but the tragedy is that today we talk about crimes in figures. It is a tragedy for the families of the killed that victims are numbers; it is a tragedy that the number of victims is the basis for the qualification of a crime" (Šaponjić 2005). Carla Del Ponte, ICTY chief prosecutor, later rejected the attempts of Čavić, the Bosnian Serbs in Kravica, and Serbian nationalists to downplay the significance and scale of the Srebrenica genocide:

> The counter-attack of the nationalist circles in Serbia was well-organized and effective. Firstly, a massive media campaign was mounted to demonstrate that there were nearly as many Serbian victims in and around Srebrenica. It was pretended that 3,000 Serbs were killed by Muslims in Srebrenica and neighboring Bratunac. What was not said is that the alleged number of Serb casualties in these two municipalities, which is probably closer to 2,000, concerns the whole period of the war, 1992 to 1995, and that it concerns both combatants and non-combatants. Secondly, a huge monument was hastily built in Kravica, a village not far from Srebrenica, and a commemoration called for July 12th. The maneuver was a success: the attention in Serbia moved to the Serb victims and the public was largely convinced that, indeed, in Srebrenica, the crimes committed against Serbs were about as important as those committed against Muslims. (Del Ponte 2005)

Del Ponte was angry at the way in which the Bosnian Serbs of Kravica and the Serbian media had, in her view, manipulated the respective numbers of victims and, in doing so, recast the Srebrenica story of victimhood and criminality. They had successfully turned the discourse away from the region's Bosniak victims to its Bosnian Serb victims by asserting parallel losses experienced by Bosnian Serbs in the region.

Since then, the monument at Kravica has become the locus not only for July 12 memorials but also for the so-called bloody Christmas. Six months after Serbian president Tadić visited the Srebrenica-Potočari Memorial Center for the tenth anniversary commemoration and mass burial, he returned to the region to attend a memorial for Bosnian Serbs killed during the war. The event was held on the Serbian Orthodox Christmas, January 7, 2006, at the recently constructed monument in Kravica. Both the date and place recalled the specific attack carried out by Srebrenica's Bosniak military leader, Naser Orić, on the village of Kravica on that same day in 1993. In the guest book President Tadić penned the note, "The whole world, not only us, should know about the suffering of our people. We have a right to that because of those who lost their loved ones in the war" (Deutsche Press-Agentur 2006). Echoing the language of Bosniak political and religious leaders, as well as that of the international community (namely the Office of the High Representative), in drawing the "world's" attention to the event of Srebrenica July 1995, the Serbian president insisted on international recognition of Serb suffering. His use of the term *right*—the Bosnian Serbs' right to grieve and commemorate and their right to international recognition—purposefully invokes the rhetoric of rights typically associated with the families of Srebrenica's missing.

For Bosnian Serbs, their right to public commemoration is as legitimate as that of the Srebrenica families and the Bosniak community. Their "facts and figures," concretized through monuments and commemorative ceremonies, work to foster a counterdiscourse. Emboldened by their leaders' efforts to offset or qualify the scale and nature of the crimes committed at Srebrenica, many Bosnian Serbs still question the validity of the term *genocide* in its application to Srebrenica and the veracity of the DNA-backed identification results. Thus, while the identification of Srebrenica's missing has forced Bosnian Serbs to temper certain claims and abandon certain practices regarding the events of July 1995, the burials at Potočari have nonetheless further entrenched divisions among Bosnian Serbs and Bosniaks concerning wartime experiences of death and suffering. Just as the coffins interred at the memorial center cemetery help forge a new nationalism among Bosniaks assembled there each July 11, so the facts and figures they embody inspire Bosnian Serbs to generate counternarratives of tabulation, suffering, and loss.

## GRAVES

With each annual burial, the graves of Srebrenica's identified victims
spread farther across the open field of the memorial center cemetery. Why are they so meaningful to so many people, especially to
the families of the Srebrenica victims? The answer lies with what a
grave itself signifies. The temporary *bašluci* (wooden markers) and
permanent *nišani* (stone markers) physically fix once and for all the
locus of mortal remains that had been unrecognizable and absent
for so many years. These markers bear inscriptions whose lettering
connects the once missing person to a specific place, a recognizable
*somewhere:* "The person in the grave and the engraving on the gravestone point to each other, in a silent spatial relationship of proximity
which exists independently of visitors and reciters. The person who
was named at birth becomes known as a name attached to a specific
body for decades in one lifetime, and forever as a name inscribed on
the gravestone at death" (Ho 2006:37). Because the genocide so violently ruptured the link between individuals' names and their corresponding physical bodies, reestablishing that connection through the
DNA-based technology makes marking each identified person's gravestone, and thereby his postmortem place, that much more significant.
The inscriptions also link the identified person with those who pass
through and enter his space. "Present on the surface of the tombstone
at one end of a chain of signification, [the inscription] enables the
dead and silent person within the graves to be launched into discourse.
Reading the name on the tombstone, a Muslim passing by can greet
the dead within. Writing is an inert switch which converts the grave
from a silent to a sonorous state, when activated by the approach of
a living Muslim person. In this sense, writing is a foundational step
in the creation and realization of potentials for signification" (Ho
2006:37).

  In the process of identifying Srebrenica's victims, the temporary
*bašluk* and the stone *nišan* are the final and most meaningful surfaces
upon which the individual names are written. The markers punctu-
ate the long, circuitous passage the remains have traveled from a state
of absence to a known space of presence. At the very beginning of
the process, we recall the sets of mortal remains were nameless and
often incomplete. Although they filled a space in Tuzla's salt mines or
mortuaries, the very fact of their recovery, let alone their whereabouts,
was unknown to families, friends, and neighbors. Coded inscriptions

FIGURE 14. The Srebrenica-Potočari Memorial Center Cemetery. Photo by the author.

marked temporary resting places along the path of identification, as the remains and the samples they yielded traveled from one ICMP facility to another.

Once identification is complete and the coffin is buried at Potočari, however, the missing person's remains inhabit a grave whose marker announces a presence even though it signals a permanent absence (Ho 2006:20). The grave and its writing put an end to the families' search for their missing and thus open up new possibilities for spiritual connection with the dead. Surviving relatives who still live in Bosnia and are able to travel to the Potočari cemetery, including returnees to the Podrinje region, often come to the gravesides on quieter days. Like the old woman who visits her son's grave to caress its earth and pray for his soul, they reconnect with their loved ones in the silence of the empty cemetery. On those days, the memorial center is a peaceful place, a field full of slender gravestones framed by hills and open sky. Describing a similar site of tranquility, Geoff Dyer ponders the transformative space of a World War I cemetery housing graves of identified and unidentified soldiers: "So strong are these feelings that I wonder if there is not some compensatory quality in nature, some equilibrium—of which the poppy is a manifestation and symbol—which means that where terrible violence has taken place the earth will sometimes generate an equal and opposite sense of peace" (1995:130).

Thus, the natural surroundings of the collective cemetery and the individual names inscribed on the tombstones connect the living to the dead, "launching" them "into discourse." And on the days when the memorial center fills with those who have come to remember the missing, a "sonorous state" pervades the space. As we see from the Bosnian Serbs' alternative commemorations on July 12, it is a compelling atmosphere with a capacity to engage the living that extends well beyond the center's gates. Even those who are purposefully absent respond to its messages.

The simple design and arrangement of the graves also contribute to the ordering effect of the memorial center cemetery. For the families, theirs is no longer a question of knowing where their sons' or husbands' or fathers' bones lie. It has become a question of *with whom* those bones lie. For reasons of their own determining, the overwhelming majority of these families have decided that burial with the other victims overrides the traditions of their own blood and homes. They thus memorialize collective loss through collective mourning. It is an understandable choice, given that so few families have returned to their prewar houses, and, by the same token, so many have been displaced to distant countries. Indeed, this centralized and public burial of the dead corresponds to the dispersal of Srebrenica's living. While Potočari offers the surviving families who live abroad a place where both they and their missing relatives can belong, it also reinforces the very violent dislocation that uprooted them from their homes and eventually from their country. Most of them have started new lives in their countries of resettlement and will come back to Bosnia only as visitors. Thus, the small villages and private family plots will eventually sink into anonymity, while the cemetery at Potočari gradually takes over the memorial center land.

Returning to Bosnia for the July 11 ceremonies, Srebrenica's diaspora recongregates, if only temporarily, to recognize its missing and commemorate the collective violence against families, friends, and neighbors. Their choice is thus grounded in the religious and political context of postwar Bosnia. They recognize that Srebrenica and its victims occupy an important place in the Bosnian Muslim community and in the nationalist discourse of Bosniak victimhood. At the same time, they come to the memorial center at Potočari because of its most intimate social meaning—that is, because its cemetery houses the gravestones that bear the names of their once missing, now identified, relatives. For as Maya Lin reminds us, the name "brings back everything someone could remember about a person." At the graveside, in the quiet days before and after July 11, families visit the memorial center to remember those individuals, just as they come on the annual commemoration to remember them among many others.

CHAPTER 8

# Technology of Repair

On October 12, 2001, as the International Commission on Missing Persons (ICMP) was on the verge of completing its first DNA-based identification, three staff members boarded a plane from Bosnia to New York City at the invitation of the National Institute of Justice.[1] In the aftermath of the September 11 attacks, efforts had begun to identify mortal remains recovered from the ruins of the World Trade Center towers, the area which soon became known as "Ground Zero." Edwin Huffine, Adnan Rizvić, and Fuad Suljetović were sent as ICMP's delegates, traveling to the United States to provide input for the Kinship and Data Analysis Panel on what kind of DNA-matching and kinship software would best identify the almost 3,000 missing.[2] The complexity of the forensic task, the object of which was to identify all recovered human remains—from a small number of intact though badly disfigured and burned bodies to the majority of charred and fragmented bits of tissue and bone—rivaled the challenges of the Srebrenica secondary mass graves.

For this reason, the Bosnian expertise promised to be a valuable source of knowledge and its technological procedures and electronic programs a useful model for comparison. Huffine, Rizvić, and Suljetović took part in several meetings, offering to share database technology developed in Bosnia for former Yugoslavia's missing persons.[3] Though the trip received little public attention, it was a proud moment for ICMP: its staff and its knowledge base had demonstrable relevance beyond the borders of former Yugoslavia. Along with other widely recognized experts in forensic science, its employees were invited to advise one of the most high-profile and politically charged mass missing persons recovery efforts since the advent of DNA-based identification technology.[4]

This moment in ICMP's history serves as the point of departure for analyzing the import of the Bosnian technology beyond the case of Srebrenica and, more importantly, beyond the Balkans. By considering the innovative identification system's subsequent application in different parts of the world, the present chapter offers a unique view of Bosnia—outside the common frames of nationalism and ethnic violence—as a country that now claims critical, indeed much sought-after, expertise in postconflict-postdisaster intervention through the process of identifying mortal remains of missing persons. In widening this scope of analysis, I use the technology to venture comment on the larger theme of identification as a means of demonstrating, actualizing, and even undermining state authority. This analysis requires that we follow the course of the Bosnian technology[5] as it extends out from former Yugoslavia, connecting places as distant as New York, Phuket, and New Orleans.

Three and a half years after being asked to consult on the World Trade Center identification efforts, the Sarajevo headquarters of ICMP received another request for its technological expertise. This time it came not in response to an armed conflict or terrorist attack, but as a consequence of a natural disaster. The tsunami that devastated the coastal communities in South and Southeast Asia on December 26, 2004, resulted in an estimated 231,452 people lost, including 181,516 dead and 49,936 missing (UNDP 2005). Faced with the enormous challenges of identifying victims whose remains had been severely damaged by the disaster and the conditions of delayed recovery, authorities in Thailand, in conjunction with Interpol (the international police organization) and police officials from the United Kingdom and Germany, asked for ICMP's assistance. On May 5, 2005, the government of Thailand formally agreed to have ICMP analyze 750 bone samples in order to obtain DNA profiles.[6] Not long afterward, families from the Maldives and the Solomon Islands followed suit. ICMP sent staff members to Phuket, Thailand, to assist in the collection of DNA samples and in designing databases. By April 2006, ICMP had received 1,891 bone samples from tsunami victims and had successfully generated DNA matching reports for 902 missing persons originating from twenty-two countries.[7] For a second time, the technological innovation developed in response to the Srebrenica graves had proven itself relevant, indeed invaluable, on an international scale.

Thus, it came as little surprise that in August 2005, following the devastation of Hurricane Katrina and the slow-moving recovery efforts by the local, state, and federal governments in the Gulf region of the United States, ICMP once again was called on to assist in identifying missing persons outside the Balkans. In the initial news coverage of the rising death toll, local authorities worried that bodies might not be recovered for days, if not weeks, after the floodwaters receded from New Orleans and the other storm-affected communities in the region (Benjamin 2005). Four months later, ICMP's laboratory in Bosnia was one of several that Louisiana state officials turned to in their search for the most accurate DNA extraction and analysis facilities available. The technologists in Sarajevo, along with other DNA specialists in US labs, were sent test samples for which they were to generate genetic profiles. Its 100 percent success rate secured ICMP the task of extracting and analyzing DNA samples from the most challenging of Hurricane Katrina's missing person cases.[8] The Louisiana Department of Health and Hospitals formally agreed to have the organization analyze some 250 bone samples to obtain DNA profiles to be used in identifying the unrecognizable victims of the hurricane.

It was an ironic role reversal: here was the United States, the world's superpower, whose former president had established the very organization responsible for developing the cutting-edge technology in Bosnia, sending DNA samples from its own missing persons to this postconflict country. Indeed, the news media were quick to highlight the story of a war-torn country's contribution to the humanitarian response taking place in the Gulf region: "Bosnia Lab to Test Katrina Bodies: A Bosnian laboratory which pioneered new techniques to identify victims of the Balkan wars is to help identify the unknown dead of Hurricane Katrina" (BBC News 2005); and "War Graves Experts to Help with Katrina IDs: Using Bone Samples, Group Expects 100 Percent Success Rate" (CNN. com 2005).[9] The latter article noted the trajectory of the Bosnian DNA technology, starting from the mass graves of former Yugoslavia to its involvement in identification efforts for victims of 9/11, the 2004 tsunami, "people missing in Iraq," and finally Hurricane Katrina.[10] The Bosnians, so it seemed, excelled at identifying dead bodies.

ICMP's expanded mandate and scope of activity illustrate not only how successful the Bosnian laboratory had become in extracting, ana-

lyzing, and matching DNA profiles, but also how the very act of identifying missing persons through genetic testing had become integral
to strategies of postconflict-postdisaster social repair. A new form of
intervention, it built on discourses of human rights and humanitarianism underwriting projects of nation (re)building. The uniqueness of
individual human genetic makeup dovetailed well with Western liberalism's insistence on the primacy of the individual: "Western (Euro-
American) imagery routinely represents individuality through people's
unique and single bodies, echoed in understandings of the unique
genetic template. No one else has quite the same combination of genes,
bar identical twins. The perception of individuality and the value of
individualism go together, and the significance of the unique genetic
template is repeated over and again, a twentieth century discovery so
easily absorbed into pre-existing notions about individuality that it
is—among other things—the possibility of compromising that uniqueness that makes cloning so threatening" (Strathern 2005:20). More
than just a synecdoche standing in for human beings, the numeric representations of individual genetic makeup, matched through computer
software to profiles of biological kin, could be used to impart order.
Restoring names to bodies by recognizing individual genetic profiles
thus promised the restitution of individual rights, namely the rights
of surviving family members. For the Srebrenica families, the project
of recovering and identifying their missing relatives was part of the
broader discourse of their "right to know"—that is, the right to know
what happened to their sons, husbands, and fathers; the right to have
their relatives' remains returned to them; and the right to a sanctified
burial of those individual sets of recovered remains.

Despite its innovative qualities, the Bosnian postmortem technology was not the first instance in which forensics had been applied in
the service of human rights, humanitarianism, and nation-building.
Rather, it fits within a broader context of forensic science and practices
of so-called postconflict social reconstruction. The first part of this
chapter explores the relationship between the system of DNA-based
identification used to recover the Srebrenica victims and other instances
of forensics employed as redress in postconflict societies, particularly
in Latin American states. Although genetic testing has played a limited
role in identification procedures in those countries, traditional methodologies within forensic anthropology and archaeology have proven
instrumental in recovering bodies and documenting human rights
abuses. Moreover, the experience gained and skills honed by forensic

anthropologists working in Latin America in the 1980s formed a critical knowledge base for subsequent exhumations in different countries. For example, several of the forensic experts who worked in Argentina and Guatemala went on to assist recovery efforts in former Yugoslavia during the 1990s. Thus, by contextualizing the technology through its antecedents, we see more clearly not only how it developed but also why its model of postmortem identification has continued to circulate across space and time.

Understanding the place of the Bosnian technology within the broader spectrum of forensic practice in postconflict societies also reveals, in a more abstract sense, its role as an intervention used by states (or their proxies) when attempting to care for and control citizens—both living and dead. The remainder of this chapter therefore examines political goals behind identification. Viewed together, as a practice gaining momentum and traction among international actors, the examples of ICMP's contribution to identifying victims of 9/11, the 2004 tsunami, and Hurricane Katrina help elucidate state-sponsored initiatives to name nameless bodies. What can DNA identification technology tell us about the relationship between states and their citizens in moments of crisis and disorder?

By juxtaposing instances when the Bosnian expertise and resources have been called on, we see the patterns and contradictions inherent in the efforts launched to identify missing persons. For alongside the invaluable act of returning remains to surviving families, there are multivalent aspects to how and why the biotechnology is applied. States may choose to employ it for reasons beyond restoring remains and protecting individual rights; identifying missing persons is also about enacting state authority and channeling, at times even manipulating, public memory. Caring for dead citizens and their surviving relatives demonstrates competence not only to domestic audiences but also to other states. In this way, state identity and individual identity become dialectically conjoined in the ordering project of naming the missing. In some instances, states undertake identification efforts to distance themselves from the violence of past regimes, setting their government apart through its ability to recover bodies and restore social order. And as we will see with the example of Hurricane Katrina, government attempts to account for missing persons can also have unexpected outcomes whereby bodies recovered and identified may in turn expose the state negligence that contributed to the death of its citizens. Thus, rather than shoring up state authority, the end results—identified remains—offer

evidence for a compelling assault on its competency. Finally, disparities
in the use of DNA testing to identify nameless remains raise questions
about the potential of the costly, though highly successful, technology
to reinscribe sociopolitical and economic inequities already in place.

## PRECEDENTS OF IDENTIFICATION TECHNOLOGY

While the DNA-based identification system proposed by ICMP in 2001
in many ways broke with conventional forensic practice, which had
used genetic testing sparingly, to confirm or exclude presumed identity,
its overall grave-to-grave approach to identification was founded in an
already well-established field of forensic practice. Many of the foreign
experts who traveled to former Yugoslavia in the early to mid-1990s
had worked on exhumation sites for victims of state-sponsored violence
in different parts of the world, in countries like Argentina, Guatemala,
Chile, East Timor, and Rwanda. They brought with them experiences
and skills that reflected the growing collaboration between forensic
science, anthropology, archaeology, and human rights.

The international experts were able to transfer their knowledge and
skills from mass grave to mass grave not only because of similarities
in the disparate sites' physical conditions, but also because of parallel
social movements in each of these different countries—campaigns for
"truth and justice" waged by surviving families and activists to locate,
identify, and commemorate missing persons.[11] Their work fit within
common discourses of redress that demanded a response to the crisis of
absence posed by individuals kidnapped, tortured, and killed by state
authorities.

In the spring of 2007, New York City hosted a museum exhibit that
captured some of the parallel experiences of both the missing and their
surviving families at the center of these human rights–based forensic
efforts. Dedicated to the theme of Latin America's disappeared *(los
desaparecidos)*, the exhibit was featured at El Museo del Barrio in
Manhattan. A few weeks before I returned to Bosnia for the twelfth
annual commemoration and mass burial at the Srebrenica-Potočari
Memorial Center, I visited the museum. Among the many installations
composed of myriad media—from photos to film, etchings to paint-
ings—one particular piece transfixed me: the work of Oscar Muñoz
entitled *Project for a Memorial*. It was simple yet powerful. Muñoz
had filmed the process of sketching a person's face onto a slab of stone
with a stylus dipped in water. Even as the artist's hand traced the lines

of the profile onto the stone, they began to disappear, to evaporate. Several monitors projected faces in different stages of being sketched and disappearing. Laura Reuter, the curator of the exhibit, noted how endless cycles of drawing and evaporating thus unfolded before the viewer's eyes, providing a visual representation of the struggle to remember against the flow of time (North Dakota Museum of Art 2006:104). As I stood before the monitors, watching the faces come to life only to fade back into the surface of the stone, I was reminded of the feeling described by some of the families of the Srebrenica victims, whose memory-images of their missing relatives seemed to slip through their fingers, the once vivid mental snapshots blurring as the years passed by.

The primary message of the exhibit centered on the violent rupture caused by the disappearances and how relatives left behind and society at large grappled with the ensuing voids. In walking through the exhibit, pausing before its various installations, I sensed for the first time the visceral connection between the human experiences of loss in places as disparate as Bosnia and Argentina. The artists provided a frame in which Srebrenica's missing joined other populations of the disappeared. Indeed, that very term, the title of the exhibit, "*Los Desaparecidos*/The Disappeared," underscored the already existent, recognized category of forced absence predating the mass graves of Bosnia and former Yugoslavia. Reuter opened her preface to the collection by focusing the viewers' attention on a telling shift in idiom, one that indexed the pervasive, insidious practice of state violence against individual citizens: "To 'disappear' was newly defined during the twentieth-century military dictatorships in Latin America. 'Disappear' evolved into a *transitive verb* describing those considered threats to the state who were kidnapped, tortured, and killed by their own military, especially in the 1970s in Argentina, Brazil, Chile, and Uruguay" (italics added; North Dakota Museum of Art 2006:25). Furthermore, the object of the transitive verb, the category of those who were disappeared, entered Latin America's lexicon as a noun: *los desaparecidos* (like the Bosnian *nestali*).

Just as language evolved to encompass the practice of "disappearing" people in these regimes of political repression, forensic science adopted new techniques and assumed new roles in searching for the whereabouts and identities of those disappeared. Scientific documentation produced through these efforts became an important resource for human rights and "truth seeking" campaigns, as missing persons represented a "major humanitarian and legal issue" (Doretti and Fondebrider 2001:139).[12] Some of the most pioneering work emerged in response to the approximately 9,000 "disappeared" of Argentina's "dirty war," the period of state-sponsored violence carried out by the military government from 1976 to 1983. Once the junta fell, the newly democratic state established a truth and reconciliation commission, CONADEP, and forensic experts participated in the commission's legal investigations of human rights violations. Limited and controversial results (Harrison 2003:145) led CONADEP and the politically mobilized group of surviving relatives, Abuelas de Plaza de Mayo, to seek international assistance with exhumations. In 1984, the American Association for the Advancement of Science sent a group of forensic specialists, including renowned forensic anthropologist Clyde Snow, to Argentina. Snow and his team of Argentine anthropologists and archaeologists dug up graves, examined bodies, and documented human rights violations that would later be presented before the judiciary (Joyce and Stover 1991).

The work carried out in Argentina in the 1980s profoundly influenced forensic efforts in other Latin American states and in other countries around the world. Forensic evidence from exhumations of unmarked mass graves in Guatemala was used to document massacres of the Maya during the period of repression known as "La Violencia," from 1978 to 1985 (Sanford 2003); during the 1990s in Chile, among the estimated thousands killed, the remains of some 400 people who "disappeared" at the hands of Augusto Pinochet's military dictatorship were identified as a part of the National Commission for Truth and Reconciliation established in 1991.[13] Beyond developing traditional forensic methodologies employed in the service of these human rights investigations, identification efforts launched for the Argentina disappeared also established DNA as an important tool for recovering victims of state violence. Indeed, genetic testing was used to resolve cases of both the living and the dead: DNA analysis was employed in the rare presumptive cases involving recovered remains, and, more frequently, in attempting to identify children of the "disappeared," usually infants who had been taken away from their biological parents and given to individuals aligned with the military regime (Smith 2008).

With increasingly sophisticated methods of exhuming graves, documenting crimes, and identifying victims of forced disappearance, investigations into human rights violations in postconflict societies signaled a reorientation in international interventionist strategies.[14] Projects of social reconstruction now sought to reform both society and the state—that is, to get "inside the head to govern the hand" (Duffield 2002:1067). Forensic science became a valuable tool for such repair, providing documentary proof of crimes and identity that fed into other reconstruction efforts—from truth and reconciliation commissions to international criminal tribunals.

Assumptions about DNA's accuracy, its "truth" in the form of distilled genetic profiles, also played into discourses of state modernity. The postconflict regime could point to its application of genetic testing in the service of excavating and excising the material and social debris of past violence. The state could illustrate not only its competence but also its sophistication, embracing genetics' high standard of proof as an emblem of technoscientific progress. For international sponsors of identification efforts, such as the Western governments funding ICMP's work, DNA testing was also heralded—much like the international criminal courts—as a preventative measure (Huffine, Crews, and Davoren 2007). Potential war criminals and repressive regimes beware: no matter how hard you try to "disappear" your undesirables, DNA can restore their identity and bear witness to your crimes.

These changes in discourse and practice surrounding forensic science reveal how DNA testing has become an integral part of the collaboration among forensics, human rights activism, humanitarian intervention, and nation-building. Like the teams of international forensic experts and investigators who traveled to Bosnia to work on the mass graves, Bosnian expertise in extracting, analyzing, and matching genetic profiles has itself begun to circulate. Its application in response to recent mass fatalities provides a useful entry point into analyzing state aims in identifying missing persons.

## IDENTIFICATION AS CARE AND CONTROL

By late 2005, ICMP's facilities in Tuzla and Sarajevo were receiving and processing bone samples from Srebrenica's mass graves and other exhumation sites in former Yugoslavia, as well as from Thailand, the Maldives, the Solomon Islands, and Louisiana. The process for each was uniform: it involved physically preparing the bone samples for testing, extracting the genetic material, taking measurements of several loci along the DNA strands, and translating those measurements into numeric representations—all to create a genetic profile of individual identity for a missing person, be it a tourist who had been vacationing on the beaches of Thailand, a body recovered from the floodwaters of Katrina, or one of the Srebrenica victims, captured and killed in the Kravica warehouse. The bone samples from these various locales became involved in a common process of knowledge production. Through its mechanized steps, the identification taking place in the Tuzla bone department and the Sarajevo laboratory had the effect of leveling the diverse human experiences of the missing persons, if only for those days, weeks, or months while the samples were transmogrified from the contents of a storage vial to dual digits filling a page.

Although the Bosnian laboratory may have become the destination point for bone samples taken from victims of natural disaster and armed conflict alike, we should not confuse or collapse the qualitatively and existentially different sources of violence that rendered those remains nameless in the first place. To so do would only buttress the hubris of those responsible for planning and carrying out genocide. Genocidal violence is often depicted in the media, and sometimes by government officials unwilling or unable to stop it, as an almost preternatural force unto itself—"unleashed," sweeping through a population like a fierce wind or tidal wave, beyond control and containment. People fleeing its destruction, namely refugees who cross into neighboring countries, are often described in terms of uprooted masses, uncontrollable flows that spill over borders, a "tide" that must be stemmed (Malkki 1992, 1996). But genocide is man-made. And however distinct the phenomena of mass executions and mass graves might be from conventional wartime violence, they are by no means supernatural in deed and in effect. The example of Srebrenica demonstrates this, with its orderly production of disorder, now well documented in court cases and commission reports. As exemplified by the "extermination machinery" of the Third Reich, "planned and perfected in all its detail long before the horror of war struck Germany herself" (Arendt 1994:166), and the Hutu-sponsored radio campaigns and systematic distribution of machetes in Rwanda in the spring of 1994, genocidal violence is neither unpredictable nor uncontrollable. Why else have such periods of intense brutality been followed by the same call, however differently worded, of "never again"? As the inscription on one of the monuments in the Srebrenica-Potočari Memorial Center reads: *Da se više nikada i nikome ne ponovi Srebrenica!* (That Srebrenica never happen again to no one anywhere!)

The fact that these different bone samples have ended up in the Sarajevo laboratory and that they undergo the same procedures as objects of the same study, however, does raise the question of *why* such a costly technological resource as DNA-based identification is being used to recognize unknown remains. The act of DNA testing, attempting to identify each and every set of remains recovered, speaks to states' capacities to regulate and respond to the needs of their citizens.

By fixing individual identity to nameless remains, states reassert their authority, authority that may have been severely undermined or challenged by earlier inaction or outright negligence. Indeed, in the case of the Hurricane Katrina victims and the Srebrenica missing, a striking parallel exists in the run-up to the violence in the form of predictive technological resources available yet unheeded—that is, the disconcerting symmetry between the Doppler radar images that tracked the course of Hurricane Katrina as it moved toward New Orleans and the satellite images that captured the ominous positioning of Bosnian Serb Army troops in the days leading up to July 11, 1995. The technological feat of looking down from above and charting the direction of the violence in both instances produced knowledge, which in turn state authorities (or, more precisely, in the case of Srebrenica, both state and international authorities) failed to act upon. Srebrenica fell and some 8,000 men and boys were killed. In New Orleans, the levees broke, the city flooded, and the community's most vulnerable (poor black residents) died in its waters, waiting for aid.

Left ignored, lists of missing persons and unidentified bodies, pulled from attics in the Ninth Ward or from one of Srebrenica's secondary mass graves, are a thorn in the government's side, a grotesque reminder of negligence. But if heeded, those same bodies present postdisaster-postconflict states with an opportunity to reestablish authority. In the eyes of Bosnia's international supporters, identifying Srebrenica's missing, along with other victims of the 1992–1995 war, brings the postconflict state one step closer to a functional democracy. The state can account for its population and, as a consequence, systematically determine how to care for surviving family members. For the state of Louisiana and the US federal government, the eventual decision to send DNA samples to a laboratory in Bosnia represented the next logical step in the pursuit to identify all bodies recovered. The act of identifying those bodies and returning them to surviving families, furthermore, shifts public attention and discourse away from passive negligence, toward active response. In both cases, identification reinserts the missing back into the embrace of the state (Torpey 2000). Identification becomes a mechanism not only for tabulating losses but also for indexing postdisaster-postconflict political will.

In recasting public discourse around the missing, the process of identifying nameless remains also feeds directly into modes of commemoration. The primary emphasis of these recovery efforts falls, first and foremost, on recognizing *individual* victims. That this process of recognizing the missing involves such a sophisticated form of forensic science reinforces the message that each and every victim must be named, even at great expense to the state. Furthermore, ensconced in the language of "hard" science, the DNA technology driving those processes imparts an air of impartiality to counter claims of political gain or manipulation. Thus, the stage is set to commemorate simultaneously both the individual and collective nature of human loss. Narratives of individual suffering become intertwined with state efforts to demonstrate its care and control over its citizens, not only through identification but also through public memory.

Herein lies one of the most provocative outcomes of the DNA-based identification technology: how these individual sets of remains—decimated, disfigured, or decomposed beyond recognition—once identified, become potential fodder for the national imagination. It is a new twist on Benedict Anderson's Tomb of the Unknown Soldier: "No more arresting emblems of the modern culture of nationalism exist than cenotaphs and tombs of Unknown Soldiers. The public ceremonial reverence accorded these monuments precisely because they are either deliberately empty or no one knows who lies inside them, has no true precedents in earlier times. To feel the force of this modernity one has only to imagine the general reaction to the busybody who 'discovered' the Unknown Soldier's name or insisted on filling the cenotaph with some real bones. Sacrilege of a strange, contemporary kind!" (2006:9).[15]

Whereas the unknown soldier, precisely because his bones are nameless, provides the discursive space for building a national imaginary around a specific event, such as a battle or a war, the DNA-identified victims' remains urge reflection not only on the scale of the violence suffered but also that of the state response. Their physical remains, the story behind their gruesome conditions, which required DNA testing to reattach individual identity to bodies, offer a unique platform for building or, equally important, diverting public discourse and specifically public dissent. Reattaching names to victims' remains places individual lives within a collectivity—such as Srebrenica's "martyrs"—by which narratives of national loss or triumph are further entrenched, effectively dampening alternative modes of remembering the individual lives lost. In other instances, identifying remains deflects attention from state inaction or even responsibility concerning how or why people went missing. For example, the Dutch government has not accepted any kind of legal responsibility for its peacekeepers' role in the fall of the enclave and thereby in the deaths of the 8,000 Bosniak men and boys, yet it allocates funds for the identification of their bodies. Helping to return remains to families subtly turns the discourse—if only slightly—away from responsibility for death and toward responsibility for social repair.

## DIFFERENT POPULATIONS
## AND DIFFERENT RECOVERY EFFORTS

Disparities in whether, how, and when DNA-based identification technology is used in response to mass fatalities reveal the complex and at times contradictory role the technology plays in mediating relationships between states and their citizens in moments of crisis and disorder. One of the most provocative examples of such disparity is found in the divergent identification efforts and national commemoration for victims of Hurricane Katrina and the World Trade Center attacks. Juxtaposed with the 9/11 response, the example of Hurricane Katrina's missing presents an extraordinary exception to the discourse of repair that typically frames the state-sponsored project of identifying nameless remains.

From the onset, the two "missing persons" populations were cast in a very different light. In the case of the 9/11 attacks at the World Trade Center, the media portrayed individual victims as national heroes, their profiles appearing on television screens and in newsprint for months after the event. The *New York Times* ran a special column dedicated to memorializing the individual dead entitled "Portraits of Grief." In an article accompanying its final edition of the consecutive daily profiles, novelist Paul Auster explained what had become for him, like many others, the daily ritual of reading victims' profiles: "We weren't mourning an anonymous mass of people, we were mourning thousands of individuals. And the more we knew about them, the more we could wrestle with our own grief" (Scott 2001).

At the same time that the media stressed the individual lives lost, the Bush administration portrayed those same people as a collectivity, victims in a "war" on terror, thereby "rendering the context of violence one of national suffering and sacrifice" (White 2004:296). Within one month of the attacks now framed as acts of war, the National Institute for Justice assembled the country's, and indeed some of the world's, top forensic and DNA scientists to plan the systematic approach to recovering mortal remains. The New York City Office of the Chief Medical Examiner (OCME) had enormous resources—intellectual and financial—available from the onset to undertake DNA testing for individual sets of remains recovered from Ground Zero (Mundoff, Zelson, and Steadman 2003). Funded out of city, state, and federal coffers, OCME coordinated the entire effort, enlisting "some of the biggest guns in biotechnology to assist in the process of analyzing the DNA" (Lee and Tirnady 2003:297), including Myriad Genetics, based in Salt Lake City, Utah, Bode Technology Group of Springfield, Virginia, Celera Genomics of Rockville, Maryland, and GeneScreen of Dallas, Texas, as well as the New York State Police Forensic Science Laboratory and the Connecticut State Police Forensic Science Laboratory.[16]

Rubble from Ground Zero was searched thoroughly for remains, first on site and then again sifted through on conveyor belts at the Fresh Kills landfill on Staten Island. In addition to DNA analysis of recovered remains and samples provided by family members, DNA samples were also taken from personal items of presumed victims. Some 15,000 such articles were collected, among them 1,400 toothbrushes, 140 razors, and 126 hairbrushes (Lee and Tirnady 2003: 297). Three and a half years later, on June 2, 2005, Chuck Hirscher, New York's chief medical examiner, announced that they had "virtually exhausted" the limits of the DNA technology available, having identified 1,591 of the 2,749 victims, with 86 percent of the identification accomplished through genetic testing (Shaler 2005:321). Nevertheless, an advancement in DNA extraction at Bode Technology Group rekindled hope for further identifications, and the Bode scientists continue to work on 9/11 samples (Dotinga 2005). Still being carried out, the identification project represents the largest, most complex DNA-led forensic effort in the history of the United States.

In terms of both resources and national attention, Hurricane Katrina's missing person recovery efforts paled in comparison. Of the more than 1,200 reported dead, the Louisiana state coroner's office initially had 897 unidentified bodies. It was obvious from the onset that DNA testing would be critical, especially given the rate of decomposition, which was accelerated by the warm weather that followed the storm as well as by the floodwaters themselves. Yet resources dedicated to such efforts were slow in arriving. Dr. Louis Cataldie, the acting state medical examiner, publicly lamented the fact that, despite his calls for DNA testing in September, it took four months before the technology was brought to bear for the unknown victims of the floodwaters.[17] At the heart of the stalled initiative lay the question of money: who was to foot the bill—the state or the federal government? The Federal Emergency Management Agency (FEMA), already being reviled by Katrina survivors for its botched recovery efforts, initially balked at the idea of funding DNA testing. After negotiations with Louisiana state officials, the agency eventually agreed to cover the $13 million expense necessary to identify approximately 150 sets of remains among the 321 still unidentified as of November 2005 (Dornin 2005).

The federal government's reluctance to support financially the identification process under way for Katrina's missing persons indexed the critical stakes of responsibility underpinning the post-Katrina recovery efforts. Simply put, the Bush administration sought to define the human and material losses experienced in the Gulf region as the results of natural disaster and not human error or negligence. The blame was on Mother Nature, not the US Army Corps of Engineers. But in the storm's aftermath, meteorologists documented that the hurricane never reached the category 4 level; even more damning, engineers documented that the levees were breached well under that scale of force and, at one point of failure, under the strain of only category-1 forces (Van Heerden and Bryan 2006:199–200). Evidence mounted that New Orleans flooded because its levee system was ineffective—poorly designed and poorly built—conditions the federal government had recognized well before Katrina.[18] Thus, the argument followed that people died trapped in their homes or swept out into the floodwaters because the levees failed, not because of the hurricane itself.

Four months later, by the time the DNA testing system was funded and in place, the hurricane's displaced persons (much like the Srebrenica survivors) were already "scattered to the winds," having been relocated to places as distant as Houston, Atlanta, New York, Utah, and Oklahoma (Casserly 2006; Crowley 2006). Obtaining DNA samples from relatives became increasingly difficult, especially given the inefficient communication system instituted in the months following the disaster (Joyce 2006). Family members struggled to report and, in turn, learn information about their missing relatives, thereby delaying even further the identification efforts. Moreover, attempts to recover bodies of the missing were haphazard, with recovery teams in some cases performing perfunctory, if not incomplete, searches for people trapped in residential homes. Family members and neighbors returned to property months later, to houses spray-painted with "0," indicating no bodies had been found in the recovery search, only to discover corpses rotting away inside.

Whereas national media coverage of the 9/11 attacks portrayed the missing as national heroes—victims of the "war on terror"—Hurricane Katrina's survivors were likened to wartime collateral damage, repeatedly called "refugees" by newscasters and print journalists (Masquelier 2006:737; Pesca 2005; Limón 2006). The label was met with immediate indignation, with activists such as Al Sharpton bristling at its implications, "They are not refugees. They are citizens of the United States" (Pesca 2005), or as one New Orleans resident quipped, "That storm came in and blew away our citizenship too?"[19] Outside the United States, the images of the rapidly deteriorating conditions at the Superdome and of people stranded on rooftops, begging the helicopters overhead to rescue them, shocked international viewers. My friends in Bosnia would later express their utter disbelief that the United States, part of the UNPROFOR mission that had air-dropped food and aid into the Srebrenica enclave, could not even protect or care for its own citizens. Echoing the international media reports, they likened what they saw on their television screens to scenes from a "third-world country." In fact, offers poured in from other governments to send aid, among them, notably, Venezuela and Cuba (Hartman and Squires 2006:1).

Seen together, both the media coverage and the DNA-based identification efforts illustrate significant differences in government responses to the two mass missing persons populations: one characterized by immediate action and the other by bureaucratic foot-dragging. In the case of the World Trade Center attacks, the public rhetoric and material resources allocated to identify victims suggest an approach of "no expense spared." Identifying and commemorating individual victims took on national import, reflecting the federal government's determination to care for its citizens and, by extension, determine modes of commemoration. On the opposite end of the spectrum, attempts to recover and identify Katrina victims speak to divided agendas and fractious politics surrounding local, state, and federal responses to the hurricane. That bodies were pulled from attics, found floating in the floodwater and abandoned on sidewalks in the heart of New Orleans, days, weeks, in some cases months after the storm, challenges the notion that those people died as a result of natural disaster (Hartman and Squires 2006). From the comparatively modest resources allocated to the endeavor to the end results of bodies belatedly returned to families, the identification process serves more as an indictment of the various government agencies' inaction than as an emblem of state ability to care for citizens.

## PRODUCING KNOWLEDGE BY NAMING BODIES: AIMS, OUTCOMES, AND INEQUALITIES

States and their proxies have embraced the DNA-based technology developed in Bosnia because, however belatedly, it enables them to identify missing citizens and, in doing so, demonstrates their authority as the arbiter of sociopolitical order in the aftermath of chaotic rupture—be it natural disaster or human violence. Science becomes the seemingly apolitical, unbiased tool of repair, producing knowledge that resolves the crisis of absence and, in turn, enabling public memory. From the World Trade Center to Srebrenica identification efforts, this form of knowledge production helps negotiate the relationship between the state and its living citizens through the medium of the dead (i.e., the missing) in moments of instability and disorder. Fixing individual identity to nameless remains renders the missing legible (Scott 1998), thereby allowing the state to account for and respond to the manner in which they died. In some cases, this means memorializing individual loss in order to memorialize national injury. In other cases, accounting for the dead redirects discussions about how and why people died, thereby forestalling criticism of state inaction. Juxtaposing these different state-sponsored initiatives of identifying missing persons through the costly procedures of DNA testing helps elucidate some of the political aims that are written into this technology.

Aims are often expressed in terms of both process and outcome, and, in the case of postconflict societies like Bosnia and Herzegovina, the explicit goal of identification is often humanitarian in nature. For example, in explaining ICMP's expanding mandate, specifically its direct contribution to the 2004 tsunami identification efforts, Deputy Chief of Staff Andreas Kleiser pointed out that the organization's involvement was a natural extension of its humanitarian mission: "We are pleased that we will be able to help in this humanitarian effort. . . . We understand how important it is for family members to know what happened to their loved ones and, if possible, to be able to bury their bodies" (ICMP 2005e). Identifying the missing thus becomes a humanitarian project, a process of delivering aid, like distributing food or providing temporary shelter. The emphasis is placed on fulfilling implicit social obligations to surviving families, and it falls to state governments to finance this application of genetic testing. The same ICMP press release goes on to note that the organization, "which is funded by 14 donor governments, would be happy to assist in the identification of tsunami victims from other countries as well" (ICMP 2005e).

Regarding Srebrenica, still an open wound in Bosnia's postconflict society, ICMP's explicit aims behind identifying the missing run deeper: according to their framing, the results of DNA matching reports—remains identified and buried—hold out the promise of social reconstruction, often expressed in the language of transitional justice or truth and reconciliation. Indeed, over the past several years, ICMP's Civil Society Initiative has increasingly embraced this rubric of social reconstruction, hosting panels and workshops dedicated to exploring the theme of transitional justice within the region.[20] The notion that identifying missing persons, victims of the 1992–1995 war, should facilitate social justice and thereby repair also underwrites the ICMP-sponsored initiative to create its local successor, the Missing Persons Institute (MPI). First established in 2000 and eventually implemented through state legislation in 2004, MPI was charged with collapsing the two separate entity missing person commissions (i.e., that of the Republika Srpska and that of the Federation) into one unified institution responsible for all exhumation and identification efforts in Bosnia and Herzegovina.[21] Upon the occasion of the signing of the MPI official agreement as co-founders, Mirsad Kebo, minister for human rights and refugees, remarked:

> The Institute will search for missing persons regardless of their religious or ethnic background and any form of discrimination. By establishing this Institute we search for institutional solutions and define the work of the Institute as an institution on the level of Bosnia and Herzegovina. . . .
>
> We emphasize the importance of the state institutions, which should lead the process of searching for the missing persons, as well as all the other processes pertinent to the citizens of Bosnia and Herzegovina. (ICMP 2005a)

Through its repeated, even redundant, emphasis on the "institutional," the underlying message in the minister's language is clear: to function as a democratic state, and more concretely, to shore up candidacy for accession to the European Union, Bosnia and Herzegovina would have to stop classifying its citizens (including its missing citizens) according to ethnic differences, but rather treat them all uniformly as

Bosnians. Its officials would need to read the DNA profiles of its missing and their relatives as the manifestation of common humanity rather than a biological expression of ethnic differentiation. Only then could Bosnia begin to act as a unified polity. In many critics' view, Bosnia's EU membership was closely tied to this transformation. An article that ran in the *Economist* in June 2003 charged, "Until [Bosnia] builds genuine cross-community government structures enabling its three groups—Serbs, Croats and Muslims—to co-operate without outsiders needing to hold the ring, it has no chance of joining the club in the foreseeable future" (*Economist* 2003). A unified, federal institution capable of searching for and identifying its missing persons would demonstrate significant progress in this realm to its outside audience. "Impartial" and "apolitical" scientific procedures of genetic analysis driving the now unified identification efforts would further support this impression.

Framed in this manner, the technological innovation of DNA testing used to recognize victims of armed conflict and natural disaster advances a particular kind of state rebuilding—that is, one directed toward strengthening governmental capacity. Furthermore, applied in postconflict societies such as Bosnia, the technology becomes another means by which the "family of nations" overseeing reconstruction and reform attempts to fashion a functional and compliant democratic state. In extolling its merits and outlining its aims, supporters of the technology draw simultaneously from discourses of civil and political rights and humanitarian intervention, as well as from scientific authority. The "ideology of technoscientific progress" (Jasanoff 2006:285) joins forces with that of Western liberalism, in which sovereign states name and care for their missing through the most accurate and sophisticated of technologies, all in an effort to demonstrate, indeed enact, political authority.

As we have seen in the case of the Srebrenica identification effort, however, this enactment of political authority has its limits. The state-sponsored initiative of identifying the missing does not necessarily produce a more stable society, a more functional democracy. Bosniak and Bosnian Serb political responses to the Srebrenica annual commemoration and mass burials may in fact confound both aims and process. The DNA technology that has helped fill the Potočari cemetery with almost 3,000 graves, the remains of once missing victims of the genocide, has in some respects deepened communal divisions at the same time that it has reconstituted physical and social beings. Moreover, the Bosnian government's Missing Persons Institute, though poised to assume the responsibility of identification previously held by the international protectorate presence, appears more concerned with its international audience, namely the European Union, than its domestic constituency. The narrative of social repair directed at its Western overseers ignores still predominant ethno-national divisions surrounding victims and perpetrators.

Beyond such unexpected outcomes, there is also the issue of who benefits from the technological innovation. Jasanoff raises the question of how advances in technology correspond with expanding power: "Will the major technological revolutions of our time—in the life sciences, information and communication technologies, computers and weaponry, and most recently nanotechnology—favor emancipation or recolonization? Will they make people around the world more or less connected, more or less free, more or less comfortable, and most important for our purposes, more or less democratic? Will the radically unequal distribution of wealth and privilege in the contemporary world reinscribe itself through technological means, continuing older forms of hegemony and dominance?" (2006:275). Jasanoff's final question speaks directly to differences in identification efforts undertaken for victims of the Srebrenica genocide, Hurricane Katrina, and the World Trade Center attacks.

On the surface, they all represent populations for whom states have determined that the costly procedures of DNA testing are necessary to reestablish authority and thereby care and control over their citizens, both living and dead. But dig a little deeper and we begin to see disparities in how and why genetic testing is being used to recognize nameless remains. The US government responded to the missing of the World Trade Center attacks and Hurricane Katrina in significantly different ways and on a significantly different scale. The former population became emblematic of national suffering, the latter of national disgrace. In asking why, we cannot help but compare the sites of violence and destruction, New York City and New Orleans, and, by extension, the political significance of the two respective populations. Do the disparities in how, when, and why DNA testing was brought to bear in the identification of both groups of missing reinforce an already "unequal distribution of wealth and privilege?" Undeniably, the financial capital of the United States, its firefighters and police officers, presented a more politically valuable constituency than the poor blacks stranded on rooftops in the lower Ninth Ward.[22]

Furthermore, DNA identification of 9/11 victims was easily worked into the narrative advanced by the Bush administration of US national injury followed by military response directed at the aggressor. In contrast, the American public never got to know the Hurricane Katrina missing in the same individuated way that it did victims of the World Trade Center attacks. The story of the recovery efforts for the Katrina missing took on a very different tone. In New Orleans, the belated funding of DNA identification fortified rather than quelled the expanding blame game. Overdue identification of bodies that had been sitting in the state coroner's office for months was rubbing salt into the wound rather than serving as a technology of repair.

Disparities exist not only in how the Bosnian DNA-based technology has been applied but also in *whether* its resources have been and will be applied. In the case of postconflict societies, the technology's costs will invariably be borne by international donors, most likely state governments. Who will determine which "missing" are politically salient enough to merit such expenses? Srebrenica is a telling example. Its mass graves became a strategic site for international intervention in postwar Bosnia, as President Clinton first established the International Commission on Missing Persons and the Dutch government earmarked its donation to the institution's Srebrenica-specific facilities. DNA testing represented a means of righting certain wrongs, specifically the inaction of the international community that led to the fall of the UN "safe area" and the eventual killing of 8,000 Bosniak men and boys. One year earlier, a different genocide took place also under the watch of a pathetically insufficient UN peacekeeping force: the 1994 Rwandan genocide, in which some 800,000 people, Tutsi and moderate Hutus, were slaughtered in a period of 100 days. Is it merely on account of cultural or religious practice that no comprehensive system of DNA testing has to this day been applied to identify the victims of that genocide?[23] While we cannot answer this question definitively—certainly not in the space and scope of this text—it is worth asking, if only to raise some of the same concerns as Jasanoff has, concerns about how the technological innovation of DNA testing may reinscribe sociopolitical and economic inequities already in place.

# Epilogue

Reattaching individual identity onto nameless physical bodies is a dynamic and multivalent process. In the case of Srebrenica, identifying the missing 8,000 Bosniak men and boys killed in the enclave has meant different things to different people in postwar Bosnia. Aims and expectations pinned to the innovative biotechnology do not always align and, indeed, are frequently at odds. Bosniak and Bosnian Serb divergent responses to the slowly filling cemetery in Potočari illustrate how the technology's results can deepen communal divisions at the same time as they reconstitute physical and social beings. And as the Bosnian technology has gone on to inform the identification efforts for mass fatalities beyond the Balkans—from the World Trade Center attacks to the 2004 tsunami and Hurricane Katrina—we see more clearly its role as an instrument of governmentality, as states employ the costly resource in their efforts to care for and control their citizens, both living and dead.

Compelling as they are, these aspects of the identification process, however, are not the main point of this study. Rather, at its core, this book is about why people seek out the remains of their loved ones—what it means to them—and how the advent of a DNA-based system of postmortem identification has helped transform this process of recovery, remembering, and reckoning. It is a reminder that among the various registers of meaning, the individual is our entry point into the social.

In its capacity to refocus our attention on individual lives and individual experiences, the technology dismantles the monoliths of collective identity—be it in the form of perceived ethnic difference or anonymous mass death. The victims of Srebrenica were killed because they were seen to belong to a collectivity: Bosnian Muslims living in an enclave located in eastern Bosnia. Individual identity was stripped away from them, removed like the identity cards from their pockets or the shirts from their backs. Thousands of their bodies were decimated, the individual integrity of each skeleton violently dismantled by the claw of a backhoe or the tilt of a dump truck. Those remains were then deposited in unmarked secondary mass graves. They lay there for months, in most cases years—some even today—nameless and unrecognizable. Yet with a few drops of blood pressed onto a stain card and a section of bone cut away from a set of recovered remains, the identification technology could begin to piece back together both a body and a life story.

This achievement not only marks an unprecedented biotechnological advance; it also reaffirms individual identity in the face of the annihilating force of collective violence. The surviving families of the Srebrenica missing demanded a response that restored individual identity to brutalized bodies. In doing so, they insisted that their missing relatives be recognized not as a collective group, as Unknown Victims entombed in a collective ossuary, but as individuals, albeit individuals who suffered and died collectively. Their need for sanctified, witnessed, and, above all, individual burial was by no means unique: across cultures and time, the recovery and proper burial of mortal remains is a social rite claimed by families, friends, and neighbors of the deceased. For this reason, we sympathize with Antigone in her decision to defy Creon's decree "that none shall entomb him or mourn, but leave unwept, unsepulchred, a welcome store for the birds, as they espy him, to feast on at will."[1]

In the case of the Srebrenica missing, propelled by different motives, people with power gradually came to support the biotechnological initiative: Bosniak political and religious leaders, the international representatives of postwar Bosnia's protectorate government, the states backing that government and intent on implementing a nation-building project of social reconstruction and rehabilitation. Whether these people in power were moved most by the idea of returning bones to mothers or by fostering reconciliation or by righting wrongs of inaction may never be entirely clear. What is clear is that these actors saw DNA testing as the resolution to the crisis of identity posed by the Srebrenica graves.

268

Epilogue

Thus, with financial and political backing secured, the biological expression of these missing persons' respective individuality became the key to recognizing their remains. The part for the whole—the synecdoche of DNA—promised literally to reassemble scattered parts into whole bodies. By matching the unique, though related, genetic profiles from blood and bone samples, names as the signpost for individual and social identity were reattached to the victims' physical remains.

As we marvel at what genetic testing has accomplished in response to the gritty, harrowing conditions of Srebrenica's secondary mass graves, the "innovation patented by the Bosnian Serbs," we must nevertheless recognize the biotechnology's social contingencies. DNA evidence of identity does not exist in a vacuum; rather, its success depends on other manifestations of individual lives, social ties, and everyday practice. Family members holding a piece of cloth, touching its fabric, whose patterns and stitching are indelibly etched into their memory, use their individual recollections to help retrieve their missing relatives' remains from the shelves of body bags that fill the Podrinje Identification Project's mortuary. Without that act of recognition, in which the family member recalls a memory-image that aligns with something among the evidence presented to her, identification relies solely on the trust she places in the DNA testing results. And if that trust is not present, no matter how certain the forensic experts themselves are in the identity of a given set of mortal remains, those remains are not officially recognized. The social, legal, and political weight of identifying missing persons ultimately depends on whether family members accept the proof offered them and acknowledge the remains as belonging to their missing relatives.

The overwhelming majority of Srebrenica families want this moment of recognition and have been awaiting it for years. As they wait, they call upon memory and imagination to maintain the social identity of their missing relatives. Recall the words of the mother who testified against General Krstić as she described how she imagined her son's hands picking strawberries. Memories and imaginings endure, despite the terrible, though partial, knowledge of the genocide. DNA endures despite the Bosnian Serb forces' attempts to erase all signs of their victims' individual identity. Combining forces, the families' subjective experiences and the DNA technology align to reconnect individual identity to physical remains and thereby counter the decimating effects of collective violence. Moreover, as we saw with the individual gravesites in the Srebrenica-Potočari Memorial Center Cemetery, the physical and metaphysical care for individual identity extends beyond the act of initial recognition. Once their whereabouts are known and marked, remains can be tended just as carefully as memories or imagined existence.

For those of us who have not experienced violence on such a scale, the nexus of technology, memory, and imagination offers a new way to think about Srebrenica's aftermath. It compels us to consider and, indeed, remember individual lives despite the brutal sweep of collective violence. It reminds us that human identity can never be reduced to the collective. Perhaps at its most arresting moments, it urges us to imagine what absence of that kind would mean in our own lives, and, in doing so, invites us to envision how we might respond to such loss.

# Notes

INTRODUCTION

1. I refer to the country of Bosnia and Herzegovina (formally, the Republic of Bosnia and Herzegovina)—which in Bosnian, Croatian, and Serbian languages is Bosna i Herzegovina (abbreviated BiH)—as "Bosnia and Herzegovina" or simply as "Bosnia."

2. The term *Bosniak (bošnjak)* refers to the ethno-national group of people known as Bosnian Muslims. Officially adopted in 1993 by the Bosniak Assembly (Bošnjački sabor), this explicitly nonreligious label became the preferred ethnonym for Bosnian Muslims after the 1992–1995 war. The ethno-national category of "Bosnian Muslims" itself arises from a complicated history of national identity formation in former Yugoslavia (Djilas 1991; Denich 1994; Donia and Fine 1994; Duijzings 2000; Hammel 2000; Hayden 1992b; Gagnon 2004). Before the rise of nationalism in the late nineteenth century, religion and language, rather than nationhood, defined ethnicity among the South Slavic people (Catholics, Orthodox, Muslim, and Jewish), and Bosnian Muslims were not considered a formal ethno-national group (Bringa 1995; Greenberg 1996). It was not until the 1960s, in socialist Yugoslavia, that Bosnian Muslims were officially recognized as a distinct national people *(narod)*. Even so, Muslims frequently included themselves in the category of "Yugoslav" when asked their ethnicity in Yugoslav censuses (Donia and Fine 1994:178; Hammel 2000:26). Throughout this text I refer to Bosnian Muslims as Bosniaks, in keeping with common usage among my informants and media representations. Nevertheless, there are instances when informants or other sources use the label "Bosnian Muslim," and I have kept the term in order to reflect their language.

3. The term *enclave* refers to the wartime area of Bosniak-controlled land that encompassed the city of Srebrenica and outlying villages and hamlets.

(See the inset on the Map of Bosnia and Herzegovina.) In January 1993, when this area was linked with Cerska, another pocket of Bosniak territory, the Srebrenica enclave stretched over 900 square kilometers in eastern Bosnia (United Nations 1999, pt. 2, sec. E, par. 36). In April 1993, the UN Security Council declared Srebrenica a "safe area" and sent peacekeeping troops to protect it. I thus refer to the wartime area of Srebrenica alternately as the enclave or safe area.

4. The number of victims in the 1992–1995 war has been a source of great debate throughout the postwar period. Recent findings of the Research and Documentation Center of Sarajevo (Istraživačko dokumentacioni centar), headed by Mirsad Tokača, provide the most definitive tabulation to date, establishing the number of human losses at 97,207 (Research and Documentation Center 2007). This represents a significant reduction from the previously accepted number of 200,000 dead.

5. The applicability of the legal term *genocide* to describe the events of Srebrenica in July 1995 derives from the conviction of Bosnian Serb general Radislav Krstić on the charge of genocide, a decision handed down by the International Criminal Tribunal for the former Yugoslavia on August 2, 2001. Although the ICTY appeals chamber subsequently overturned that conviction for the lesser charge of aiding and abetting genocide, they upheld the trial chamber's initial finding that genocide was committed in Srebrenica in 1995 (ICTY Prosecutor v. Radislav Krstić 2004). Article 4(2) of the tribunal's statute defines genocide as follows: "any of the following acts committed with the intent to destroy, in whole or in part, a national, ethnical, racial or religious group, as such: (a) killing members of the group; (b) causing serious bodily or mental harm to members of the group; (c) deliberately inflicting on the group conditions of life calculated to bring about its physical destruction in whole or in part; (d) imposing meaures intended to prevent births within the group; (e) forcibly transferring children of the group to another group" (ICTY Updated Statute 2007).

6. The phrase "surface graves" refers to remains recovered on the surface of the earth (i.e., remains that had not been intentionally buried). In the case of Srebrenica, most surface graves were located along the trek made by the column of men attempting to flee to Bosniak-controlled territory.

7. Tone Bringa's film *Returning Home: Revival of a Bosnian Village* explores the complicated experience of returning to prewar residences, as well as relations among neighbors of different ethnicities in a postwar village in central Bosnia (Bringa 2001; reviewed by Helms 2003). For an ethnographic study of refugee return experiences more generally, see Laura Hammond's *This Place Will Become Home* (2004).

8. Hajra's husband was identified a little more than a year later, in December 2004.

9. When referring to the family association, I use the shortened name of Women of Srebrenica. All citations of material published by the Women of Srebrenica, however, are listed under the organization's name in Bosnian (i.e., Žene Srebrenice).

10. As of December 7, 2007, the International Commission for Missing

Persons had generated a total of 20,315 DNA match reports for 12,927 different missing individuals from across former Yugoslavia. These matches were derived from a database of 84,740 DNA profiles from surviving family members seeking 28,422 missing persons.

11. Unless otherwise noted, all translations of interviews and published and unpublished material in Bosnian/Croatian/Serbian (BCS) are my own.

12. Kešetović is not the first person to observe that a "person cannot go missing." The US ambassador to Croatia at the time of the enclave's fall later remarked, "People don't just disappear. . . . Once we didn't hear from them and once we couldn't get access to the area, we knew. How could we not know?" (quoted in Power 2002:412).

13. I use the masculine personal pronoun to refer to a single missing person because the overwhelming majority of the victims from Srebrenica were men and boys. ICMP's Podrinje Identification Project registers a total of four women missing after the fall of the Srebrenica enclave. The Women of Srebrenica's records indicate that approximately 600 women died in the enclave from April 1992 to July 1995.

14. See Paul Sant Cassia's discussion of the defilement of corpses of the missing in Cyprus (2005:97–98).

15. The Dayton Peace Agreement divided Bosnia and Herzegovina into two separate political and territorial entities: the Federation of Bosnia and Herzegovina (Federacija Bosne i Herzegovine), with 51 percent of the country's territory, and the Republika Srpska (RS), with 49 percent. The interentity boundary (see the map of Bosnia and Herzegovina) demarcates the two entities.

16. In the early period of its operations in 1996–1997, ICMP established an agreement to support Physicians for Human Rights' forensic activities in Bosnia.

17. Because the physical matter recovered is in different states of decomposition and often not complete, throughout this work I use the term *mortal remains* or simply *remains* to describe what is exhumed from mass or surface graves. When I felt the context required it or to reflect an informant's language, however, I have employed different terms, including *body* and *skeletal remains*.

18. Given the disarticulation caused by the secondary mass graves and the scattering of bones associated with the surface graves, the total number of reference samples taken from recovered skeletal remains will likely well exceed 8,000.

19. This translation is the English version of the prayer that appears on one of the three sides of the stone monument. Robert Hayden noted that the word *tuga* is better translated as "sadness" or "sorrow" as opposed to "grievance"; the meaning, therefore, shifts subtly but significantly, as the line should read "may sorrow [rather than grievance] become hope!"

20. The term *expert* also entails a sense of authority—but "expert for whom, and to whose benefit?" (Brodwin 2000:329). Both it and the label "technologist," used throughout this study, are indicative of an authority and concomitant social capital granted to the DNA-based identification technology

(Bourdieu 1985; Verdery 1991:17–18), themes I will explore in the proceeding chapters.

## CHAPTER 1. THE FALL OF SREBRENICA

Epigraph: The English translation of Advija Ibrahimović's speech was provided to representatives of the local and international press; I received a copy of the translation from Sadik Salimović, a journalist and returnee living in Srebrenica.

1. Erdemović pleaded guilty and agreed to testify before the ICTY; after appeal he received a five-year prison sentence and was released in August 2000. Upon entering his guilty plea, Erdemović remarked to the court, "Your Honour, I had to do this. If I had refused, I would have been killed together with the victims. When I refused, they told me: 'If you are sorry for them, stand up, line up with them and we will kill you too'. I am not sorry for myself but for my family, my wife and son who then had nine months, and I could not refuse because then they would have killed me. That is all I wish to add" (ICTY Prosecutor v. Dražen Erdemović 1998, par. 14; see also Drakulić 2004: 106–120). In total, there are nineteen cases related to the Srebrenica enclave at the ICTY, including indictments against Radovan Karadžić and Ratko Mladić. Karadžić was captured by Serbian authorities in July 2008; Mladić remains at large.

2. Several copies of the tape were allegedly available at a video rental shop in Šid, the hometown of the Scorpion unit on the Serbian-Croatian border; members of the unit and their friends borrowed and viewed the video for ten years before it fell into the hands of a "neutral" party, who decided to turn the tape over to the Belgrade human rights activist Nataša Kandić, who subsequently gave it to authorities at the tribunal (Williams 2005).

3. The same decision for the case (CH01–8365 et al. Selimović and 48 Others v. the Republika Srpska) compelled the RS government to pay 2 million KM *(konvertibilne marke)* to the Foundation of the Srebrenica-Potočari Memorial Center (Human Rights Chamber for Bosnia and Herzegovina 2003).

4. Čavić's statement was included in the Government of the Republika Srpska Conclusions, adopted October 28, 2004 (Government of the Republika Srpska 2004:3).

5. Rohde won the Pulitzer Prize for International Reporting for his coverage of the Srebrenica genocide and its mass graves. See his article "Evidence Indicates Bosnia Massacre," *Christian Science Monitor,* August 18, 1995. Rohde was captured and detained by Bosnian Serb officials while investigating the whereabouts of the Srebrenica mass graves.

6. In 2005, Nuhanović published a book from this initial research, *Pod zastavom UN-a: međunarodna zajednica i zločin u Srebrenici* (Under the UN Flag: The International Community and the Srebrenica Genocide), and the Women of Srebrenica followed suit in 2007, publishing *Ujedinjani narodi na srebreničkom stubu srama* (The United Nations on Srebrenica's Pillar of Shame), based on the testimony of Srebrenica survivors.

7. The Independent State of Croatia (Nezavisna Država Hrvatska, NDH) was established in April 1941 following the occupation of Yugoslavia by Fas-

cist Italy and Nazi Germany. Led by Croatian fascist Ante Pavelić, the NDH encompassed Croatia, Bosnia and Herzegovina, and parts of Slovenia and Serbia. It pursued the systematic elimination of Jews, Gypsies, and Serbs within its boundaries; by 1944, most of the 30,000 Jews of NDH had been transported to Nazi labor or extermination camps (Donia and Fine 1994:139).

8. On the disintegration of Yugoslavia, see V. P. Gagnon's *The Myth of Ethnic War* (2004), Sabrina Ramet's *Balkan Babel* (2002), and Ivo Banac's 1992 article "The Fearful Asymmetry of War: The Causes and Consequences of Yugoslavia's Demise."

9. The term *narod* is translated as "people" and, in the context of postwar Bosnia, often refers to nationality or ethno-national groups such as *srpski narod* (Serbian people) or *bošnjački narod* (Bosniak people). See Bringa (1995:2–27); Bougarel, Helms, and Duijzings (2007:1); Lockwood (1975); and Denich (1994).

10. These figures come from the 1991 census for Bosnia and Herzegovina. Its prewar minority populations included Montenegrins, Roma, Albanians, Ukrainians, and "Yugoslavs" (Bringa 1995:26).

11. The Bosnian Croat branch of the Croatian Democratic Union (Hrvatska demokratska zajednica, or HDZ) established the "Croat Republic of Herzeg-Bosna" on November 18, 1991.

12. The term *ethnic cleansing* (*etničko čišćenje*) predates the wars in former Yugoslavia in the 1990s. The term *čišćenje* (or the verb *rasčistiti*) "was used in the vernacular during World War II to describe a military action akin to 'mopping up,' as in the term *rasčistiti teren* ('mopping up the terrain')" (Bringa 2002:204). See also Pamela Ballinger's analysis of the term applied to violence carried out by Yugoslav forces against Italians in Istria and Dalmatia during World War II (2003:73, 119, 145–156).

13. These numbers are taken from the Yugoslav 1990 census.

14. An estimated 1,000 to 2,000 troops from three brigades of the Bosnian Serb Army's Drina Corps were deployed in the area surrounding the Srebrenica enclave.

15. In 2006, the tribunal convicted Orić of failing to take steps to prevent the murder and cruel treatment of a number of Serb prisoners in the enclave; he was acquitted of several other related charges and, having already served the imposed sentence of two years imprisonment, he was released from custody.

16. Sudetic quotes surviving Serbs from Kravica as having pledged to exact revenge on the Muslims of Srebrenica for the raid. " '*Kad tad*,' the men swore to one another. '*Kad tad*. Sooner or later, we'll get our five minutes' " (1998:164). In his epilogue, Sudetic recounts a conversation with two men, a father and son from Kravica who had survived the raid. They discuss Srebrenica and the participation in the torture and mass killing by men from Kravica. " 'Was it honorable to kill them all?' I asked the father. 'Absolutely,' he said. 'It was a fair fight' " (1998:352).

17. The Finding of Fact in the Krstić judgment cites the number of refugees in the enclave following the Serb capture of Konjević Polje and Cerska at 50,000 to 60,000 (ICTY Prosecutor v. Radislav Krstić 2001, par. 14).

18. From the onset, the French government appeared to adopt a pro-Serb

approach to the war, epitomized by President Mitterand's visit to Sarajevo in July 1992, a gesture intimating that military intervention was not required. This impression was compounded by France's initial reluctance to condemn the Serbs even upon the discovery of Bosniak concentration camps in the summer of 1992.

19. The Krstić judgment states that "between March and April 1993, approximately 8,000 to 9,000 Bosnian Muslims were evacuated from Srebrenica under the auspices of the UN High Commissioner for Refugees (UNHCR). The evacuations were, however, opposed by the Bosnian Muslim government in Sarajevo as contributing to the 'ethnic cleansing' of the territory" (ICTY Prosecutor v. Radislav Krstić 2001, par. 16).

20. Security Council Resolution 824 of May 6, 1993, established the other enclaves as safe areas; Resolution 836, passed on June 4, 1993, extended the UN mission's mandate to include the safe areas, detailing the terms of "peace enforcement" that would prove crucial to the decision-making process in June and July of 1995. Resolution 836 stipulated that the UN troops were to "deter attacks against the safe area" (UN Security Council 1993b, par. 5) and authorized "acting in self-defense, to take necessary measures, including the use of force, in reply to bombardments against the safe areas by any of the parties or to armed incursion into them or in the event of any deliberate obstruction in or around those areas to the freedom of movement of UNPROFOR or of protected humanitarian convoys" (par. 9).

21. The UNPROFOR troops were to oversee the disarming of the Bosniak forces within the enclave.

22. In contrast to the estimated 1,500 total (Honig and Both 1996:130), the United Nations report estimates this number to be higher, with 3,000 to 4,000 men in the 28th Division (United Nations 1999, pt. vi, par. 230).

23. In addition to the raids on Serb villages surrounding the enclave, a steady stream of goods flowed back and forth between Srebrenica and the other Muslim-held safe area of Žepa. "The enclave was certainly not hermetically sealed" (Honig and Both 1996:131).

24. Beyond simply launching raids on Serb villages from the enclave, Orić and his top military commanders "had the disconcerting habit of taking up positions close to the Dutch and then opening fire on the Serbs, hoping to entice them and the Dutch into a firefight"; furthermore, they would turn off the Dutch compound's water supply and stop Dutch patrols when they saw fit (Honig and Both 1996:133).

25. These words appeared alongside other graffiti and murals sketched by Dutchbat soldiers during the period of 1994–1995, with the texts penned in both English and Dutch. This particular piece of graffiti became the subject of Bosnian artist Šejla Kamerić's critique of the Dutch peacekeeping forces in the Srebrenica enclave. Working with photographer Tarik Samarah, Kamerić superimposed the text onto her own photograph, a striking image of the young woman dressed in a sleeveless white shirt, staring intently at the camera. The piece appeared on billboards, in magazines, and as posters and postcards, both in Bosnia and abroad.

26. A friend from Srebrenica once described to me how, at the most des-

perate stage during her three years in the enclave, she and another woman survived an entire month on 1 kilo of flour as their only food staple.

27. The Dutch NIOD report also details the deterioration of relations between the enclave's civilian authorities and the staff of the few NGOs providing aid to the refugee population, including Médecins Sans Frontières, the International Committee of the Red Cross, and the Swedish Rescue Services (NIOD 2002: pt. 2, chap. 7). Naser Orić appeared to have the most political power. A staff member of Médecins Sans Frontières wrote that "the king of the place is without competition Commander Naser. . . . Without his official consent, nothing can be done in this town! . . . He controls the black market, the prostitution and Opstina. All of this, of course, under the cover of the official authorities" (NIOD 2002: pt. 2, chap. 7).

28. In his memoir *The Reawakening,* Primo Levi describes the grueling thirty-month journey from Auschwitz to his hometown, Turin, and the heartbreaking disappointment of life immediately after liberation from the Nazi death camp: "Liberty, the improbable, the impossible liberty, so far removed from Auschwitz that we had only dared to hope for it in our dreams, had come, but it had not taken us to the Promised Land. It was around us, but in the form of a pitiless deserted plain. More trials, more toil, more hunger, more cold, more fears awaited us" (1987:26). See also Mark Wyman's analysis of this period in *DPs: Europe's Displaced Persons* (1998).

29. In analyzing psychosocial mechanisms of such moral disengagement in the context of violent conflict (i.e., specifically terrorism), Albert Bandura examines the dissociative practices of the diffusion or displacement of responsibility for violence (1990).

30. Mustafić's remark about the Dutchbat (UNPROFOR) colleagues being tied up was a reference to an incident a month before. UNPROFOR air raids on Bosnian Serb ammunition depots near the city of Pale had resulted in the Bosnian Serbs taking a total of 375 UNPROFOR troops hostage throughout the country (Honig and Both 1996:8). Fears of hostage taking and the use of UNPROFOR hostages as human shields would play into the UN commanders' decisions about whether to protect the enclave through the use of air strikes in July 1995.

31. In the months leading up to July 1995, Bosnian Serb forces prevented soldiers from returning to the enclave after they had gone out of the area on leave, thus reducing their numbers substantially.

32. The special representative of the secretary general received a telephone call from the Dutch minister of defense, who requested that the air strikes be discontinued "because Serb soldiers on the scene were too close to the Dutch troops, and their safety would be jeopardized. . . . The Minister made similar calls to the Under-Secretary-General for Peacekeeping Operations in New York and his Military Adviser (a Dutch Major-General) at the same time, which were echoed in demarches by the Permanent Representative of the Netherlands" (United Nations 1999, pt. vii, sec. F, par. 306).

33. Mladić was referring to the first Serbian uprising (1804–1813) against the *dahis,* Turkish local military, or high-ranking janissary. In appendix IV of the NIOD report, anthropologist Ger Duijzings analyzes Mladić's historical

framing of the Bosnian war and in particular the cultural significance of his army's occupation of Srebrenica (NIOD 2002: app. 4, intro. and chap. 1).

34. The United Nations report lists the age range as seventeen to sixty (1999, pt. viii, sec. A, par. 320).

35. Sandići is a village located on the Bratunac–Konjević Polje road. In June 2004, after receiving information provided by the RS Commission on Srebrenica, the Federation Commission for Missing Persons, along with ICMP staff, exhumed a primary mass grave at Sandići. The grave contained eighteen bodies thought to be victims from Srebrenica (Hadžić 2004a). It also contained several unexploded genades and grenade launchers, presumably placed among the bodies by those who dug and filled the grave. "All of the explosive devices found were among the bodies of the victims, which leads one to the conclusion that they were left there intentionally. Until now mines had been found in the immediate vicinity of mass graves, but Sandići is the first location at which explosive material was found in the grave itself" (Huremović 2004). The practice was not a new one in the region; Pamela Ballinger details the example of a mine shaft in Basovizza, near Trieste, which contains the remains of Istrian Italians killed by Slovenes during World War II. Sealed off after the war because of rumored explosives and other weaponry, the site has never been exhumed, so the total number of victims has never been determined (2003:138).

36. Rohde describes how the Dutch detail to accompany the convoy of buses quickly fell apart: "The Dutch attempt to escort convoys of civilians was turning into a farce" (1997:255). The Bosnian Serb forces stopped the Dutch vehicles, demanding the peacekeepers' flak jackets and helmets, and in some cases, their vehicles. Two Dutch soldiers were forced to ride with Bosnian Serbs in a stolen Dutch armored personnel carrier while they went "Muslim hunting"—that is, trying to find and kill Bosniak men in the column trekking along the Bratunac–Konjević Polje road (Rohde 1997:275).

37. One of the saddest and most oft-recounted stories of the inconsistencies in the deportation of the final group of Bosniaks inside the compound is that of the young translator Hasan Nuhanović. Hasan's father, Ibro Nuhanović, who had served as one of the three representatives in the final meeting with Mladić, was to be included among the protected UN staff, as was Hasan because of his role as a translator with the Dutchbat. But Hasan's younger brother and mother were not. After Hasan's unsuccessful pleas to several of his Dutch colleagues to gain protection for his entire family, Ibro decided to leave with his wife and younger son. None of the three survived; Hasan's younger brother was identified and buried at the Srebrenica-Potočari Memorial Center in July 2007, but both parents remain missing. Shortly after watching his father, brother, and mother walk out of the compound and into the Serbs' hands, Hasan found out that other local UN and NGO staff had managed to include their family members among the group of protected personnel. (See Neuffer 2002; Rohde 1997.)

38. It should be noted that the Drina Corps Bratunac Brigade had compiled a list, dated July 12, 1995, of 387 Bosniaks in the enclave suspected of war crimes (ICTY Prosecutor v. Radislav Krstić 2001, par. 156).

39. Rohde recounts a telling conversation between a Dutch soldier, Lieutenant Leen van Duijn, and a Bosnian Serb soldier about the import of the confiscated identity cards: " 'You're going to try to identify the people?' van Duijn asked. 'Yes,' Mane said. 'We have a list of war criminals.' 'Then you'll need their passports to identify them,' van Duijn said. 'I don't follow you,' Mane said. 'Those passports,' van Duijn said, pointing at the pile on the ground. 'You're going to need to identify the Muslims or they'll just give you false names.' 'You're crazy,' Mane said, shaking his head and laughing. 'They don't need those passports anymore' " (1997:277).

40. According to information collected from surviving family members by the International Commission on Missing Persons, 25 percent of the total number of Srebrenica missing were detained at Potočari, while the remaining 75 percent were captured as they tried to escape through the forest.

41. The bullet-point descriptions of the execution and burial sites summarize the more comprehensive material presented in the Krstić judgment. Since the Krstić case, the Federation Commission for Missing Persons and ICMP have located and exhumed several additional mass graves, including, among others, ten found in the Kamenica valley near Zvornik (the largest of which, Kamenica-9, contained at least 600 sets of incomplete and complete remains) and in the villages of Potočari, Zeleni Jadar, and Budak.

42. To avoid using too many acronyms, I refer to the International Committee of the Red Cross at times as simply the "Red Cross" as opposed to ICRC.

43. The misspelling of Potočari (Potochari) is presumably a parody of the Dutchbat and international pronunciation and spelling of the name.

44. It later came out that the film containing the photographs of the nine dead bodies was "accidentally" destroyed at a processing lab. "Outraged members of the Dutch Parliament accused the Ministry of Defense of a cover-up" (Rohde 1997:336).

CHAPTER 2. THE PEOPLE AND PLACE OF POSTWAR SREBRENICA

1. The word *srebro* means silver. Srebrenica got its name from the silver mines run by the Sasi (Saxons primarily from Hungary) who came to the region in the late thirteenth and early fourteenth centuries. It was considered the most important silver mining center in the region (Fine 1994:283). There is a mining village near Srebrenica named Sasa, a direct reference to its Saxon founders. Until the war, much of the region's economy depended heavily on bauxite and zinc mining, but only a fraction of the mines have since reopened. They are owned and run by Bosnian Serbs and allegedly employ only Bosnian Serbs. See Peric (2007) for a historical analysis of the nexus of mining and mass graves in western Bosnia and Herzegovina.

2. The phrase *minority return* refers to the return of members of the minority ethnic group to their prewar residences in the entity controlled by another, majority, ethnic group. For example, in the Podrinje region, located within the Bosnian Serb–controlled entity of the Republika Sprska, Bosniaks who return to their prewar houses are considered minority returnees. By the same logic,

Bosnian Serbs returning to the Bosniak and Croat–controlled Federation are also minority returnees.

3. When I visited the city in July 2007, residents told me that the spa no longer officially housed displaced Bosnian Serbs and that many of the longtime residents had moved out over the previous few months.

4. During and after the war, collective centers such as the Argentaria (the former Banja Guber spa) in Srebrenica or complexes like Mihatović on the outskirts of Tuzla were built or designated as temporary housing for internally displaced persons.

5. As Bosnian Serbs departed from Sarajevo's southern suburbs in late 1995, many burned their own homes, leaving them uninhabitable for potential Bosniak occupants. Rid of its Bosniak population, Serb Sarajevo (Srpsko Sarajevo) still fell within the territory of the RS. Serbian Orthodox archdeacon Jovan Ćulibrk explained the significance of this situation: "*Serbian* Sarajevo is . . . the symbol of a town cleansed by fire. Its survival (through the Republika Srpska) is the ruin of the *political* charge of pop-culture: proof of the impotence of the West to realize its fiction through the tools of politics" (italics in the original; Čolović 2002:255).

6. After the fall of the enclave, Serbs declared Petrovdan (July 12) the official patron saint day of Srebrenica (NIOD 2001: app. 4, n. 1).

7. As one example of their continued support, in the immediate postwar years, residents of the Milići municipality in the RS allegedly paid a fee listed on their monthly electricity bill as the "Radovan Karadžić fund."

8. The nursing outreach project was part of a larger program run by the Dutch NGO Werkgroep Nederlands-Srebrenica (WNS). Headed by activist and mediator Abel Herzberger, WNS first began working with Srebrenica survivors in 1996, waging public awareness campaigns before Dutch audiences. In and around the city of Srebrenica, the organization sought to address the needs of Bosniak returnees and vulnerable Bosnian Serb residents through several related programs: funding micro-economic projects, running educational and recreational activities, and implementing a "Civil Foreign Presence" (CFP) initiative, of which the nursing outreach project was an important element. The main goal of the CFP was to diminish tensions in the city during the early period of return. To that end, from 2000 to 2003, volunteers from the Netherlands and the UK lived and worked in Srebrenica, constituting the only international organization whose staff took up full-time residence in the postwar city. WNS eventually helped establish a locally run and staffed successor organization called Prijatelji Srebrenice (Friends of Srebrenica).

9. The *vikendaši* criticism also applied to Bosnian Serb political representatives who left the municipality on the weekends for homes in places such as Bajina Bašta in Serbia.

10. See Elissa Helms on the image of female victimhood in Bosnian public discourse and, more particularly, in Bosnian politics (2007).

11. Many prewar residents of Srebrenica had been employed in the car brake, car battery, and zinc processing factories located in nearby Potočari (Rohde 1997:xiv).

12. The question of representation—whether the Sarajevo- and Tuzla-

based organizations indeed spoke for the majority of surviving families—arose repeatedly during my fieldwork. I encountered people who disagreed with public positions taken by the leaders of both organizations; I also met people who were not active members of either group but who nevertheless supported their work. Furthermore, as Delpla notes, membership numbers are ineffective evidence of representation; many of the officially listed members do not participate in regular activities and meetings (2007:220).

13. Although less prominent in the media and with fewer members, the Women of Srebrenica and Podrinje (Žene Srebrenice i Podrinja) and the Mothers of Srebrenica (Srebreničke majke) are two other notable family associations that also use the categories of motherhood and women in their association titles.

14. A collection of his poems, *Ljudi beznađa*, written during the war, was published posthumously in 2005.

15. When I first began visiting the association in the fall of 2003, its staff still occupied both sides of the apartment. A cut in funding from ICMP, the group's major donor, forced them to move into one side, effectively reducing their office space by half.

16. As of October 2007, the Women of Srebrenica had collected over 3,500 photographs, some sent to them from overseas or passed along through distant relatives or friends. The collection will one day be a part of a display in the Srebrenica-Potočari Memorial Center Museum.

17. Elissa Helms drew my attention to the specifically gendered significance of the pillowcases and embroidery during a discussion at the November 2005 conference "Politics and Society Ten Years after Dayton," held at the Human Rights Centre, University of Sarajevo.

18. Another major donor to the Women of Srebrenica was the Interchurch Peace Council (IKV); prior to ICMP's support, IKV funded the group's major activities and expenses, including the office space.

19. Caught up in a divisive struggle for public attention further aggravated by personal politics, the leaders of the two main Srebrenica advocacy organizations (the Women of Srebrenica and the Mothers of the Srebrenica and Žepa Enclaves) often regarded one another as rivals rather than partners in their campaigns for truth and justice.

## CHAPTER 3. A TECHNOLOGICAL INNOVATION

1. According to PIP staff, a total of 150 cases were closed during the period of 1996–2001; 99 of those cases were completed through out-of-country DNA testing and 51 by classical forensic methods (i.e., without DNA testing).

2. ICMP records indicate that from 2002 to 2006 a total of 2,689 Srebrenica victims were found and identified. As of July 15, 2005 (coinciding with the ten-year anniversary of the fall of Srebrenica), ICMP had generated 4,249 DNA matching reports for 2,981 different individuals from the enclave. By that same date, a total of 2,079 cases had been formally closed, of which 2,026 had been buried: 1,887 at the Potočari memorial center and 139 in other locations.

3. Hayden notes that atrocities committed in the Bosnian war have fre-

quently elicited comparison to the "official histories" of World War II, for example by juxtaposing " 'ethnic cleansing' and the Serbian-run death camps in Bosnia and Herzegovina with the Nazi practices of genocide" (Hayden 1994:181–182). He argues that there are more apt parallels to be drawn from that same period of violence in Yugoslavia, a point to which I will return in chapter 6. Other scholars have analyzed rhetorical strategies of invoking and comparing ethnic violence in former Yugoslavia to the Holocaust (Živković 2000; Ballinger 2003; Miller 2006).

4. The satellite imagery could have alerted UN peacekeepers to the increase in Bosnian Serb troops around the enclave in the days leading up to July 11, 1995. UN Dutchbat major Robert Franken recalled that the Dutch had in fact requested UN and NATO intelligence—aerial surveillance—concerning the possibility of a buildup twice in June and again on July 4. " 'Someone had to have seen what was going on,' said Franken. 'That they didn't is fucking nonsense' " (Rohde 1997:371). Immediately after the fall of the enclave, satellite imagery could have pinpointed the whereabouts of at least one substantial group of Bosniak captives: "One [US] spy photo showed several hundred prisoners gathered on the Nova Kasaba soccer field. Several days later, the prisoners were gone and four areas of fresh digging appeared conspicuously nearby" (Rohde 1997:334).

5. By the late fall of 1996, fewer than 550 sets of remains had been found in approximately one-third of the known and exhumed gravesites. Rohde writes, "If bodies were found at roughly the same ratios [the following year], approximately 1,650 victims of the mass executions would be located, a fraction of the 7,079 men reported missing to the Red Cross. According to the ICRC, 2,935 of the missing were last seen in Serb custody" (1997:347).

6. In 2004, the estimated ICMP cost per DNA match was $1,010; the necessary chemicals cost approximately $150 per bone sample and $70 per blood sample. The cost for the latter has since gone down and was estimated in 2007 to be $25 per sample.

7. The Federation government included these percentages, figures generated by the International Red Cross in Bosnia and Herzegovina, in a resolution about the Fund for Support for Families of the Missing (Fond za podršku porodicama nestalih osoba), passed during its forty-third session on January 23, 2008 (Vlada Federacije Bosne i Herzegovine 2008). The Sarajevo-based Research and Documentation Center has also carried out a project on population losses in Bosnia and Herzegovina from 1991 to 1995; its preliminary report, *Bosnian Book of the Dead*, documented that killed and missing Bosniaks totaled 64,036, Serbs 24,905, Croats 7,788, and other nationalities 478 (Research and Documentation Center 2007).

8. See Annex 4: Constitution of Bosnia and Herzegovina in the Dayton Peace Agreement (Office of the High Representative 1995).

9. The RS commission web site explains that the Office of the High Representative ordered the change in name, specifically that the word "state" be removed: "Поменимо и то да је Комисија, на инсистирање Канцеларије високог представника, промијенила назив тако што је из њеног имена избрисана ријеч *државна*. Истовремено, формирањем Федералне комисије за тражење несталих није

стављена ван снаге одлука о формирању Државне комисије за нестала и заробљена лица БиХ сто је, донедавно, служило за манипулацију проблемом несталих на подручју БиХ." (We would also mention that the Commission, at the insistence of the Office of the High Representative, changed its title so that the word *state* was erased from its name. At the same time, with the formation of the Federation Commission for Missing Persons, the decision to form a State Commission for Missing Persons and Prisoners of Bosnia and Herzegovina was not invalidated, thereby making it easier to manipulate the problem of Bosnia and Herzegovina's missing persons.) (Office for Tracing Detained and Missing of Republic of Srpksa 2007.)

10. See Article I of Annex 10 for the types of activities falling within the realm of the civilian peace settlement, including, among others, humanitarian assistance, reconstruction, refugee return, and promotion of human rights (Office of the High Representative 1995).

11. The Office of the High Representative's authority increased significantly when in May 1997 the Peace Implementation Council authorized OHR to crack down on an RS public media outlet that had been accused of broadcasting messages intended to incite violence. Knaus and Martin argue that OHR's intervention (its insistence that the Serb broadcaster's entire management resign) resulted in the significant expansion of OHR authority to the point that its newly extended powers soon became "instruments of bureaucratic convenience," as much as measures for structural reform (2003:63–65). Indeed, the Bonn powers, as they were called, enabled the High Representative to undertake drastic executive measures, including dismissing elected officials deemed obstructive (Chandler 1999; Campbell 1999:427). Several decisions made by the OHR under this expansion of power directly related to Srebrenica. For example, in 2003 High Representative Paddy Ashdown demanded that ownership of the former UN peacekeepers' compound, Battery Factory "AS" a.d.-Srebrenica, be handed over to the Foundation of the Srebrenica-Potočari Memorial Center for inclusion in the memorial complex (Office of the High Representative 2003a). In 2004, Ashdown also intervened into the RS fact-finding commission on Srebrenica, removing Serb members and demanding revisions to its final report (Office of the High Representative 2004).

12. Comparisons made between Bosnia's protectorate and nineteenth-century European imperialism, specifically British colonial administration in India, have sparked debate among Balkan scholars and members of the international community in Bosnia; see Gerald Knaus and Felix Martin's 2003 article, "Travails of the European Raj," in the *Journal of Democracy,* and Keith Brown's (2003) response, "Unraveling Europe's Raj" in *Foreign Policy.* Regarding the European face of OHR, Coles (2007b) notes that "as of February 2006, there have been five High Representatives, all male and all European politician/diplomats." Appointed in June 2007, the latest successor, Miroslav Lajčák, is a Slovak diplomat who previously served as Slovakia's ambassador to the Federal Republic of Yugoslavia (later Serbia and Montenegro); having learned Serbian in that post, Lajčák is the first High Representative who does not use a translator but instead regularly addresses the public in BCS.

13. For a detailed explanation of eligibility for this monetary support,

as well as information on other rights accorded families of the missing, see *Primjena zakona o nestalim osobama BiH: Vodić za porodice nestalih osoba* (Application of the Law on Missing Persons of Bosnia and Herzegovina: Guide for Family Members of Missing Persons), which includes the text of the Missing Persons Law, passed by the Bosnian Parliamentary Assembly in October 2004 (Ministarstvo za ljudska prava i izbjeglice 2006).

14. Power describes the Red Cross presence as a "small nongovernmental organization with no muscle behind it and a library of conventions that had gone unheeded in the past. It was tapped to perform the function it had always performed—negotiating access with the Serbs, compiling lists of missing, and inspecting prisoner conditions" (2002:411).

15. ICMP's records on cases of missing persons based on blood samples collected are larger in number than those represented by ICRC tracing requests. The Srebrenica missing are relatively well represented in ICRC's *Book of Missing*, which lists close to 95 percent of ICMP names. The missing from the enclave in 1992, however, were not as well represented; only about 75 percent of ICMP names from 1992 are included in earlier editions of the ICRC published list of tracing requests received.

16. Despite the urgency of the situation, the Red Cross's work also suffered because many relatives of the enclave's refugees already harbored deep distrust and skepticism. Nura Begović of the Women of Srebrenica described a revealing encounter with a Red Cross director in the Tuzla headquarters in late March 1993. Nura and two other women participating in a protest outside the ICRC building were summoned inside to meet with the head of the office. As the three women made their case, pleading for assistance, the international staff member, with his back turned to the visitors, played a game on his computer. Nura recounted, "I remember some ladybugs on the computer screen—I will never forget that." As their pleas became more strident, he finally turned away from the computer and told them flatly, "How do I know what the situation in Srebrenica is? We can't do anything to help you. You can protest as much as you want but nothing can be done." With that, the meeting was concluded and he went back to playing the computer game. Two years later, in the days following the Bosnian Serb Army's attack on the enclave, the refugees who arrived in Tuzla believed the Red Cross should have been doing more to signal to the outside world what was happening in Srebrenica. "When requests for access were ignored, the organization did not blare an alarm. . . . Despite the repetitiveness of the sequence [of the Bosnian Serb forces thwarting ICRC access to the prisoners], diplomats and ICRC officials joined in the pantomime, failing to grasp that they had a very short time to influence Serb behavior" (Power 2002:411).

17. Laurie Vollen, former director of Physicians for Human Rights's program for the Srebrenica missing, explained that the "documents were intended to help the next of kin obtain legal benefits such as pension. But the death attestation program caused a backlash; many, although not all, of the families were unwilling and unable to accept a 'paper death.' They claimed that their missing were being written off, that the search for places of hidden detention was inadequate, and that information was no substitute for bodies" (Vollen 2001).

See also Eric Stover's explanation of ICRC's "death attestation" program and the angry response it drew from families of the missing (1998:195–196).

18. For many years, ICRC's *Book of Missing* was considered the most complete and centralized record of missing persons from throughout former Yugoslavia. By 2004, surviving family members scattered across the globe were accessing the document, then in its sixth edition, on the organization's web site (www.familylinks.icrc.org).

19. The public response of documenting missing persons, specifically soldiers, has a complex history predating twentieth-century forensic practices and bureaucratic strategies. For example, in *This Republic of Suffering*, Drew Gilpin Faust details efforts to name and account for Civil War soldiers, whose designation of "Unknown" became increasingly significant and problematic in the aftermath of the war (2008:102–136).

20. There were earlier limited efforts by NGO representatives in 2002 to compile a comprehensive list of the Srebrenica missing, and in 2004 the "RS Commission for the Investigation of the Events in and around Srebrenica between 10 and 19 July" produced a list based on multiple sources.

21. The list drew from several sources, including the Red Cross, the family associations, the International Commission on Missing Persons, and the Federation commission's own archives. As Amor Mašović explained before an assembly of media representatives at the memorial center on June 9, 2005, each name had to have appeared in at least two other sources in order for it to be included in the commission's list (Hadžić 2005).

22. By 2007, the number on the commission's list had in fact increased to 8,400. Apparently, the list contained names of individuals who had died in the enclave before July 11, 1995 (i.e., during the period of 1992–1995). By including names of individuals who were not victims of the July 1995 genocide on this list, the Federation Commission for Missing Persons opened up the possibility of burying the pre–July 1995 enclave victims in the Srebrenica-Potočari Memorial Center. See chapter 7 for a discussion of the debate surrounding burials at the memorial center.

23. The organization Physicians for Human Rights (PHR) was contracted by ICMP to carry out its initial identification efforts. PHR left Bosnia in 1999, though many of its local staff members went on to work for ICMP, which took over the direction and implementation of its programs in former Yugoslavia.

24. In *The Graves: Srebrenica and Vukovar* (1998), Eric Stover provides a compelling chronicle of the early forensic efforts undertaken to identify the Srebrenica missing, describing the work of various individuals, mostly foreign forensic experts and investigators, who traveled to the region in the immediate postwar years.

25. *Making Things Public* is a volume of essays based on an exhibition held March 20–October 3, 2005, at the ZKM (Center for Art and Media Karlsruhe) in Karlsruhe, Germany. Bruno Latour and Peter Weibel were the exhibition's curators (Latour 2005).

26. In the years immediately following the war's end, institutions such as ICMP and its various programs worked together toward a complete accounting and recovery of the victims of Srebrenica; other institutions and individu-

als sought to deny or thwart such efforts, including Serbian authorities, the Bosnian Serb government officials of the Republika Srpska, Bosnian Serb civil associations, and private citizens. The numbers and lists of names were a particular point of contention. The Bosnian Serb public took their cues from the politicians and nationalist-oriented media in gauging their response to the "alleged" massacre. In September 2002, for example, the Bureau of the Government of Republika Srpska for Relations with the ICTY issued a report refuting the assertion that between 6,000 and 8,000 Bosniak men had been executed, instead claiming the number of missing to be 1,800. The RS bureau also maintained that "the number of Bosnian Muslim soldiers who were executed by Bosnian Serb forces for personal revenge or for simple ignorance of international law . . . would probably stand at less than 100" (Human Rights Chamber for Bosnia and Herzegovina 2003, par. 94).

27. Such rumors were grounded in wartime practice; the Bosnian Serb Army and police forces had used Bosniak prisoners as forced laborers to dig trenches and sometimes graves. The 2003 film *Gori vatra* (Fuse), directed by Pjer Žalica, incorporates this theme: the father of a missing man searches in vain for his son, imagining him trapped in an abandoned mine.

28. Mark Skinner and John Sterenberg, both former staff members of ICMP who worked on Srebrenica graves, analyze the exhumation process and the overlapping areas of forensic expertise present at exhumations of mass graves in their 2005 article "Turf Wars: Authority and Responsibility for the Investigation of Mass Graves."

29. Several companies have made in-kind donations of laboratory equipment: Applied Biosystems, Millipore Corp., Life Technologies Inc., GS Laboratory Equipment, Promega Corp., VWS Scientific Products, Techno Plastic Products AG, Revco, and Qiagen.

30. In 2004 ICMP began an initiative to use satellite imagery more systematically to uncover mass graves. By splitting satellite images into 270 color bands, technicians are able to detect where the ground has been disturbed. ICMP then sends a team to test for variations in electrical conductivity in the soil; the results provide an indication of where the remains are located. In her memoir of her experiences working as a forensic anthropologist at the exhumation sites of Srebrenica's mass graves Courtney Brkic describes how archaeologists read the earth's vegetation: "Sometimes there will be a perfect circle of flowers in an otherwise unremarkable field, a neon sign that can tell [them] where to start digging" (2004:127).

31. In collaboration with PIP, the Red Cross published a second volume of *Book of Belongings* in 2001; the book contained photographs of possessions found with the mortal remains of people who went missing during the fall of the enclave.

32. During this early period, the Physicians for Human Rights identification project, based in Tuzla, sent samples from presumptive cases to its Molecular Genetics Laboratory, which fell under the auspices of the laboratory of Mary-Claire King at the University of Washington, Seattle (Physicians for Human Rights 1997; see also Huffine et al. 2001:274).

33. Often the early presumptive cases involved remains found on the sur-

face in the woods, those of individuals who fled through the forest toward Tuzla; eyewitness testimony about the exact location where the person perished led the forensic experts to the grave. Clothing and personal possessions would also strengthen the presumption of identity. In other, rarer presumptive cases, a distinguishing physical feature such as a prosthetic limb aided identification.

34. In 1998, Ed Huffine was among the AFDIL scientists who identified the remains of Vietnam serviceman First Lieutenant Michael Blassie, exhumed from the Tomb of the Unknown Soldier at Arlington National Cemetery. Upon that occasion, Secretary of Defense William S. Cohen remarked, "It may be that forensic science has reached the point where there will be no other unknowns in any war" (US National Library of Medicine 2006).

35. In 2003, ICMP made the following projection: "The ICRC list of the missing currently contains approximately 20,000 names [missing persons throughout former Yugoslavia]; of these 17,424 are unresolved. The ICMP DNA Program is being designed to have the ability to *process* 20,000 bone specimens and 100,000 family blood references within a 5–7 year timeframe" (italics in the original; 2003a). For cases across former Yugoslavia, as of December 7, 2007, ICMP had generated a total of 20,315 DNA match reports for 12,927 different missing individuals, using a database of 84,740 DNA profiles from surviving relatives seeking 28,422 missing persons. Region-wide updates for these figures are available on ICMP's web site (www.ic-mp.org).

36. As of December 7, 2007, ICMP had collected 21,209 blood samples from surviving family members for 7,789 different missing persons from Srebrenica.

37. ICMP established the threshold of 99.95 percent statistical certainty for a DNA match to advance a case into the phase of antemortem-postmortem data comparison; 99.949 percent would not be considered a satisfactory blind match.

38. In cases for which nuclear DNA analysis is impossible, ICMP has occasionally employed Y-chromosome DNA testing. Furthermore, the organization's forensic science division is currently developing the capacity of mitochondrial testing for exclusive use in presumptive cases lacking sufficient reference samples. For a more technical explanation of the nuclear short tandem repeat (STR) typing method used by ICMP, see Davoren et al. 2007.

39. To address this obstacle, in 2004 ICMP launched an outreach campaign in the European Union, sending several mobile blood collection teams to countries throughout the EU. In late 2005 additional teams were sent to the United States. Encompassing several cities scattered throughout the country, their itinerary included St. Louis, which has the largest concentration of Srebrenica families in the United States. See *After the Fall: Srebrenica Survivors in St. Louis,* Patrick McCarthy and Tom Maday's striking compilation of photographs and personal testimonies of Srebrenica refugees resettled in St. Louis (2000).

40. There were exceptions among ICMP staff: a colleague at the International Coordination Division had herself lived in Srebrenica during the war. Another young man working in Sarajevo as part of the mobile blood collection teams was missing his father. Undoubtedly, they and other staff members

periodically encountered the names of people they knew among the databases of missing during their tenure with ICMP.

41. This was not the case; rather, all the victims were from Zvornik, 1992.

42. In this type of DNA extraction and testing, only six loci are measured as opposed to the bone-blood/bone analysis of the general ICMP DNA matching program, which measures sixteen different loci. The task is much more limited—that is, the goal is to determine if the two samples are a genetic match rather than analyzing them against the more than 84,000 discrete samples, as in the case of the general program. Also, this type of analysis utilizes full band, rather than half band, matching, and thus requires fewer loci as points of comparison.

43. ICMP findings demonstrate that the highest DNA typing success rates were observed with samples from dense cortical bone of weight-bearing leg bones (femur 86.9 percent), whereas long bones of the arms showed significantly lower success (humerus 46.2 percent; radius 24.5 percent; and ulna 22.8 percent). Intact teeth also exhibited high success rates (82.7 percent) (Miloš et al. 2007).

44. When ICMP first established its DNA analysis system for identifying missing persons from former Yugoslavia, it set up four laboratories: in Belgrade (Serbia), Sarajevo, Tuzla, and Banja Luka. Ed Huffine explained that while it was financially more costly to conduct the analyses at the different laboratories, it was the "least expensive route socially." Testing completed in these locations would ensure that the results would be more politically acceptable than if they were conducted only in Sarajevo or Tuzla (i.e., cities located in the Bosniak and Croat–controlled Federation). By 2003, however, all samples were being sent to the Sarajevo and Banja Luka laboratories for DNA extraction and analysis.

45. "Physiochemical testing for geographic origins (long-time residence) can provide an additional line of evidence to prove that, e.g., mortal remains recovered are from a missing person who lived for a long time in northwest Bosnia, was last seen in northwest Bosnia, and was never known to have traveled to eastern Bosnia even though the body was recovered in eastern Bosnia" (ICMP 2005b).

46. Dr. Tom Parsons, director of ICMP's Forensic Sciences Division, provided this explanation of the DNAView software, emphasizing that the program obviates the need for manual reconstruction of missing profiles.

47. For example, with Srebrenica, the number of missing is set at 8,000. The statistical analysis calculates the possibility of another human having the identical set of genetic coding within the parameters of the population of former Yugoslavia as well as additional factors including the number and relation of the donors. A combination of traits occurs within a determinable proportion; when compared with the contributing population, that proportion gives an idea of how many times such a combination can be expected.

48. In "The Eye of Everyman: Witnessing DNA in the Simpson Trial," the "stark signifier of truth" Jasanoff refers to is not the individual identity of nameless mortal remains, but rather DNA samples used in the criminal justice system (1998).

CHAPTER 4. MEMORY AT WORK

1. A portion of the article's text is superimposed on a second, smaller photograph of Đemila's hands holding a human skull, presumably that of one of her sons.

2. Some of ICMP's current staff began their careers working on the missing persons issue as local employees of the Boltzman Institute back in 1996.

3. For reasons still somewhat unclear, when Physicians for Human Rights finished its work in Bosnia in 2000, its directors decided to transfer all antemortem data to the Red Cross, effectively outsourcing an integral aspect of the identification process then under ICMP's direction to a different international organization. This division of labor caused further friction between the Red Cross and ICMP, organizations already caught up in an implicit rivalry concerning authority over the missing person issue in the region.

4. Former PHR staffer Mary Ellen Keough helped develop the questionnaire and helped train the local interviewing staff. She noted that despite the fixed structure of the questionnaire, Physicians for Human Rights staff conducted the interviews in very informal social settings, such as people's homes and in collective centers. Often the interviewer gathered the data in a more conversational manner as opposed to following a strict question-answer formula, especially because families reacted differently to the various questions.

5. Ricoeur writes, "In my eyes, Bergson remains the philosopher who has best understood the close connection between what he calls 'the survival of images,' and the key phenomenon of recognition" (2004:430). Beyond Bergson's *Matter and Memory*, the following studies of memory, especially its interrelations with images and imagination, are particularly valuable: F. C. Bartlett's *Remembering: A Study in Experimental and Social Psychology* (1967), Paul Ricoeur's *Memory, History, and Forgetting* (2004), and the chapter "Memory" in William James's *The Principles of Psychology* (1983). For the ancient Greek understanding of the memory-image as imprint, see Frances Yates's *The Art of Memory* (1966), especially the chapter "The Art of Memory in Greece: Memory and the Soul." James Tatum's *The Mourner's Song* (2003) helpfully explores memory in classical literature such as Homer's *Iliad*, as well as in more contemporary fiction such as the "The Heart's Intermissions" in Proust's *Remembrance of Things Past (Cities of the Plain)* (1970).

6. In his analysis of interpretive memory, Bolles uses the phrase "memory chunks"—borrowed from George Miller—to refer to a "unit of associations whose constituent elements can be derived simply by recalling the chunk" (1988:82); chunking thus depends on both recognition and recall, which, working together, construct a detailed memory.

7. The clothing exhumed with remains is rinsed to remove soil, dried, and then stored in large paper sacks. PIP does not use detergent because of its potential to damage the already fragile fibers of the recovered articles. Personal possessions are likewise cleaned off and stored separately from the clothing in smaller plastic bags.

8. Many of the enclave's residents thought the Serb assault was only temporary and that they would return to their homes within a couple of days. Power

quotes a fifty-five-year-old man as saying, " 'It was a U.N. 'safe haven,' there is no way it will be allowed to fall,' I thought. That's why I didn't take anything with me when I left my house. I just locked my door and figured I'd be back in a few hours or a few days at the longest" (2002:399).

9. Ešefa is referring to the parachutes attached to the pallets of food and aid air-dropped into the enclave during the war. The refugees would use the material from the parachutes to sew pants and other articles of clothing.

## CHAPTER 5. WHERE MEMORY AND IMAGINATION MEET

Epigraph: Proust 1970:115.

1. The UN Security Council granted the International Criminal Tribunal for the former Yugoslavia jurisdiction over the offenses identified in Articles 2 through 5 of the Updated Statute of the International Tribunal: Grave breaches of the Geneva Conventions of 1949 (Article 2); Violations of the laws or customs of war (Article 3); Genocide (Article 4); and Crimes against humanity (Article 5). It is important to note that both genocide and crimes against humanity are addressed in different articles, indicating the separate legal concepts encompassed in each (ICTY Updated Statute 2007).

2. The findings of the judgment provided a factual basis for several official reports about the events of July 1995, including the Dutch NIOD report and the RS-sponsored Srebrenica commission's final report, issued in June 2004. As mentioned in chapter 2, the latter report prompted the first Bosnian Serb official statement recognizing the crimes made by then Bosnian Serb president Dragan Čavić in June 2004. His statement was followed by the RS government's official acknowledgment of the commission's finding in October 2004.

3. As I will explain further in chapters 6 and 7, the Bosnian Muslim practice of ritual cleansing and preparation of the body for burial usually takes place in the home of the deceased, as do the ritual prayers for the dead (Bringa 1995:188–189).

4. My friend explained what I had not realized while translating: the second person singular imperative form for the verb *ući* would have been *uđi*, not *ući*. Furthermore, it made more sense in the context of the dream that the son was commanding his mother to pray, rather than to enter the grave or study/learn.

5. It is also important to note Mašović's affiliations with the Bosniak nationalist political party, SDA. A member of the party, he stood for the Bosnian Parliament in the November 2000 election. See Nerzuk Ćurak's interview with Mašović in the August 25, 2000, issue of *Dani* (Ćurak 2000).

6. An article in the first edition of the Women of Srebrenica's *Bilten Srebrenica* tackled the issue of responsibility for the search for missing persons *(traženje nestalih osoba)*. "A number of questions arise in relation to the activities of these organizations, particularly having in mind that the majority of the families of the missing do not even know the names of the organizations that they should be addressing. . . . One of the reasons that our people don't understand 'who drinks and who pays' is because these organizations most

often give their names in English and in an abbreviated form: ICMP, ICRC, OHR, UN, PHR, ICTY, etc." (Žene Srebrenice 1998a:7).

7. The confusion partially stems from their initial contact with the Red Cross when filing missing persons claims and was more recently compounded by the overlapping responsibility of the antemortem data collection efforts. Furthermore, the Red Cross has been issuing a final identification certificate, a document without legal or official value with local courts or local and federal institutions. The chief pathologist at PIP, Dr. Rifat Kešetović, has authorization to issue an official death certificate; this capacity within ICMP has streamlined the families' ability to verify the identification before local authorities, such as when they attempt to access social welfare benefits as relatives of missing persons.

8. In her memoir *The Stone Fields*, forensic anthropologist and writer Courtney Angela Brkic (2004) describes her uneasiness in the presence of Bosnian Serbs at exhumations of Srebrenica graves in 1996. Her troubling account of the international team's decision to hire Serbs to work at these sites illustrates the lack of understanding and sensitivity toward the families' concerns during those early stages of the identification process.

9. Lockwood describes the same vocabulary differences among villagers in western Bosnia: "When a Moslem enters a gathering of both Moslems and Christians, he will invariably say *merhaba i dobar dan*—'good day [Moslems] and good day [Christians]'—thus automatically categorizing his listeners into ingroup and outgroup. In similar circumstances, a Christian will use only *dobar dan*" (1975:53).

10. In Bosnia, hiding and playing to ethnicity often entail telling jokes. Sabrina Peric argues that the constructions of separate, essentialized ethnic and national identities in this practice of joke-telling actually enable a cross-ethnic intimacy, whereby "social actors can identify with each other through the memory of social suffering" (2006:9).

11. When I returned to Tuzla in the summer of 2005, I attended the Women of Srebrenica's June 11 protest and once again met with Emina. She had taken that same photocopy of her son's recovered clothes to a photo shop, where the staff had created a collage conjoining the images of the clothing with a photograph of her son. She hung the laminated picture around her neck as she walked with the other women through the streets of Tuzla.

12. The story of Martin Guerre has appeared in both fiction and film, including Janet Lewis's *The Wife of Martin Guerre*, Alexandre Dumas's accounts in both *Celebrated Crimes* and *The Two Dianas*, and the French movie *Le Retour de Martin Guerre*.

13. Ricoeur's discussion of the image as imprint draws from the famous metaphor of the block of wax in Plato's *Theaetetus*. Socrates explains to Theaetetus that "we may look upon it, then, as a gift of Memory *[Mnemosyne]*, the mother of the Muses. We make impressions upon this of everything we wish to remember *[mnēmoneusai]* among the things we have seen or heard or thought of ourselves; we hold the wax under our perceptions and thoughts and take a stamp from them, in the way in which we take the imprints [marks, *sēmeia*] of signet rings. Whatever is impressed upon the wax we remember

and know so long as the image *[eidōlon]* remains in the wax; whatever is obliterated or cannot be impressed, we forget *[epilelēsthai]* and do not know" (quoted in Ricoeur 2004:9). See also Frances Yates for Aristotle's use of the metaphor of the signet ring's imprint on wax (1966:36).

14. Tone Bringa provides a detailed ethnographic description and analysis of Bosnian Muslim practices of caring for the dead both physically and spiritually (1995:185–196); see Bougarel (2007:177–178) for a discussion of burial rituals accorded to *šehidi* (Bosnian Muslims who are considered martyrs, a point I will return to in chapter 7). More generally, Jane Idleman Smith and Yvonne Yazbeck Haddad explain Islamic burial practices in *Islamic Understanding of Death and Resurrection* (2002).

## CHAPTER 6. RETURN TO POTOČARI

1. The battery factory is a significant site because it was part of the UN peacekeepers' compound, where the refugees sought shelter when the enclave fell to the Bosnian Serb forces.

2. Engseng Ho provided this insight into the memorial center cemetery as a space commemorating collective injury (blood spilled) as much as kin ties (blood inherited), whereby caring for the returned bodies of the Srebrenica victims entails caring for the body politic of the Bosniak people.

3. The term *legacy* intimates both a specific historical context as well as an overlapping, interconnected historical process. For example, in her introduction to *Balkan Identities: Nation and Memory,* Maria Todorova defines the concept and legacy of Eastern Europe as "the most important medium through which the recent debate over Central Europe and the Balkans has to be historicized," just as she acknowledges that its "socialist legacy is the latest in a sequence of historical legacies" that cannot be separated from the phenomenon of capitalism and its associated effects of industrialism, urbanism, modernization, and globalization (2004:15–16).

4. Earlier in her book's namesake chapter, "The Culture of Lies," Ugrešić comments on the politics of exhumations: "The necrophiliac Yugoslav passion for digging up old bones (and burying new ones!) spares no one: the Serbs threatened the Croats by saying they will dig up Tito's bones, buried in Belgrade, and send them to the Croats" (1998:69).

5. See also Ballinger's account of the 1991 division of the Istrian Peninsula as it echoed with the post–World War II partition of the Julian March; she examines how contemporary Istrians and exiles, like other actors in the region, deploy memories as a part of the "politics of submersion" (2003:12).

6. For a careful analysis of Milošević's rise to power and his populist rhetoric, see "The Destruction of Political Alternatives" in Eric Gordy's *The Culture of Power in Serbia: Nationalism and the Destruction of Alternatives* (1999:21–28).

7. The Kosovo epic provides Serbs with "a mental framework" that "establishes continuity with the past and projects a predestined future"; furthermore, "There are constant and direct equations made between the main protagonists of the Kosovo legend and present-day political and military leaders" (Duijz-

ings 2000:194). For the poems of Vuk Karadžić on the Battle of Kosovo, see Milne Holton and Vasa Mahailovich's collection of Serbian poetry, *Songs of the Serbian People* (1997).

8. Robert Donia and John Fine argue that unlike in Western Europe and the United States, where WWII was "experienced principally as a colossal struggle against Nazi Germany and its fascist allies," the war in Yugoslavia was "multidimensional, involving three distinct conflicts": first, the struggle against the Axis occupation by Yugoslav resistance forces; second, a "civil war" among "rival nationalist extremists and the competing domestic resistance movements"; and third, "a struggle for a revolutionary social transformation," led by Tito's Communist Party and Partisan forces (1994:136).

9. Duijzings explains that "Serb victims were commemorated because the great majority of Serbs had been on the Partisan side at the end of the war, even though many of them had been *četnici* before and had participated in massacres against the Muslim population" (2007:148).

10. See also Pamela Ballinger's analysis of the debates surrounding the *foibe*, the karstic pits that were used as tombs by Yugoslav Partisans in Istria in 1943 and in Trieste in 1945 (2003:129–167).

11. In 1990 Tudjman published a book in which he attempted both to minimize the number of Serb victims of the Croatian forces and to offset the "absolute criminality of genocide itself" by contextualizing the killings at Jasenovac in relation to other massacres and crimes (thereby relativizing it) (Hayden 1994:176; see also Ballinger 2003:110 and Donia and Fine 1994:141).

12. In July 1998, a commemorative ceremony was in fact held in Kladanj; attendees included Reis Cerić and Alija Izetbegović (Duijzings 2007:158).

13. See Duijzings on the Bosniak nationalist political party's (SDA) initial opposition to locating the memorial center in the RS (2007:157–158).

14. Fiona Ross notes that when commissioned by a state, truth and reconciliation campaigns often seek to "forge a common memory predicated on making public particular kinds of knowledge" (2003:251); the representatives of the Srebrenica family associations, however, refused to engage in crafting such a common memory until certain aspects of the "truth," namely the whereabouts of the remaining mass graves, had been made public by the RS government.

15. State governments that donated money to the memorial center foundation included, among others, the United States, The Netherlands, and the United Kingdom (Duijzings 2007:158). In 2003, when these initial contributions were made, the average exchange rate for the KM was 1.73 US dollars.

16. One of the advertisement images used in the campaign displayed hundreds of the Women of Srebrenica's emblematic pillowcases spread out along even rows in a lush green valley. The serene panorama simulated the scale of the crime (number of victims) yet promised a peaceful and orderly return to the Drina valley for their mortal remains.

17. The forty-nine families agreed to the OHR proposition because, according to the directors of the Women of Srebrenica, they recognized the inappropriateness of so few families receiving reparations.

18. When people use the term *complex* to refer to the memorial center,

typically they are speaking about its physical grounds—that is, the land and buildings included as part of the foundation's property. For example, once the memorial center site was established in Potočari, debates arose about whether the battery factory should also be included in the complex.

19. Milica Bakić-Hayden argues against such interpretations of the Kosovo theme as merely "fictive," or "myth," but illustrates how both fictive and factual dimensions of experience are inextricably bound together in the "constitution of Serbian cultural and national identity" (2004:25).

20. From the onset, several international consultants—in both formal and informal capacities—participated in discussions concerning the design and content of the memorial center. Among them was Suzanne Bardgett, project director of the Holocaust Exhibition and Crimes against Humanity Exhibition at London's Imperial War Museum; she played an instrumental role in coordinating the memorial room (see below) eventually established in the battery factory. She credits a former High Representative with inspiring the original idea behind the permanent exhibit: "It was Lord Ashdown's visit to the Holocaust Exhibition at London's Imperial War Museum, which first set the making of the Srebrenica Memorial Room in motion" (Bardgett 2005).

21. See classicist James Tatum's study, *The Mourner's Song* (2003), especially chapter 1, "Mourners and Monuments," for a rich and compelling analysis of literary and physical memorials to the dead, including those of Maya Lin's Vietnam Veterans Memorial and the Memorial to the Missing of the Somme; see also Robert Pogue Harrison's analysis of the Vietnam Veterans Memorial (2003:136–141).

22. In the case of at least one missing person profile, where the remains had not yet been recovered, family members donated the personal article of a school notebook to complete the display.

23. Commemorative ceremonies and mass burials were held on March 31, 2003 (600 identified victims); July 11, 2003 (282); upon the official opening of the memorial center on September 20, 2003 (107); July 11, 2004 (338); July 11, 2005 (611); July 11, 2006 (505); and July 11, 2007 (465). As of December 7, 2007, ICMP records indicate that of the 3,105 Srebrenica cases it has processed and closed (i.e., the identification completed), 2,985 individuals have been buried: 2,819 of those individuals were buried in the Srebrenica-Potočari Memorial Center cemetery, while 166 were individual burials in a location other than the memorial center. The difference between ICMP's official number of individuals buried in the memorial center and the total reported in the news media arises because the Federation Commission for Missing Persons has completed identifications for Srebrenica victims independent of ICMP.

24. Bringa notes that a *tabut* is a lidless coffin; the basic meaning in Arabic is "box." Among Muslims in her field site of Dolina, the *tabut* was "covered by a large green cloth with the Islamic profession of faith *lailahe illallah* ('there is no God except for the one Allah') printed on it in Arabic." Apparently, "in the past only women were placed in a *tabut*. This was so that the men would not have to touch the female body when carrying it to the mosque and the grave" (1995:185).

25. This can also be observed at the memorial center on the recently

erected panels displaying the names of the victims that encircle the *musala*. Literally rows upon rows of common names such as Alić, Begić, Hasanović, and Mehmedović fill entire panels among the display.

26. The extended family household, *zadruga,* common in the former Yugoslavia, represented a kinship structure and economic cooperative, both of which were heavily shaped by patrilocal and patrilineal practices (Halpern 1967; Hammel 1972).

27. Bringa also notes that the Bosnian word *tevhid* "comes from the Arabic *tawhid,* which means 'faith in one supreme God,' but is often translated more freely as 'praise of God' " (1995:187).

28. "The possible polluting effect of certain thoughts or memories related to the Islamic belief that the soul does not leave the body until the fortieth day after death and that during this time the deceased is still a sentient being. The living, especially those emotionally close to the deceased, should therefore avoid saying, doing, or even thinking anything that may upset the deceased" (Bringa 1995:185).

29. Over the years, as reconstruction aid in Bosnia has been significantly scaled back, older single women such as Rufejda are the lowest priority for the few donor agencies still offering reconstruction packages. Families with school-age children are much more likely candidates; the international community, supported by local politicians (such as the Bosniak SDA party), hope to foster higher minority return rates, for example, Bosniaks to the RS and Bosnian Serbs to the Federation. Old women, the sad logic goes, will die within a few years and their property will probably fall back into the hands of the majority ethnic group, reinforcing the demographic shifts initially caused by the ethnic violence and the policies of "ethnic cleansing."

CHAPTER 7. 'THAT YOU SEE, THAT YOU KNOW, THAT YOU REMEMBER'

Epigraph: Ho 2006:8.

1. This quotation is translated from the roundtable's presentations, including that of Mufti Kavazović (Kavazović 2003), which the Mothers of the Srebrenica and Žepa Enclaves published in English and Bosnian. At the time that I visited their office, I was able to obtain only an English version. All subsequent citations of Mufti Kavazović's presentation are taken from that same version.

2. In his discussion of the postwar "cult of *šehidi*"—an unexamined phrase that runs throughout his analysis—Bougarel traces the origins and multiple meanings of the term *šehid,* drawing particular attention to how its usage is linked to expressions of both the meaning and memory of war (2007:167–191). He notes that the Bosnian *ulemas* have designated "first-rank" and "second-rank" *šehidi,* which according to his explanation would relegate the Srebrenica missing to "second-rank" status (2007:178–179). Aside from the issue many, including myself, would take with his footnote 13, in which he claims that "most of the men slaughtered by the Bosnian Serb Army after the fall of Srebrenica on 11 July 1995 were Bosnian Army soldiers," his application of these "ranks" does not correspond with the position articulated

by Mufti Kavazović at the March 2003 roundtable discussion. Rather, as the Tuzla mufti expressly underscored, the Srebrenica victims' status as martyrs means that ritual cleansing and removal of clothing are not required for proper burial.

3. Kavazović elaborates, "I'm finding basis for such a statement in the praxis of God's prophet in the case of the victims of Uhud."

4. The line is from Al-Baqarah 154. As Bougarel notes, the inscription appears on standardized permanent gravestones *(nišani)* erected for *šehidi* (i.e., replacing temporary wartime markers) by state institutions since 1997 (2007:179). Their form, a slender column of white marble, lacks the ornamental and symbolic motifs that characterize Bosnian Muslim gravestones *(nišani* and *bašluci)* of earlier centuries. Many of those older tombstones reflect the Bosnian *stećak* tradition—that is, the form and style of the huge stone monoliths that served as gravestones in medieval times (Lovrenović 2001:117).

5. See Elissa Helms's work on women's activism for insight into the gendered politics within the NGO sector in postwar Bosnia (2007:241–43), a realm often dominated by the emblematic "Mothers" and "Women" of Srebrenica.

6. From the context of the speech, I understand "they" to refer implicitly to those Bosnian Serbs, Serbs, and others who refuse to recognize the crimes of Srebrenica. In a related section Cerić says, "There is no answer to the question why they do not want to recognize genocide, but there is an answer to the question why war criminals have the right to punishment."

7. Since that commemoration, other members of the Dutchbat force have attended the July 11 ceremonies at Potočari. On July 11, 2007, a delegation from the Dutch interfaith organization IKV met with members of the Women of Srebrenica at the memorial center foundation office before the commemorative ceremony; among their party were two former members of the peacekeeping force. The men broached the subject of a possible trip organized for a small group of Dutchbat soldiers to travel to Srebrenica with their families. The suggestion prompted an unusually candid conversation between the women assembled and the two former soldiers. In one of the most poignant exchanges of the meeting, one woman responded to the proposed trip by saying simply, "Let them come, let them visit the cemetery, and let them sleep in peace if they had no hand in enabling the genocide."

8. At the July 11, 2007, ceremony and burial, the practice of transporting the coffins to the individual gravesites was slightly different. Although still following a carefully scripted order, male relatives and friends began carrying the coffins from their resting place near the *musala,* bearing them above their heads as they walked the entire distance into the cemetery and toward the individual plots. Watching this procession, I was struck by the poignant disparities across the entourages. In some cases, family and friends crowded around the slender box, wedging themselves together so that each person could bear some portion of the weight. In other, rarer instances, two, three, or four men would carry the *tabut.* Perhaps the saddest sight for me that day was watching a group of three men, one of whom must have been in his seventies, walk a coffin—presumably that of a relative or friend—through the grassy

field toward the cemetery. Because of the differences in height between the two men on either end of the humble procession, the coffin was pitched at a severe angle. The sight of it bobbing above their upheld arms, receding into the distance, was hard to watch; it was hard to contemplate a lonely burial in that place, on that day.

9. In conversations I had with Bosnian Serbs on this subject, they were critical of this change in practice—that is, the Bosnian Muslim women's presence at the gravesites. My Serb informants saw this as a direct result of the war, and, more implicitly, the politics of the war. They seemed to fault the Bosnian Muslims for not adhering to their traditions, but also saw the change as one inspired by political motives, such as the public demonstration of victimization.

10. Bringa explains that through honoring and remembering the dead, Bosnian Muslims earn *sevap* (a good deed or religious merit) on behalf of the deceased and, in turn, for themselves: "The living and dead are thus connected in a mutual relationship of spiritual exchange which ensures the continuity and indivisibility of life and death, the world of the living and the world of the dead, and of the past, present, and future" (1995:196).

11. Diaspora groups held activities in North America, Australia, and throughout Europe.

12. An early draft of the commemoration activities schedule listed the event of an "opening of a mass grave." The description was later changed to a "visit to a mass grave." Nevertheless, the Federation Commission for Missing Persons, responsible for deciding when and which mass graves to exhume, began working on a secondary mass grave located in Potočari, near the memorial center, in the days leading up to the tenth anniversary ceremony. On the morning of July 11 Mašović personally conducted a tour of that same mass grave for a group of VIP (predominantly international) guests.

13. Most Bosniaks resented the pressure placed on their government by the Bush administration to send troops to the war in Iraq (Nettelfield and Wagner 2004).

14. Most of those attending the July 12, 2005, Petrovdan celebration were Bosnian Serbs who traveled to the city from nearby villages and towns, while the majority of Bosnian Serb residents of Srebrenica were not present for the occasion.

15. The 2002 report commissioned by the RS government, which claimed only 1,800 persons to be missing, best epitomizes the official Bosnian Serb discourse of minimizing and downplaying the events of Srebrenica July 1995.

16. The site for the monument built in Kravica in 2005 had actually been dedicated four years earlier when a plaque was laid memorializing the 1,300 Bosnian Serbs killed in the Srebrenica-Bratunac region during the war (Duijzings 2007:162).

CHAPTER 8. TECHNOLOGY OF REPAIR

The title of this chapter comes from a collaborative project with Lindsay Smith and Jason Cross on the theme of technologies of repair.

1. The National Institute of Justice is the research, development, and evaluation agency of the US Department of Justice.

2. On June 2, 2005, at the end of the three-and-a-half-year long DNA identification effort, the chief medical examiner for the city of New York, Chuck Hirsch, reported the total number of missing persons from the World Trade Center attacks to be 2,749 (Shaler 2005:321).

3. In his memoir of the World Trade Center identification efforts, *Who They Were*, Robert Shaler explains that in the end, the Bosnian software program was not suited for the task: "It had not been designed to address the problems I was anticipating from the World Trade Center samples, though it did track samples and do direct matching" (2005:116).

4. The preface to the NIJ report, "Lessons Learned from 9/11: DNA Identification in Mass Fatality Incidents," explains that "the number of victims, the condition of their remains, and the duration of the recovery effort made the identification of the victims the most difficult ever undertaken by the forensic community in this country" (National Institute of Justice 2006:4).

5. I refer to the DNA-based identification system developed by ICMP as the "Bosnian technology," reflecting the fact that the laboratory and resources used to conduct DNA extraction, analysis, and matching procedures are located in Bosnia (in the cities of Tuzla and Sarajevo) and the overwhelming majority of ICMP staff members working with the genetic profiles are Bosnian nationals.

6. Director general of ICMP Kathryne Bomberger explained the decision to extend ICMP's scope of work to include identification efforts for victims of natural disaster according to the logic of humanitarianism: "Although our mandate is to assist in the identification of persons missing as a result of conflict or human rights abuses, . . . we have the capability and the capacity to help in the identification of tsunami victims and as a humanitarian measure we are all willing to help" (ICMP 2005d).

7. According to the April 27, 2006, report "Tsunami Victim Identification Tracking Chart," posted on ICMP's web site, DNA reports were generated for missing persons from the following countries: Austria (6); Burma (72); Czech Republic (1); China (1); Denmark (2); Finland (14); France (8); Germany (21); Hong Kong (3); Italy (6); Japan (3); Kazakhstan (2); Norway (1); Nepal (2); Philippines (2); Russia (2); Sweden (42); Singapore (2); Switzerland (3); Thailand (702); United Kingdom (5); and United States (2) (ICMP 2006).

8. "When the State of Louisiana sent test bone samples from Katrina victims to DNA laboratories in November 2005, ICMP achieved a 100 percent success rate in obtaining DNA profiles from them" (ICMP 2005f).

9. After the 9/11 attacks, a BBC headline drew a similar connection directly to Srebrenica: "DNA tests: Srebrenica to Ground Zero" (Thorpe 2001).

10. At that time (late 2005), ICMP had begun working with Iraqi officials in the Ministry of Human Rights and the Medico-Legal Institute in Baghdad on the issue of missing persons; it has subsequently assisted in training Iraqi technical experts in the "fields of forensic archaeology, anthropology and database management, as well as institution building" (ICMP 2007).

11. Some of most striking parallels within these social movements are found

among the Argentine and Bosnian family associations, namely the Mothers of the Plaza de Mayo and the Grandmothers of the Plaza de Mayo, and the Tuzla-based Women of Srebrenica and the Sarajevo-based Mothers of the Srebrenica and Žepa Enclaves. From their peaceful protests to their representations of the missing through testimonies and photographs, the organizations employ similar strategies to raise awareness about their missing relatives and the state-sponsored violence behind their forced disappearance (Smith 2008; see also Harrison 2003:144–145).

12. See also Thomas Lacquer (2002) and Buchli and Lucas (2001) on human rights, forensics, and the *corpus delicti,* "the body of the crime."

13. Human activists have criticized the limited scope of the commission and an ineffective identification process. Indeed, recently, some of the identifications have been proven incorrect: "In April 2006, the Chilean Bureau of Forensic Services determined that at least 48 out of 96 disappeared persons whose remains had been found at the General Cemetery of Santiago in the 1990s had been wrongly identified" (Correa 2007).

14. In addition to Clyde Snow, several forensic anthropologists played key roles in developing the collaboration between forensic science and human rights investigations. One of the most recognized is Mercedes (Mimi) Doretti, who worked with Clyde Snow in the 1980s. Doretti cofounded the Argentine Forensic Anthropology Team (EAAF), which has participated in identification efforts in over twenty countries, including South Africa, East Timor, Kosovo, and Bosnia and Herzegovina. At the nexus of DNA testing and human rights investigations, American geneticist Mary-Claire King was instrumental in bridging the Argentina identification efforts with those in other postconflict societies, including among others El Salvador, Chile, Guatemala, Haiti, and former Yugoslavia. As part of her involvement in former Yugoslavia, King's laboratory at the University of Washington conducted DNA analysis for early presumptive cases from Srebrenica.

15. It was Ed Huffine (the DNA scientist who later joined ICMP) and the team of AFDIL scientists who accomplished that "sacrilege" in identifying the remains of First Lieutenant Michael Blassie. Blassie's family had lobbied the government to perform the genetic testing and, upon receiving the news that Blassie's remains had been identified, requested to remove them from the Tomb of the Unknown Soldier for burial in their hometown of St. Louis, Missouri. The crypt's former inscription, "Here Rests Honored Glory, an American Soldier Known but to God," has since been replaced with "Honoring and Keeping Faith with America's Missing Servicemen."

16. See Robert Shaler (2005) for a comprehensive explanation of these various laboratories' involvement in the identification efforts, and Holland et al. (2003) and Budimlija et al. (2003) on the DNA testing methods used.

17. Cataldie remarked, "I need DNA results. I'm not the money man. I find myself in a position where money is holding me up" (Dornin 2005). See also Cataldie's interview in Spike Lee's (2006) documentary film *When the Levees Broke.*

18. The federal government had received reports well before Hurricane Katrina that the system was in serious danger if indeed a hurricane

on the scale of Katrina should hit the Gulf region (Van Heerden and Bryan 2006:206–210).

19. The New Orleans resident was interviewed in Spike Lee's documentary film *When the Levees Broke* (2006).

20. This aim is captured in ICMP's "Main Achievements," previously listed on its web site, which highlight efforts at "building civil society structures" as a means of "persuading inter-regional cooperation" (ICMP 2005c).

21. The subsequent Agreement on Assuming the Role of Co-Founders of the Missing Persons Institute of Bosnia and Herzegovina and ICMP was passed in 2005.

22. See the edited volume *There Is No Such Thing as a Natural Disaster: Race, Class, and Hurricane Katrina* (Hartman and Squires 2006) for an in-depth analysis of post-Katrina policies and responses that compounded already existent structural racism and social inequality.

23. DNA testing was used in a very limited capacity in response to the Rwanda genocide; forensic experts led by William Hagland of Physicians for Human Rights (who also participated in the exhumations of Srebrenica graves) and Robert Kirschner, a medical examiner from Chicago, turned to mitochondrial DNA analysis for the presumptive cases at the Kibuye mass graves (Lee and Tirnady 2003:324).

EPILOGUE

1. From R. C. Jebb's translation of Sophocles' *Antigone* (1976:15).

# References

OFFICIAL PUBLICATIONS AND DOCUMENTS

Assemblée nationale
> 2001 *Srebrenica: Rapport sur un massacre*. Documents d'information de l'Assemblée nationale, no. 3413. www.assemblee-nationale.fr/11/rap-info/i3413–01.asp; accessed October 2007.

Government of the Republika Srpska
> 2004 Conclusions. 99th Session. Banja Luka. October 28. www.vladars.net/pdf/srbren_zaklj_e.pdf; accessed December 2005.

Human Rights Chamber for Bosnia and Herzegovina
> 2003 CH01–8365 et al. Selimović and 48 Others v. the Republika Srpska. Decision on Admissibility and Merits, The "Srebrenica Cases." March 7. www.hrc.ba/ENGLISH/DEFAULT.HTM; accessed January 2006.

International Commission on Missing Persons (ICMP)
> 2003a The DNA Identification Program. International Commission on Missing Persons, Sarajevo.

> 2003b General Fact Sheet. International Commission on Missing Persons, Sarajevo.

> 2005a Press Release: Missing Persons Institute Launched on International Day of the Disappeared. August 30. www.ic-mp.org/?p=300; accessed May 2008.

> 2005b Exhumations and Examinations: The Postmortem Examination. www.ic-mp.org/home.php?act=exhum; accessed December 2005.

2005c ICMP's Main Achievements. www.ic-mp.org/home.php?act= achievements; accessed December 2005.

2005d Press Release: Interpol Visits ICMP to Discuss Disaster Victim Identification. May 16. www.ic-mp.org/?p=274; accessed May 2008.

2005e Press Release: ICMP to Identify Tsunami Victims. May 24. www .ic-mp.org/?p=277; accessed May 2008.

2005f Press Release: ICMP Helping to Identify Hurricane Katrina Victims. December 29. www.ic-mp.org/?p=333; accessed May 2008.

2006 Tsunami Victim Identification Tracking Chart. www.ic-mp.org/ home.php; accessed August 2007.

2007 Iraq: Countries and Regions. www.ic-mp.org/home.php?act=gov_ rel#iraq; accessed August 2007.

International Criminal Tribunal for the former Yugoslavia (ICTY)
2005 ICTY Weekly Press Briefing. July 7. www.un.org/icty/briefing/2005/ PB050706.htm; accessed January 2008.

2007 Updated Statute of the International Criminal Tribunal for the former Yugoslavia. www.un.org/icty/legaldoc-e/index.htm; accessed January 2008.

ICTY Prosecutor v. Dražen Erdemović
1998 Case no. IT-96–22-Tbis. Sentencing Judgment. March 5. International Criminal Tribunal for the former Yugoslavia. www.un .org/icty/erdemovic/trialc/judgement/erd-tsj980305e.htm; accessed September 2005.

ICTY Prosecutor v. Radislav Krstić
2000a Case no. IT-98–33-T. Transcript. April 13. International Criminal Tribunal for the former Yugoslavia. www.un.org/icty/transe33/ 000413ed.htm; accessed January 2005.

2000b Case no. IT-98 – 33-T. Transcript. July 26. International Criminal Tribunal for the former Yugoslavia. www.un.org/icty/transe33/ 000726ed.htm; accessed January 2005.

2001 Case no. IT-98 – 33-T. Judgment. August 2. International Criminal Tribunal for the former Yugoslavia. www.un.org/icty/krstic/TrialC1/ judgement/krs-tj010802e.pdf; accessed January 2005.

2004 Case no: IT-98 – 33-A: Appeals Chamber Judgment. April 19. International Criminal Tribunal for the former Yugoslavia. www.un .org/icty/krstic/Appeal/judgement/index.htm; accessed January 2005.

Ministarstvo za ljudska prava i izbjeglice
2005 *Uporedna analiza pristupa pravima izbjeglica i raseljenih osoba.* December. Sarajevo.

2006 *Primjena zakona o nestalim osobama BiH: Vodić za porodice nesta-lih osoba.* September. Sarajevo.

National Institute of Justice
    2006 Lessons Learned from 9/11: DNA Identification in Mass Fatality
        Incidents. President's DNA Initiative. September. http://massfatality
        .dna.gov/; accessed September 2006.

Nederlands Instituut voor Oorlogsdocumentatie (NIOD)
    2002 Srebrenica, a "Safe Area"—Reconstruction, Background,
        Consequences and Analyses of the Fall of a Safe Area. Amsterdam.
        www.srebrenica.nl/en; accessed November 2004.

Office for Tracing Detained and Missing Persons of Republic of Srpksa
    2007 Briefly about History and Work of Office. www.nestalirs.com/en/
        onama.html; accessed September 2007.

Office of the High Representative
    1995 The Dayton Peace Agreement. December 14. www.ohr.int/dpa/
        default.asp?content_id=380; accessed January 2008.

    2000 Decision on the Location of a Cemetery and a Monument for the
        Victims of Srebrenica. October 25. www.ohr.int/print/?content_id219;
        accessed December 2005.

    2003a Decision Ordering the Transfer of Ownership of the Battery Factory
        "AS" a.d.-Srebrenica to the Foundation of the Srebrenica-Potocari
        Memorial and Cemetery and Establishing an ad hoc Battery Factory
        "AS" a.d.- Srebrenica Compensation Commission. March 25. www
        .ohr.int/decisions/plipdec/default.asp?content_id=29527; accessed
        February 2008.

    2003b Remarks by the High Representative on the Occasion of the
        First Burials at Potocari Cemetery of Victims of the 1995 Srebrenica
        Massacre. Press Office. March 31. www.ohr.int/print/?content_
        id=29588; accessed January 2006.

    2004 Press Release: High Representative Announces Srebrenica
        Commission Support Measures. April 16. www.ohr.int/ohr-dept/
        presso/pressr/default.asp?content_id=32294; accessed February 2008.

Physicians for Human Rights
    1997 Medical Group Announces First Identifications of Victims of
        Srebrenica Massacre. July 17. http://physiciansforhumanrights.org/
        library/news-1997–07–17.html; accessed October 2007.

Research and Documentation Center
    2007 Bosnian Book of the Dead. Sarajevo: Research and Documentation
        Center.

United Nations
    1999 Report of the Secretary General pursuant to General Assembly
        Resolution 53/35: The Fall of Srebrenica. United Nations General
        Assembly. November 15. www.un.org/peace/srebrenica.pdf; accessed
        November 2004.

UN Development Program (UNDP)
   2005 Survivors of the Tsunami: One Year Later. UNDP's Regional Bureau
      for Asia and the Pacific. www.undp.org/tsunami/; accessed October
      2007.

UN Security Council
   1993a Resolution 819. In S/Res/819 (1993). April 16. http://daccessdds.un
      .org/doc/UNDOC/GEN/N93/221/90/IMG/N9322190.pdf; accessed
      March 2005.

   1993b Resolution 836. In S/Res/836 (1993). June 4. http://daccessdds.un
      .org/doc/UNDOC/GEN/N93/330/21/IMG/N9333021.pdf; accessed
      March 2005.

US National Library of Medicine
   2006 Visible Proofs: Forensic Views of the Body. May 23. www.nlm.nih
      .gov/visibleproofs/galleries/cases/blassie.html; accessed October 2007.

Vlada Federacije Bosne i Herzegovine
   2008 Saopćenje o radu. 43 sjednica Vlade Federacije BiH. Sarajevo,
      January 23. www.fbihvlada.gov.ba/bosanski/sjednica.php?sjed_
      id=64&col=sjed_saopcenje; accessed February 2008.


GENERAL PUBLICATIONS

Anderson, Benedict
   2006 *Imagined Communities: Reflections on the Origin and Spread of
      Nationalism.* London: Verso.

Arendt, Hannah
   1994 *Eichmann in Jerusalem: A Report on the Banality of Evil.* Rev. ed.
      New York: Penguin Books.

Auerbach, Erich
   2003 *Mimesis: The Representation of Reality in Western Literature.*
      Trans. Willard R. Trask. Princeton, NJ: Princeton University Press.

Bachelard, Gaston
   1994 *The Poetics of Space.* Boston: Beacon Press.

Bakić-Hayden, Milica
   2004 National Memory as Narrative Memory. In *Balkan Identities:
      Nation and Memory.* Ed. Maria Todorova. New York: New York
      University Press.

Ballinger, Pamela
   2003 *History in Exile: Memory and Identity at the Borders of the
      Balkans.* Princeton, NJ: Princeton University Press.

Banac, Ivo
   1992a The Fearful Asymmetry of War: The Causes and Consequences of
      Yugoslavia's Demise. *Daedalus* 121 (2): 141–174.

   1992b Historiography of the Countries of Eastern Europe: Yugoslavia.
      *American Historical Review* 97 (4): 1084–1104.

Bandura, Albert
1990 Mechanisms of Moral Disengagement. In *Origins of Terrorism: Psychologies, Ideologies, Theologies, States of Mind*. Ed. W. Reich. Cambridge: Cambridge University Press.

Bardgett, Suzanne
2005 Memorial Room for Battery Factory at Potocari. *The Muslim News*, no. 195, July 29. www.muslimnews.co.uk/paper/index.php?article= 2061; accessed September 2007.

Barnett, Michael
1997 The UN Security Council, Indifference, and Genocide in Rwanda. *Cultural Anthropology* 12 (4): 551–578.

Bartlett, F. C.
1967 *Remembering: A Study in Experiment and Social Psychology*. Cambridge: Cambridge University Press.

Bašović, Almir
2003 *Priviđenja iz srebrenog vijeka*. Sarajevo: Narodno pozorište Sarajevo.

BBC News
2005 Bosnia Lab to Test Katrina Bodies. December 29. http://news.bbc.co .uk/2/hi/europe/4567442.stm; accessed August 2007.

Benjamin, Mark
2005 The Gravest Job. *Salon.com*. September 3. http://dir.salon.com/story/ news/feature/2005/09/03/dead/index.html; accessed September 2007.

Bergson, Henri
1991 *Matter and Memory*. New York: Zone Books.

Biserko, Sonja
2005 *Srebrenica—From Denial to Confession*. Belgrade: Helsinki Committee for Human Rights in Serbia. Chronicles 22.

Black, Richard
2001 Return and Reconstruction in Bosnia-Herzegovina: Missing Link, or Mistaken Priority? *SAIS Review* 21 (2): 177–199.

Boban, Ljubo
1990 Jasenovac and the Manipulation of History. *East European Politics and Societies* 4 (3): 580–592.

Bolles, Edmund Blair
1988 *Remembering and Forgetting: An Inquiry into the Nature of Memory*. New York: Walker and Company.

Bose, Sumantra
2002 *Bosnia after Dayton: Nationalist Partition and International Intervention*. London: Hurst.

Bougarel, Xavier
2007 Death and Nationalism: Martyrdom, War Memory and Veteran Identity among Bosnian Muslims. In *The New Bosnian Mosaic: Identities, Memories and Moral Claims in a Post-War Society*. Ed.

Xavier Bougarel, Elissa Helms, and Ger Duijzings. Hampshire, UK: Ashgate.

Bougarel, Xavier, Elissa Helms, and Ger Duijzings, eds.
2007 *The New Bosnian Mosaic: Identities, Memories and Moral Claims in a Post-War Society.* Hampshire, UK: Ashgate.

Bourdieu, Pierre
1985 The Social Space and the Genesis of Groups. *Theory and Society* 14: 723–744.

Bowker, Geoffrey C., and Susan Leigh Star
1999 *Sorting Things Out: Classification and Its Consequences.* Cambridge, MA: MIT Press.

Bringa, Tone
1995 *Being Bosnian the Muslim Way.* Princeton, NJ: Princeton University Press.

2001 *Returning Home: Revival of a Bosnian Village.* With Peter Loizos, consultant. Sarajevo: Saga Film and Video Productions.

2002 Averted Gaze: Genocide in Bosnia-Herzegovina. In *Annihilating Difference.* Ed. Alexander L. Hinton. Berkeley and Los Angeles: University of California Press.

Brkic, Courtney Angela
2004 *The Stone Fields.* New York: Farrar, Straus and Giroux.

Brodwin, Paul
2000 Genetics, Identity, and the Anthropology of Essentialism. *Anthropological Quarterly* 75 (2): 323–330.

Brown, Keith
2003 Global Newsstand: Unraveling Europe's Raj. *Foreign Policy* 139 (November–December): 84–85.

Buchli, Victor, and Gavin Lucas
2001 Bodies of Evidence. In *Archaeologies of the Contemporary Past.* Ed. Victor Buchli and Gavin Lucas. London: Routledge.

Budimlija, Zoran M., Mechthild K. Prinz, Amy Zelson-Mundorff, Jason Wiersema, Eric Bartelink, Gaille MacKinnon, Bianca L. Nazzaruolo, Sheila M. Estacio, Michael J. Hennessey, and Robert C. Shaler
2003 World Trade Center Human Identification Project: Experiences with Individual Body Identification Cases. *Croatian Medical Journal* 44 (3): 259–263.

Campbell, David
1999 Apartheid Cartography: The Political Anthropology and Spatial Effects of International Diplomacy in Bosnia. *Political Geography* 18 (4): 395–435.

Caplan, Jane, and John Torpey
2001 *Documenting Individual Identity.* Princeton, NJ: Princeton University Press.

Casserly, Michael
  2006 Double Jeopardy: Public Education in New Orleans before and after
    the Storm. In *There Is No Such Thing as a Natural Disaster: Race,
    Class, and Hurricane Katrina*. Ed. Chester Hartman and Gregory D.
    Squires. New York: Routledge.

Chandler, David
  1999 The Bosnian Protectorate and the Implications for Kosovo. *New Left
    Review* 235 (May–June): 124–134.

Chipman, John
  2005 The Bones of Srebrenica. *CBC News*, July 11. www.cbc.ca/news/
    background/balkans/bones.html; accessed August 2007.

Clinton, William J.
  1996 Statement on the International Commission on Missing Persons in
    the former Yugoslavia. *Public Papers of the Presidents of the United
    States: William J. Clinton*. Vol. 1:997–998. Washington, DC: US
    Government Printing Office. www.gpoaccess.gov/pubpapers/wjclinton,
    accessed November 2005.

CNN.com
  2005 War Graves Experts to Help with Katrina IDs: Using Bone Samples,
    Group Expects 100 Percent Success Rate. December 29. www.cnn.
    com/2005/US/12/29/bosnia.katrina/index.html; accessed August 2007.

Coles, Kimberley
  2004 Election Day: The Construction of Democracy through Technique.
    *Cultural Anthropology* 19 (4): 551–581.

  2007a Ambivalent Builders: Europeanization, the Production of Difference
    and Internationals in Bosnia-Herzegovina. In *The New Bosnian
    Mosaic: Identities, Memories and Moral Claims in a Post-War Society*.
    Ed. Xavier Bougarel, Elissa Helms, and Ger Duijzings. Hampshire, UK:
    Ashgate.

  2007b *Democratic Designs: International Intervention and Electoral
    Practices in Postwar Bosnia-Herzegovina*. Ann Arbor: University of
    Michigan Press.

Cooper, Frederick
  2005 *Colonialism in Question: Theory, Knowledge, History*. Berkeley and
    Los Angeles: University of California Press.

Correa, Cristian
  2007 The Ghosts of the Past: Forensic Obstacles to the Truth in Chile.
    International Center for Transitional Justice. September. www.ictj.org/
    en/news/features/1313.html; accessed October 2007.

Crowley, Sheila
  2006 Where Is Home? Housing for Low-Income People after the 2005
    Hurricanes. In *There Is No Such Thing as a Natural Disaster: Race,
    Class, and Hurricane Katrina*. Ed. Chester Hartman and Gregory D.
    Squires. New York: Routledge.

Čekić, Smail, Muharem Kreso, and Bećir Macić
    2001 *Genocide in Srebrenica, United Nations "Safe Area," in July 1995.*
        Trans. K. Hadžić. Sarajevo: Institute for Research of Crimes against
        Humanity and International Law.

Čolović, Ivan
    2002 *Politics of Identity in Serbia: Essays in Political Anthropology.*
        Trans. Celia Hawkesworth. New York: New York University Press.

Ćatić, Nihad Nino
    2005 *Ljudi beznađa.* Oud-Beijerland, The Netherlands: Stichting Steun
        Bewoners van Bosnië-Herzegovina..

Ćurak, Nerzuk
    2000 Priča iz sredista zemlje. *Dani,* no. 169, August 25.

Das, Veena
    1995 *Critical Events: An Anthropological Perspective on Contemporary
        India.* Delhi: Oxford University Press.

Davis, Natalie Zemon
    1983 *The Return of Martin Guerre.* Cambridge, MA: Harvard University
        Press.

Davoren, Jon, Daniel Vanek, Rijad Konjhodžić, John Crews, Edwin Huffine,
    and Thomas J. Parsons
    2007 Highly Effective DNA Extraction Method for Nuclear Short Tandem
        Repeat Testing of Skeletal Remains from Mass Graves. *Croatian
        Medical Journal* 48 (4): 478–485.

Delpla, Isabella
    2007 In the Midst of Injustice: The ICTY from the Perspective of Some
        Victim Associations. In *The New Bosnian Mosaic: Identities,
        Memories and Moral Claims in a Post-War Society.* Ed. Xavier
        Bougarel, Elissa Helms, and Ger Duijzings. Hampshire, UK: Ashgate.

Del Ponte, Carla
    2005 Keynote Speech by Carla Del Ponte, Prosecutor of the International
        Criminal Tribunal for the former Yugoslavia. Annual Conference of
        Political Affairs Division IV, "Civilian Peace-Building and Human
        Rights in South-East Europe." Bern. September 1. www.un.org/icty/
        pressreal/2005/p1001-e.htm, accessed January 2006.

Denich, Bette
    1994 Dismembering Yugoslavia: Nationalist Ideologies and the Symbolic
        Revival of Genocide. *American Ethnologist* 21 (2): 367–390.

Deutsche Press-Agentur
    2006 Serbian President Commemorates Serb Victims in Bosnia. January 7.

Djilas, Aleksa
    1991 *The Contested Country.* Cambridge, MA: Harvard University Press.

*Dnevni avaz*
    2004a Amor nam je jedina nada. February 4.

2004b Zločinac nema ni nacije ni vjere. July 12.

2004c Šehidsko mezarje nije naš kult nego bunt protiv genocida. July 12.

Donia, Robert J., and John A. Fine Jr.
1994 *Bosnia and Herzegovina: A Tradition Betrayed.* New York: Columbia University Press.

Doretti, Mercedes, and Luis Fondebrider
2001 Science and Human Rights: Truth, Justice, Reparation and Reconciliation, a Long Way in Third World Countries. In *Archaeologies of the Contemporary Past.* Ed. Victor Buchli and Gavin Lucas. London: Routledge.

Dornin, Rusty
2005 Deal Made on Plan to ID Katrina Dead: FEMA Will Cover Most of Cost for DNA Testing. *CNN.com,* November 17. www.cnn.com/2005/US/11/17/katrina.dna/index.html; accessed August 2007.

Dotinga, Randy
2005 Tech May ID More 9/11 Victims. *Wired,* December 20. www.wired.com/medtech/health/news/2005/12/69877; accessed October 2007.

Drakulić, Slavenka
2004 *They Would Never Hurt a Fly: War Criminals on Trial at The Hague.* New York: Viking Penguin.

Duffield, Mark
2002 Social Reconstruction and the Radicalization of Development: Aid as a Relation of Global Liberal Governance. *Development and Change* 33 (5): 1049–1071.

Duijzings, Ger
2000 *Religion and the Politics of Identity in Kosovo.* New York: Columbia University Press.

2007 Commemorating Srebrenica: Histories of Violence and the Politics of Memory in Eastern Bosnia. In *The New Bosnian Mosaic: Identities, Memories and Moral Claims in a Post-War Society.* Ed. Xavier Bougarel, Elissa Helms, and Ger Duijzings. Hampshire, UK: Ashgate.

Dyer, Geoff
1995 *The Missing of the Somme.* London: Penguin Books.

*Economist*
2003 The Regatta Sets Sail: The Balkans and the European Union. June 28.

2005 A Chronicle of Deaths Foretold. July 9–15.

Faust, Drew Gilpin
2008 *This Republic of Suffering: Death and the American Civil War.* New York: Alfred A. Knopf.

Fine, John V. A., Jr.
1994 *The Late Medieval Balkans.* Ann Arbor: University of Michigan Press.

Fletcher, Laurel E., and Harvey M. Weinstein
    2002 Violence and Social Repair: Rethinking the Contributions of Justice
        and Reconciliation. *Human Rights Quarterly* 24: 573–639.

Foucault, Michel
    1981 *The History of Sexuality: Volume I.* Trans. R. Hurley. London:
        Penguin.

Gagnon, V. P., Jr.
    2004 *The Myth of Ethnic War: Serbia and Croatia in the 1990s.* Ithaca,
        NY: Cornell University Press.

*Glas Srpske*
    2004 Nestao krst. February 28–29.

Goffman, Erving
    1959 *The Presentation of Self in Everyday Life.* New York: Doubleday
        Anchor Books.

Gordy, Eric D.
    1999 *The Culture of Power in Serbia: Nationalism and the Destruction of
        Alternatives.* University Park: Pennsylvania State University Press.

Greenberg, Robert
    1996 The Politics of Dialect among Serbs, Croats, and Muslims in the for-
        mer Yugoslavia. *East European Politics and Societies* 10: 393–415.

Hadžić, Almasa
    2004a Ešdaun: Ima još tajni sakrivenih u ormarima vinovnika zločina.
        *Dnevni avaz,* June 17.

    2004b Majke dočekale 338 tabuta. *Dnevni avaz,* July 10.

    2005 Mašovićev spisak nestalih. *Dnevni avaz,* June 10.

Halbwachs, Maurice
    1980 *The Collective Memory.* Trans. Francis J. Ditter Jr. and Vida Yazdi
        Ditter. New York: Harper and Row.

Halpern, Joel M.
    1967 *A Serbian Village.* New York: Harper and Row.

Hammel, Eugene
    1972 The Zadruga as Process. In *Household and Family in Past Time.* Ed.
        Peter Laslett. Cambridge: Cambridge University Press.

    2000 Lessons from the Yugoslav Labyrinth. In *Neighbors at War.* Ed. Joel
        Halpern and David Kideckel. University Park: Pennsylvania State
        University Press.

Hammond, Laura
    2004 *This Place Will Become Home: Refugee Repatriation to Ethiopia.*
        Ithaca, NY: Cornell University Press.

Handžić, H.
    2005a Fotografije koje su uzdrmale Beograd. *Dnevni avaz,* July 5.

    2005b Priča se u autobusima, Parlamentu i cijeloj Srbiji. *Dnevni avaz,*
        July 6.

Harrison, Robert Pogue
  2003 *The Dominion of the Dead*. Chicago: University of Chicago Press.

Hartman, Chester, and Gregory D. Squires, eds.
  2006 *There Is No Such Thing as a Natural Disaster: Race, Class, and Hurricane Katrina*. New York: Routledge.

Hayden, Dorothy
  1999 Landscapes of Loss and Remembrance: The Case of Little Tokyo in Los Angeles. In *War and Remembrance in the Twentieth Century*. Ed. Jay Winter and Emmanuel Sivan. Cambridge: Cambridge University Press.

Hayden, Robert
  1992a Balancing Discussion of Jasenovac and the Manipulation of History. *East European Politics and Societies* 6 (2): 207–212.

  1992b Constitutional Nationalism in the Formerly Yugoslav Republics. *Slavic Review* 51: 646–673.

  1994 Recounting the Dead. In *Memory, History, and Opposition*. Ed. Rubie Watson. Santa Fe: School of American Research Press.

Helms, Elissa
  2003 Film Review: "Returning Home: Revival of a Bosnian Village." Tone Bringa (Producer, Anthropologist) with Peter Loizos (Consultant). *Anthropology of East Europe Review* 21 (2).

  2007 "Politics Is a Whore": Women, Morality and Victimhood in Post-War Bosnia-Herzegovina. In *The New Bosnian Mosaic: Identities, Memories and Moral Claims in a Post-War Society*. Ed. Xavier Bougarel, Elissa Helms, and Ger Duijzings. Hampshire, UK: Ashgate.

Herzfeld, Michael
  1997 *Cultural Intimacy: Social Poetics in the Nation-State*. New York: Routledge.

Ho, Engseng
  2006 *The Graves of Tarim: Genealogy and Mobility across the Indian Ocean*. Berkeley and Los Angeles: University of California Press.

Holland, Mitchell M, Christopher A. Cave, Charity A. Holland, and Todd W. Bille
  2003 Development of a Quality, High Throughput DNA Analysis Procedure for Skeletal Samples to Assist with the Identification of Victims from the World Trade Center Attacks. *Croatian Medical Journal* 44 (3): 264–272.

Holton, Milne, and Vasa D. Mihailovich
  1997 *Songs of the Serbian People*. Pittsburgh: Pittsburgh University Press.

Honig, Jan Willem, and Norbert Both
  1996 *Srebrenica: Record of a War Crime*. London: Penguin Books.

Hoskins, Janet
  1998 *Biographical Objects*. New York: Routledge.

Huffine, Edwin, John Crews, and John Davoren
    2007 Developing Role of Forensics in Deterring Violence and Genocide. *Croatian Medical Journal* 48 (4): 431–436.

Huffine, Edwin, John Crews, Brenda Kennedy, Kathryne Bomberger, and Asta Zinbo
    2001 Mass Identification of Persons Missing from the Break-up of the Former Yugoslavia: Structure, Function, and Role of the International Commission on Missing Persons. *Croatian Medical Journal* 42 (3): 271–275.

Huremović, Elvir
    2004 Granate i trombloni ostavljeni medju tijela. *Dnevni avaz,* June 18.

James, William
    1983 *The Principles of Psychology.* Cambridge, MA: Harvard University Press.

Jasanoff, Sheila
    1998 The Eye of Everyman: Witnessing DNA in the Simpson Trial. *Social Studies of Science* 28 (5–6): 713–740.

    2006 Biotechnology and Empire: The Global Power of Seeds and Science. *Osiris* 21 (1): 273–292.

Joyce, Christopher
    2006 Genetics IDs Katrina Victims: Some Were Long Missing. *All Things Considered.* NPR, May 11.

Joyce, Christopher, and Eric Stover
    1991 *Witnesses from the Grave: The Stories Bones Tell.* Boston: Little, Brown.

Kavazović, Husejn ef.
    2003 Address by Husejn ef. Kavazović. Roundtable, "Between Truth and Justice—Memories and Hope." Sarajevo. Association of the Mothers of Srebrenica and Žepa Enclaves.

Keane, Webb
    2005 Estrangement, Intimacy, and the Objects of Anthropology. In *The Politics of Method in the Human Sciences: Positivism and Its Epistemological Others.* Ed. George Steinmetz. Durham, NC: Duke University Press.

Knaus, Gerald, and Felix Martin
    2003 Travails of the European Raj. *Journal of Democracy* 14 (3): 60–74.

Komar, Debra
    2003 Lessons from Srebrenica: The Contributions and Limitations of Physical Anthropology in Identifying Victims of War Crimes. *Journal of Forensic Science* 48 (4): 713–716.

    2008 Patterns of Mortuary Practice Associated with Genocide: Implications for Archaeological Research. *Current Anthropology* 49 (1): 123–133.

Lacquer, Thomas
  2002 The Dead Body and Human Rights. In *The Body*. Ed. Sean T.
    Sweeny and Ian Hodder. Cambridge: Cambridge University Press.

Latour, Bruno
  1996 *Aramis or the Love of Technology*. Trans. Catherine Porter.
    Cambridge, MA: Harvard University Press.

  2005 From Realpolitik to Dingpolitik; or, How to Make Things Public. In
    *Making Things Public: Atmospheres of Democracy*. Ed. Bruno Latour
    and Peter Weibel. Cambridge, MA: MIT Press.

Laušević, Mirjana
  2000 Some Aspects of Music and Politics in Bosnia. In *Neighbors at War*.
    Ed. Joel Halpern and David Kideckel. University Park: Pennsylvania
    State University Press.

Lee, Henry C., and Frank Tirnady
  2003 *Blood Evidence: How DNA Is Revolutionizing the Way We Solve
    Crimes*. Cambridge, MA: Perseus.

Lee, Spike
  2006 *When the Levees Broke: A Requiem in Four Acts*. HBO
    Documentary Films. 40 Acres and a Mule Filmworks.

Levi, Primo
  1987 *The Reawakening*. Trans. Stuart Woolf. New York: Collier Books.

Limón, Lavinia
  2006 We Ain't Refugees. In *World Refugee Survey 2006*. US Committee
    for Refugees and Immigrants.

Lockwood, William G.
  1975 *European Muslims: Economy and Ethnicity in Western Bosnia*. New
    York: Academic Press.

Longinović, Tomislav
  2001 Music Wars: Blood and Song at the Ends of Yugoslavia. In *Music and
    Racial Imagination*. Ed. Rod Radano and Phil Bohlman. Chicago:
    Chicago University Press.

Lovrenović, Ivan
  2001 *Bosnia: A Cultural History*. New York: New York University Press.

Lyon, David
  2001 Under My Skin: From Identification Papers to Body Surveillance. In
    *Documenting Individual Identity*. Ed. Jane Caplan and John Torpey.
    Princeton, NJ: Princeton University Press.

Malkki, Liisa
  1992 National Geographic: The Rooting of People and the
    Territorialization of National Identity among Scholars and Refugees.
    *Cultural Anthropology* 7(1): 24–44.

  1996 Speechless Emissaries: Refugees, Humanitarianism, and
    Dehistoricization. *Cultural Anthropology* 11(3): 377–404.

Masquelier, Adeline
    2006 Why Katrina's Victims Aren't Refugees: Musings on a "Dirty"
        Word. *American Anthropologist* 108 (4): 735–743.

Matton, Sylvie
    2005 *Srebrenica, un génocide annoncé.* Paris: Flammarion.

McCarthy, Patrick, and Tom Maday
    2000 *After the Fall: Srebrenica Survivors in St. Louis.* St. Louis: Missouri
        Historical Society Press.

Miller, Paul
    2006 Contested Memories: The Bosnian Genocide in the Minds of Serbs
        and Muslims. *Journal of Genocide Research* 8 (3): 311–324.

Miloš, Ana, Arijana Selmanović, Lejla Smajlović, René L. M. Huel, Cheryl
Katzmarzyk, Adi Rizvić, and Thomas J. Parsons
    2007 Success Rates of Nuclear Short Tandem Repeat Typing from
        Different Skeletal Elements. *Croatian Medical Journal* 48 (4): 486–493.

Morrison, Toni
    1988 *Beloved.* New York: Plume.

Mundoff, Amy Zelson, and Dawnie Wolfe Steadman
    2003 Anthropological Perspectives on the Forensic Response at the World
        Trade Center Disaster. *General Anthropology* 10 (1): 1–5.

Mustafić, Mirsad
    2003 *Sjećanje na Srebrenicu.* Tuzla: JU NUB "Derviš Sušić."

Mustafić, M.
    2007 Četnička ikonografija u gradu genocida. *Dnevni avaz.* July 13.

Nettelfield, Lara
    2006 Courting Democracy: The Hague Tribunal's Effects in Bosnia-
        Herzegovina. PhD diss., Columbia University.

Nettelfield, Lara, and Sarah Wagner
    2004 For Bosniaks, the US Ideal Is in Ruins. *LA Times,* September 19.

Neuffer, Elizabeth
    2002 *The Key to My Neighbor's House.* New York: Picador.

North Dakota Museum of Art
    2006 "*Los Desaparecidos*/The Disappeared." Exhibit.

Nuhanović, Hasan
    2003 Uloga međunarodih elemenata u Srebrenici "zaštićenoj
        zoni"—hronologija, analiza i komentari. Tuzla.

    2005 *Pod zastavom UN-a: međunarodna zajednica i zločin u Srebrenici.*
        Sarajevo: Preporod.

Peric, Sabrina
    2006 Sex, Death and Ethnicity: Post-War Joke-telling and Balkan Intimacy.
        Paper presented at the Eighth Annual Kokkalis Graduate Student Work-
        shop, February, Kennedy School of Government, Harvard University.

2007 Subterranean Encounters: Geological Landscapes and the Political Life of the Western Balkans. Paper presented at the conference Historical Continuities, Political Responsibilities: Unsettling Conceptual Blindspots in Ottoman Studies, May, Graduate Center, City University of New York.

Pesca, Mike
2005 Are Katrina's Victims "Refugees" or "Evacuees"? NPR report, September 5. www.npr.org/templates/story/story.php?storyId=4833613; accessed August 2007.

Petrović, Edit
2000 Ethnonationalism and the Dissolution of Yugoslavia. In *Neighbors at War*. Ed. Joel Halpern and David Kideckel. University Park: Pennsylvania State University Press.

Petryna, Adriana
2002 *Life Exposed: Biological Citizens after Chernobyl*. Princeton, NJ: Princeton University Press.

Pollack, Craig Evan
2003a Returning to a Safe Area? The Importance of Burial for Return to Srebrenica. *Journal of Refugee Studies* 16 (2): 186 – 201.

2003b Burial at Srebrenica: Linking Place and Trauma. *Social Science and Medicine* 56 (4): 793 – 801.

2003c Intentions of Burial: Mourning, Politics, and Memorials Following the Massacre at Srebrenica. *Death Studies* 27 (2): 125–142.

Power, Samantha
2002 *"A Problem from Hell": America and the Age of Genocide*. New York: HarperCollins.

Proust, Marcel
1970 *Remembrance of Things Past*. Vol. 2. Trans. C. K. Scott Moncrieff. New York: Random House.

Rabinow, Paul
1999 *French DNA: Trouble in Purgatory*. Chicago and London: University of Chicago Press.

Ramet, Sabrina
2002 *Balkan Babel: The Disintegration of Yugoslavia from the Death of Tito to the Fall of Milošević*. Boulder, CO: Westview Press.

Ricoeur, Paul
2004 Memory, History, Forgetting. Trans. Kathleen Blamey and David Pellauer. Chicago and London: Chicago University Press.

2005 *The Course of Recognition*. Trans. David Pellauer. Cambridge, MA: Harvard University Press.

Riles, Annelise
2001 *The Network Inside Out*. Ann Arbor: University of Michigan Press.

Rohde, David

  1995 Evidence Indicates Bosnia Massacre. *Christian Science Monitor*,
       August 18.

  1997 *Endgame: The Betrayal and Fall of Srebrenica, Europe's Worst
       Massacre since World War II*. New York: Farrar, Straus and Giroux.

Ross, Fiona C.

  2001 Speech and Silence: Women's Testimonies in the First Five Weeks of
       Public Hearings of the South African Truth and Reconciliation
       Commission. In *Remaking a World: Violence, Social Suffering, and
       Recovery*. Ed. Veena Das, Arther Kleinman, Margaret Lock,
       Mamphele Ramphele, and Pamela Reynolds. Berkeley and Los Angeles:
       University of California Press.

  2003 Using Rights to Measure Wrongs: A Case Study of Method and
       Moral in the Work of the South African Truth and Reconciliation
       Commission. In *Human Rights in Global Perspective: Anthropological
       Studies of Rights, Claims and Entitlements*. Ed. R. A. Wilson and J. P.
       Mitchell. London and New York: Routledge.

Salimović, Sadik

  2002 *Knjiga o Srebrenici*. Srebrenica: Skupština opštine Srebrenica.

Sanford, Victoria

  2003 *Buried Secrets: Truth and Human Rights in Guatemala*. New York:
       Palgrave Macmillan.

Sankar, Pamela

  2001 DNA-Typing: Galton's Eugenic Dream Realized? In *Documenting
       Individual Identity*. Ed. Jane Caplan and John Torpey. Princeton, NJ:
       Princeton University Press.

Sant Cassia, Paul

  2005 *Bodies of Evidence: Burial, Memory and the Recovery of Missing
       Persons in Cyprus*. New York: Berghahn Books.

Sartre, Jean-Paul

  1961 *The Psychology of Imagination*. New York: Citadel Press.

Scott, James

  1998 *Seeing like a State: How Certain Schemes to Improve the Human
       Condition Have Failed*. New Haven, CT: Yale University Press.

Scott, James, John Tehranian, and Jeremy Mathias

  2002 The Production of Legal Identities Proper to States: The Case of
       the Permanent Family Surname. *Comparative Studies in Society and
       History* 44 (1): 4–44.

Scott, Janny

  2001 Closing a Scrapbook Full of Life and Sorrow. *New York Times*,
       December 31. http://query.nytimes.com/gst/fullpage.html?res=9505E7D
       A1730F932A05751C1A9679C8B63; accessed December 2006.

Shaler, Robert
    2005 *Who They Were: Inside the World Trade Center DNA Story*. New York: Free Press.

Skinner, Mark, and Jon Sterenberg
    2005 Turf Wars: Authority and Responsibility for the Investigation of Mass Graves. *Forensic Science Journal* 151: 221–232.

Smith, Jane Idleman, and Yvonne Yazbeck Haddad
    2002 *Islamic Understanding of Death and Resurrection*. Oxford: Oxford University Press.

Smith, Lindsay
    2008 Subversive Genes: Forensic DNA and Human Rights in Post-Dictatorship Argentina. PhD diss., Harvard University.

Sophocles
    1976 *Antigone*. Trans. R. C. Jebb. Cambridge: Cambridge University Press.

Steffanson, Anders
    2004 Refugee Returns to Sarajevo and Their Challenge to Contemporary Narratives of Mobility. In *Coming Home? Refugees, Migrants, and Those Who Stayed Behind*. Ed. Lynellen D. Long and Ellen Oxfeld. Philadelphia: University of Pennsylvania Press.

Stover, Eric
    1998 *The Graves: Srebrenica and Vukovar*. New York: Scalo.

Stover, Eric, and Rachel Shigekane
    2002 The Missing in the Aftermath of the War: When Do the Needs of Victims' Families and International War Crimes Tribunals Clash? *International Review of the Red Cross* 48 (848): 845–866.

Stover, Eric, and Harvey M. Weinstein
    2004 *My Neighbor, My Enemy: Justice and Community in the Aftermath of Mass Atrocity*. Cambridge: Cambridge University Press.

Strathern, Marilyn
    2005 Kinship, Law and the Unexpected: Relatives Are Always a Surprise. Cambridge: Cambridge University Press.

Sturken, Marita
    1997 *Tangled Memories: The Vietnam War, the AIDS Epidemic, and the Politics of Remembering*. Berkeley and Los Angeles: University of California Press.

Sudetic, Chuck
    1998 *Blood and Vengeance: One Family's Story of the War in Bosnia*. New York: Penguin Books.

Suljagić, Emir
    2005 *Postcards from the Grave*. London: Saqi.

Šaponjić, Z.
    2005 Srbi sami ožalili svoje. *Glas javnosti*, July 13.

Tate, Winifred
    2007 *Counting the Dead: The Culture and Politics of Human Rights Activism in Colombia*. Berkeley and Los Angeles: University of California Press.

Tatum, James
    2003 *The Mourner's Song*. Chicago: University of Chicago Press.

Thorpe, Nick
    2001 DNA Tests: Srebrenica to Ground Zero. *BBC News*, Europe, November 16. http://news.bbc.co.uk/1/hi/world/europe/1660833.stm; accessed August 2006.

Toal, Gerard, and Carl Dahlman
    2004 The Effort to Reverse Ethnic Cleansing in Bosnia-Herzegovina: The Limits of Return. *Eurasian Geography and Economics* 45 (6): 434–464.

Todorova, Maria
    2004 Introduction: Learning Memory, Remembering Identity. In *Balkan Identities: Nation and Memory*. Ed. Maria Todorova. New York: New York University Press.

Tokača, Mirsad
    2005 An Analysis of Population Losses in the Middle Drina Valley with a Special Look at the Srebrenica Killings 11th to the 18th of July 1995. Conference, "Genocide against Bosniaks in the US Safe Area Srebrenica in July 1995." Sarajevo.

Torpey, John
    2000 *The Invention of the Passport*. Cambridge: Cambridge University Press.

Ugrešić, Dubravka
    1998 *The Culture of Lies*. Trans. Celia Hawkesworth. University Park: Pennsylvania State University Press.

Van Heerden, Ivor, and Mike Bryan
    2006 *The Storm: What Went Wrong and Why during Hurricane Katrina—The Inside Story from One Louisiana Scientist*. New York: Viking.

Verdery, Katherine
    1991 *National Ideology under Socialism*. Berkeley and Los Angeles: University of California Press.
    1999 *The Political Lives of Dead Bodies*. New York: Columbia University Press.

Vollen, Laurie
    2001 All That Remains: Identifying the Victims of the Srebrenica Massacre. *Cambridge Quarterly of Healthcare Ethics* 10: 336–340.

White, Geoffrey M.
  2004 National Subjects: September 11 and Pearl Harbor. *American Ethnologist* 31 (3): 293–310.

Williams, Daniel
  2005 Srebrenica Video Vindicates Long Pursuit by Serb Activist. *Washington Post*, September 25. www.washingtonpost.com/wp-dyn/content/article/2005/06/24/AR2005062401501.html; accessed January 2006.

Winter, Jay
  1995 *Sites of Memory, Sites of Mourning.* Cambridge: Cambridge University Press.

  1999 Forms of Kinship and Remembrance in the Aftermath of the Great War. In *War and Remembrance in the Twentieth Century.* Ed. Jay Winter and Emmanuel Sivan. Cambridge: Cambridge University Press.

Winter, Jay, and Emmanuel Sivan, eds.
  1999 *War and Remembrance in the Twentieth Century.* Cambridge: Cambridge University Press.

Wyman, Mark
  1998 *DPs: Europe's Displaced Persons, 1945–1951.* Ithaca, NY: Cornell University Press.

Yates, Frances A.
  1966 *The Art of Memory.* Chicago: Chicago University Press.

Žalica, Pjer
  2003 *Gori vatra* (Fuse). Refresh Productions, Sarajevo.

Žene Srebrenice
  1998a Kratak opis organizancija i agencija u BiH čiji mandat podrazumijeva traženje nestalih osoba. *Bilten Srebrenica* 1:7–9.

  1998b *Samrtno Srebreničko ljeto '95.* Tuzla: PrintCom Tuzla.

  1999 Moj prvi odlazak u rodni grad. *Bilten Srebrenica* 6:9.

  2000 Majka Đemila ovih dana pronašla posmrtne ostatke od svoja dva sina Sulje i Sadika. *Bilten Srebrenica* 10:9.

  2001 Šta mislite o Memorijalnom kompleksu? *Bilten Srebrenica* 18:6.

  2003 Kolekcija 107 izjava o ulozi međunarodne zajednice u Srebrenici "zaštićenoj zoni" UN-a. Tuzla.

  2004 Za četvrtu fazu ukopa do sada identifikovano 70 osoba. *Bilten Srebrenica* 31:8.

  2007 *Ujedinjani narodi na srebreničkom stubu sram.* Tuzla: Harfo-graf.

Živković, Marko
  2000 The Wish to Be a Jew: The Power of the Jewish Trope in the Yugoslav Conflict. *Cahiers de l'Urmis,* 6: 69–84. http://urmis.revues.org/document323.html, accessed August 2007.

# Index

International Criminal Tribunal for
the former Yugoslavia (ICTY): and
Carla Del Ponte, 239; and Dražen
Erdemović, 241n1; findings of, 4,
22, 23, 151, 216, 272n5; indictment
against Karadžić, 274n1; indictment
against Naser Orić, 29, 234, 275n15;
investigations, 49–51, 98; jurisdiction
of, 290n1; outstanding indictment
of Mladić, 41, 274n1; and plea
bargains, 98; role in exhumations, 93,
95–96, 177; and Scorpions tape, 22;
testimony before, 22, 26, 152–56. See
also Krstić, Radislav; Witness DD
international intervention: in postconflict-
postdisaster societies, 18, 89, 246,
248–49, 252–53, 263–65; in postwar
Bosnia, 2, 8, 12, 88–89, 128
Iraq, 234, 247, 298n10
Islamic Community, 17, 89, 223; and
establishment of the memorial center,
195–96; and July 11 burials, 202, 223;
response to Srebrenica's missing, 180,
198, 215–19, 295n2, 296n3
Islamska zajednica. See Islamic
Community
Izetbegović, Alija, 37, 44, 293n12

Jaglići, 41
James, William, 133
Janvier, Bernard, 38–40, 46, 56
Jasanoff, Sheila, 264–65, 288n48
Jasenovac, 211–12, 293n11
Jugoslovenska narodna armija (Yugoslav
People's Army, or JNA), 25

Kamp Westerbork, 202
Karadžić, Radovan, 26, 237, 280n7;
capture of, 274n1; and disappearance
of Bosniaks, 27, 43; and ICTY, 274n1;
and relocation of Bosnian Serbs, 62;
and Srebrenica, 34–35, 56
Karremans, Tom, 35–36, 38–39, 42–43,
53–54, 64
Kavazović, Mufti Husejn ef., 195, 199,
216–18, 232, 295n1, 296nn2–3
Kebo, Mirsad, 262
Kešetović, Rifat: on early identification
efforts, 100, 103; and families of missing, 116–17, 180; on missing persons
(nestali), 6–7, 95, 156, 183, 273n12;
supervising case managers, 137, 150,
170; and trust, 161–63
kinship, 114, 117, 295n26; "fictive,"
193; patrilineal, 14, 205, 295n26;
software, 245

Kinship and Data Analysis Panel, 245
Kladanj, 43–44, 195, 206, 214, 293n12
Kleiser, Andras, 261
knowledge production, 10, 12, 83, 120–
21, 214, 254, 261
Komunistička partija Jugoslavije (Com-
munist Party of Yugoslavia, or KPJ),
190–91
Konjević Polje, 29–30, 46–47, 49
Konjhodžić, Rijad, 82
Koran, 76, 142, 210, 219
Kosovo Polje, 189–90, 199, 292n7,
294n19
KPJ. See Komunistička partija
Jugoslavije
Kravica: Bosnian Serb commemoration
in, 238–40, 297n16; 1993 attack
on, 29, 238, 275n16; warehouse as
detention and execution site, 47, 49,
149, 254
Krstić, Radislav, 22, 41, 49, 151, 153–
54, 155, 268, 272n5

Latin America, and forensic science, 18,
248–52
Latour, Bruno, 13, 94, 121–22,
285n25
liberalism. See Western liberalism
ligature, 49, 50, 95–96, 140, 178
Lin, Maya, 200–201, 244
los desaparecidos, 250–51
Louisiana, 247, 253, 255, 258–59. See
also Hurricane Katrina
Lukavac, 109–11

Malkić, Abdulrahman, 185
Mandžić, Nesib, 42, 43
Marš smrti, 23, 210
martyr, 187, 217, 219, 232, 256,
292n14, 295n2
mass burial: families' decisions regarding, 182, 186–88, 230–31; and mass
killings, 2, 48–51, 54, 55, 56–57, 83–
85, 254; at memorial center, 185–86,
202, 225–29, 243–44
mass graves: creation of, 4, 49–51, 54,
56–57, 85, 254, 278n35, 279n41;
detection and discovery of, 55, 98,
286n30; exhumation of, 95–98, 108–
9, 179, 286n28, 297n12; images of,
174, 175; in Latin America, 250, 252;
primary, 4; twentieth century commemoration of, 189; World War II (in
Yugoslavia), 17, 188–89, 191, 192,
293n10. See also secondary mass
graves; surface graves